WITHDRAWN

BETWEEN FRANCE AND GERMANY

The Jews of Alsace-Lorraine, 1871-1918

BETWEEN FRANCE AND GERMANY

The Jews of Alsace-Lorraine,
1871-1918

VICKI CARON

Stanford University Press ◆ Stanford, California
1988

DS
135
.F85
A 4715
1988

Stanford University Press
Stanford, California
© 1988 by the Board of Trustees of the
Leland Stanford Junior University

Printed in the United States of America

Published with the assistance of the
Andrew W. Mellon Foundation

CIP data appear at the end of the book

To My Parents
and
In Memory of Jay

The map shows all communities with Jewish populations of over 200 in 1895 and several other towns that are frequently mentioned in the text. Current French place-names are used. The Jewish populations are based on data in *Das Reichsland Elsass-Lothringer* (Strassburg, 1898–1901).

Preface

I would like to extend my most sincere gratitude to the many individuals and institutions who contributed to the completion of this book. First and foremost, I would like to thank those professors who served as my dissertation advisers at Columbia University, without whose steady encouragement and guidance this work would not have come about. From Robert O. Paxton, I learned to think critically about modern French history. His insightful criticisms and scrupulous reading of the manuscript inspired me to situate this study within the larger contexts of French and German history. Similarly, it was primarily under the influence of Paula Hyman that I was ushered into the world of modern Jewish history. Her dynamic teaching constantly stimulated me to ask new types of questions of the discipline, and her in-depth knowledge of French Jewish history proved indispensable at every stage of this study. The opportunity to have worked with two such fine scholars, both of whom always gave graciously of their time, has made the years devoted to this project especially rewarding.

Generous financial support from the Fulbright Foundation, the Whiting Foundation, and the Memorial Foundation for Jewish Culture provided me with valuable time and funding for travel, research, and writing, without which this book could never have come to fruition. I would also like to thank Brown University and the Jewish Studies Program at the University of Washington for financial help in the final preparation of the manuscript.

The patient and generous assistance of the staffs of many libraries and institutions was crucial to the completion of this work. These include the Bibliothèque nationale et universitaire in Strasbourg; the

Bibliothèque municipale in Strasbourg; the Bibliothèque nationale in Paris; the Columbia University Library; the New York City Public Library; the Departmental Archives of Bas-Rhin, Haut-Rhin, and the Moselle; the Municipal Archives of Strasbourg; the Foreign Ministry Archives in Paris; the Leo Baeck Institute in New York; and the Jewish Theological Seminary in New York. In particular I would like to thank the Honorary Grand Rabbi of Strasbourg, Max Warschawski; Gilbert Cahen of the Departmental Archives of the Moselle; and Roger Kohn, the former archivist at the Central Consistory in Paris, for their considerable personal assistance in helping me locate pertinent information.

Many colleagues and friends gave generously of their time to read the manuscript and offer critical suggestions. Here I would like to thank Michael Hanagan; Jack Wertheimer; Calvin Goldscheider; Mark Stein; Roger Kohn; Sigmund Diamond; Joseph Rothschild; Michael Stanislawski; David Pinkney; Roger Errera; Jay Schechter; Phyllis Albert; and Bob Stoll. I would also like to thank those who offered valuable advice and suggestions at the initial stages of research, especially Dan P. Silverman, Alfred Wahl, Simon Schwarzfuchs, Freddy Raphael, Paul Leuilliot, John Craig, Victor Treschan, David Cohen, and Arthur Hertzberg. I am particularly grateful once again to Paula Hyman for permitting me to cite her statistical data on Alsace-Lorraine Jewry during the pre-annexation period, as well as for her collaboration on our article "The Failed Alliance: Jewish-Catholic Relations in Alsace-Lorraine, 1871–1914," published in the *Leo Baeck Institute Yearbook* (1981), which constitutes much of the foundation for Chapter 6 of this book. I am also indebted to Simon Schwarzfuchs for his willingness to share with me the manuscript of Elie Scheid's, *Mémoires d'un juif alsacien* (1906).

I would also like to extend my appreciation to the Leo Baeck Institute, and in particular, to Dr. Arnold Paucker, editor of the *Leo Baeck Institute Yearbook*, and Dr. Fred Grubel, director of the Institute's New York branch for their long-standing interest in this project. Chapters 3, 6, and 8 of this book are based on articles originally published in the 1981, 1983, and 1985 volumes of the *Yearbook*, and I would like to thank the Institute and especially Dr. Paucker for permission to publish those materials in somewhat altered form.

A heartfelt debt of gratitude must also be extended to Grant Barnes, Director of Stanford University Press, and to Norris Pope,

Preface

Assistant Director, for their unflagging confidence in and support of this project. Barbara E. Mnookin, Stanford's production editor, and Shirley Taylor, the copy editor, also deserve special praise for their care and attention to detail during the final stages of revising the manuscript.

I would also like to thank my colleagues in the Judaic Studies Program at Brown University for providing a most stimulating environment in which to complete the final draft of the manuscript. In particular, Ernest Frerichs, the Director, and Calvin Goldscheider took great care to ensure that all means would be made available to facilitate the completion of this project.

Finally, I would like to thank my parents, Sidney and Annette Caron, for their constant support, and my friend Bob Stoll, for his help and patience over the years.

A word on the conventions used in the text. French place-names have been employed throughout, since these are the names currently in use. In some instances, the German names of cities and towns have been given in parentheses. The terms Alsatians and Lorrainers refer to people native to the territories of Alsace and Lorraine annexed by Germany following the Franco-Prussian War. "Old Germans" refers to people from Germany (pre-1871 borders) who came and settled in Alsace-Lorraine after 1871.

V.C.

Contents

1. The Task of Becoming Citizens   1
2. The Challenge of Patriotism: Responses to the Annexation   27
3. Patriotism or Profit? Emigration to France, 1871–1872   45
4. Emigration Patterns, 1873–1914   75
5. The Persistence of French Loyalties   96
6. The Failed Alliance: Jewish-Catholic Relations   118
7. The Politics of Accommodation   136
8. Social Transformations   157
9. Resurrected Conflicts: The First World War   178
10. Reflections on Jews and National Identity   187

Appendixes

A. Option and Emigration, 1871–1872   197
B. Emigration, 1872–1914   199

Notes   201
Bibliography   248
Index   270

Tables

3.1	Distribution of Jewish Optants and All Alsace-Lorraine Optants by District, 1871–1872	51
3.2	Age and Sex Structure of Jewish Optants and All Bas-Rhin Optants	53
3.3	Marital Status of Jewish Optants	53
3.4	Age Distribution of Jewish Optants	53
3.5	Distribution of Jewish Optants by Hometown City Size	56
3.6	Occupational Distribution of Urban Jewish Male Optants Compared with That of All Strasbourg Jews	59
3.7	Occupational Distribution of Rural Jewish Male Optants Compared with That of All Jews in Three Selected Towns	60
3.8	Occupational Distribution of Jewish Optants Compared with That of All Bas-Rhin Optants	61
3.9	Size of the Jewish, Catholic, and Protestant Populations of Bischwiller Before and After the Annexation, 1863–1873	65
3.10	Occupational Distribution of Jewish Optants Compared with That of Pre-1870 Alsatian Jewish Migrants to Paris and the United States	70
4.1	The Jewish Population of Alsace-Lorraine, 1871–1910	76
4.2	Size of the Jewish and Total Populations of Alsace-Lorraine by Province, 1871 and 1910	76
4.3	Jewish and Non-Jewish Emigration from Haguenau District by Two-Year Periods, 1873–1898	78
4.4	Jewish and Total Legal Emigration from Bas-Rhin by Year, 1883–1892 and 1903–1910	78
4.5	Distribution of Jewish and Non-Jewish Emigrants by Hometown City Size	79

4.6	Distribution of Jewish Emigrants by Town	80
4.7	Distribution of Jewish Optants and Emigrants by Jewish Population Density	81
4.8	Occupational Distribution of Jewish Emigrants Compared with That of Three Other Populations	82
4.9	Occupational Distribution of Rural and Urban Jewish Emigrants Compared with That of Rural and Urban Jewish Male Optants	84
4.10	Destinations of Jewish and Non-Jewish Emigrants	86
4.11	Distribution of Jewish Emigrants by Destination and Hometown City Size	87
4.12	Distribution of Non-Jewish Emigrants by Destination and Hometown City Size	88
4.13	Age Distribution of Jewish and Non-Jewish Emigrants	92
8.1	Distribution of Households with Two or Fewer Resident Children by City Size and Religion, 1910	160
8.2	Growth of the Urban Jewish and Total Populations of Alsace-Lorraine by Province, 1871–1910	163
8.3	Size of the Jewish Population in the Major Cities of Alsace-Lorraine, 1871 and 1910	163
8.4	Size of the Jewish and Total Populations of Alsace-Lorraine by District, 1871 and 1910	165
8.5	Decline of the Rural Jewish Population of Alsace, 1871–1905	166
8.6	Occupational Distribution of Alsace-Lorrainers by Religion, 1907	170
8.7	Composition of the Student Body of Kaiser Wilhelm University, Mid-December 1898	174
8.8	Jewish Converts to Protestantism in Alsace-Lorraine, 1889–1907	176
8.9	Jewish Marriages and Mixed Marriages in Strasbourg, Mulhouse, and Alsace-Lorraine as a Whole, 1872–1919	177

BETWEEN FRANCE AND GERMANY

The Jews of Alsace-Lorraine, 1871-1918

One will see first of all that it is wrong in our day to speak of *Jews*. It is necessary to speak of English Jews, Italian Jews, French Jews, who differ in language and sentiments as much as the people among whom they live. Within the soul of a Jew, you will rediscover the soul of the nation itself, of which it makes up a part. Formerly, the Jew bought his right of residence through annual taxes; today, he conquers those rights of citizenship on the battlefields.

—Maurice Bloch

ONE

The Task of Becoming Citizens

The contours of modern European Jewry were forged by emancipation—the struggle to secure citizenship rights for European Jews that began in the late eighteenth century and continued for the next hundred years. The emergence of Jewish communities with distinctive national identities was perhaps the single most important outcome of the process of emancipation.[1] Until the last quarter of the eighteenth century, Jews throughout the world still perceived themselves to be members not only of a common religious community but also of a shared national group. The two most salient features of Jewish life during the Middle Ages and into the early modern period highlight the inseparability of the national and religious components of Judaism. First, the primary institution of medieval Jewry was the semi-autonomous local Jewish community. Since Jews were defined as a corporation within the hierarchy of feudal society, membership in the Jewish community was involuntary; therefore the problem of defining one's identity did not exist for traditional Jews. Moreover, the rabbi was not only a religious leader but a civil authority as well, and nearly all aspects of life in Jewish communities everywhere were governed by the edicts of Jewish law. To be sure, Jews respected the civil laws of their respective countries of residence, maintaining the principle that "the law of the land is the law." But this dictum rarely conflicted with the civil aspects of Jewish law, because the cultural, religious, and social affairs of Jews, if not their commercial activities, were restricted entirely to the confines of the Jewish community.[2]

The second important feature of medieval and early modern Jewish life was that Jewish residence in Europe was tenuous and impermanent, from both the Jewish and the Gentile point of view. Jewish existence prior to emancipation was based on privilege rather than on right. Merely tolerated by the rulers of their respective lands of settlement, Jewish communities confronted the ever-present threat of expulsion.[3] What enabled Jews to endure this constant insecurity was an unshakable faith in the coming of the messiah who would bring about the political restoration of the Jewish nation in Palestine. For the meanwhile, Jews felt they were living in a situation of *galut* or exile. The fact that the *galut* had persisted for centuries did nothing to impair this faith. Consequently, despite the communal fragmentation of the medieval Jewish world, collective adherence to Jewish law, together with Jewish messianic expectations stimulated by the precarious nature of Jewish existence, provided the religio-national components of a Jewish identity. Frequent exchanges between members of one Jewish community and another for the purposes of commerce, education, marriage, or religious consultations reinforced this supranational sense of Jewish peoplehood.[4]

Toward the end of the eighteenth century, the process of emancipation began to dissolve these two bonds that had cemented Jews into a single people. With the rise of the modern nation-state in the sixteenth and seventeenth centuries, monarchs eager to centralize authority progressively chipped away at the autonomous rights of all medieval corporations, including the Jewish community. Jewish emancipation, according to Salo Baron, "was as much a historic necessity for the modern state as it was for the Jews. . . . Jewish equality of rights was not a bounty bestowed upon the Jews by benevolent governments but rather an exchange of an outworn, no longer tenable status for another which better fit the modern conditions."[5] Clermont-Tonnerre, a major proponent of Jewish emancipation, declared before the French National Assembly in 1789: "To the Jews as individuals—everything; to the Jews as a group—nothing. They must constitute neither a body politic nor an order; they must be citizens individually." If Jews refused to give up their communal autonomy, he continued, the only recourse left open to the state would be expulsion.[6] As Baron has noted, it is a paradox that the same political, economic, and cultural forces that contributed to the rise of the modern nation-state made imperative the complete eradication of the traditional Jewish community, the basis for the sense of peoplehood among premodern Jewry.[7]

Since the debate regarding emancipation revolved essentially around the question of whether Jews could become "useful" and patriotic citizens, advocates of emancipation further expected Jews to alter those aspects of their law that would conflict with their new civil status. In his 1782 treatise *Concerning the Amelioration of the Civil Status of the Jews*, Christian Wilhelm Dohm argued that Jewish law was indeed flexible enough to adapt to the new circumstances of citizenship. Even that most serious objection to the extension of civil equality to Jews—whether Jewish law would permit Jews to fulfill their military obligations on the Sabbath—could be overcome, according to Dohm. In ancient times, he argued, Jews had interpreted the law on this question to allow them to serve in the armies of their respective countries. Surely, contemporary European Jews could reinterpret the laws once again to conform to changing times. Dohm concluded his tract with the prophecy that "as soon as wider horizons are opened to the Jews, as soon as they are accepted as members of the political society and can make its interests their own, they will then reform their religious laws and regulations according to the demands of society."[8] The Abbé Grégoire, a central figure in the crusade for Jewish rights in France, agreed with Dohm on this matter. Grégoire believed that Judaism had only three fundamental dogmas: the coming of the messiah, the unity of God, and the immortality of the soul together with the belief in divine retribution. Otherwise, Grégoire concluded, the majority of Jewish laws were relative and would not conflict with civil functions.[9]

Not all observers of eighteenth-century Jewry were as sanguine as Dohm and Grégoire. Reviewing Dohm's essay, Johann David Michaelis of Göttingen retorted, "As long as Jews keep the laws of Moses, as long as for instance they do not take their meals with us at mealtimes or are not able to make friends with simple folk over a glass of beer, they will never (I do not speak of individuals but of the greater part) fuse with us like Catholics and Lutherans, Germans, Wends, and Frenchmen living in the same State." Both dietary laws and proscriptions against Sabbath work, Michaelis argued, would make it impossible for Jews to serve in the army. In contrast to Dohm, Michaelis held that Jewish law could not be amended to meet the demands of emancipation, and he concluded that membership in the Jewish community would forever preclude citizenship in the state.[10] Even Moses Mendelssohn, who ardently believed the demands of citizenship could be reconciled with continued adherence to Jewish law, nurtured some reservations. In his famous redefinition of Judaism in terms of enlightenment ideals, *Jerusalem*, Mendelssohn declared to his fellow Jews, "Adopt the mores and constitution of the country in which you find yourself, but be steadfast in upholding the religion of your fathers, too." But to Christians he warned, "If we can be united with you as citizens only on the condition that we deviate from the law which we still consider binding, then we sincerely regret the necessity of declaring that we shall renounce our claim to civil equality and union with you."[11]

Jewish messianic expectations evoked even stronger doubts about the possibility of transforming Jews into patriotic citizens. According to Michaelis, Jews could never feel true loyalty toward their country of residence because "they hope one day to leave, to their great happiness, and return to Palestine.... A people that has such hopes never will feel entirely at home or have patriotic love for the paternal soil."[12] Countering Michaelis's argument, Grégoire retorted, "If you expect a Jew to love a country, give him one." Grégoire agreed that Jews hoped for their eventual return to Palestine, but, he said, "Their return is set for an uncertain epoch," and in the meantime most Jews were primarily concerned with securing their livelihoods and possessions wherever they currently resided. If Jews could be convinced that peace, security, liberty, and comfort were attainable in the diaspora, they would abandon messianism, for "Too often the advantages of this life make them forget the promised future." On a more mundane level, some opponents of Jewish emancipation also held that the international business connections among Jews would prevent them from becoming "zealous patriots." Grégoire's reply to this charge was that if European society allowed Jews to participate in trades other than commerce, they would gladly abandon their economic activities in favor of agriculture. As peasants, Jews would develop the love of the land that is the basis for all patriotic sentiments. Thus for Grégoire, the two factors that above all made Jews into a sort of transnational nation—messianism and commerce—did not constitute insurmountable obstacles to their becoming good citizens.[13]

Both advocates and opponents of civic equality for the Jews in the late eighteenth century were in agreement on at least two points, although they interpreted them differently. They both concurred that Jewry in its present condition was corrupt and debased, and that this corruption grew out of Jewish particularism. Opponents of emancipation, like Michaelis, maintained that Jewish degeneration was innate, and that it was in fact responsible for Jewish separateness. Their view spawned the familiar nineteenth-century antisemitic charge that Jews would always constitute a "state within a state."[14] Liberal, pro-emancipation forces, on the other hand, argued that the degenerate nature of Jewish society was the result of centuries of persecution at the hands of intolerant Christians. If Jews were granted legal and economic equality and treated by Christians in a tolerant and humane manner, they could be expected to "regenerate" or refashion themselves into rational, enlightened human beings fit to be citizens. Under such circumstances, Jews would voluntarily shed those particularistic traits of their culture and religion that had kept them separate throughout the ages, and would wholeheartedly enter the mainstream of Gentile society. Furthermore, these physiocratic enlightenment thinkers predicted, Jews would renounce their traditional commercial trades, particularly usury, to become "useful" as either artisans or peasants. They would also move out of their autonomous communities and enthusiastically adopt the laws of their new residences, including the fulfillment of their military duties. Naturally, Jews were expected to give up their messianic hopes as well as special legal proscriptions that might interfere with their full participation in civic duties. Having done all that, so said the enlightened protagonists of emancipation, Jews would then fraternize with their Christian countrymen and would abandon their impure Yiddish dialects in favor of the language of their country. Some even hoped that in the not too far distant future, Jews might take that final leap, conversion, and fully integrate themselves into the culture of their newly adopted nations. In short, Gentile society expected assimilation in return for emancipation.[15] Continued tensions between Christians and Jews in the nineteenth century were due in no small measure to conflicting interpretations over precisely what assimilation entailed.

This implicitly contractual nature of emancipation imposed tremendous pressures on Jews to prove their worthiness to become citizens. In the late eighteenth and early nineteenth centuries, two prevailing theories arose in western and central Europe about the most efficacious manner of bringing about the regeneration of that refractory people. In France, the majority of pro-emancipation spokesmen, including Grégoire, Malesherbes, and Mirabeau, argued that equality should precede regeneration: grant Jews rights and assimilation will follow naturally. Many in France harbored reservations about this view, which explains why the Sephardi Jews of southern France acquired their emancipation almost two years before their more traditional Ashkenazi coreligionists in eastern France. Nevertheless, the momentum of revolutionary events prodded the National Assembly into passing a wave of legislation in 1791, including complete and immediate civic equality for all Jews.[16]

In Germany, where the question of emancipation arose in a period of reaction against the ideas of the French Revolution, only a few liberal thinkers, most notably Alexander von Humboldt and Karl August von Hardenberg, who played an influential role in the Prussian Reform movement (1807–12), advocated following the example of the French. Instead, the prevailing German ideology on emancipation held that regeneration must precede civic equality. Jews would have to prove themselves worthy of citizenship before government officials would consider any changes in the legal status quo. Central European administrations thus adopted a piecemeal and gradualistic approach to emancipation that placed the entire burden of this implicit contract on one party alone, the Jews.[17]

Even in France, despite the more unconditional nature of emancipation, there were setbacks and fluctuations in policy. When it became apparent that the transformation of French Jewry was not as immediate and complete as Gentile society had originally anticipated, Napoleon decided to make explicit the demands and expectations. In a typically pompous and grandiose gesture, Napoleon convened the Sanhedrin between 1806 and 1807, an assembly of carefully selected lay and religious leaders called upon to clarify the position of French Jewry vis-à-vis the state. As in past debates over emancipation, national identity emerged as the central theme of the Sanhedrin's deliberations. Delegates to the Sanhedrin refused to condone the total social and cultural fusion of Jews into French society by rejecting Napoleon's suggestion that they sanction intermarriage. They did comply, however, with his political demands intended to ensure that the primary allegiance of Jews be to the state and not to international Jewry. In answer to the question of whether Jews recognized civil law in divorce cases, the Sanhedrin declared: "Submission to the prince is the first of duties. It is a principle generally acknowledged among them, that, in everything relating to civil or political interests the law of the State is supreme." In answer to the question whether "Jews born in France, and treated by law as French citizens, regard France as their homeland, feel an obligation to defend France, and to obey the laws and provisions of the civil code," the Sanhedrin responded unequivocably in the affirmative. It was the sacred duty of Jews to defend their country: "Men who have adopted a country, who have resided in it these many generations,... cannot but consider themselves as Frenchmen in France.... The love of the country is in the heart of Jews a sentiment so natural, so powerful, and so consonant to their religious opinions, that a French Jew considers himself, in England, as among strangers, although he may be among Jews; and the case is the same with English Jews in France." To diminish practical obstacles impeding Jewish army service, the Sanhedrin decreed that Jewish conscripts be exempted from all religious obligations that might conflict with military duties.[18]

Ironically, Napoleon believed that Jews could be made equal only by means of exceptional legislation. So as not to repeat the error of relying solely on the voluntary compliance of Jews to bring about their own self-regeneration, Napoleon passed the "Infamous Decree" of 1808. That legislation placed ten-year restrictions on Jewish commercial activities, and particularly the charging of interest on loans; limited Jewish immigration into France and the Jews' freedom of movement within France; and forbade Jews (in contradistinction to all other French citizens) from purchasing military replacements. Napoleon further mandated that Jews abandon their Hebrew names and assume permanent French family names. To ensure the complete divestiture of all political and national elements from Judaism, Napoleon decided to create a state-supervised Jewish Consistory on the Protestant model.[19] As a result of the Napoleonic legacy, full legal equality was not achieved in France until the end of the July Monarchy. Although both Catholic and Protestant clerical personnel had received state salaries since the 1801 Concordat, it was only in 1831 that the government first began to remunerate Jewish clergy. Moreover, the last juridical discriminatory measure against the Jews, the oath *more judaico*,* was abolished only in 1846. Thus even in France, as in Germany and elsewhere in central Europe,

---

* A special form of oath required of Jewish witnesses testifying in non-Jewish courts of law. This oath, instituted during the Middle Ages, was frequently accompanied by humiliating rituals and self-deprecatory formulations. In some ceremonies, Jews were forced to swear while standing on a sow's skin; they were also often required to invoke terrible biblical curses on themselves should they give false testimony. With emancipation in the nineteenth century, these oaths gradually fell out of practice.

Jews felt the continued need to prove themselves worthy of emancipation in the eyes of non-Jewish society.[20]

The formulation of assimilationist ideologies among nineteenth-century western and central European Jews reflects the degree to which at least one segment of the Jewish population internalized the Enlightenment critique of Jews and Judaism. In Germany this ideology received expression primarily from the new religious movements, Reform and neo-Orthodoxy, associated respectively with Abraham Geiger and Samson Raphael Hirsch. Although these movements differed substantially on the nature of Jewish law, they both maintained that assimilation did not necessarily demand the complete denial of all Jewish particularism and eagerly sought to redefine Judaism in terms compatible with the demands of citizenship. The most marked feature of both Reform and neo-Orthodoxy was the thorough reduction of Judaism to a creed, stripped of all national and political elements. Differing with their Enlightenment predecessor, Moses Mendelssohn, who had argued that what was unique to Judaism was the ceremonial law, Geiger and Hirsch maintained that it was "ethical monotheism"—the universal rational and ethical principles of Judaism as espoused by the prophets—that constituted the "essence of Judaism." No longer were Jews to wait for the coming of a distinctively Jewish messiah who would bring about the ultimate restoration of the Jewish polity in Palestine. Now, in the modern age of enlightenment, Geiger and Hirsch announced that Jews had embraced a new mission—to spread prophetic Judaism's universal values of brotherhood and justice among all the peoples of the world. Thus denuded of its particularist implications, messianism symbolized, to Reformers and neo-Orthodox alike, not merely the redemption of the Jewish people but the spiritual redemption of all humankind.[21] Exemplifying this new attitude, the Reformers at the 1845 Frankfurt Rabbinical Conference even declared, "The Messianic idea should receive prominent mention in the prayers, but all petitions for our return to the land of our fathers and for the restoration of a Jewish state should be eliminated from the prayers."[22]

In France at about the same time, ideologists of assimilation formulated the doctrine of Franco-Judaism, which couched the concepts of ethical monotheism and the mission of Judaism in more secular language. Perhaps because legal emancipation had not yet been achieved, Reform and neo-Orthodox Jews in Germany continued to believe in a solitary mission for contemporary Jews. By contrast, spokesmen for Franco-Judaism, such as Théodore Reinach, James Darmsteter, and Joseph Salvador, argued that although Jews in the modern era continued to have a special mission, they no longer had to work alone to promulgate their message of universal justice and peace. France, now transfigured by the Revolution into the nation of liberalism and progress, had joined Israel in the vanguard of civilization. Having taken upon itself the promulgation of those prophetic values "liberté, egalité, fraternité," France would lead the crusade to eradicate once and for all those barbaric prejudices, residues from the medieval past. According to Franco-Judaism, Jewish messianic hopes and prophetic ethical ideals culminated in the Enlightenment and the French Revolution. Emancipation thus marked the end of Jewish exile, and just as in Germany, messianism would be realized in the diaspora. France became the "Promised Land," the "New Jerusalem." With this complete fusion of Jewish religious tenets with French republican and democratic values, patriotism became a quasi-religious duty. The Consistory accordingly adopted as its motto, "Patrie and Religion," and by the second half of the nineteenth century, French rabbis could proclaim, "If Palestine is no longer our fatherland, France, mother so tender and generous, has become for us a second fatherland."[23] On the whole, however, advocates of Franco-Judaism did not envision the complete disappearance of Judaism. Rather, as one rabbi put it, "The spirit of France is that which best protects the spirit of Judaism." Another added that to be a patriotic Frenchman a Jew must simply "remain faithful to the past of Israel."[24]

This universalization of the messianic idea, which dramatically altered the Jewish view of *galut* (exile), entailed significant political repercussions. Traditionally Jews had conceived of the *galut* as divine punishment for their sins. Now, Reform and neo-Orthodox Jews in Germany as well as theoreticians of Franco-Judaism maintained that dispersion offered the arena in which the Jewish mission would be carried out. Terminology reflected this new positive connotation; the word *diaspora* increasingly supplanted *galut*, just as the term *Israélite* supplanted *Jew*.[25] Politically, the shift symbolized the virtual denationalization of Judaism, and Jews themselves came to adopt Clermont-Tonnerre's view that in the postemancipation era collective Jewish interests were illegitimate, except those that were purely religious. Abraham Geiger pushed this denial of Jewish solidarity to its logical conclusion when the Jewish community of Damascus came under bloody attack in 1840 as the result of a ritual murder charge. Explaining his decision not to join leaders of French and British Jewry who interceded on behalf of the Syrian Jews, Geiger wrote to his friend Joseph Derenbourg in France: "While it is very honorable of these gentlemen to take up the cause of the persecuted and the oppressed, it is not and has never been a specifically Jewish question. . . . That Jews in Prussia may have the chance to become pharmacists or lawyers is much more important to me than the rescue of all the Jews of Asia and Africa."[26]

In another letter to Derenbourg, written during the Franco-Prussian war, Geiger summed up his views on the relationship of Judaism to German nationalism thus: "Over and above everything else, I am a human being; it is only second to that, or in constant relation to it, that I am a German and then a Jew."[27] During the Dreyfus Affair in France, the Consistory adopted a similar policy of neutrality, refusing to consider domestic antisemitism a collective Jewish interest. Although German Jews modified this position in the late nineteenth century when they created Jewish self-defense organizations to combat rising antisemitism, native French Jews maintained this policy until the 1930's.[28] Some post-Holocaust historians have vehemently criticized western European Jewry for this stance of political neutrality on what today are considered national Jewish issues, condemning it as passivity and naïveté.[29] Yet in light of the weighty pressures emancipation exerted on nineteenth-century Jews, constantly subjecting them to suspicions of "dual loyalties," political neutrality seemed a reasonable and workable solution.

The articulation of the ideology of assimilation did not remain limited to theoretical formulations; it quickly received institutional expression as well. The enlightened elites of German and French Jewry created religious, educational, philanthropic, and intellectual institutions in order to regenerate Jews in conformity with the expectations of Gentile society and to inculcate patriotic virtues simultaneously with religious ones. Although no major reform movement emerged in France comparable to that in Germany, the Consistory itself initiated many of the same religious modifications. In accordance with the aesthetic criterion of the Protestant model, reformers in France and Germany abbreviated synagogue services by eliminating many of the *piyuttim* (liturgical poetry), introduced sermons and prayers in the vernacular, preached the need for more discipline and order in the service, and deemphasized the political aspects of messianism.[30] To produce modern rabbis, who above all would be able to deliver edifying and patriotic sermons, French and German Jews established new types of rabbinical seminaries in which secular learning in French or German strongly complemented a modernized religious curriculum.[31] In Jewish primary schools, teachers required students to recite daily a catechism that outlined patriotic obligations owed to the state and they made every attempt to suppress Alsatian Yiddish.[32] To stimulate economic regeneration among Jews, reformers in Germany and the Consistory in France created vocational schools to encourage poor Jews to become artisans and manual laborers.* New journals and academic societies promulgated the ideals of regeneration and assimilation.† Ironically, even the Alliance Israélite Universelle, which recognized the ties of Jewish solidarity and sought to combat anti-Jewish persecution in eastern Europe, the Near East, and North Africa, propagated the ideology of patriotism and assimilation. Confident of having proved their own worthiness to be citizens, the younger generation of French Jews who had created the organization in the mid-nineteenth century believed the time was ripe to spread the ideology of regeneration among their more backward and "oriental" coreligionists. Thus they hoped that Jews throughout the world would ultimately ac-

---

*In 1825 three societies were created in France to encourage poor Jews to go into artisanry and manual labor: the Société Israélite des Amis du Travail in Paris, the Société d'Encouragement au Travail Parmi les Jeunes Israélites Indigents du Bas-Rhin in Strasbourg, and the Société pour l'Encouragement des Arts et Métiers Parmi les Israélites de Metz. In 1825 the Consistory established an Ecole de Travail in Strasbourg. A similar school was founded in Mulhouse in 1842 on independent initiative. See Patrick Girard, *Les Juifs de France*, p. 119; and Albert, *Modernization*, p. 136. On efforts in Germany, see Kober, "Emancipation's Impact."

†The two major French journals were the *Archives israélites* and the *Univers israélite*. Their efforts were paralleled in Germany by the *Allgemeine Zeitung des Judentums*. The Verein für Cultur und Wissenschaft der Juden was founded in 1819 by Leopold Zunz in Germany. The Société des Etudes Juives was founded in Paris in 1880. A major purpose of both groups was to prove that Jews had made valuable contributions to European culture as a whole. On the influence of German Haskalah and German Reform Judaism on French Jewry, see Helfand, "Symbiotic Relationship."

quire emancipation under the aegis of the most progressive and enlightened of all European Jews—the French.[33]

Clearly, the ideology of "Patrie and Religion" had achieved a secure foothold on both theoretical and institutional planes. Nevertheless, it is necessary to raise several crucial questions. First, did the Jewish response to the challenge of national identity differ substantially from that of the non-Jewish population? Was there anything peculiar in the nineteenth-century Jewish experience that caused Jews to adopt a particular brand of nationalism? Second, to what degree did the ideology spread beyond the confines of the capital cities? Since a significant portion of western European Jewry resided outside the capitals, is it not likely that their experience of acculturation was distinct from that of Jews in either Berlin or Paris? Third, to what extent did the ideology filter down to the less articulate Jewish masses? Is it not possible that the formulation and institutionalization of the ideology remained restricted to one segment of European Jewry, that is, to those upwardly mobile and essentially urban middle-class Jews? Or, if the ideology did indeed penetrate to the lower classes, did it do so in the same manner and to the same extent as it did among the urban elites?

In order to begin providing answers to these questions, so central to an understanding of the relationship between national identity and emancipation, we will focus attention on a single population of European Jews caught up in a change of national allegiance—the Jews of Alsace and Lorraine between 1871 and 1918. The annexation of France's eastern provinces by the newly formed German empire in 1871 provides an opportunity to study the first major challenge to the Franco-Jewish symbiosis in the ideology of nineteenth-century French Jewry. The transition from French to German sovereignty offered an occasion not only for Alsace-Lorraine Jews, who constituted 57 percent of all French Jewry in 1866,[34] but also for Catholics and Protestants in the provinces to publicly manifest their patriotic sympathies. Besides emigration, which was of course the most overt demonstration of national loyalties, other more subtle forms of protest continued throughout the nearly one-half century of German rule. The Reichsland, as Alsace-Lorraine was officially called during this period, thus affords a unique locale in which to carry out a comparative study of reactions to the German annexation to determine whether the Jewish minority, constituting slightly less than

The Task of Becoming Citizens

3 percent of the total population, had a different notion of its Frenchness from that of non-Jews.

In addition to the opportunity for comparative analysis with Christians, Alsace-Lorraine constitutes an ideal case study of Jewish national identity because the Jews of these provinces had always been regarded as those most in need of regeneration. Following the expulsion of Jews from France in 1394, many fled to Alsace and Lorraine, then largely within the boundaries of the Holy Roman Empire. After the treaty of Westphalia in 1648, these territories increasingly fell under French dominion, and a sizable Jewish population was reintroduced into France. When the question of Jewish emancipation first arose during the National Assembly debates between 1789 and 1791, doubts regarding the assimilability of the Jews focused specifically on the Jews of these regions, who at that time constituted nearly 90 percent of all French Jewry. Under the ancien régime, these Jews had been excluded from owning land and from entering artisan guilds, and they had been denied residence rights in the major cities of the provinces, with the exception of Metz. As a result of these restrictions, the majority of eighteenth-century Jews lived in semirural villages and engaged in petty commerce such as cattle, horse, and grain dealing, trade in secondhand clothing, peddling, and moneylending. While Christian conservatives denounced the religious stubbornness of the Jews, radical Jacobins from Alsace and Lorraine, under the leadership of Jean François Reubell, excoriated the Jews as the principal exploiters of the peasantry. Reubell argued that the parasitical economic behavior of the Jews, and in particular their propensity toward usury, made them entirely unfit for the rights and obligations of citizenship.[35]

Another cause for concern was that the Jewish community in Alsace and Lorraine had not expressed any willingness to abandon its communal autonomy at the time of the French Revolution. The more assimilated Sephardi communities of Bordeaux and Bayonne, which had been naturalized since the mid-sixteenth century,* as

---

*The first *lettres patentes* granted to the Sephardim of southern France by Henry II in 1550 recognized these recently arrived refugees of the Iberian Inquisition not as Jews but as *conversos*, or New Christians. These documents authorized them to reside "wherever they desired," even though the 1394 edict expelling the Jews remained in effect. It was only in 1723 that the Sephardim of southern France first received *lettres patentes* recognizing them officially as Jews rather than as New Christians. See Hertzberg, *French Enlightenment*, pp. 16–17, 25–28, 50–51.

well as the small Jewish community of Paris, had voluntarily renounced their right to corporate autonomy in their *cahiers* sent to the National Assembly in 1789. The Jews of Alsace and Lorraine, by contrast, did not initially perceive any necessary conflict between autonomy and citizenship and showed themselves to be far more concerned with economic rather than political equality. While requesting freedom of residence and an end to all arbitrary and discriminatory taxes, the Jews of eastern France listed among their original demands "that we will be maintained in the free exercise of our laws, rites, and customs, and that we conserve our Synagogues, our Rabbis, and our Syndics, in the same manner that they exist today."* Non-Jewish opponents of emancipation, like Reubell, seized on this petition to prove the disinclination of Jews to become citizens—"You will see that it is not I who exclude the Jews, they exclude themselves."[36] The Sephardim, sensible to the danger such demands posed to their emancipation, immediately dissociated themselves from their northern Ashkenazi coreligionists, whom they had long regarded as inferior in manners and morals.[37]

Although the campaign to regenerate the Jews of France was thus targeted specifically at the refractory economic, cultural, and religious behavior of those in Alsace-Lorraine as a whole, various sectors of that Jewish population responded to the challenge in significantly different ways. Without a doubt, the middle- and upper middle-class urban elite imbibed the ideology of Patrie/Religion and made it their task to work for the regeneration of their poorer coreligionists. In the 1830's Simon Bloch, future editor of one of Franco-Jewry's most influential publications, the *Univers israélite*, created a monthly in Strasbourg called *La Régénération*. Preaching the moral and religious betterment of Jews, Bloch launched the first installment with the appeal: "Israelites of Alsace, fully recognize your obligations. The Fatherland has adopted you as its children. Show yourselves worthy of that reception, so that you are not obliged

---

*Three months later the Ashkenazim abandoned these demands. Two Lorraine Jewish communities, however, Sarreguemines and Lunéville, dissociated themselves from the Ashkenazi position at the outset in an effort to acquire greater autonomy from the larger community of Nancy, which they felt had been subjecting them to unfair and excessive taxation. "Adresse à l'Assemblée . . . 31 août 1789," pp. 13–14. See also Helfand, "Symbiotic Relationship," pp. 336–39, 342–43; and Hertzberg, *French Enlightenment*, p. 345.

to receive as a favor that which you ask for as a right."[38] Similarly, Maurice Bloch, a prominent Alsatian Jewish educational reformer and publicist, appealed to his coreligionists in Alsace: "You all know that the French Revolution emancipated the Jews. But is the decree that accorded them the rights of citizenship sufficient to render them worthy of those rights? Much more is needed than a stroke of the pen to change, along with their civil and political situation, their morals, their manners, their sentiments, fruits of long centuries of misery and humiliation."[39]

To encourage their own regeneration, Jewish writers in Alsace and Lorraine created a new genre of didactic literature urging Jews to abandon commerce in favor of the liberal professions, artisanry, and even peasantry, and praising the virtues of military service and patriotism. Paradigmatic of this literature is the novel published in 1865 by Rabbi Isaac Lévy, soon to become Grand Rabbi of Colmar. *Isaïe ou le travail*, set in the 1840's, is the story of an orphaned Jewish *schnorrer* (beggar) of German parentage who, under the guidance of the local rabbi, is "regenerated" into an honorable French Jewish citizen. After his Bar Mitzvah, Isaïe attends the Ecole de Travail to become an artisan, distinguishes himself as a military hero in Algeria, instills discipline into the prayer service, marries and cultivates a garden, and finally becomes a lay member of the Consistory. In that post, he works assiduously to wipe out that scourge of the Alsatian countryside—Jewish mendicancy.

Lévy's call for "regeneration" received practical implementation as well. Léon Werth, a prominent lay member of the Colmar Consistory, went so far as to advocate in 1868 the creation of an agricultural colony for Jews to complement the efforts of the *écoles de travail* in Strasbourg and Mulhouse.[40] At the Strasbourg Ecole de Travail, instructors urged their students to speak French, not Alsatian Yiddish, which Maurice Bloch condemned as "that barbaric idiom, left over from more barbaric times," a language that "created something like a masonic link among those who spoke it" but "separated like a moat Jews and Christians, Jews and Frenchmen."[41] By the mid-1830's one fanatically assimilationist Alsatian Jewish writer proclaimed that the transformation of the Jews had been successfully accomplished within only forty years. That collective entity known as the Jewish people, he declared confidently, would dissolve entirely in the very near future.[42]

Despite this enthusiasm, a significant gap seems to have existed between the perceptions of the Alsace-Lorraine elite and the lives and circumstances of the majority of Jews who resided in the provinces. Historians of French Jewry, who have focused almost exclusively on urban elites, stress the rapidity with which French Jews assimilated to French culture. But in Alsace and Lorraine urbanization proceeded far more slowly than elsewhere in France. In 1851 only 24 percent of the Jews in Alsace-Lorraine lived in the capital cities of their districts; as late as 1871–72, only 31 percent did so.* Taking such demographic data into account, a growing number of recent studies, more oriented toward social history, have begun to look beyond the confines of the city. Their findings offer a quite different picture of social transformation. Without denying that essential changes occurred among rural Jews, these historians stress the gradual nature of change, and claim that socioeconomic, religious, cultural, and linguistic traditionalism persisted well into the nineteenth century.[43]

Pointing to Alsace as a test case, Jacob Katz, for example, has argued that notwithstanding a few isolated instances, the program of economic regeneration proved an overwhelming failure. Although great numbers of Jews did indeed take advantage of new opportunities in the liberal professions, very few entered artisan trades, and scarcely any became peasants. Moreover, despite the expectations of both Jewish and Gentile reformers that the Jews would "normalize" their occupational distribution if allowed to, nineteenth-century Jews actually became increasingly concentrated in certain professional categories, and commerce remained the main field of Jewish economic activity. Concurring with the view of Simon Kuznets, Katz argues that a noneconomic factor—the sociological status of Jews as a minority group—was preeminently responsible for maintaining the lopsided Jewish economic distribution. Even though legal disabilities disappeared, social prejudices continued to exclude

---

*Szajkowski, "Growth of the Jewish Population," p. 311. The 1871–72 figures are based on the pre-annexation borders of the provinces. Urbanization proceeded slowly in Germany too. At the beginning of the nineteenth century, 90 percent of the Jews in German-speaking Central European countries resided in rural or semi-rural villages, and as late as 1895 almost one-half of the Bavarian Jews were still considered rural. See Cahnman, "Village and Small-Town Jews in Germany," p. 107. For the view that French Jews assimilated rapidly, see Roblin, Les Juifs de Paris.

Jews from traditionally Christian occupations. Christian masters were reluctant to take on Jewish apprentices, and the practice of Saturday work made artisanry unattractive to Jews. Nor would it have been easy for Jews to enter into the tightly knit peasant community. Kuznets and Katz agree that the social, religious, and cultural cohesiveness of Jews as a minority group, together with their desire for endogamy, encouraged their continued concentration in specific economic pursuits. Economic considerations further compounded these sociological ones. First, in a nonindustrial and noncapitalistic economy, Jews performed essential economic functions as creditors and middlemen. Second, it made little sense for Jews to compete with Christians for already saturated economic niches. To have abandoned commerce in favor of artisanry and peasantry would have been to swim against the economic currents of the nineteenth century. Because of their traditional commercial occupations, Jews in fact found themselves particularly well suited to take advantage of new economic opportunities made available by the rising tides of capitalism. In this situation, Katz points out, legal access to enter hitherto proscribed professions was rendered meaningless by the complete absence of economic incentives.[44]

Furthermore, ascendence up the ladder of socioeconomic success, even in preeminently commercial pursuits, did not take place as rapidly as some historians have argued. Social mobility did indeed occur, and Alsace-Lorraine Jews began to rise into the new and more prestigious occupational categories of the liberal professions, public service, and manufacturing all the while abandoning petty commerce for wholesale and retail trades.[45] Yet recent social historical studies of Alsace-Lorraine Jewry during the first half of the nineteenth century indicate that the pace of socioeconomic amelioration among Alsace-Lorraine Jews in general, and rural Jews there in particular, was slower than anywhere else in France.[46] Despite the embourgeoisement of one segment of recently urbanized Jews, especially during the economic upsurge under the Second Empire, most Jews continued to live on the edge of poverty.[47] Writing in the mid-nineteenth century, the celebrated Alsatian Jewish writer and journalist Alexandre Weill commented ironically: "One can reproach the Jews in Alsace for many things. First of all they are poor."[48] (Zadoc Kahn, Grand Rabbi of France at the end of the nineteenth century, related that his father, a rural peddler who worked from dawn till dusk, sustained himself on one piece of bread daily.[49]) Subject to constant price fluctuations and victims of periodic famines, most rural Jews barely eked out a living. On the eve of the Revolution, Isaiah Berr Bing, a proponent of Jewish enlightenment, estimated that two-thirds of all Alsatian Jews existed on the brink of starvation. Thirty percent of the Jews in the district of Colmar in 1828 were unable to pay their consistorial taxes; in Metz, 50 percent found themselves in similar straits. The Bas-Rhin Consistory estimated that in 1850 there were two hundred families of wandering beggars and six hundred families living on partial charity. As late as 1858, some 13 percent of Bas-Rhin Jews were indigent in comparison with 9 percent of Catholics and 5 percent of Lutherans.[50] The pace of socioeconomic change in the countryside thus remained decidedly slow.

Cultural habits also lingered, as evidenced by the persistence of linguistic traditionalism. It is true, as Paul Lévy points out, that although the Catholic and Protestant clergy systematically opposed the introduction of French into the schools, the Alsace-Lorraine rabbinate in general actively supported it, earning the commendation of official school inspectors.[51] But in 1810 only 10 percent of all Jewish children attended public schools, and school attendance did not become prevalent until the 1830's with the promulgation of the Guizot law, which mandated that every municipality create and support a primary school.[52] It is hardly surprising, therefore, that in spite of significant efforts on the part of religious and educational leaders, Alsatian Yiddish continued to be spoken on a wide scale, particularly by rural Jewry. When compelled by law to adopt non-Hebrew family names, Jews in the provinces generally chose German names like Braun, Kaufmann, Berger, and Schuler, rather than French ones.[53] One not too sympathetic critic of the Jews declared before the Chamber of Deputies in 1818: "They generally know only German and the jargon they use among themselves. . . . They have few notions of the French language."[54] Jewish literary evidence lends further credence to this view, which cannot be dismissed as mere antisemitic rhetoric. As late as 1848, the reform-oriented *Archives israélites* continued to carry scathing attacks on Alsatian rabbis for their persistence in delivering sermons in the Yiddish "jargon."[55] In *Scènes de la vie juive en Alsace* (1860), Daniel Stauben portrays a Jewish beggar in the countryside vehemently denouncing the translation of the Bible and other holy books into French: "That's an abomination! Can God and does God want to be prayed to in a language other than the language of our ancestors in Palestine? . . . And to say . . . that the majority of those who buy them [the holy books] understand no more French than you or me!"[56] According to another Alsatian Jewish writer, Georges Stenne, even by the mid-nineteenth century, knowledge of French among the generation of Jews born before the Revolution was extremely rare. In his novel *Perle* (1877), in describing the inn of one rural Jew, Stenne writes, "All that he had done for the prosperity of the establishment was the choice of the sign: *Au Cheval Blanc*, the only French words that his rebellious memory could ever retain."[57]

Since German remained the predominant language in the provinces until the 1830's, better-educated rural Jews often spoke German to the exclusion of French.[58] We have evidence that in 1828 a Lauterbourg Jew dictated his will in German and the local notary subsequently translated it into French.[59] Zadoc Kahn declared that his mother possessed a good working knowledge of German in the 1830's—"a rare thing in those surroundings where scarcely anything but jargon was spoken."[60] Stenne's novel *Perle* relates that a young Jewish factotum of the Wertheim municipal councilor knew only German in the mid-nineteenth century.[61] Isaac Lévy makes a similar point in *Isaïe ou le travail*. He has children in the village of Odratzheim, which lacked its own Jewish school, learning at their *cheder* (traditional Jewish school) how to write German in Hebrew letters; those who wanted to learn French had to attend the Catholic school. He also portrays a funeral service where the rabbi of Marmoutier reads prayers in Hebrew and translates certain Talmudic passages into German, not French.[62] Given Lévy's pro-emancipation views, one assumes that these details were intended to show how hard it was for the hero, Isaïe, to become regenerated into a good French citizen.

Alsace and Lorraine also remained the bastion of religious traditionalism in the nineteenth century. The persistence of ritual observance among rural Jewry is, of course, legendary,[63] but strong orthodox currents surfaced even in the cities. Most symbolic of the differences between the elites of Paris and the provinces was the rift that developed between the Central Consistory and the Grand Rabbi of Colmar, Salomon Klein, although it should be pointed out that Klein presided over an overwhelmingly rural constituency. In 1847 the Strasbourg and Colmar consistories proposed to establish their own Talmudic preparatory schools for students planning to enter the Central Consistory–supervised Ecole Rabbinique in Metz. The Central Consistory staunchly refused to authorize this change and advised the two departmental consistories to subsidize the attendance of prospective rabbinical students at public secondary schools, all the while providing them privately with religious training.

Although the Strasbourg Consistory complied with the Central Consistory's directive, the Colmar Consistory, under the leadership of Grand Rabbi Klein, proceeded to open its school in 1853. The conflict grew into open rebellion when Klein, together with other conservative Jewish rabbis from the provinces, publicly denounced the reformist decisions of the 1856 rabbinical conference in Paris. Klein then took the step of transforming his preparatory school into an independent seminary to train orthodox rabbis from Alsace-Lorraine, who would not want to study at the too liberal Ecole Rabbinique, which was soon to be transferred to Paris. Unable to tolerate this challenge to its hegemony, the Central Consistory threatened Klein with dismissal and forced him to retreat. Despite Klein's failure, the affair nevertheless indicates the extent to which orthodoxy continued to compete with the liberal version of Judaism propagated by the Consistory as well as with the more radical voices for religious reform that had emerged earlier from Metz.[64]

Nor did deep-seated hostilities toward military service change as quickly as the apostles of regeneration would lead us to believe. Like their Gentile neighbors, Jews were often less than enthusiastic about serving in the armies of the Directory and Napoleon I. In the Year XI (September 1802–September 1803) the Prefect of the Moselle did indeed commend the patriotic commitment of Jews in his district and concluded a governmental survey by saying, "They have shown themselves worthy of the French name by their bravery."[65] In Bas-Rhin, on the other hand, the prefect reported in 1806 that "the great majority of that sect [the Jews] constantly seeks to elude the laws and particularly those *regarding conscription*."[66] More than a decade later, a non-Jewish observer concurred, explaining the two sides of the problem: Jews in general "have manifested an aversion for military service, to which they had not been subject at all prior to the Revolution," yet at the same time "the young soldiers have seemed little disposed to receive Jews into their ranks, and the officers in charge of the examination of the conscripts likewise have been loath to admit those of that religion."[67] A sympathetic portrayal of Jewish distaste for military service is presented in *Le Blocus* (1867) by Erckmann-Chatrian. In that novel, a Jewish secondhand dealer counsels his two sons to emigrate to the United States to avoid having to take up arms in what he considers Napoleon I's senseless battles against Prussia.[68] The provision of Napoleon's "Infamous Decree" forbidding Jews to purchase military replacements was clearly intended to counteract such attitudes.

Fictional evidence substantiates the view that despite Napoleon's measures, traditional hostility on the part of Alsace-Lorraine Jewry toward military service continued well into the nineteenth century. To cite *Isaïe ou le travail* once again, the protagonist's adoptive mother, Malkele, represents the well-intentioned but unenlightened point of view. When twenty-year-old Isaïe becomes eligible for conscription to fight in Algeria in 1845, she counsels him to obtain a military dispensation on the legitimate grounds that his parents were of foreign birth. Malkele's main concern is the welfare of her immediate family, for she has only a limited knowledge of foreign affairs: "It's said that our king is making war with the king of a country where it's quite hot and of which I have been told the name, but I have forgotten it."[69] Like other traditional Jews, Malkele recites prayers before the draft lottery in which Isaïe's number is included. Although Lévy shows sympathy for Malkele's maternal apprehensions, he sharply rebukes her narrow-mindedness.

Lévy's fictional portrayal of Malkele's attitude is borne out by the inscription on a *huppah*, or marriage canopy, from the Jewish community of Soultz-sous-Forêts that was discovered by Freddy Raphael and Robert Weyl. The inscription along its four sides reads: "Offered by Naphtali, son of Juda Polak, and of his wife Nanel, daughter of Meir, in the year 5620 of the creation [1860] when their son Joseph drew by lot for the war and obtained a lucky number. They have offered this *huppah* to the community of Soultz."[70]

Jewish supporters of regeneration did their best to combat such traditionalism. Isaac Lévy's fictional hero, Isaïe, the enlightened foil to the traditional Malkele, refuses to heed Malkele's advice to apply for a military dispensation. Explaining his decision to a friend, he proclaims: "Wasn't it in France that I was born, wasn't it there that I was raised, that I was truly protected to this day by laws that are the same for all? And because France today demands my support, will I tell her: I don't wish to be counted among the number of your children? That would be ingratitude; even worse, that would be bad faith." Isaïe is by no means enthusiastic about becoming a soldier and adamantly refuses to glorify militarism, but he considers it his duty to serve if called. By his patriotism, he hopes to improve the image of Alsatian Jews: "I will try to do my duty to show that a Jew (Israélite) knows how to give his blood to his country" in the tradition of the ancient Maccabees.* Yet it is clear from Lévy's novel that Isaïe's patriotic decision remained the exception, particularly among the older generation of rural Jews.

Finally, the pace of social and political assimilation was not a uniform process, and it varied in accordance with socioeconomic factors such as class, urbanization, and religiosity.† Although Alsace-Lorraine Jews generally scorned mixed marriages and conversions, the two most overt forms of social assimilation, at least one sector of the Jews in the provinces did embrace less radical types of acculturation.[71] Responding to an inquiry sent out by the Ministry of Interior in 1843 regarding the social status of the Jewish population, the prefect of Bas-Rhin lavishly praised the "immense" progress of "the richest and most enlightened Israelites." Not only did the Jewish urban middle and upper middle class work to improve the condi-

---

*Isaïe ou le travail, pp. 76, 80, 95. For a general discussion of Jews and military service before 1870 and a good summary of the Isaïe section on conscription, see Raphael, "Les Juifs d'Alsace," especially pp. 139–40. In Perle, Stenne similarly writes (pp. 85–86): "The Jew dearly loves the uniform; each button, the least bit of braiding, seems to remind him of his emancipation and constitutes a visible symbol, a palpable witness of his status as a French citizen, of which he is as happy as he is proud."

†In contemporary parlance, the term assimilation can have negative connotations, suggesting the total abandonment of one's identity and heritage. The vast majority of nineteenth-century Western and Central European Jews, however, understood assimilation to be a process that would enable them to integrate into the majority society without losing their Jewish identity. I have therefore decided to use the term assimilation in a neutral sense, to refer interchangeably to both acculturation and integration. As Stephen Poppel has pointed out, Jewish assimilation has a dual nature: it entails, on the one hand, acculturation, a process that Jews themselves control, and on the other, integration, a dynamic that remains dependent on the receptivity of the host society. For more on this subject see Gordon, *Assimilation in American Life*, pp. 65–73; Poppel, *Zionism in Germany, 1897–1933*, pp. 12–13; Rozenblit, *Jews of Vienna, 1867–1914*, pp. 3–4; and Hyman, *From Dreyfus to Vichy*, pp. 6–8.

tions of life for their more impoverished coreligionists, but by "improving their appearance, by accustoming themselves to habits that correspond to their new position, [they] have brought about a noticeable rapprochement between that class and the part of the Christian population whose social position is materially analogous."[72] Similarly, the prefect of the Moselle noted with satisfaction the considerable social progress of the urban middle classes of Jews. Increasingly, "the rich or even only well-to-do families" were abandoning their ancestral Jewish quarters to live among their Christian compatriots. Moreover, he noted, "this class lodges, dresses, and supports itself, except in solemn circumstances where it is necessary to perform external religious acts, exactly like the Catholic population. It very willingly frequents public places and above all the cafés."[73] Together with this greater degree of social integration, Alsace-Lorraine Jewry increasingly participated in local and even national politics.[74] In 1866 the economic historian Xavier Mossmann exclaimed: "The Revolution was not mistaken. . . . Assimilation has taken place slowly, but surely." All classes within the Jewish population had made progress, but "the elite led the way. You can recognize them everywhere, those men who were ahead of their times and who preceded their coreligionists in the letters, in the arts, in education, in the sciences, in industry, in finance, in the magistracy, in the army, at the bar."[75] In his contemporary study of Lorraine, Henry Contamine goes so far as to state, "It is possible to confirm that in 1870 the Jews of Metz had become integrally French, in their life and their civilization and not only in law."[76]

This picture contrasts sharply with the portrayal by these same commentators of the condition of the impoverished rural Jews. The 1843 report of the prefect of Bas-Rhin described these Jews as "a species of scum wallowing in ignorance, nourishing its old prejudices and in whom one again encounters in a somewhat modified degree, all the original sins of the Jewish nation." The comments of the prefects of Meurthe and Moselle were no less scathing. Lower-class Jews in the villages, these prefects said, were almost entirely untouched by the emancipation: "Jews of this class live only among themselves and have no other relations with Christians except those required by their commerce or their industry."[77] The prefects blamed the retrograde behavior of these poor village Jews on their fervent religiosity, but it is more likely that their entire social nexus, of which religiosity was but one aspect, explains their failure to integrate more fully into Christian society. The considerable antisemitism that reigned in the Alsace-Lorraine countryside, and had erupted into open violence during the Revolution of 1848, also played a significant role in reinforcing social barriers between Jews and Christians.[78]

By the time of the German annexation in 1871, assimilation in Alsace-Lorraine had clearly proceeded at an uneven pace, affecting urban middle-class and upper middle-class Jews far more than their rural coreligionists. Embedded in a traditional culture, the rural Jews of France's eastern provinces continued to maintain linguistic, cultural, religious, and even to some extent economic ties to the larger Ashkenazi Jewish community. Werner Cahnman, explaining his decision to include Alsace-Lorraine in a recent study of rural Jewish life in nineteenth-century Germany, notes, "Their socioeconomic status and their mental habit were not different from the status and habit of other Jewish communities along the Rhine."[79] Since the market network in this frontier land remained essentially local, it is not surprising that national boundaries did not significantly interfere with petty commerce, which was concentrated primarily in the hands of the Jews.[80] Moreover, evidence suggests that ignorance of German was nearly universal in the French-speaking districts of Lorraine, except among the Jews who used it to carry on business with their coreligionists across the Rhine.[81] In one of Albert Neher's stories set around the turn of the last century, the wife of an Alsatian cattle dealer remarks to her husband, "In the land of Baden, cattle are more expensive than here; if not, Baden merchants wouldn't come to provision themselves in Alsace."[82] The steady emigration of German Jews westward to Alsace-Lorraine throughout the French period served to strengthen these connections.[83]

In light of these considerations, the annexation of Alsace and Lorraine affords an excellent test case for examining three major questions relating to Jewish national identity. First, it allows us to determine whether ordinary Jews subscribed to the ideology of patriotism in the same fashion and to the same degree as the Jewish elite. Like the question of Alsace-Lorraine generally, discussion of the Jewish role in Alsace-Lorraine has been subjected to a cross fire of competing French and German patriotic polemics.[84] This rhetoric of patriotism is, of course, one expression of the ideology of Jewish emancipation, but it is also necessary to decipher how accurately the rhetoric reflects historical reality.[85] As recent studies demonstrate, Alsace-Lorraine was not the monolithic society depicted by the patriotic enthusiasts. Rather, it was composed of diverse social, economic, religious, and political groups, each reacting distinctively to the German annexation.[86] It is therefore likely that a similar situation prevailed within the Jewish community of the annexed provinces. Since the ideology of "Patrie/Religion" was integrally related to other aspects of assimilation, socioeconomic factors such as class, urbanization, and social mobility, as well as generational differences, probably played a major role in determining national consciousness. Thus, although more conventional literary sources—newspapers, periodicals, fiction, and administrative reports—afford us the opportunity to study the sentiments of urban Jewish elites, statistical data, particularly on emigration, enable us to determine the degree to which nationalism touched the lives of ordinary, less literate Jews.

Second, this study permits us to address the question whether Jews thought of their national identity in the same fashion as non-Jews. Most often, the patriotism of nineteenth-century Jews assumed a liberal cast, but fin-de-siècle Europe also witnessed the rise of radical right-wing nationalisms tinged to varying degrees with anti-semitism. Clearly, patriotism could manifest itself in diverse ways. An analysis of Jewish notions of patriotism as compared with those of Catholics or Protestants can increase our understanding of the general political function of patriotism in the Reichsland following the annexation.

Finally, recent scholarship also suggests that the population of Alsace-Lorraine was not irreconcilably hostile to Germany. At least until the eve of the First World War, chances for integrating the provinces into the German Reich grew increasingly favorable.[87] Jews, too, probably experienced some sort of accommodation to German rule. Yet this issue has until now remained buried beneath layers of pro-French patriotic polemics. Therefore, another of our goals will be to assess whether the Reichsland's Jewish community exhibited any signs of rapprochement to German rule, or whether it remained recalcitrantly pro-French throughout the entire 47-year-long period, as publicists of Franco-Judaism have argued.

In sum, this study will shed new light on the degree to which French patriotism exercised a real, rather than a merely rhetorical, influence on the political and cultural life of both Jews and non-Jews caught up in this battle of competing national identities. In doing so, it may also offer glimpses into the nature of patriotism itself.

TWO

The Challenge of Patriotism: Responses to the Annexation

The political and literary reactions of Alsace-Lorraine Jewry to the annexation prove that Franco-Judaism had indeed made significant inroads among the most articulate sector of Jews in France's eastern provinces. Despite the close social, economic, and cultural bonds that had linked Alsace-Lorraine and south German Jewry since the Middle Ages, national identity in 1871 triumphed over religious identity. The common experience of the battlefield shared by Frenchmen of all faiths solidified these national affinities, and the enlightened elites of Alsace-Lorraine Jewry unhesitatingly manifested their pro-French sympathies.* Jews and non-Jews alike adhered to French patriotism, but an analysis of Jewish responses as compared with those of Catholics and Protestants reveals that Jewish pro-French proclivities in 1871–72 were deeply rooted in the nineteenth-century Franco-Jewish experience. Above all, spokesmen for Jews in the annexed provinces feared that the transfer to German sovereignty would mean a reversal of their civil rights won in 1791. It was the emancipation that had secured their loyalties to France, and it was the persistence of legal disabilities against Jews in Germany that made them wary of entry into the newly created Reich. Although the leaders of German Jewry energetically vied for the loyalties of their coreligionists in the conquered

---

*Helfand, "Symbiotic Relationship," pp. 331–50, argues that despite the extremely close relations between German and French Jewish enlightened elites during the late eighteenth and early nineteenth centuries, the growing patriotism on both sides had severely weakened these bonds by the 1830's and 1840's. German Jewish spokesmen frequently accused French Jews of laxity in carrying out religious and educational reforms; French Jews retorted by pointing to their undeniably superior civil and political status.

territories, and the new provincial government strove to placate their fears, the political and cultural elites of Alsace-Lorraine Jewry emerged as a major reservoir of anti-German sentiment throughout 1871–72.

National allegiances did not break down precisely along religious lines, but there were important differences between Catholic, Protestant, and Jewish responses to the annexation.[1] Since the Catholic clergy in Alsace-Lorraine had fiercely resisted efforts to impose the French language in schools and churches, it is not surprising that the Catholic majority—80.6 percent of the 1871 civil population—initially adopted a modern wait-and-see attitude toward the new government in the hope of winning political concessions.[2] All chances for appeasement dissipated, however, when Bismarck introduced the *Kulturkampf*, his aggressive anti-Catholic campaign, into the annexed territories in late 1871. Political Catholics consequently became the backbone of the pro-French movement in the Reichsland in the years following the annexation.

Protestant reactions to the annexation were more diverse. Some Protestant spokesmen manifested a decisively pro-French attitude in 1871–72,[3] but others accommodated rapidly to the new German regime. Protestants—16.5 percent of the 1871 civil population—had formed close religious ties with their coreligionists across the Rhine, and like the Catholics, had resisted the French government's gallicization efforts.[4] These bonds, together with the prospect of becoming members of the majority religious group, eventually brought about the conciliation of this important minority to the annexation.[5] Economic interests also led some Protestants to adopt a more favorable outlook on the transition to German sovereignty. Not only did some members of the predominantly Protestant industrial class look forward to profiting from membership in the Zollverein, the powerful German customs union; many also hoped that the new imperial government would subdue the labor unrest that had plagued Alsatian industry since 1869. The impotence of the weakened French administration to deal with these problems stimulated industrialists to turn increasingly to Germany.[6] Consequently, both religious and economic concerns helped reconcile Protestants to the new political situation.

Jewish leaders, in accordance with their earlier expressions of francophile sentiments, also vociferously voiced pro-French sympathies in the wake of the annexation. Not surprisingly, the French Jewish press applauded the patriotism of the Jewish minority— 2.6 percent of the civil population in 1871. Less expected, however, was the lavish praise it received from the non-Jewish French press. The *Journal des débats* exclaimed: "It's remarkable! The Jews, who according to their organization are rather inclined to be cosmopolitans, have demonstrated great repugnance toward becoming Germans, and a large number of them have preferred expatriation."[7] The *Siècle*, too, praised the attitude of the Jewish elites: "All the leaders of the Jewish religion in Lorraine and in Alsace have declared the most unwavering war against the invader."[8] Although the French loyalties of Alsace-Lorraine Jews were occasionally impugned,[9] the generally accepted view was quite the contrary. That Jews did not become scapegoats for France's defeat in the war, in contrast to the oft-repeated recriminations voiced in other instances of national humiliation,* proved all the more that they had succeeded, at least temporarily, in convincing their French compatriots of their worthiness of French citizenship.

Unlike the responses of the Catholic and Protestant leadership to the annexation, the reaction of the Jewish elites was free of all ambivalence, for in no respect did these Jews feel they had anything to gain from a German regime. An extended analysis in a German security report from the summer of 1871 depicted Jews as constituting a large proportion of the pro-French element in Alsace.[10] The report asserted that Jews "judged the worth of their domicile solely in terms of pecuniary advantage . . . and considered the political transformation of this territory dangerous." As the most important commercial class, they particularly "feared the impending inundation of the recently won provinces by German businessmen and German capital [which would] impair . . . their business circumstances. . . . At the same time the extensive business contacts of these Jews with

*A notable case is Germany. Despite the German victory in 1870, Jews in the following years were often blamed for their country's economic problems. Again, Germany's defeat in the First World War was followed by an outburst of antisemitic propaganda reproaching Jews for the debacle. Jews were also held responsible for the French defeat of 1940. Alexandre Weill claims that some clerical papers in France blamed Jews for France's defeat in 1870, and Emile Durkheim took note of similar charges in French Alsace. Yet these remarks seem to have been extremely restricted, and there is no further evidence of a widespread antisemitic campaign after this date. See A. Weill, "Actualités," p. 420; and Wilson, *Ideology and Experience*, p. 663.

France and with all classes of the native population make them appear a preeminently suitable tool of agitation." Politically, Jews "were afraid of stricter control of their conduct because of their close connections with French officials and agents who have been totally expelled." Finally, the report noted that the persistence of anti-Jewish discrimination in Germany, which proscribed Jews from access to high-ranking positions in government, academe, and the army, exacerbated the misgivings of Alsace-Lorraine Jewry about the new situation. Jews were thus classified, along with ultramontanes and the Socialist International, as a major source of potential anti-German agitation.

The fear that Jewish emancipation would be attenuated under German rule was a very real one. Although German Jews had been legally emancipated in 1870, Jewish leaders in the annexed provinces remained skeptical of imperial Germany's commitment to constitutional equality for its Jewish citizens. One Colmar Jew openly expressed these fears in a letter to the Parisian paper the *Revue israélite*: "And lawyers, attorneys, bailiffs, and other officials, what will become of them if Prussian rule is applied to us and systematically excludes us from public offices? What taste could our young people have for military service if they are denied advancement in the army?"[11] Similarly, a Jewish teacher from Lauterbourg lamented the French defeat in his diary in 1870, adding, "For us Frenchmen, for us Jews, this is an enormous sorrow. God will that we not have to sacrifice our civil and religious conquests, [based on] the principles of '89."[12]

Jews and non-Jews on the other side of the Rhine likewise expressed anxiety regarding the status of Jewish civil liberties under the new regime. Describing his recent journey through Alsace-Lorraine, a German Jew reported in a Stettin newspaper that Jews in the annexed provinces "consider Prussia the personification of hatred toward the Jews . . . they fear . . . that Germany will not maintain the practical realization of the emancipation in as liberal a manner as France. As long as the Prussian state does not in reality accord to its Jewish citizens the same measure and weight as to its other nationals, the Jews of the annexed provinces will at least have a valid pretext for fear."[13] In the same vein, a letter printed in the *Kölnische Zeitung* commented that the majority of Jews worried that their "citizenship rights, even if formally guaranteed, could not be interpreted in practice . . . as they had by the French."[14]

In light of these apprehensions, Jewish elites as well as political liberals closely scrutinized the policies of the new government and severely excoriated every hint of anti-Jewish intolerance.* When a Jewish landowner from Lorraine submitted a declaration of war damages at the town hall shortly after the annexation, the German court clerk responded, "I don't write anything for Jews."[15] Simon Bloch, editor of the French Jewish paper, the *Univers israélite*, himself a native of Alsace, commented, "But could one have seriously believed for an instant that it would be otherwise? It's inbred."[16] Likewise, when it was reported at first that no Jews were to be appointed to judicial positions, in contrast to the situation under the French administration, a letter in the *Kölnische Zeitung* admonished, "Should the rumor be confirmed, we must recognize this rejection as nothing other than an extremely serious blunder."[17]

Even greater concern was expressed about German Civil Commissioner Kühlwetter's plan, in the spring of 1871, to transform Alsace-Lorraine's confessionally mixed normal schools into confessionally segregated institutions. Although Jews were to be allowed to attend either the Protestant school in Colmar or the Catholic one in Strasbourg, the fact that religion would play a greater role in the curriculum and that nearly all the teachers were to be priests stimulated fears that Jewish students would be "continually wounded in their religious convictions and forced . . . to renounce their studies."[18] A liberal spokesman at an assembly of Colmar notables in 1871 strongly criticized the measure as "a blow to the liberal principle of the freedom of religion and the equality of citizens. In dividing the Catholic and Protestant colleges, the Jewish population, who for more than a century has enjoyed a civil status equal to all other inhabitants, would be virtually excluded."[19] A Colmar Jew commented bitterly that, although Protestants and Catholics might be satisfied with this plan, the Jewish population viewed it as an affront to their religious rights:

> We do not foresee that the Jews will . . . be any better off in the German Reich. We must not forget that we are dealing here not only with teaching institutions . . . but also with the entire civil position that Jews occupy in the eyes of their fellow Christian citizens. If Jews are perceived to be treated

---

*A common complaint was that German civil servants often publicly employed the qualification "Jew" in official proceedings. See *Archives israélites*, Sept. 1, 1871, p. 230, and Aug. 15, 1872, pp. 483–84.

as an excluded and neglected group, deprived of their former rights without any further ado, this [attitude] then has immediate repercussions on a whole host of other situations. Let it be remembered that we are dealing with the Alsatian population, which is still highly susceptible to religious malice, as the year 1848 proved.[20]

The introduction of the Kulturkampf reversed Kühlwetter's decision, but Jewish apprehensions regarding the new government's policies were not so easily dispelled.

It is somewhat ironic that Alsace-Lorraine Jewry perceived German antisemitism to be so menacing, since it was in these same French provinces that anti-Jewish sentiments had taken deepest root. Most Jewish intellectuals in the conquered territories, however, considered German antisemitism different in kind from the homegrown Alsatian variety; it was legal rather than merely social discrimination and therefore of a far more serious nature. Celebrating the tolerance of French Alsace, the writers Léon Cahun and Honel Meiss were but two of many Alsatian Jews who attributed the spread of antisemitism in the provinces to the German conquest. In his book *La Vie juive* (1886), Cahun declared, "It took the war of 1870 and admiration for the genius of M. de Bismarck . . . for that barbaric word antisemitism to receive letters of naturalization in France."[21] In the same vein, Meiss, a rabbi, railed on the eve of the First World War: "That horrible thing, that German plaything chiseled with love by Bismarck and that is called 'antisemitism,' did not exist formerly in Alsace! It's a shoddy piece of exported merchandise with which the *Boches* have flooded France."*

Jewish misgivings were publicly articulated in the petitions of French Jewish authorities to the French representatives at the Brussels Peace Conference. In March 1871 the Grand Rabbi of Metz, Benjamin Lipman, appealed to the French plenipotentiary at the conference to safeguard Jewish rights and institutions in Alsace-Lorraine.[22] The Central Consistory of French Jews followed suit and even recommended the inclusion of a special clause in the peace

---

* Meiss, *Choses d'Alsace*, pp. 7–8. Jonathon Helfand has recently illustrated that similar anti-German polemics had actually begun to appear several decades earlier. The editor of the *Archives israélites* went so far as to blame the anti-Jewish riots of 1848 in Alsace on the "Germanic blood" of the local peasantry. *Archives israélites* 9 (1848), pp. 467–69, cited in Helfand, "Symbiotic Relationship," p. 350. See also Helfand, "French Jewry," p. 57.

treaty to protect Jewish interests because "the Jewish religion is not treated [in Prussia] equally with other religions and does not enjoy there the rights guaranteed by French law." Otherwise, continued the memoir, "in the passage [of Jews] from liberal French legislation to the restrictive legislation of Germany there would occur not only a considerable diminution of rights they already possess but also a profound and irreparable disturbance of their organization and interests." The Central Consistory concluded by soliciting both the French and German delegates to declare openly that "Jewish citizens inhabiting the territories ceded by France will enjoy, in their new nation, the same civil and political rights as their fellow citizens of other religions, and their religious belief will never be for them a cause of inequality before the law."[23]

Nonsectarian committees in Strasbourg and Colmar for the defense of Alsatian interests likewise decided to include the safeguard of Jewish interests as one of their demands to be presented in Berlin.[24] Even the *Allgemeine Zeitung des Judentums*, the major organ of German Jewry, counseled the local Jewish communities of Alsace-Lorraine to petition the Reichstag to protect Jewish civil rights and to maintain the existing consistorial structure.[25] The fate of the French consistorial system was of deep concern to the Jewish leadership of the annexed provinces, since Jewish religious officials and institutions received financial support from the state, in contrast to the German model of autonomous self-supporting religious communities.

Given this attitude, it is not surprising that several Jewish notables played a prominent role in protesting the annexation, becoming symbols of French patriotism not only for French Jews but for French nationalists everywhere. Two of the most prestigious members of this group were Dr. Edouard Bamberger, republican deputy from Moselle, and Isidore Wolff, a lawyer from Sarreguemines.

Bamberger was a staunch liberal and anticlerical republican and an outspoken critic of Napoleon III. Although a freethinker and Mason, he was for a time an active member of the Jewish community in Strasbourg, his native town, and served as an administrator of the Ecole Israélite des Arts et Métiers there in 1852. Later, after moving to Metz in 1858, where he practiced medicine, he became the leading force behind the delegation of deputies from Alsace-Lorraine protesting the annexation at the National Assembly at Bordeaux on

March 1, 1871, convoked to ratify the Treaty of Frankfurt. Denouncing the treaty as "one of the greatest iniquities that the history of peoples and diplomatic annals will have recorded," Bamberger presented the assembly with a petition signed by 200,000 inhabitants of Moselle protesting the cession of Alsace-Lorraine. When the Bordeaux assembly voted to accept the treaty, Bamberger, together with all the representatives of Alsace-Lorraine, resigned. At the invitation of the new president, Adolphe Thiers, Bamberger emigrated to France and resumed his post as deputy at Versailles, where he remained active in French politics until 1881.[26]

Isidore Wolff was a member of the Sarreguemines municipal council and an important figure in the local Jewish community who served as a representative to the Jewish Consistory of Moselle. In February 1871, on the eve of the elections to the Bordeaux National Assembly, Wolff wrote two protests against the eventual annexation, the first of which was signed by 32,000 electors from the districts of Sarreguemines and Forbach. In this address to the members of the government of National Defense, Wolff declared: "It is against the monstrosity of such an eventuality [the annexation] that the undersigned . . . protest with all their force, in placing themselves under the aegis of your glorious patriotism. Moreover, what interest would Germany have in annexing a country where French sentiments are and will remain forever at the bottom of all hearts?" As a consequence of this petition, Wolff was thrown into prison by the German authorities for treason. He was able to avoid conviction by proving that the publication of the petition preceded the signing of the preliminary peace treaty by one day, and shortly thereafter he emigrated to France to maintain his French citizenship.[27]

Bellicosity was not characteristic of traditional Jewish culture, but *revanche*, the ardent hope that France would reconquer the annexed provinces, emerged as a major theme of Jewish writers and religious leaders from Alsace-Lorraine after 1871. One of the eminent spokesmen of French chauvinism and anti-Germanism was the well-known Jewish author and polemicist Alexandre Weill. Weill, who had a command of both languages, became an important figure in French and German intellectual circles and was one of those Alsatians who served as a bridge between the two cultures in the mid-nineteenth century.[28] Despite Weill's insistence that even as a young boy he nourished a violent hatred of Germany imparted by his father,[29] he nevertheless spent a good portion of his life in that country.

He was born in a small village in Alsace in 1811 and during his adolescence devoted several years to studying both secular and Jewish subjects in Frankfurt.[30] Later, as a fervent opponent of Napoleon III, he returned to Germany to live in self-imposed exile, since "under the Second Empire, to leave France for Germany . . . was to escape a suffocating prison to breathe the fresh air of a free and poetic country."[31]

Although Weill never abandoned his scathing criticism of Napoleon III and French decadence under the Second Empire, his pro-French sentiments resurfaced during the Franco-Prussian War. Later, in an introduction to a collection of letters written during the war (the "terrible year"), Weill wrote: "I did not know that Alsace was being demanded, even less Lorraine, a surrender I never would have signed, even if I were forced to cut off my hand."[32] He was bitterly critical not only of the imperial government for having launched France into the debacle, but also and in particular of Bismarck and German militarism, and he swore vengeance for the annexation of Alsace.[33] In his *Lettres de vengeance d'un alsacien* (1871), he promised the Alsatian patriots, "Sleep in peace, you can wait! You will be avenged, doubly, triply avenged," and he repeated the prophecy in "Lamentation d'un alsacien" (1895), modeled on the lamentations of Jeremiah after the fall of Jerusalem: "France, in the blood of fire, will find her revenge."[34] He warned that within no more than ten years a terrible fate would be visited on Prussia that would cause it to "vomit like a flood all the innocent blood . . . devoured."[35] Defending the Frenchness of Alsatians against German claims that culturally, linguistically, and historically they were Germans, Weill wrote in rhyme:

> Mais qu'on parlât français, ou bien même allemand,
> On n'avait qu'un seul coeur et qu'un seul battement.
> Les habitants brulaient tous, de la même flamme.
> On n'était que Français, Français de corps et d'âme.
>
> (But whether one speaks French or German,
> We have but one heart with but a single beat.
> All inhabitants burn with the same flame.
> We are only Frenchmen, Frenchmen in body and soul.)[36]

Weill's patriotism undoubtedly stemmed from his dual identity as an Alsatian and a Frenchman, but it was also deeply rooted in his Jewishness. Prussia symbolized the land of hereditary anti-Jewish hatred, whereas France, despite occasional lapses, essentially represented the ideals of the French Revolution, including the emancipation of the Jews.[37]

The Alsatian Jewish writer Léon Cahun, writing some years later from Paris, envisioned revanche in terms more specifically Jewish, although no less violent, than Weill's. In his *La Vie juive* he extolled the French Revolution for having rescued Jews from the debased conditions under which they had lived during the Middle Ages, "reduced to humble trades, to the humiliation of bank and office." It was France, too, that enabled Jews to become "soldiers and scholars, artists and poets, engineers, workers." For Cahun, the Emancipation marked an event in Jewish history comparable to the exodus from Egypt, and he believed that in response, French Jews had come to love France as much as "their ancestors had loved the Jewish nation" before the Roman conquest of the first century.[38] It was therefore natural that Cahun should become an advocate of revanche, which he picturesquely evoked: "One of these days, France, . . . having slept off that heavy Bavarian beer, and having cleaned her stomach with a good swig of honest Burgundy wine, will rub her eyes, shaking off all that Teutonism in one great burst of laughter. . . . On that day when the French sublieutenant erects the flag on the rampart of Strasbourg, whether he be Jewish, Catholic, or Huguenot, . . . the three colors [of the French flag] will be illuminated atop churches, temples, and synagogues." Above all, Cahun's chauvinistic rage was stimulated by his view of Germany as the archenemy of the Jews. Paradoxically, he declared himself ready to sacrifice even German Jews in his crusade against the foe of France, the homeland of antisemitism: "And if it is a Jewish soldier who is the first to mount the breach, the first German who wants to bar his way, whether he be the greatest Talmudist in Germany [or] the most devout rabbi of Frankfurt, [will get] six French sword thrusts in the belly. . . . Amen; this is our way . . . of understanding antisemitism." Cahun's description of revanche concluded with an apocalyptic vision: Alsatian Jews would ascend from their graves, playing the *Marseillaise* and emptying "the barrels of Bavarian beer and refilling them with the beer of Strasbourg" in celebration of the French victory.[39]

The most influential of these Jewish apostles of French patriotism and revanche was the Grand Rabbi of Haut-Rhin, Isaac Lévy.[40] Born in 1835 in the small Alsatian village of Marmoutier, Lévy was the scion of a long line of Alsatian rabbis. He came to Colmar in 1869, after serving as rabbi in Verdun and Lunéville. From the moment of France's defeat in 1870 until his emigration to France in October 1872, Lévy preached French patriotism in synagogues throughout Alsace and Lorraine. Comparing the annexation to the destruction of Jerusalem and the Babylonian Exile of biblical times, Lévy proclaimed, "Like the Israelites sitting on the shores of Babylon mourning the memory of Zion, today we shed tears just as bitter for the memory of our nation." "For us there is no longer joy," he said, "nor true happiness as long as we remain separated from the mother from whom we have been violently torn away."[41] In his most famous sermon, Lévy, following the tradition of Franco-Judaism, exhorted French Jews to remember that the French nation should occupy second place only to God in their hearts: "It is France who first redressed the iniquities of which Israel had been the victim throughout the centuries. She is the first to have invited our ancestors to the banquet of social life; the first to have promised them to develop the faculties that they were burning to place at the service of the nation."[42] Jewish soldiers who died on the battlefields in 1870 glorified not only the nation but Judaism as well, and proved to all that "the Jew understands and practices his duties to his country, that he is endowed with those warlike virtues that he has long been reproached for not possessing."[43]

As was true of Weill and Cahun, the persistence of German antisemitism nurtured Lévy's French chauvinism, reinforcing the dichotomy in his mind between France, the repository of liberalism, justice, and tolerance, and Germany, the bastion of barbarism, militarism, and oppression.[44] Revanche thus provided Lévy with a constant theme for sermons and prayers: "Request of God, my brothers, often ask Him in this temple that the hope [*revanche*] not be in vain, that it be promptly realized, that it arrive as soon as the happy day when we press in our arms 'the hostages of the Eternal,' whom the Eternal will deliver from the hand of the adversary."[45] Lévy, like his colleague in Metz, Grand Rabbi Benjamin Lipman, refused to take the loyalty oath to the Kaiser or to lead synagogue prayers in his honor.[46] Ultimately, despite his strong attachment to his congregation and to his native Alsace, he decided to preserve his French nationality by emigrating.[47]

German Jewish leaders, though no less patriotic than their enlightened French coreligionists, recognized Alsace-Lorraine Jews as a strongly francophile population and made vigorous efforts to reconcile them to the new situation. The *Israelitische Wochenschrift* of Breslau carried an article in October 1870 entitled "The Jews in Alsace and in German Lorraine."[48] The *Wochenschrift* conceded that although the "oldest habitation" of Alsace-Lorraine Jewry had been Germany, those Jews had justifiably come to look favorably on their status as French citizens: "In all administrative spheres as well as in society, every consideration of religious distinction has been abolished . . . and our coreligionists there must regard their position with proud satisfaction in comparison with the situation in Germany."

Nevertheless, Germany could still hope to win over the sentiments of the Jewish population of the conquered territories by following the strategy that the *Wochenschrift* then proceeded to outline. First, Germany itself would have to become more liberal:

> As long as Herr von Muhler [the conservative Prussian Minister of Religion] remains at the helm, protecting the idea of the Christian state with his authority, the hope of a liberal change in Prussian Jewish circumstances is slight. Therefore, our coreligionists who have been separated from the French body politic could only suffer a loss in their formerly undisputed rights. What sort of impression could be made upon our brothers in Alsace-Lorraine if . . . through their return to the German homeland they risk forfeiting their rights?

Second, the *Wochenschrift* suggested that the German government should exploit the single factor that allegedly differentiated Alsace-Lorraine Jews from the non-Jewish population and provided a special link to Germany, that is, language: "Although the greater part of the inhabitants in the formerly German region really have lost their knowledge of their mother tongue to some extent, and the other portion has renounced it with deliberate ostentation, the Jews, with rare exceptions, have remained true to their old German language, which at most has been mixed with a corrupted French."* Recognition of this crucial fact, the *Wochenschrift* argued, could

---

*This argument glosses over the fact that although many Jews, particularly in small villages, did not know French, the rural Christian population, especially in Alsace, also spoke mainly German. In one sense, however, this statement is justified. Roth, *Lorraine*, p. 46, points out that in the French-speaking parts of Lorraine it was only Jews who knew German, since they carried on business with their coreligionists across the Rhine.

"hasten their reconciliation to the German homeland." In conclusion, the *Wochenschrift* warned the government against treating the not-uninfluential Jewish population of the annexed provinces in a "brusque manner" by overt affronts to their civil rights.

In the spring of 1871 an even stronger article appeared in the prominent *Allgemeine Zeitung des Judentums*, written by the paper's editor, Dr. Ludwig Philippson. Couched in the language of fervent German patriotism and entitled "To Our Coreligionists in Alsace and German Lorraine," the article greeted the Jews of the two provinces "with the warmest sympathy and invited them to at least meet Germany and particularly ourselves with neither reluctance nor hostile sentiments."[49] Like the *Wochenschrift*, Philippson recognized that the annexation was not a welcome change to the Jews of Alsace and Lorraine, who were deeply devoted to France. It was both natural and honorable that their loyalties should not change overnight, and he predicted that these attitudes would be modified only after many years, perhaps even generations. Nevertheless, Philippson thought it necessary to justify the German point of view on the annexation as a way of easing the transition.

First, he pointed out that Germany had not been the aggressor but had been egged on by France, which therefore bore full responsibility for the outbreak of hostilities and for having forced Germany into a defensive war. Reiterating historical arguments set forth by German nationalists, Philippson declared that it was not "lust for conquest" but historical right that had induced Germany to annex France's eastern provinces: "[Germany] has remained standing upon the border of its original property, and its hand has fallen on the region where Germans originally resided and where the German language is still spoken today as the popular tongue." Since culturally, linguistically, and historically, Alsace-Lorraine was more German than French, the principle of nationality had not been violated. As proof of Germany's integrity, Philippson pointed to the fact that only "German" Lorraine had been demanded. The second, and no less valid, motive for the annexation was national security: Germany needed to take precautions against future French attacks, "which had repeatedly threatened Germany throughout so many centuries." Concluding this section of his argument, Philippson noted that the unification of Germany, a result of the war, would benefit all its citizens by creating improved conditions for personal freedom and growth.

Philippson then turned his pen specifically to the annexed Jewish populations, asking, "But even you, Jews of Alsace and Lorraine, are you not preeminently of German origin?" Had it not been Germany, he argued, that once had shown itself to be more tolerant of Jews than France? "And if our fathers also all too often suffered difficult bloody persecutions on German soil, yet they were never completely expelled and banished and their return prohibited as was the case in France. So it was that only south and east France could be inhabited by Jews, since these territories only later became French possessions." Jews in Alsace-Lorraine, therefore, had Germany alone to thank for their right of domicile there. Philippson, too, like the *Wochenschrift* before him, argued that the Jews of Alsace-Lorraine had preserved much of their German cultural background. They followed the Ashkenazi religious rites in their synagogues, some of their most important rabbis came from Germany, their education was based on German models, and during the Napoleonic period they had forged close bonds with German Jews in the parts of Germany that were then under French dominion. Thus, "the connection between them and German Jewry never died out." Philippson claimed that his sole wish was "to resume once again this bond in friendship and harmony." In conclusion, he expressed his hope that German and Alsace-Lorraine Jewry would work together toward their two shared goals: "support of our holy religion" and "equality in state and society," which could serve as a future basis for unity.*

The reaction of the major organs of French Jewry to the German Jewish press's justification of their government's policy showed what a tremendous gulf nationalism had already wedged between the Jewish elites of the two countries. The *Archives israélites* protested Philippson's "tendency of annexation" and condemned what it perceived as the excessive chauvinism of German Jews, who "in order to draw more favor to themselves from triumphant Teutonism and to persuade themselves that they are pure Germans, have opted for the same excesses of language and violence that characterize nearly all German papers."[50] The *Presse israélite* refuted Philippson's claim

---

*There is a certain tragic irony in Philippson's acceptance of the cultural-historical definition of German nationhood. German antisemites used exactly these same arguments in their attempt to prove that German Jews were inherently alien to the German nation. For an excellent discussion of this brand of nationalism, see Mosse, *Crisis of German Ideology*.

that Germany had fought a defensive war: "The series of events that have come to pass in the last six months . . . has demonstrated which side has so long made hostile preparations and amassed murderous devices. All was coldly foreseen, with the cruelty of wild beasts."[51] Above all, the French Jewish press contested Philippson's imputations about the Germanic character of Alsace-Lorraine generally and of the Jewish population in particular. Defending the Frenchness of the annexed territories, Simon Bloch wrote: "The truth is that the German origin of Alsace and Lorraine was effaced forever after the blessed day when the breath of France there proclaimed its noble laws of justice and liberty! The germanic *original sin* of Alsace no longer exists, and the Alsatian population has become French in its soul, its heart, and its virtues."[52]

The *Presse israélite* criticized what it perceived as a racial claim of Teutonic origin, arguing that such ascriptions could not apply to Jews living "where the homogeneity of race and blood has been maintained intact throughout the centuries."[53] As a final blow to German Jewish patriotism, the French Jewish press invoked the issue of civil rights for Jews in the Empire. Addressing German Jews directly, Simon Bloch asked how it was possible to accept the cultural argument of the Germanness of Alsace-Lorraine Jewry, since "in your country, in your legislative assemblies, and in all gatherings of civil, political, military, and scientific societies, . . . you are told 'You are not Germans, but Jews.'"[54] In a similar vein, one Alsatian rabbi attacked the ingratitude of certain German Jewish editors who "forget too easily that whatever rights they enjoy in a country that has long been the foyer of intolerance they owe to France."*

* *Univers israélite*, March 1, 1872, p. 410. These arguments were reiterated in an interesting exchange of letters between the Jewish scholar Joseph Derenbourg and Abraham Geiger, leader of the Jewish Reform movement in Germany. Although born in Germany, Derenbourg had lived in France for a number of years and had chastised German Jews for their chauvinism, accusing them of ingratitude toward France, "the country to which they owe everything they've acquired in the domain of civil liberty." Geiger's response, written on Aug. 2, 1871, defended the "brilliant" intellectual achievements of German Jewry as opposed to "the dryness of French Jews who derive their only nourishment from German sources." Conceding that Germany was more intolerant than France, Geiger blamed this situation on Germany's corrupt Christian religious institutions and predicted greater liberalism in the near future. *Revue israélite*, Oct. 13, 1871, pp. 739–43. See also Wiener, *Abraham Geiger*, pp. 70–72, 88–90, 133.

The Jews of Alsace-Lorraine thus became pawns in a debate between French and German Jewish elites that persisted throughout the annexation era and gave rise to a substantial rhetorical literature on the true loyalties of Jews in the annexed territories. The *Allgemeine Zeitung des Judentums* and other German Jewish papers consistently downplayed the negative impact of the annexation on Alsace-Lorraine Jewry, stressing every sign of accommodation and lauding the new regime's apparently liberal attitude toward Jews. Just as consistently, the French Jewish press insisted that Jewish life in the provinces had suffered an irreparable blow and held firm to its conviction that Alsace-Lorraine Jewry would remain forever loyal to France.[55] Thus, the *Presse israélite* pointed out, the only hope of future cooperation between French and German Jewry was to draw a radical distinction between religion and politics.[56] Concerning the long-range repercussions on relations between French and German Jews, Isidore Cahen of the *Archives israélites* concluded: "Between hate and affection there is a middle ground: my religion prohibits me from detesting you, my patriotism from loving you. Until the reparation of the evil of which you have rendered yourself guilty . . . nothing but cold and constrained relations."[57]

Similarly aware of the need for appeasement, the new German authorities heeded the advice of the German Jewish press to take note of the significant Jewish minority in Alsace-Lorraine. As one local correspondent remarked in the autumn of 1871, scarcely a week went by without the publication of an article in the official *Strassburger Zeitung* designed to win the sympathies of the local Jewish population in "friendly and benevolent ways."[58] In one conciliatory article of September 1871, the *Strassburger Zeitung* proclaimed antisemitism a relic of the past and lauded Jewish assimilation: "The rise of the present generation of Jews into the fields of science, literature, art, and large-scale commerce demonstrates a strong reaction to the disgraceful persecutions of the Middle Ages."[59]

Another article in that same month reassured Alsace-Lorraine Jews that their civil rights and religious institutions would be protected.[60] Speaking of the fear expressed by the Jewish community that confessional distinctions would resurface under the new regime, the *Strassburger Zeitung* declared: "The German government has done absolutely nothing that could justify it, and for the future as well it is far from entertaining the thought of offending and alienating such an important segment of the population by the diminution of its rights." Not only would the new imperial constitution of 1873 leave the religious domain untouched, but if any new institutions were to be established in Alsace-Lorraine, they too "would include the equality of rights, next to the equality of obligations of all citizens." Indeed, the *Strassburger Zeitung* said, one had only to ask German Jews whether they viewed the annexation as a misfortune. Had not the *Allgemeine Zeitung des Judentums* already provided an answer "in that it impressively invites Jews here to rally to the annexation to Germany, and in so doing, simultaneously reminds them that according to descent and rite they belong to the Germanic branch of their people?" Now that German Jews "enjoy the same privileges and rights as other religions," Jews in the annexed provinces were certain to share the same freedom and independence as Jews elsewhere in Germany.

Deed was consistent with word, and by the mid-1870's, the government had successfully dispelled many of the original fears nourished by the Jewish population. As the *Archives israélites* conceded in November 1871, the German authorities, "not at all wanting to offend the Jews," maintained the equality of religions as well as the consistorial system.[61] The only significant change in the administrative structure was that the three departmental consistories of Bas-Rhin, Haut-Rhin, and Lorraine, formerly under the governance of the Central Consistory in Paris, were detached from that authority and placed under the direct supervision of the district governor.[62] Not only did the state continue to remunerate religious personnel, but it in fact raised the salaries of rabbis a full 50 percent.[63] It also endeavored to appoint Jews to posts in the civil administration, leading one local correspondent from Colmar to remark, "Prussian officials are becoming accustomed to taking the Jews into account."[64]

As this survey of initial Jewish political and literary responses to the annexation indicates, the principal ingredient in the pro-French patriotism of the most articulate classes of the Alsace-Lorraine Jewish population was the fear that emancipation would suffer a setback in the transition to German sovereignty. For these Jews, membership in the French body politic had thus come to signify not merely symbolic but very concrete and pragmatic advances in civic equality.

Even the German government was acutely aware that the conciliation of the Jewish minority in the Reichsland would require considerable time and effort.

Two questions, nevertheless, remain to be answered. First, to what extent did the enlightened elite of Alsace-Lorraine Jewry actually act on these francophile proclivities? What measures did they take to preserve their French citizenship? And second, did these literary and political responses to the annexation accurately reflect the reactions of the less articulate rural and urban masses of Jews? Was there, in fact, a unified Jewish response in Alsace-Lorraine to the political events of 1871? To answer these questions, we must turn to an examination of the connection between French national identity and Jewish emigration in the wake of the annexation.

THREE

Patriotism or Profit? Emigration to France, 1871-1872

Following the lead of their non-Jewish counterparts, French and German Jewish patriots in the wake of Germany's annexation of Alsace-Lorraine heatedly debated the significance of Jewish emigration from the conquered territories. The Franco-Jewish press of the period, as well as Jewish commentators like Georges Delahache and Sylvain Halff, made strong and insistent claims for the political motivations of post-1871 Alsace-Lorraine Jewish emigrants and argued that this migration was entirely distinct from earlier, economically induced out-migrations of Jews from the region.[1] Refuting antisemitic charges leveled during the Dreyfus Affair, the president of the Lille Consistory declared: "Cosmopolitans! Those Jews from Alsace and from Lorraine, who at the moment of the mutilation of the *patrie* abandoned their native soil, sacrificed their dearest interests in order not to become Germans."[2] Even present-day historians of French Jewry maintain this view. Zosa Szajkowski, for example, writes: "The migration can hardly be attributed to material causes, for what could a conquered and ruined France offer the newcomers? Nor did antisemitism in Alsace-Lorraine become more virulent under German rule. We must, therefore, endorse the interpretation given by contemporary Franco-Jewish journalists and writers, namely, that the Alsatian Jews left for patriotic reasons."[3] Similarly, Freddy Raphael deemphasizes economic motivations of emigration and stresses what he considers to be the primary cause—"fidelity toward the country that was the first in the world to emancipate them."[4]

German Jewish periodicals like the *Allgemeine Zeitung des Judentums*, for their part, stressed the importance of economic concerns in

Jewish migration. Along with non-Jewish German historians and publicists, German Jewish patriots argued that Jewish emigration following the annexation was essentially a continuation of a longstanding out-migration of Jews from the provinces for socioeconomic reasons and had little to do with the constellation of political events in 1871.[5]

Trickles of Jews had indeed begun to emigrate from Alsace-Lorraine by the early nineteenth century.[6] During the French period, although the Jewish population of Alsace-Lorraine increased in absolute numbers, it decreased in relation to the total French Jewish population. In 1808 Jews in the eastern provinces constituted 79 percent of all French Jewry, whereas by 1866 they totaled only 57 percent.[7] The poorest Jews usually went to the United States; those who had already experienced some upward social mobility most often headed to Paris.[8] By the 1860's, Alsace-Lorraine Jews made up approximately one-third of all Parisian Jewry.[9] A number of Jewish migrants also gravitated to the departments bordering Lorraine and to southern France.

Unfortunately, the subject of pre-1871 Alsace-Lorraine Jewish migration has not yet been studied systematically. Pull factors, that is, the forces attracting emigrants to new places of settlement, certainly served as one stimulus to Jewish emigration from the provinces before 1871. For peasants, the most important pull factors were higher wages in cities or the availability of cheap uncultivated land in some new frontier; for Jews, because of their commercial background, the pull factor emanated almost exclusively from cities. Urban life, whether in France or abroad, offered Jews not only greater economic and cultural opportunities but also a haven from the virulent antisemitism of the Alsace-Lorraine peasantry.[10]

Scholars who have touched upon the subject of pre-1870 Jewish emigration from eastern France agree, however, that push factors—those socioeconomic conditions in the place of origin that propel emigration—were primary. To understand these push factors, it is useful to view the situation of Alsace-Lorraine Jewry within the larger European context. Sociologists and social historians have fixed the origin of the twin demographic phenomena of urbanization and emigration in the processes of industrialization and capitalistic expansion. Specifically, the source of these changes lies in the inability of an economy only beginning to undergo industrialization and capitalistic development to absorb the surplus rural population that resulted from the post-1800 population boom. Khristian Hvidt, an authority on Danish migration, explains the problem thus: "Pressure from a surplus European population might have been absorbed through the contemporary Industrial Revolution, but actually industrialization lagged behind population growth during most of the nineteenth century. The surplus rural population looked to the urban culture for employment, but the transformation of craft trades to mass production did not keep pace with the rush of people to the towns."[11] Hvidt points out that although this lag between demographic growth and economic opportunity often gave the impression of rural overpopulation, a factor commonly alleged to be responsible for migration, the overpopulation was not absolute in the Malthusian sense, but only relative in light of the existing economic conditions in the countryside. It was this temporarily surplus population that searched out new economic opportunities by migration, made easier in the second half of the century by the greater availability of cheap transportation.[12]

As an overwhelmingly commercial group, the rural Jewish population of Alsace-Lorraine was affected more by the incipient infiltration of capitalistic institutions into the countryside than by any direct connection with the industrial revolution. After the creation of the first rural banks during the Second Empire, Jews were no longer the almost sole moneylenders and commercial middlemen in rural areas. Although these banks did not become widespread until the German period, competition in these traditional Jewish occupations created a sense of overpopulation. Between 1846 and 1855, a period of economic crisis, some poor rural Jews fled the eastern provinces, primarily for the United States.[13] The Bas-Rhin Consistory even established an organization in 1853 to facilitate the emigration of the poorest Jews to that country.[14] Clearly, the sphere of economic opportunity in the countryside was beginning to shrink for Jews as well as for Christians. It was not simply the existence of poverty that caused Jewish and Gentile migration; poverty had always existed. Rather, it was, as Simon Kuznets has pointed out, "the worsening of economic and social conditions at home, not their low absolute level, that provides the push needed to initiate migration on a significant scale."[15]

The key to unraveling the problems of continuity and discontinuity and the relative weights of economic and political motivations in post-1871 Jewish emigration from the newly annexed territories lies in the distinction between emigration linked to the campaign for option in 1871-72 and long-term emigration after 1872. Article Two of the Treaty of Frankfurt, the peace settlement that was signed by France and Germany on May 10, 1871, granted to all citizens of Alsace-Lorraine who had reached the age of majority (twenty) the opportunity to maintain their French citizenship on the condition that they, first, filed a formal declaration with the recently installed German authorities of their intention to opt for it, and, second, moved their domicile to France by October 1, 1872. Using the techniques of social statistics, together with more traditional historical sources, I shall attempt to show that Jewish emigration by option was to a large extent motivated by political sentiments rooted in pro-French patriotism.* Sociological factors support this view, since it can be demonstrated that there was little social continuity between these Jewish migrants, overwhelmingly recruited from the urban bourgeoisie, and their pre-1871 rural, lower-class forerunners. Moreover, the pattern of Jewish option and emigration in 1871-72 closely parallels the sociological model of political migration, characterized by nearly equal numbers of men and women and by a high percentage of people not in the labor force—children, the elderly, and women without professions.[16] Even when economic motives did play a role in stimulating this migration, they were not the traditional ones that had sparked earlier Jewish migrations from the countryside. Finally, it is essential to stress that the existence of economic factors does not in itself negate the importance of political considerations. Rather, in the case of option, the two factors generally complemented one another. By contrast, as the next chapter will illustrate, long-term Jewish emigration throughout the German period indeed constituted an extension and even an intensification of previously established socioeconomic migration patterns, although political reasons continued to enter in.

A quantitative study of Jewish emigration in this period also provides the basis for a comparative analysis of Jewish and overall emigration from Alsace-Lorraine, which in turn makes it possible to determine whether Jews had particular reasons for leaving that dif-

*For a discussion of the population, the sources, and the methodology employed, see Appendix A.

fered from those of the general population.[17] In numerical terms, such a statistical analysis will contribute to substantiating or refuting the claims made by the contemporary Franco-Jewish press and numerous historians of French Jewry that Alsace-Lorraine Jews emigrated in far greater proportions than their non-Jewish compatriots, thus proving their exceptional patriotic attachment to France.[18]

Finally, a quantitative examination of Jewish option and emigration in 1871-72 affords an opportunity to study whether the Jewish response to the annexation was as monolithic as Franco-Jewish historians and publicists have portrayed it to be. If it can be demonstrated that emigration was indeed one type of political reaction to the annexation, a quantitative analysis may reveal important distinctions among the ways in which diverse sectors of the Jewish population greeted the transition to German sovereignty. As we achieve an understanding of the relationship of such factors as urbanization, age, gender, marital status, occupation, and social class to emigration, we can also begin to address the larger question of the impact of socioeconomic assimilation on the development of a sense of national identity among Jews.

Religion was one of several considerations that influenced 11 percent of Alsace-Lorraine's total population to opt for French citizenship in 1871-72.* The different ways in which Catholics, Protestants, and Jews initially perceived the new German regime were reflected in the propensity of members of those groups to file option declarations. Municipalities with large Catholic populations contributed the greatest numbers of optants and emigrants, reflecting above all fears about the introduction of the Kulturkampf into the provinces in late 1871. This event caused some members of the ultramontane clergy to agitate for emigration as a means of protesting the annexation, despite the opposition of several important Catholic leaders who argued that a mass exodus would facilitate the "germanization" of the provinces.[19] On the other hand, as one might expect, Protestant regions of Alsace and Lorraine accounted for the fewest options. Option and emigration thus mirrored, to a

*Language also influenced the choice. French-speaking communes contributed the most optants. See A. Wahl, *L'Option et l'émigration*, p. 154; Roth, *La Lorraine annexée*, p. 99; and D'Elstein, *L'Alsace-Lorraine sous la domination allemande*, pp. 91-92.

large degree, the traditional Catholic-Protestant cleavage in Alsace-Lorraine.[20]

In 1871–72 Jewish sentiments about the annexation more closely resembled those of Catholics than those of Protestants. Most Jewish community leaders in the provinces looked favorably on option and emigration. Two of Alsace-Lorraine's three Grand Rabbis, Isaac Lévy of Colmar and Benjamin Lipman of Metz, turned down Prussian offers to remain at their posts at doubled salaries in order to opt for French citizenship. Neither Lévy nor Lipman overtly counseled his constituency to emigrate, cognizant of the difficulties involved in leaving one's family, business, and home. Their farewell speeches and effusive praise for those who opted clearly indicate, however, that they viewed emigration as the highest manifestation of French patriotism.[21] The Grand Rabbi of France, Lazare Isidore, himself of Alsatian origin, warmly welcomed Jews fleeing German rule and expressed his hope that they would establish new and vibrant communities in the French interior to compensate for the loss of the eastern provinces.[22]

In light of the pro-option attitudes held by many Jewish communal leaders, as well as of the more general apprehensions of Jews about the transition to German sovereignty, it is not surprising that Jews opted and emigrated in disproportionately high numbers. Commenting on the considerable contingent of Jewish optants from the district of Strasbourg-campagne (Bas-Rhin), a French police report noted, "It is known that the Jews of Alsace feared that Germany would confer upon them a less liberal legal status."[23] In Molsheim (Bas-Rhin), where the signing of option declarations was frequently accompanied by cries of "Vive la France!," the Kreisdirector observed that, although the majority of emigrants were departing for the United States during the summer of 1872, Jews constituted the greatest proportion of those headed for France.[24] Several local newspapers noted the massive emigration of Jews from Mulhouse (Haut-Rhin) to French-speaking Basel. The *Courrier du Bas-Rhin* reported on October 1, 1872:

The effect of the emigration was noticed only on Saturday; during the other days of the week, one has only to go to the National Café to be convinced that there are really people leaving. Until now, whoever was accustomed to promenading in town on Saturday used to encounter a large number of

TABLE 3.1
Distribution of Jewish Optants and All Alsace-Lorraine Optants by District,
1871–1872

District	Jewish optants[a]	All optants	Jews as percent of all optants	Jews as percent of 1871 civil population
Strasbourg-ville (B-R)	126 – 185	2,032	6.2 – 9.1%	4.0%
Strasbourg-campagne (B-R)	18 – 22	212	8.5 – 10.4	4.2
Haguenau (B-R)	97 – 130	1,021	9.5 – 12.7	4.1
Wissembourg (B-R)	21 – 32	930	2.3 – 3.4	3.5
Saverne (B-R)	18 – 31	557	3.2 – 5.6	3.2
Altkirch (H-R)[b]	67 – 74	678	9.9 – 10.9	13.7
Colmar (H-R)	143 – 224	3,956[c]	3.7 – 5.7	4.2
Sarreguemines (Lorr.)	27 – 29	864	3.1 – 3.4	1.5
TOTAL	517 – 727	10,250		

SOURCES: *Jewish optants.* See Appendix A. *All optants,* Archives départementales du Bas-Rhin, AL 69 604; Archives départementales du Haut-Rhin, Altkirch 7510; Alfred Wahl, *L'Option et l'émigration des Alsaciens-Lorrains, 1871–1872* (Paris, 1974), p. 101. *1871 civil population,* Statistischen Bureau des Kaiserlichen Ministeriums für Elsass-Lothringen, *Statistische Mitteilungen über Elsass-Lothringen, 1871.*

NOTE: The term optants signifies heads of households in all tables except where otherwise noted.

[a] Since the actual number of Jewish optants is uncertain, I have given the minimum (517) and maximum (727) figures. All statistics in this study are based on the minimum.

[b] Only three communes of the district were analyzed: Altkirch, Durmenach, and Wittersdorf. According to the 1871 census, Wittersdorf had no Jewish inhabitants; Jews who opted from that commune probably resided in both Alsace and Switzerland.

[c] This is the actual number of options declared. But 50 of the declarations were missing from the dossiers. The percentages in the next column are therefore based on the surviving 3,906 declarations.

richly dressed persons, for the most part with opulent jet black hair and black eyes, whom one quickly recognized as the children of Israel celebrating the Sabbath. But yesterday the number of these promenaders was very small. At the National Café, where the male descendants of Israel likewise habitually gathered on weekdays, today there wasn't a soul.[25]

The *Neue Mülhauser Zeitung* even compared the flight of Jews from Mulhouse to the exodus of the Hebrews from Egypt.[26]

A glance at the statistical data on Alsace-Lorraine Jewish optants corroborates these reports. Table 3.1 shows that Jews constituted a disproportionately large number of those who opted in the provinces of Bas-Rhin and Lorraine, with the single exception of the rural district of Wissembourg.[27] In Haut-Rhin, Jews were slightly underrepresented, probably as a result of the more massive option of residents in that province generally owing to the propaganda of the Ligue d'Alsace, the most vociferously pro-French organization in the Reichsland, which advocated option as a form of an anti-German plebiscite regardless of whether or not one intended to emigrate.[28] Furthermore, Jews numbered 13 percent of the first wave of optants from the city of Strasbourg who registered between May 10, 1871, and the end of March 1872. Similarly, Jewish merchants from the district of Haguenau, including André Maurois's grandparents, Solomon Herzog and his wife Emilie née Fraenkel, were among the first to file their declarations.[29] Between 1866 and the end of 1871, the Jewish population of Alsace and those territories of Lorraine incorporated into the Reichsland declined from approximately 47,000 to 40,938, leading the *Archives israélites* to conclude that some 6,000 Jews had emigrated following the war.[30] Whereas Alsace-Lorraine Jews constituted 57 percent of all French Jewry in 1866, they totaled only 45 percent by 1871.[31]

Who were the Jews who opted for French nationality in 1871–72? One of the most obvious features of this emigration, for both Jews and non-Jews, is the relatively high proportion of women and minors. As indicated above, this is characteristic of political migrations generally. Table 3.2 shows the ratio of Jewish men to women involved in option to have been 160 to 100, compared with 150 to 100 for the general population of optants. Indicative of the familial nature of option are the facts that over 40 percent of Jewish optants were married couples, and over 40 percent of all people involved in option, Jews and non-Jews, were under the age of twenty (Tables 3.2–3.4). That Gentile optants shared these sociodemographic traits strongly suggests the political nature of option in general.

Despite high proportions of women and children, the majority of people concerned in option were men. Among the Jewish option declarants, single men (including widowers) constituted the largest contingent—48 percent—a fact repeatedly noted by the French Jewish press.[32] The decline of the Jewish male population is also apparent from the German census figures. In 1871 there were 94.9 Jewish males for every 100 females; by 1875 the ratio had dipped to 91.7. In France at the same time, as Szajkowski points out, the ratio was 97.7 females to 100 males.[33] Moreover, most of these males were

TABLE 3.2
Age and Sex Structure of Jewish Optants and All Bas-Rhin Optants

Group	Jewish optants[a]		All Bas-Rhin optants	
	Number	Percent	Number	Percent
Males				
Under 20	317	26.4%	9,914	25.3%
20 or over	423	35.2	13,642	34.9
Total males	740	61.6	23,556	60.2
Females				
Under 20	203	16.9%	7,382	18.9%
20 or over	258	21.5	8,192	20.9
Total females	461	38.4	15,574	39.8
TOTAL	1,201	100.0%	39,130	100.0%

SOURCE: *Bas-Rhin optants*. Alfred Wahl, *L'Option et l'émigration des Alsaciens-Lorrains, 1871–1872* (Paris, 1974), p. 103.
[a] Optants here refers to heads of households (N = 517) and their families (N = 684).

TABLE 3.3
Marital Status of Jewish Optants

Marital Status	Number	Percent
Married, male and female	210	40.6%
Widows	59	11.4
Single men, widowers[a]	248[a]	48.0
TOTAL	517	100.0%

[a] Includes 5 male minors with guardians.

TABLE 3.4
Age Distribution of Jewish Optants

Year of birth	Number	Percent	Cumulative percent
Before 1800	2	0.4%	0.4%
1800–1809	32	6.2	6.6
1810–1819	65	12.6	19.2
1820–1829	92	17.8	37.0
1830–1839	85	16.4	53.4
1840–1849	164	31.7	85.1
1850 and after	77	14.9	100.0%
TOTAL	517	100.0%	

NOTE: Any minor discrepancies between the percent and cumulative percent columns in this and subsequent tables are due to rounding.

young. Not only were 26.4 percent of those Jews who opted for French citizenship male minors (Table 3.2), but of the primarily male heads of household who filed option declarations a full 46.6 percent were thirty-two years of age or younger (Table 3.4).

The preponderance of young Jewish males among the optants seems at first to be explicable in wholly economic terms. It is a general demographic rule that young men in search of improved economic circumstances are the most geographically mobile segment of the population.[34] Khristian Hvidt points out that push factors need not be as great for young bachelors as for married men, who have "all the economic and social ties that make breaking out of the old life so difficult, particularly if there are children."[35] Moreover, young males in their peak wage-earning years would be the ones best suited to taking advantage of the pull factors, those economic and cultural opportunities that made the new cities of destination so attractive. Therefore, one might be led to conclude that option and emigration in 1871–72 merely accelerated traditional demographic patterns.

It is unquestionable, however, that in the minds of young male optants there were political considerations as well, the most important being to evade service in the German military.[36] Against the recommendation of several advisers, Bismarck decided to extend compulsory military service into the Reichsland, and in the fall of 1872 the German army began to recruit Alsace-Lorraine males born in 1851–52. In an effort to mitigate resentment, the German military offered a special one-year term of service, in contrast to the normal three years, to those who enlisted before October 1, 1872, and as a further concession it exempted men who had previously served in the French army.[37]

Unwillingness to be conscripted into the German army was indeed one of the main reasons for option and emigration among the general population. A popular saying of the time was, "He who had sons departed."[38] Out of 33,475 names on the German recruitment lists of 1872, only 7,454 men registered.[39] Those who did not appear were considered draft evaders and could not legally return to the provinces until they had passed military age. In every district, over 70 percent of all those eligible to serve in the German army emigrated, and this trend continued throughout the 1870's.* Minors in

---

*A. Wahl, *L'Option et l'émigration*, p. 182. Between 1871 and 1880, the 20-to-40-year-old category in Alsace-Lorraine declined from 102,178 to 86,506. Silverman, *Reluctant Union*, p. 70. This trend will be discussed more fully in Chapter 4.

particular, as the local press frequently reported, were departing from the Reichsland en masse to evade military service, necessitating the issuance of a government circular in March 1872 clarifying the conditions under which they were permitted to opt.[40] The *Courrier du Bas-Rhin* pointed out that even men who had been granted exemptions were afraid "that in case of a renewed outbreak of war, they would be forced to serve in the German army against their former compatriots."[41]

This apprehension was, of course, very compelling to Jews. In February 1872 Grand Rabbi Isidore addressed the Minister of Foreign Affairs on behalf of his coreligionists in Alsace and Lorraine, who were "doubly distressed about the disasters of France." Isidore explained that he had received numerous queries from parents asking whether they could legally emancipate their minor sons so the latter could opt independently. He added, "You understand . . . how important this question is to these poor Alsatians, and how fortunate it would be for it to be resolved favorably."[42] The fact that among Jewish optants, 25.5 percent of all the minors would have turned twenty years old (the age of army recruitment) in 1872 and 1873 suggests that many Jewish parents opted expressly for the sake of their sons of military age.

Although Alsace-Lorrainers in general and Alsace-Lorraine Jews in particular bore a reputation throughout the nineteenth century for an aversion to serving in the French army, evasion of the German draft in 1871-72 cannot be explained away as a mere continuation of this traditional hostility, as some commentators have tried to do.[43] In 1872 the French government passed a conscription law that was stiffer than the German one, requiring up to five years of service of all males between the ages of twenty and forty and making the purchase of replacements, common under the Second Empire, more difficult. The fact that many Alsace-Lorrainers who opted and emigrated, including many Jews, soon enlisted in the French army or the Foreign Legion suggests that their desire to escape the German draft was largely political in nature.* In the case of Jews in particular,

---

*Those inducted in 1871 were the first to feel the impact of the new law. Since the length of service was determined by lot after the first year of military duty, only a minority of recruits had to serve the full five-year term. Between 1870 and 1914, an average of 500 Alsace-Lorrainers per year enlisted in the French Foreign Legion; between 1882 and 1908, approximately 45 percent of all the Legion's troops were Alsace-Lorraine emigrants.

there is also substantial evidence indicating a general acceptance of French military service by the time of the Second Empire, at least among the younger generation, who had actively participated in the Crimean War.[44] Moreover, only a small minority of Jews possessed sufficient economic means to buy military replacements.[45] Edmond Uhry, a village Jew who grew up in Alsace during the first years of the annexation, recalls in his memoirs that his uncle, "a patriotic Frenchman," enlisted in the *franc tireurs* for the duration of the Franco-Prussian war despite the opposition of his entire family.[46] Another memoir from the Jewish community of Hegenheim, dated 1870–71, relates that since so many sons went off to fight for their "beloved Fatherland," significant numbers of parents were left without means of support.[47] These accounts suggest that Jews who opted to avoid conscription into the German army did not act out of traditional hostility toward military service, but rather were responding to a new political situation in a decidedly untraditional manner.

Another striking feature about the option of Alsace-Lorraine Jews is its urban character (Table 3.5): some 69 percent of Jewish optants came from cities with over 5,000 inhabitants and 53 percent came from cities with over 10,000 inhabitants, but only 28.9 percent and 21.7 percent of the total Jewish population of the provinces in 1871 resided in cities of those respective sizes (see Table 8.2). Approximately 25 percent of all Jewish optants surveyed came from Strasbourg itself, though Strasbourg accounted for only 16.2 percent of the total Jewish population of those regions on which this study is based. Also, not a single Jew opted from the rural villages of the district of Haguenau, which included the sizable Jewish commu-

TABLE 3.5
Distribution of Jewish Optants by Hometown City Size

Hometown city size (population)	Jewish optants		
	Number	Percent	Cumulative percent
0–1,999	87	16.8%	16.8%
2,000–4,999	72	13.9	30.8
5,000–9,999	83	16.1	46.8
10,000–49,999	149	28.8	75.6
50,000 or more	126	24.4	100.0%
TOTAL	517	100.0%	

nities of Niederbronn, Herrlisheim, and Schirrhofen. The urban nature of option also accounts for the low percentage of Jews who opted from the rural district of Wissembourg. By contrast, Jewish emigrants from Bas-Rhin to the United States between 1827 and 1837 had been entirely rural.[48] This high degree of urbanization characterized the population of optants in general.[49]

The most probable explanation for the highly urban character of Jewish as well as Gentile option is that those living in the largest cities were the most economically and culturally assimilated to France. The urban bourgeoisie was the chief victim of the economic repercussions of the annexation. Suddenly detached from French markets and the French tariff system and incorporated into the German customs union, the Zollverein, many industries and businesses found it advantageous to move to France or at least to establish one subsidiary there in order to trade on both French and German markets. Moreover, German tariffs remained low until 1879, whereas French tariffs were extremely protectionist. The 10 percent import duty imposed by France on all Alsace-Lorraine products as of 1873 had serious consequences particularly for the textile and brewing industries of the German-annexed provinces.[50] The impact of these economic factors on specific groups of Jewish merchants and industrialists will be discussed more fully below.

Cultural attachments reinforced these economic interests. Since the urban bourgeoisie in general had always been in the forefront of propagating French language and culture in the provinces, it is not surprising that many in this class preferred to retain their French nationality. For Jews as well, the urban-rural dichotomy was apparent. A correspondent for one German Jewish paper wrote in 1874:

> There is a distinction to be made between the towns and the villages. In the towns the majority of Jews are still extremely French in sentiment; and although they are glad of the tranquility, order, and security that the German administration has ensured for the country, the problems and contentions among the parties in France cannot extinguish their French sympathies. If anything, they serve to keep them alive, all the more so because their [the Jews] industrial interests continually steer them more toward France than Germany.

The correspondent went on to explain that the situation in the countryside was altogether different. Jews there were far more satisfied with the new government because, he argued, German judges in rural localities discriminated less against them than their French predecessors had—a claim heatedly contested by the Franco-Jewish press.[51]

Because of the lack of information on wealth or social status, one cannot draw any definitive conclusions about the class composition of the optants; nevertheless, an examination of the occupational structure of Jewish optants reveals distinctions in the responses to the annexation between Jews and non-Jews, as well as within the Jewish community itself, that can ultimately shed light on the way social class influenced option. Broadly speaking, the occupational categories in which Jewish optants were overrepresented in comparison with the general Jewish population were the liberal professions, public service, and land and investments. In rural areas, a disproportionately large number of Jewish optants were recruited from artisanry and manufacturing. Although this group was slightly underrepresented in relation to the base urban Jewish population, urban Jewish optants in these professions nevertheless constituted a sizable contingent (Tables 3.6–3.8). Jewish optants were underrepresented in the categories of unskilled labor and nonprofessional services, at least from urban areas. Most significantly, a disproportionately low number of optants from both rural and urban areas were recruited from the commercial professions. Whereas the proportion of Jews greatly outweighed that of the general population of optants in this field, making Jews the most numerically significant group of merchants who opted, this pattern merely reflects the skewed occupational structure of the general Jewish population in favor of commerce. Alfred Wahl hypothesizes that merchants often hesitated to emigrate because of the enormous commercial risks involved.[52]

In order to interpret these data, we have to examine more closely the major considerations impelling option and emigration. Some Jews who opted and emigrated, especially in certain of the liberal professions and civil service posts, expressed a profound sense of being integrated into French culture. Prodding his colleagues to emigrate in 1871, a Jewish teacher from Durmenach proclaimed: "Are not the Jews of unfortunate Alsace French at heart? Will they not remain so? They will never forget their brothers in Paris, Lyon, Nancy, Marseille; they will not separate themselves from them, but will draw closer to them. They will even emigrate to help France recover, to establish useful institutions there for the development of the coun-

TABLE 3.6
Occupational Distribution of Urban Jewish Male Optants Compared with That of All Strasbourg Jews
(Cities of 5,000 or more inhabitants)

Sector	Male optants		All Strasbourg Jews, 1846 (N = 424)
	All cities (N = 309)	Strasbourg only (N = 100)	
Commerce	55.7%	50.0%	63.8%
Nonspecified independent	23.3	20.0	31.1[a]
Nonspecified employee	14.2	17.0	—
Agricultural produce[b]	5.2	1.0	4.2
Books[c]	1.9	3.0	0.0
Food[d]	4.2	2.0	3.4
Inns, restaurants	1.0	0.0	0.0
Jewelry	0.0	0.0	0.4
Leather	0.3	0.0	0.2
Metal	0.0	0.0	0.9
Money[e]	3.2	5.0	6.8
Porcelain, glass	0.3	0.0	0.0
Street trades[f]	1.0	1.0	10.4
Textiles	1.0	0.0	6.4
Land, investments	7.4	12.0	4.0
Liberal professions	10.0	11.0	4.7
Manufacturing, artisanry	12.9	12.0	15.3
Nonprofessional services	0.6	1.0	5.1
Public service	6.8	12.0	0.5
Unskilled labor	1.9	2.0	6.1
Without, unknown, not stated	4.5	0.0	0.5

SOURCE: *Strasbourg, 1846.* Paula Hyman, "Migration and Social Mobility of Alsatian Jewry, 1820–1866" (paper presented to the Social Science History Association, Nov. 3, 1978), Table 4, p. 12. Cited with the author's permission.

NOTE: In this table and the ones that follow, percentages may not sum to 100 because of rounding.

[a] Includes nonspecified commercial employees as well as nonspecified independent merchants.
[b] Horse and cattle traders, grain merchants, etc.
[c] Both publishers and book sellers.
[d] Butchers, bakers, etc.
[e] Bankers, brokers, moneylenders, etc.
[f] Peddlers, second-hand dealers, etc.

TABLE 3.7
Occupational Distribution of Rural Jewish Male Optants
Compared with That of All Jews in Three Selected Towns
(Towns of fewer than 5,000 inhabitants)

Sector	Male optants, all towns (N = 146)	All Jews of Bischheim, Niederrödern, and Itterswiller, 1846 (N = 230)
Commerce	67.8%	87.4%
Nonspecified independent	39.0	17.6[a]
Nonspecified employee	4.1	—
Agricultural produce	11.6	23.9
Food	8.9	1.3
Inns, restaurants	0.7	0.0
Leather	0.7	1.7
Metal	0.0	0.8
Money	1.3	0.8
Street trades	0.0	27.4
Textiles	1.4	13.9
Land, investments	4.8	0.0
Liberal professions	2.1	3.5
Manufacturing, artisanry	11.6	4.6
Nonprofessional services	0.7	0.8
Public service	0.7	0.0
Unskilled labor	5.5	3.9
Without, unknown, not stated	6.8	0.0

SOURCE: *3 towns, 1846.* Same as Table 3.6.
[a] Includes nonspecified commercial employees as well as nonspecified independent merchants.

try and for the prosperity of the nation."[53] Dr. Samuel Bernheim, a celebrated Jewish psychologist at the University Strasbourg, enthusiastically supported the proposal to transfer the university's entire medical faculty to Nancy and declared, "We are not a Strasbourg faculty, but a French faculty, an integral part of the French university, residing in Strasbourg."[54] He and other prominent Jewish doctors associated with the Strasbourg medical faculty, such as Paul Aronssohn and Mathieu Hirtz, gave up their posts and practices in order to move to France.[55]

One compelling influence on the decision of Jews and non-Jews in certain liberal professions or holding public service appointments was the introduction of German as the official language of the Reichsland. According to Civil Commissioner Kühlwetter, the main reasons for the option of lawyers in general were a lack of proficiency in German and the new government's intention to introduce the German penal code.[56] One of the first to opt, despite the German government's attempts to induce him to remain in Strasbourg, was David Maase, a highly respected lawyer and president of the Strasbourg bar, who also happened to be a lay member of the Bas-Rhin Consistory.[57] Legislation imposing German as the compulsory language of school instruction made it difficult for teachers to remain at their posts, notwithstanding considerable increases in their salaries.[58] As the correspondent for the *Revue israélite* pointed out, few Jewish teachers in public schools knew German in 1871; German was the language spoken most frequently on the streets, but French had long

TABLE 3.8
Occupational Distribution of Jewish Optants Compared with That of All Bas-Rhin Optants

Sector	Jewish optants (N = 517)	All Bas-Rhin optants (N = 21,284)[a]
Commerce	52.8%	2.6%
Nonspecified independent	25.7	
Nonspecified employee	9.8	
Agricultural produce	6.6	
Books	1.7	
Food	4.8	
Inns, restaurants	0.8	
Leather	0.3	
Money	1.9	
Porcelain, glass	0.2	
Street trades	0.6	
Textiles	0.6	
Land, investments	6.8%	13.1%
Liberal professions	6.6	1.1
Manufacturing, artisanry	11.0	31.8
Public service	4.3	5.0
Transportation	0.0	0.2
Unskilled labor, nonprofessional services	3.5	12.1
Without, unknown, not stated	15.1	34.1

SOURCES: *Bas-Rhin optants.* Archives départementales du Bas-Rhin, AL 69 604; Alfred Wahl, *L'Option et l'émigration des Alsaciens-Lorrains* (Paris, 1974), p. 103. The German officials aggregated the occupations, but the categories were discrete enough to fit into my categorization.

[a] In the German records, all people involved were assigned to an occupational group, not just the declarants. Minors, who never listed profession, have therefore been subtracted from the "Without" category.

since become the language of the classroom.⁵⁹ Language also posed a problem to the publishing industry, which employed several Jews. Following the annexation, Félix Alcan of Metz, a distinguished editor and publisher and a member of the Lorraine Consistory, refused to publish any materials in German and eventually opted for French citizenship. Although Alcan's gesture was no doubt motivated by patriotic sentiments, he may also have anticipated practical problems arising from the transition to German.⁶⁰

All civil servants and teachers feared expulsion and replacement by German personnel, but Jews in these positions nourished particularly strong anxieties because they remained uncertain of the imperial government's commitment to legal equality. The Jewish teacher of Lauterbourg remarked in his diary of 1870: "To what extent is my salary assured, inasmuch as I am a Jewish teacher? Will Prussian law allow the equality of cults to survive so that the municipality will have to see to paying three instructors of three different religions?"⁶¹ The *Archives israélites* reported in 1871 that most Jewish teachers were emigrating from the provinces because of rumors (which proved unfounded) that with the introduction of the new constitution in 1873, Jewish instructors would no longer be paid by the state or the municipality, and it urged the French government to grant those who departed preferential treatment for posts in France and Algeria.⁶² The French government did indeed accord preference to civil servants who emigrated "either in new posts or in reparative advances," and this gesture accounted in part for the large number of people who opted and emigrated from this occupational category.⁶³ Initial fears over the loss of French pensions similarly motivated some retired civil and military servants to opt, although an agreement was soon worked out whereby the German government promised to pay the pensions of those who remained.⁶⁴

Particularly for Jews involved in those sectors of commerce and industry most adversely affected by the annexation, economic considerations weighed heavily in the decision to opt or not to opt. One illustration of these economic repercussions is the case of the Jewish hops dealers from Haguenau. In 1867, when the hops exchange opened in that city, all except one of the ten major houses trading in this commodity were in the hands of Jews.⁶⁵ For several reasons, the annexation dealt a severe blow to the Alsatian brewery industry and to the commerce in hops. Not only was the industry cut off by the new customs frontier from the French markets upon which it had entirely depended, but it had no chance of successfully competing with the formidable brewing industry of Germany. This already dire situation was made worse by a series of bad harvests in the early 1870's, and the Haguenau and Bischwiller hops merchants emigrated en masse. Their emigration alone accounts for the disproportionately high number of urban Jewish optants involved in agricultural commerce. The industry stagnated as a result, and it was not until the beginning of the twentieth century that dealers were once again in a position to export hops from Alsace.[66]

The changes in the tariff frontier also motivated many industrialists—Jews and non-Jews—to opt and emigrate. Despite their underrepresentation in comparison with the total population of optants, as well as with the general Jewish population, Jewish industrialists still formed an important contingent of Jewish optants. Of the forty urban Jewish optants from manufacturing and artisanry, nearly half were industrialists. One of the most notable optants from Sarreguemines was the Jewish lime manufacturer Emmanuel Durlach, who kept his business in Lorraine intact but created a sizable subsidiary in Nancy so as to maintain his French clientele.[67] The iron forge of Ars-sur-Moselle in Lorraine, owned by René Dreyfus and Pierre Mayer Dupont, president of the Lorraine Consistory, was one of the most important Jewish enterprises that moved to France in wake of the annexation.[68]

The industry that most immediately experienced the harmful impact of the annexation was the Alsatian textile industry, which included several important Jewish manufacturers.* This industry was noted for its fine black cloth, intended for luxury markets, and for which there was little demand in Germany. The cutting off of the French markets after the annexation left the industry in the position of trying to compete against German textile manufacturers in a market for which it was ill-suited. Consequently, many Alsatian textile

*This industry proved to be a particularly attractive avenue of upward social mobility for Jews for two reasons: it required a relatively small initial outlay of capital, and, as the first industry to mechanize, it attracted individuals seeking new types of commercial endeavors. A number of rural Jews who had traditionally traded in agrarian and textile products eventually invested capital earned from this commerce into the building of textile factories. Richarz, "Jewish Social Mobility in Germany," p. 73.

manufacturers opened branch factories in France or simply emigrated from the annexed provinces altogether, relocating either in France or in Switzerland.[69]

In Mulhouse, Haut-Rhin's most important textile center, several Jewish textile manufacturers were among the sizable contingent of industrialists who opted. Although Jews were generally excluded from Mulhouse's textile industry, which was dominated by a Calvinist oligarchy,[70] several Jewish mavericks had penetrated this closed caste, and they were among the most prominent textile magnates who opted from that city. One of the first firms to move its spinning and weaving mills to France was that of Les Fils d'Emmanuel Lang. Like Emmanuel Durlach, the Lang brothers established a branch in Nancy while maintaining their operation in Alsace. In the paternalistic fashion of Alsatian textile manufacturers, the Langs accommodated their 396 employees and associates who moved to Nancy by constructing an entirely new industrial village around their factory—"a veritable Alsatian quarter," according to Odette Voilliard.[71] Similarly, Raphael Dreyfus, an eminent Mulhouse textile manufacturer (and father of Alfred Dreyfus, who several decades later would become the cause célèbre of nineteenth-century France's most infamous "affair"), opted and moved to Basel with his wife and minor-aged children in 1872. He opened a factory there, but he also maintained his home branch in Alsace under the direction of his eldest son, Jacques.[72]

The most intriguing example of the option and emigration of Jewish textile manufacturers is provided by the town of Bischwiller, the nucleus of the Bas-Rhin textile industry. Jews had only recently settled in Bischwiller: the first arrived there in 1826; a formal community was established only in 1850, the synagogue in 1856. As the town's general population expanded from 3,008 in 1800 to 11,500 in 1867, the Jewish community grew rapidly in size.[73] Between 1846 and 1861, the number of Jews quadrupled, going from 53 to 216. The primary source of this demographic explosion was immigration from the neighboring municipality of Schirrhofen, in which Jews constituted 69 percent of the population in 1871, as well as from the nearby villages of Herrlisheim, Offendorf, and Wittersheim. During that same period—the 1840's through the 1860's—Bischwiller's textile industry experienced its greatest boom, stimulated by the completion of a railroad line in 1855 that enormously facilitated the transport of merchandise to both French and German markets. Because Bischwiller's textile industry was relatively young, social mobility within the entrepreneurial class was far easier there than in Mulhouse, so that Jews were able to participate with amazing success in the town's burgeoning industrial opportunities.[74]

Bischwiller's textile industry suffered even more than Mulhouse's as a result of the annexation. Unlike the owners of the wealthier and more established Mulhouse mills, who could open branches across the border in France or Switzerland, most of the Bischwiller textile manufacturers had to transplant their entire operations to France in order to maintain their clientele and avoid high French duties. Almost the whole textile industry, including the masses of workers and foremen, emigrated to France, relocating primarily in Sedan and Reims in eastern France, Vire and Elbeuf in Normandy, and Tourcoing in the north.[75]

The migration of the textile industry had immediate demographic repercussions. Between 1871 and 1873, the Bischwiller population in general dropped by 15 percent. Of all groups in the population, the Jewish community experienced the most precipitous relative decline, losing close to half its numbers in that period (Table 3.9).[76] Of the thirty-three Bischwiller manufacturers who opted in Alsace, twelve were Jews and nearly all were involved in the production of textiles. The most prominent of these Jewish textile magnates were David and Edgar Bloch, Maurice and Théodore Blin, Henri and Louis Fraenkel, and Ernst Herzog, André Maurois's father.[77] A large number of Jewish merchants, many of whom were also involved in the textile trade, opted as well. Several of these optants were active in civic affairs: both Maurice and Théodore Blin were

TABLE 3.9
Size of the Jewish, Catholic, and Protestant Populations of Bischwiller Before and After the Annexation, 1863–1873

Population	1863	1871	1873	Loss, 1871–73 (percent)
Jews	216	267	143	−46.4%
Catholics	1,886	1,994	1,603	−19.6
Protestants	6,661	6,881	6,025	−12.4

SOURCE: Alfred Wahl, *L'Option et l'émigration des Alsaciens-Lorrains* (Paris, 1974), p. 188.

members of Bischwiller's chamber of commerce, the former also serving on that city's municipal council.[78]

The case of the Jewish textile manufacturers raises the central question of the relative weights to be assigned to political and economic considerations in motivating option and emigration. Although economic considerations undoubtedly played an important role in the decision to opt, journalistic and literary sources attest to the importance of the patriotic incentive. Jean-Richard Bloch's well-known novel *"— & Co."* offers a vivid semi-autobiographical account of the experience of one family of textile manufacturers, the Simlers, who opted for France in 1872. Describing the reaction of Hippolyte Simler, the patriarch of the family, Bloch writes:

He had not ceased to rage since the Prussians had invaded the little town.
At the first report from Wissembourg, he had stopped his looms, dismissed his workmen, locked his gate. . . . And nobody could have told, even then, whether the fury of the father and sons was not due to the silence of the looms, to the suspension of business and to the rapid approach of bankruptcy, as much as to the misfortunes of their country.[79]

Even though the material prospects for the textile manufacturers who remained in Alsace looked bleak in 1871, leaving was not easy, either financially or emotionally. Relocating an entire mill involved a sizable initial outlay of capital, and often considerable debt. Also, because of the urgency of leaving, many industrialists often had to sell their firms at significant losses. This is depicted in *"— & Co.,"* when the two young Simler brothers return to Alsace from Normandy after buying a new factory there in 1871: "They did not admit to themselves that they were returning to their native land to hasten the moment in which they would abandon it forever. Nor that every expense which they incurred, from then onward, must add to the burden of their debts and constituted, strictly speaking, a crime against their future."[80]

Bloch's cousin André Maurois similarly describes in his memoirs his father's great reluctance to leave his homeland for Elbeuf in Normandy, where his uncles, the Fraenkels, had relocated in 1871 with their 400 workers: "But nothing ever consoled him for having had to leave Alsace. Our house was full of engravings showing the cathedral of Strasbourg, storks nesting on gabled roofs, and girls with straw colored hair tied with huge black ribbons. Every year the Alsatians in Elbeuf gathered for a big celebration at which they would sing their native songs and dance Alsatian dances. At such times I would see tears in my father's eyes."[81] Years later, just prior to a serious medical operation, Ernst Herzog voiced his great contentment because, "whatever happens now, I have seen the thing I hoped for more than anything else in the world: the return of Alsace to France."[82]

Cultural factors further aggravated the difficulties of the textile manufacturers who made the decision to opt and emigrate. In *"— & Co.,"* for example, everyone in Normandy refers to the Alsatian newcomers as "the Prussians."[83] On the day of the Paris commune uprising in March 1871, Théodore Blin and Henri Fraenkel, who were making a brief stopover in Paris on their way back to Bischwiller from Normandy, were even arrested as Prussian spies on account of their Alsatian accents.[84]

Besides the general xenophobia to which all emigrating Alsatians were exposed, Jews had to deal with an additional prejudice—antisemitism. In *"— & Co.,"* Bloch shows how fears of competition on the part of French industrialists frequently assumed the form of anti-Jewish prejudice. One of the leading antirepublican notables in Normandy, speaking of the newly arrived Simlers, describes them scornfully as

the fine flower of Rhineland business, the very best type of what they have been turning out, ever since the Revolution of Eighty-nine, in the ghettos of Frankfurt, the first fruits of M. Thiers' government, a pretty German warp on a Jewish weft, one of those reversible stuffs, don't you know, usury on one side, swindling on the other, with a broad selvage of meanness, stuffs that look well enough, I don't deny, smooth to the touch, that take in the purchaser, but the expert can detect for certain the end of all honest and conscientious work.[85]

Items in the local Alsatian press attest to the accuracy of Bloch's fictional account of the difficulties encountered in emigrating. While on a short visit to Bischwiller a year after his emigration, one anonymous but socially eminent Jewish textile manufacturer declared that he and his family now regretted their decision to leave. Expressing his profound disillusionment with France, he explained: "We were ignited by patriotism and the hope of finding in France, if not affection, at least an amiable reception, but we have been bitterly enlightened. I can say without presumption that here, in Alsace, we live esteemed and in good relations with our neighbors and our competitors; there, in France, we haven't found that at all. We are looked upon with a scornful air, and we occasionally hear expressions like the following: 'What do we care about the Alsatian Jews!'" Most of all, he regretted having to pay his workers wages 30 to 40 percent higher than those he had paid in Bischwiller. He lamented that despite these increases, his workers constantly complained that they had been better off before leaving.[86]

Several commentators have concluded that commercial considerations alone cannot explain the massive exodus from Bischwiller. The historian Eugène Bourguignon, for example, argues that Bischwiller's textile industry could have survived the augmented French tariffs without much difficulty because the merchandise was so highly specialized that the clientele could not have turned elsewhere.[87] In fact, for some textile manufacturers, such as Bloch's fictional half-Jewish family the Altermanns, there were powerful economic disincentives to emigrate: "The Altermanns opted *preuss.* A competitor the less and a debt on the competitor's balance sheet made this morose man quite cheerful." For Bloch, the actions of the Simlers and other Jewish textile manufacturers who emigrated cannot be understood without taking into account their patriotism: "These men had abandoned everything in order to remain citizens of France."[88] Supporting this view, the Bischwiller police commissioner said in 1875, "The first emigrations cannot be attributed to the aggravation of the situation of industry, but must rather be explained by political motives."[89] In sum, it is unlikely that economic considerations could have triggered the decision to opt for France without the added impulse of the political factor—patriotism.

Although substantive data on wealth are lacking, it is possible to draw some conclusions about the optants' class composition. Jewish optants, like their non-Jewish peers, appear to have been recruited mainly from the ranks of the urban middle classes, and option was therefore a migration of elites. Not all the migrants were wealthy, to be sure. In 1872 the Jewish community of Saint-Dié in the Vosges complained to the Minister of Public Education and Religion that 275 of its 300 members lived in poverty and needed to be supported by charity. The poor Jews were "far more numerous today," the community explained, "because the annexation brought to Saint-Dié a great number of indigent coreligionists."⁹⁰ Similarly, Doris Bensimon-Donath comments that the high proportion of working women among the Alsatian migrants to Paris indicates that many of the migrant families were not well off. French government subsidies of transportation costs for the optants facilitated the emigration of those without significant means.⁹¹

In general, however, both literary and statistical sources suggest that the Jews who opted were "the richest, the most important, and the most respected."⁹² One member of the Metz community reported: "The news from our community is sad; this is a mass emigration, and from the whole of our beautiful *Kehilla* [community] there will soon remain only the indigent population. The well-to-do and intelligent sector that has abandoned an intolerant soil will not be replaced."⁹³ Metz did in fact lose most of its wealthiest Jews, many of whom were or had been members of the Lorraine Consistory. These included the lawyer Eliezer Lambert, the industrialists Dreyfus and Dupont, the publisher Félix Alcan, the banker Justin Worms, the former pharmacist Olry Terquem, the doctor and leading protester among Alsace-Lorraine deputies Edouard Bamberger, and the director of the newspaper *L'Indépendent de la Marne et de la Moselle*, Joseph Mayer.⁹⁴

The financial problems the communities subsequently faced further illustrate that it was in fact the wealthiest classes that emigrated.* In 1876 the Strasbourg Jewish community requested a government subsidy to construct a new synagogue. The Consistory explained that although the size of the community had increased since 1871 owing to the in-migration of German Jews, its income had declined "since many rich families have opted for France that have not been replaced by other rich families."⁹⁵ A few years later, in 1873, the Jewish community of Metz unsuccessfully requested a subsidy for the synagogue administration in 1873 on the grounds that the families that had previously contributed most to the synagogue's revenue had opted for French citizenship and emigrated.⁹⁶

---

*The emigration of the wealthiest sector convinced the Ratisbonnes, one of the most prominent families of the Strasbourg Jewish elite, to abandon their court proceedings against the Alsatian consistories through which they had for years attempted to recover long-standing debts owed them. See Patrick Girard, *Les Juifs de France*, p. 70.

TABLE 3.10
Occupational Distribution of Jewish Optants Compared with That of
Pre-1870 Alsatian Jewish Migrants to Paris and the United States

Sector	Jewish optants (N = 517)	Alsatian Jews in Paris, 1872[a] (N = 1,825)	Bas-Rhin Jewish emigrants to U.S., 1828–37[b] (N = 62)
Property Owners, rentiers	6.8%	8%	1.6%
Liberal and superior professions	11.2	7	1.6
Independent commerce	41.1	35	12.9
Employees (government and commerce)	13.4	19	1.6
Artisans, skilled labor	7.9	20	32.3
Unskilled, street trades	4.5	11	41.9
Without, unknown	15.1	—	8.1

SOURCES: Doris Bensimon-Donath, *Socio-démographie des juifs de France et d'Algérie, 1867–1907* (Paris, 1976), p. 150; Archives départementales du Bas-Rhin, 3 M 703, "Emigration en Amérique d'habitants du Bas-Rhin—États numériques et nominatifs, 1828–1837."
NOTE: The occupational categories are Bensimon-Donath's.
[a] This group includes the Jewish optants who emigrated, as well as Jews who had moved to Paris earlier in the 19th century.
[b] Personal names and surnames were used to determine the Jewish migrants.

A comparison of the socioprofessional structure of Jewish optants from Alsace-Lorraine with that of earlier Alsatian Jewish emigrant groups lends further credence to the hypothesis correlating high social class with the propensity to opt (Table 3.10). Although property owners and *rentiers* among the optants were slightly underrepresented in comparison with all Alsatian Jews who had migrated to Paris by 1872, the optants were significantly overrepresented in the two occupational categories that would have embraced the wealthiest segments of the population—the liberal and superior professions and independent commerce. Concomitantly, Jewish optants were underrepresented in comparison with earlier Alsatian Jewish migrants to Paris in the lower-status occupations—salaried government and commercial employment, artisanry and skilled labor, and unskilled labor and street trades.[97]

The occupational and class structure of Jews who emigrated to the United States from Bas-Rhin earlier in the nineteenth century also reveals sharp differences when compared with the occupational structure of the Jewish optants. The majority of the earlier emigrants possessed 600 francs or less or had only enough money for the sea voyage. They were overwhelmingly concentrated in the lowest-status occupations: artisanry (there were no industrialists), unskilled labor, and street trades. The observation that Jewish optants were recruited from a higher socioeconomic bracket than pre-1871 Jewish migrants from the provinces led one late-nineteenth-century German Jewish commentator to argue that class rather than religion was the primary determinant of the relatively high proportion of Jewish optants.[98]

Option and emigration in 1871-72 had profound repercussions on the shape of the Alsace-Lorraine Jewish community. The emigration of numerous lay members of the three departmental consistories, as well as many synagogue officials, threw the Jewish communities of the provinces into what Lorraine Jewish leaders called "a sort of disarray."* It is estimated that in Metz alone 1,000 Jews departed out of a total Jewish population of 2,500.[99] Once-vibrant organizations like Metz's Société de Bienfaisance de la Jeunesse Israélite (Jewish Youth's Benevolent Society) felt the impact of emigration not only in a dramatic decline in membership but also in a significant loss of income.[100] Moreover, the option of nearly all the Alsace-Lorraine candidates at the Ecole Rabbinique in Paris, described by a wartime report as "animated by the purest patriotic sentiments," created a severe shortage of rabbis in the Reichsland. This problem was only partly alleviated by the creation of a rabbinical preparatory school in Colmar in 1880.[101]

The contours of the French Jewish community were also remolded as a result of the annexation. Although the German conquest severed 45 percent of the total French Jewish population, the migration of Jewish optants caused the Jewish population of the

*In Strasbourg, the Consistory lost two of its lay members, Achille Ratisbonne and David Maase. Simon Lévy and Marx Haarscher, the president and the beadle of the synagogue, respectively, also opted and emigrated to France. The Colmar Consistory lost two of its lay members, Abraham Lévy and Leopold Rueff. In Lorraine, the cantors of Metz and Sarreguemines opted and emigrated. Moreover, only one member of the Consistory remained—Louis Morhange—and even he emigrated to Marseille in the early twentieth century. Lorraine Consistory to Bezirkspräsident, Lorraine, March 23, 1874, Archives départementales de la Moselle, 7 AL 4; Roth, *La Lorraine annexée*, p. 143.

French interior to increase proportionately more than either the Catholic or the Protestant population.* Most Jews who opted in Alsace-Lorraine emigrated to Paris and its suburbs. Between 1866 and 1872 the Jewish population of Paris increased from 20,615 to 23,434, a jump of 16 percent.[102] The Paris Consistory requested the creation of two new rabbinical posts in 1872 to better serve a community whose numbers had swollen as a result of the recent influx of immigrants.[103]

Significant numbers of Jews headed toward cities and towns in the departments bordering the annexed provinces, especially Vosges, Meurthe-et-Moselle, Ardennes, and Haute-Saône. Some, particularly the industrialists, ventured farther to the north and east of France.[104] In contrast to earlier migrations of Alsace-Lorraine Jews into the French interior, Jewish optants frequently gravitated to small towns that had no Jewish communities or tiny ones at best.[105] Jewish optants also headed to Algeria, where the *Archives israélites* predicted the "creation of a new Alsace-Lorraine" as an "affirmation of Jewish patriotism."[106]

With the demographic shifts in France came institutional changes. In order to accommodate the two Grand Rabbis who opted, Benjamin Lipman and Isaac Lévy, the Consistory created two new consistorial seats, at Lille (department of the Nord) and Vesoul (the Vosges).[107] The Ecole Rabbinique not only lost its principal source of income and students, but was also faced with a diminution of employment opportunities for the remaining students, since 75 percent of all rabbinical posts in the country had been situated in Alsace-Lorraine.[108] To deal with the problem of organizing new communities and establishing new rabbinical seats, the Grand Rabbinate of France, together with the Paris Consistory, established the Missions Rabbiniques des Communautés de France in 1872.[109] The membership of the Central Consistory itself was affected by the Treaty of Frankfurt. Faced with the loss of the three delegates from the annexed provinces, including its president, Max Cerfberr, the Consistory simply

*Although the number of Catholics in France (post-1871 borders) decreased by 1.3 percent between 1866 and 1872 and the number of Protestants 5.1 percent, the Jewish population actually increased substantially—by 11.4 percent—owing to the immigration from the annexed provinces. Szajkowski, "Growth of the Jewish Population," pp. 304, 309.

decided in 1871 to continue to recognize those delegates. Furthermore, it invited Cerfberr, who had resigned just after the annexation, to become its honorary president.[110]

Despite arguments by historians and commentators who have attempted, with some justification, to disengage the question of Alsace-Lorraine from nationalistic polemics, literary as well as statistical evidence attests to the centrality of political considerations in the option and emigration of Jews in 1871–72. Even those factors impelling option that were ostensibly economic or cultural were often inseparably intertwined with political motivations. In this respect, option marks a sharp departure from previous socioeconomically induced Jewish migrations from the provinces. Hence, although the Franco-Jewish patriotic polemics oversimplify to the extreme the motives of Jewish optants and emigrants, their emphasis on the essentially political factor of French national identity accurately reflects historical reality.

Nevertheless, these same Franco-Jewish nationalistic polemics err in portraying the Jewish response to the annexation as a monolithic one. Certainly Jews as a group shared an initial mistrust of the new German regime, fearing a downgrading of their legal status, but very clearly the urban middle and upper-middle classes constituted the greatest proportion of optants and emigrants. This tendency suggests a strong relationship between a high level of socioeconomic assimilation and acculturation, including the development of a sense of French national identity. Since national identity represented not only an abstract ideal for Jews but also a set of practical advances in terms of civil rights, it follows that the Jews who had benefited most from the cultural and economic opportunities opened up by emancipation would also have felt most threatened by the shift from French to German sovereignty. By the same token, it appears that rural Jews, less assimilated to France linguistically, culturally, and economically, possessed a less developed national consciousness.* Thus,

---

* This may have been true of the rural French in general, as Eugen Weber argues in *Peasants into Frenchmen, 1870–1914*. On the other hand, a statistical survey of Jewish emigration from the Reichsland between 1872 and the First World War shows that rural Jews were not at all loath to move, and indeed emigrated in disproportionate numbers throughout the period. The nature of this emigration will be discussed in Chapter 4.

the political responses of Jews to annexation, although on the whole pro-French, were far more varied than they are made out to be in the patriotic polemics of French Jewish historians and publicists. Above all, those responses reflected the uneven pace of the development of a sense of French national identity among different sectors of the Jewish community.

FOUR

Emigration Patterns, 1873-1914

Large-scale emigration from Alsace-Lorraine continued long after the October 1, 1872, deadline for the filing of option declarations. According to government calculations, approximately 460,000 persons emigrated from the annexed provinces between 1871 and 1910, nearly 30 percent of the total 1871 population.[1] Jewish emigration is similarly reflected in the sharp decline of the general Jewish population, both in proportion to the total population and in absolute numbers. Although declining fertility played a role in this trend, French and German Jews alike agreed that emigration was the main cause of this constant diminution.[2] Between 1871 and 1910 the Jewish population of Alsace-Lorraine fell from 40,938 to 30,483 (Table 4.1). But since nearly one-quarter of the 1910 Jewish population consisted of in-migrants from Germany, the decline of the native population was far greater than these figures indicate.[3] Furthermore, whereas the Jewish population was 25.5 percent smaller by the end of the period, the general population of the three provinces increased 20.9 percent. Haut-Rhin experienced the most precipitous decline, losing more than a third of its Jews, while Bas-Rhin and Lorraine each lost approximately one-fifth (Table 4.2).

Many historians of Alsace-Lorraine have seen this post-1872 emigration as a continuation of option, but there is substantial evidence that the two were distinct, at least in the case of Jews.* Unlike the

*Hiegel, "Option" (1975), suggests that the two migrations were distinct, although he does not establish a conceptual framework for differentiating them. Roth, *La Lorraine annexée*, pp. 112–13, makes the distinction more clearly. The nineteenth and early-twentieth-century historians of Alsace-Lorraine, including Reuss, Delahache, and Moch, do not distinguish between option and post-1872 migration in general. They argue that both movements were essentially political protests against the German annexation.

TABLE 4.1
The Jewish Population of Alsace-Lorraine, 1871–1910

Year	Total population[a]	Jewish population	Jews as percent of total population
1871	1,549,738	40,938	2.6%
1875	1,531,804	39,002	2.5
1880	1,566,670	39,278	2.5
1885	1,564,355	36,876	2.4
1890	1,603,506	34,645	2.2
1895	1,640,986	32,859	2.0
1900	1,719,470	32,264	1.9
1905	1,814,564	31,708	1.7
1910	1,874,014	30,483	1.6

SOURCE: Statistischen Bureau des Kaiserlichen Ministeriums für Elsass-Lothringen, *Statistisches Jahrbuch für Elsass-Lothringen, 1913/14*, pp. 1, 16.
[a] Includes military personnel.

TABLE 4.2
Size of the Jewish and Total Populations of Alsace-Lorraine by Province, 1871 and 1910

Population	1871	1910	Absolute change	Percent change
Jewish population	40,938	30,483	−10,455	−25.5
Bas-Rhin	20,189	15,779	−4,410	−21.8
Haut-Rhin	12,103	7,689	−4,414	−36.5
Lorraine	8,646	7,015	−1,631	−18.9
Total population	1,549,738	1,874,014	+324,276	+20.9%

SOURCES: Statistischen Bureau des Kaiserlichen Ministeriums für Elsass-Lothringen, *Statistisches Handbuch für Elsass-Lothringen, 1885*, p. 39; *Statistisches Jahrbuch für Elsass-Lothringen, 1913/14*, pp. 3, 16.

Jewish optants of 1871–72, the Jews who emigrated after 1872 from the Bas-Rhin district of Haguenau (the population selected for this study) tended to head, not for France, but for the New World, generally the United States. Moreover, whereas the Jewish optants had been essentially urban and middle class, the Jews who emigrated after October 1872 were overwhelmingly rural and lower class. Post-1872 Jewish migration also closely resembled the sociological model of migrations caused by the lack of economic opportunities in the countryside and the inhabitants' perception of a condition of overpopulation. Such population movements are characterized by greater numbers of men than women, small numbers of the occupationally inactive, and either a preponderance of men or a mixture of both sexes among working-age migrants.[4] Jewish option had marked a radical break with earlier nineteenth-century socioeconomic migration patterns linked to the incipient spread of capitalism and industrialization; post-1872 Jewish emigration constituted an extension and even an intensification of these earlier tendencies. Indeed, rural Jewish migration assumed the proportions of a mass movement only in the German period, when capitalistic institutions became well entrenched in rural districts. Although the Franco-Jewish press persisted in its attempts to use post-1872 Jewish emigration as proof of the continued French patriotism of Alsace-Lorraine Jewry, the insistence of the German Jewish press upon the importance of material motivations now carried more weight than it had in the case of option.

That post-1872 Jewish emigration exhibited discontinuities in relation to Jewish option and continuities with pre-1871 population trends further substantiates the argument that there was no monolithic Jewish response to the annexation. The choice of the United States as the principal destination suggests that these rural and lower-class Jews felt less of a sense of French national identity than did their urban, middle-class coreligionists who had opted in disproportionate numbers. Even when political motives played a role in stimulating post-1872 Jewish emigration, they were essentially of a negative nature, expressed primarily as an anti-German animus rather than as a positive avowal of French patriotism. The fact that this sector of the Jewish population was the least assimilated to France culturally and economically lends credence to the hypothesis that the rise of national identity among Jews was in fact closely linked to other aspects of assimilation.

Jews found themselves overrepresented among the applicants for *Entlassungsurkunde*, or emigration permits, to an even greater extent than they had been among the optants. Of a total of 1,575 applicants for emigration permits from the district of Haguenau between 1873 and 1898, almost 20 percent (316) were Jews, even though in 1875 Jews constituted only 3.9 percent of the total population of the district (Table 4.3).* According to published census figures, between

*For a discussion of the population, the sources, and the methodology employed, see Appendix B.

TABLE 4.3
Jewish and Non-Jewish Emigration from Haguenau District by Two-Year Periods, 1873–1898

Period	Jews	Non-Jews	Total	Period	Jews	Non-Jews	Total
1873–74	20	49	69	1887–88	30	193	223
1875–76	11	52	63	1889–90	26	140	166
1877–78	42	146	188	1891–92	29	109	138
1879–80	14	53	67	1893–94	24	89	113
1881–82	30	97	127	1895–96	27	55	82
1883–84	25	118	143	1897–98	15	38	53
1885–86	23	120	143	TOTAL	316	1,259	1,575

SOURCES: See Appendix B. The other tables in this chapter are based on these sources unless otherwise noted.

TABLE 4.4
Jewish and Total Legal Emigration from Bas-Rhin by Year, 1883–1892 and 1903–1910

Year	Jews	Total	Jews as percent of total	Year	Jews	Total	Jews as percent of total
1883	106	837	12.7	1903	17	145	11.7
1884	81	706	11.5	1904	15	101	14.9
1885	89	604	14.7	1905	24	95	25.3
1886	69	568	12.1	1906	26	177	14.7
1887	70	632	11.1	1907	38	125	30.4
1888	51	592	8.6	1908	14	115	12.2
1889	57	479	11.9	1909	25	170	14.7
1890	54	404	13.3	1910	20	147	13.6
1891	66	400	16.5	TOTAL	179	1,075	16.7
1892	53	400	13.3				
TOTAL	696	5,622	12.4				

SOURCES: Archives départementales du Bas-Rhin, D 49 49, D 98-16a.

1871 and 1910 the Jewish population of Haguenau declined from 2,970 to 1,911, a drop of 35.7 percent, which was in large part due to emigration. The proportion of Jews who emigrated from Haguenau, although it was somewhat higher than that from other Bas-Rhin districts, was by no means atypical. For Bas-Rhin as a whole between 1883 and 1892, Jews constituted 696 out of 5,622 legal emigrants— 12.4 percent. Between 1903 and 1910, they numbered 179 out of

1,075 legal emigrants—16.7 percent (Table 4.4). Throughout the period of the annexation, Jews never represented more than 3.5 percent of Bas-Rhin's entire population.

The yearly emigration figures must be analyzed with an awareness that young men usually emigrated several years before they actually petitioned for the *Entlassungsurkunde*. Nevertheless, some of the fluctuations in Table 4.3 can be explained by the political and economic conditions in certain periods. The large number of emigrants from Haguenau in 1878 (42 Jews, 133 non-Jews) may be related to the economic depression that gripped Alsace-Lorraine in the mid- to late 1870's; the large number in the years 1887 and 1888 was almost certainly due to the Franco-German political crisis and the mounting threat of war sparked by the militantly anti-German and revanchist political campaign of General Boulanger; and the notable tapering-off in the late 1890's may reflect a growing accommodation to German rule as well as increased economic prosperity.[5]

Perhaps the most striking characteristic of post-1872 Jewish emigration is that it was overwhelmingly a rural phenomenon, in contrast to the preeminently urban nature of option for both Jews and Christians. Whereas only 16.8 percent of all Jewish optants had come from towns with fewer than 2,000 inhabitants, a full 54.4 percent of Jewish emigrants from the district of Haguenau came from towns of that size (Table 4.5). Similarly, whereas towns with under 5,000 inhabitants had recruited only 30.8 percent of all Jewish optants, 75.3 percent of all Jewish emigrants fell into this category. Post-1872 Jewish emigration, in contrast to option, thus closely mirrored the situation within the general Jewish population, where 71 percent of

TABLE 4.5
Distribution of Jewish and Non-Jewish Emigrants by Hometown City Size

Hometown city size (*population*)	Jews (N = 316)	Non-Jews (N = 1,253)[a]
Less than 2,000	54.4%	49.2%
2,000–4,999	20.9	17.8
5,000–9,999	9.5	22.8
More than 10,000	15.2	10.2

NOTE: City size based on 1875 census figures, Statistischen Bureau des Kaiserlichen Ministeriums für Elsass-Lothringen, *Statistische Mitteilungen über Elsass-Lothringen, 1875.*

[a] The city size was not available for 6 of the 1,259 non-Jewish emigrants.

TABLE 4.6
Distribution of Jewish Emigrants by Town

Town	Number (N = 316)	Percent of total	Town	Number (N = 316)	Percent of total
Schirrhofen	66	21%	Oberbronn	8	3%
Haguenau	47	15	Batzendorf	5	2
Herlisheim	36	11	Offendorf	4	1
Reichshofen	30	9	Uhrwiller	4	1
Bischwiller	29	9	Offwiller	2	1
Mertzwiller	21	7	Schweighausen	2	1
Niederbronn	20	6	Walk	2	1
Gundershofen	14	4	Windstein	1	0
Wittersheim	13	4	Wintershausen	1	0
Dauerndorf	8	3	Other[a]	3	0

NOTE: Percent column does not sum to 100 because of rounding.
[a] One emigrant each from Surbourg, in the district of Wissembourg; Bushswiller, in the district of Saverne; and Metz. The first two were probably included out of confusion over the redistricting after the Franco-Prussian War. The emigrant from Metz had probably resided in the district of Haguenau at one time.

all Jews in 1871 lived in towns with fewer than 5,000 inhabitants.[6] According to Doris Bensimon-Donath, what most distinguished post 1872 Alsace-Lorraine Jewish immigrants to Paris from other internal Jewish migrants was their rural provenance. Whereas about 30 percent of other provincial Jews drawn to the capital came from rural or semirural backgrounds, at least 70 percent of Reichsland Jews arriving in Paris fitted this category.[7]

The Jews who emigrated from the district of Haguenau came from a large number of towns (Table 4.6). Schirrhofen, whose population in 1875 was 65 percent Jewish, supplied the most Jewish emigrants.[8] Significantly, not a single Jew from this town had opted for French citizenship in 1871–72. On the other hand, only 24.1 percent of the Jewish emigrants came from the two largest cities, Haguenau and Bischwiller, which between them had supplied all the district of Haguenau's optants in 1871–72. Although proportionately more Christian emigrants, 33 percent, were drawn from Haguenau and Bischwiller, the fact remains that rural areas were the major source of emigration.*

*The decline of the rural Jewish population in general will be discussed in Chapter 8. On this tendency for the population as a whole, see D'Elstein, *L'Alsace-Lorraine sous la domination allemande*, p. 104.

TABLE 4.7
Distribution of Jewish Optants and Emigrants by Jewish Population Density

Jewish population density	Jewish population, selected districts, 1871[a]		Jewish population, Haguenau District, 1875	
	Total (N = 19,045)	Optants (N = 517)	Total (N = 2,748)	Emigrants (N = 316)
Less than 3%	5.7%	11.0%	8.3%	13.9%
3%–9.9%	51.7	73.1	65.4	53.5
10%–24.9%	31.7	9.5	13.3	11.1
25% and over	10.9	6.4	13.0	21.5

SOURCES: Columns 1 and 3 calculated from census data in Statistischen Bureau des Kaiserlichen Ministeriums für Elsass-Lothringen, *Statistische Mitteilungen über Elsass, 1871* and *1875*.
[a] For the districts, see Table 3.1.

Not only were the Jewish emigrants more rural than the optants; they also were more likely to come from areas of high Jewish population density (Table 4.7). In contrast to Jewish option, which drew primarily from cities and towns with low Jewish population densities, post-1872 emigration drew a disproportionate number of people from heavily Jewish villages (more than 25 percent representation). To some extent this trend reflects the more rural nature of emigration, since the areas of highest Jewish concentration were small rural villages; the pattern further suggests that population pressures, linked to the increasing competition among Jews for a progressively limited number of rural occupations, played an important role in propelling emigration. This positive correlation between Jewish population density and emigration lends additional support to the contention that the post-1872 outflow was primarily an economically based migration.

A clue to why rural Jews from heavily Jewish villages were particularly likely to emigrate from the Reichsland emerges from an examination of the occupational structure of the emigrant population (Table 4.8). The professional distribution of the emigrants, both Jews and non-Jews, far more closely mirrors that of their nonmobile counterparts than had that of the optants. According to a 1907 survey of the general Alsace-Lorraine population, 34.8 percent of all non-Jews were involved in agriculture and landed investments, 35.7 percent in industry and artisanry, and 9.1 percent in trade and commerce (calculated from data in Table 8.6). Although Christian emigrants were underrepresented in the agricultural sector, their

TABLE 4.8
Occupational Distribution of Jewish Emigrants
Compared with That of Three Other Populations

Sector	Haguenau emigrants[a]		Jews of Strasbourg-campagne, 1874 (N = 554)	Haguenau Jewish optants (N = 97)
	Jewish (N = 316)	Non-Jewish (N = 1,259)		
Commerce	85.8%	10.3%	85.2%	55.7%
Nonspecified independent	52.8		39.0	
Nonspecified employee	0.3		1.1	
Agricultural produce	13.0		4.7	
Food	7.3		16.1	
Inns, restaurants	1.3		1.1	
Leather	0.3		0.0	
Metal	0.3		1.3	
Money	5.4		9.7	
Notions	0.3		0.0	
Real estate	0.0		0.2	
Street trades	3.5		11.4	
Textiles	1.3		0.7	
Land, investments	2.2	24.9	1.1	3.1
Liberal professions	1.6	2.1	3.6	2.1
Manufacturing, artisanry	2.8	38.6	7.0	18.5
Nonprofessional services	0.6	0.9	0.9	0.0
Public service	0.3	2.4	0.2	3.1
Transportation	0.0	1.1	0.2	0.0
Unskilled labor	0.3	9.8	1.6	0.0
Without, unknown, not stated	6.3	9.8	0.2	17.5

[a] The occupation of the father was counted for emigrants too young to work.

proportions in manufacturing, artisanry, and commerce closely resemble those of the Christian population as a whole. A significant number of Christian emigrants—9.8 percent—also fell into the unskilled labor category.

The same relationship also characterized Jewish emigrants. In comparing them with the 1874 general Jewish population from a similar region, Strasbourg-campagne (Bas-Rhin), the most striking feature is that over 85 percent of both groups were involved in commercial pursuits.[9] Jewish emigrants were noticeably underrepresented only in manufacturing and artisanry and the liberal professions, suggesting that, unlike the optants, these migrants were not recruited primarily from the economic and cultural elites. It therefore appears that emigration of both Jews and non-Jews drew fairly proportionately from all occupational groups in the population.

Thus, whereas Jewish optants (Table 3.6) had been disproportionately represented in the highest-status professional categories of land and investments, public service, manufacturing and artisanry, and the liberal professions, post-1872 Jewish emigrants were concentrated in the lower-status commercial professions, indicating their lower social-class background. Also, these trends characterized urban as well as rural Jewish emigrants, although a greater proportion of urban emigrants were employed in the liberal professions and in manufacturing and artisanry (Table 4.9). There was a higher percentage of Jewish emigrants than of optants in independent commerce, but in the countryside independent commerce usually implied marginal petty commerce. The other commercial profession overrepresented among the emigrants was agricultural produce, that is, trading in cattle, horses, wood, and grain, which were traditional rural Jewish occupations. On the other hand, a disproportionately low number of Jewish emigrants made their livelihoods in the traditional Jewish street trades, in moneylending or brokerage, or in the food business.

Poverty clearly had a great deal to do with Jewish emigration. The fact that in only fourteen cases in my study was the worth of the family's property even estimated (and most of those estimates fell between 2,000 and 8,000 marks) attests to the relative penury of most emigrants. Moreover, of the 95 Jewish emigrants who discussed their motivations, 84 listed economic considerations—the desire to secure a better livelihood. Some poorer parents expressed the hope that, once abroad, their sons would make so much money that they could contribute not only to the upbringing of the siblings remaining in Alsace-Lorraine, but also to the care of the parents. Others declared that they were too poor, too old, or too sickly to look after young children properly, and that the interests of the children would be better supervised by brothers or sisters who had already emigrated.[10]

Poverty alone, however, does not sufficiently explain this emigration. The poorest of the Alsace-Lorraine Jews were surely those involved in the street trades and employed in unskilled jobs, and these categories were underrepresented among the emigrants. Rather, it was precisely those Jews who had once played a prominent and secure role in the rural economy who were in the forefront of emigration. It was the shrinking of economic opportunities, rather than their complete absence, that was the main stimulus to emigration. The progressive infiltration of capitalistic institutions into the Alsace-

TABLE 4.9
Occupational Distribution of Rural and Urban Jewish Emigrants Compared with That of Rural and Urban Jewish Male Optants

Sector	Rural		Urban	
	Emigrants (N = 238)[a]	Male optants (N = 146)	Emigrants (N = 78)[a]	Male optants (N = 309)
Commerce	88.2%	67.8%	78.2%	55.7%
Nonspecified independent	55.0	39.0	46.2	23.3
Nonspecified employee	0.0	4.1	1.3	14.2
Agricultural produce	14.3	11.6	9.0	5.2
Books	0.0	0.0	0.0	1.9
Food	6.7	8.9	9.0	4.2
Inns, restaurants	1.7	0.7	0.0	1.0
Leather	0.0	0.7	1.3	0.3
Metal	0.4	0.0	0.0	0.0
Money	5.0	1.3	6.4	3.2
Notions	0.0	0.0	1.3	0.0
Porcelain, glass	0.0	0.0	0.0	0.3
Street trades	4.6	0.0	0.0	1.0
Textiles	0.4	1.4	3.8	1.0
Land, investments	2.1	4.8	2.6	7.4
Liberal professions	0.4	2.1	5.1	10.0
Manufacturing, artisanry	2.5	11.7	3.8	12.9
Nonprofessional services	0.0	0.7	2.6	0.6
Public service	0.4	0.7	0.0	6.8
Unskilled labor	0.4	5.5	0.0	1.9
Without, unknown, not stated	5.9	6.8	7.7	4.5

NOTE: Urban is defined as cities with 5,000 inhabitants or more; rural as anything smaller.
[a] The occupation of the father was counted for emigrants too young to work.

Lorraine countryside that had begun during the Second Empire and assumed formidable proportions after the annexation was part of the change. These developments will be described fully in Chapter 8. Suffice it to say here that the rise of new types of agricultural credit banks and cooperatives, together with increased government regulation of both cattle and horse dealing and peddling, resulted in the erosion of rural Jewry's economic base.

The economic interests of the Jewish optants had drawn them toward France; the entirely different economic concerns of the essentially rural Jewish emigrants attracted them to the New World, and this choice also indicates a lesser degree of cultural as well as economic assimilation to France. Among the Haguenau district Jewish emigrants in the years 1873–98, only 30.7 percent went to France, whereas 62.5 percent sailed to the New World, most often to the United States, but also to Latin America (Table 4.10).* Describing Jewish emigration from his village of Ingwiller, in the district of Saverne, Edmond Uhry told this story: "When a new synagogue was being built, he [Karl Clemmer, a saddler] told a visiting American native of the town that in the court of the *shul* the Jewish people would erect a monument. That sounded very Catholic. The visitor inquired: 'To whom?' He answered, 'Christopher Columbus. Hasn't every Jewish family in this town a good investment in America, having sent so many of its sons?'"[11] The New World, of course, much more than France, symbolized the land of golden opportunity. As one not very well-off Jewish cantor remarked, in America his son "would earn much money."[12] For the most adventuresome of Jewish youths who hoped to make a quick fortune, the gold fields of Brazil and Argentina proved even more enticing.[13]

*The choice of destination did not vary over time. The preferred destinations of Jewish emigrants to France were Paris (60.6%), Nancy (9.0%), Macon (4.5%), and Sedan (4.5%). Those of non-Jews were Paris (37.3%), Nancy (9.7%), Elbeuf (6.0%), Clermont (6.0%), and Lunéville (6.0%). The favored destinations of Jewish emigrants to the United States were New York City (35.9%), New Orleans (20.3%), San Francisco (12.5%), Galveston (6.3%), and Brooklyn (6.3%). The most popular destinations of non-Jewish emigrants to the United States were New York City (38.7%), Buffalo (9.8%), Philadelphia (12.3%), and St. Louis (6.1%). In Latin America the favored countries of destination of Jewish emigrants were Brazil, Argentina, Mexico, Chile, and Uruguay. Judith Elkin reports that Alsace-Lorraine Jewish emigrants also headed to Peru after 1872. See Elkin, *Jews of the Latin American Republics*, pp. 40–42, 46.

TABLE 4.10
Destinations of Jewish and Non-Jewish Emigrants

Destination	Jews (N = 309)[a]	Non-Jews (N = 1,224)[a]
United States	56.0%	38.1%
France	30.7	54.3
Latin America	6.5	0.3
Europe (other than France)	6.5	5.6
Africa	0.3	1.6
Canada	0.0	0.2

[a] The destinations of 7 Jewish emigrants and 35 non-Jewish emigrants are unknown.

That proportionately more non-Jewish emigrants headed to France suggests that they were more economically and culturally assimilated to that country. Religion in part explains this trend, since a considerable number of non-Jewish emigrants claimed they intended to emigrate in order to receive a Catholic education in a French seminary.* The degree of urbanization before emigration also partly accounts for the discrepancy between Jewish and Gentile choices of destination. Proportionately more Jewish than Christian emigrants came from small villages, and for both groups there is a clear correlation between urbanization and destination (Tables 4.11 and 4.12). In general, a disproportionately high number of Jewish emigrants from the smallest towns tended to go to the United States. Indeed, 63 percent of all the district's Jewish emigrants to the United States came from towns of under 2,000 inhabitants. Jewish emigrants from towns of this size were over three times more likely to go to the United States and Latin America combined than to France.

On the other hand, Jews from larger cities were overrepresented significantly among the group of emigrants that felt the attractions of France. Jews from cities with between 5,000 and 9,999 inhabitants were almost equally divided between the New World and France. Those from the largest city, Haguenau, were 1.2 times more likely to go to France than to the New World. For Christian emigrants, the correlation between urbanization and destination was even stronger,

*For non-Jewish emigrants, I noted the motives only when they were readily apparent in their dossiers. Of these, 93 non-Jews stated the desire to attend a Catholic seminary as the reason for emigration.

TABLE 4.11
Distribution of Jewish Emigrants by Destination and Hometown City Size
(N = 308)[a]

	Hometown city size			
Destination	Less than 2,000 (N = 167)	2,000–4,999 (N = 64)	5,000–9,999 (N = 30)	10,000 or more (N = 47)
United States	65.3%	51.6%	43.3%	38.3%
France	21.6	32.8	40.0	55.3
Latin America	6.0	7.8	6.7	6.4
Europe (other than France)	7.2	7.8	10.0	0.0
TOTAL	100.0%	100.0%	100.0%	100.0%

	Destination			
Hometown city size	United States (N = 173)	France (N = 95)	Latin America (N = 20)	Europe (except France) (N = 20)
Less than 2,000	63.0%	37.9%	50.0%	60.0%
2,000–4,999	19.1	22.1	25.0	25.0
5,000–9,999	7.5	12.6	10.0	15.0
10,000 or more	10.4	27.4	15.0	0.0
TOTAL	100.0%	100.0%	100.0%	100.0%

[a] The total omits the 1 other emigrant whose destination was known. That person went to Africa.

with the exception that even Christians from small villages were slightly more likely to go to France than to the United States, or Latin America. As was true of their Jewish counterparts, the largest contingent of Christian emigrants to the United States came from the smallest villages.*

A final important influence on the choice of destination was the presence of either relatives or fellow townsmen already abroad.[14] Thirty-two percent of Jewish emigrants said they had relatives al-

*Occupation does not appear to have been a major influence on the choice of destination. The only significant socioprofessional distinctions between the Jews moving to France and those who went to the United States were that 5.3 percent of the emigrants to France were in the land and investments category, compared with only 0.6 percent of the emigrants to the United States. Furthermore, a somewhat higher proportion of the U.S. immigrants were involved in commerce—89.6 percent against 81.1 percent. Jewish emigrants to France, therefore, may have been recruited from a slightly higher social class.

TABLE 4.12
Distribution of Non-Jewish Emigrants by Destination and
Hometown City Size
(N = 1,218)[a]

	Hometown city size			
Destination	Less than 2,000 (N = 602)	2,000–4,999 (N = 211)	5,000–9,999 (N = 279)	10,000 or more (N = 126)
United States	45.2%	39.8%	30.1%	20.6%
France	47.7	55.5	60.9	69.8
Latin America	0.2	0.5	0.4	0.8
Europe (other than France)	4.5	4.3	8.2	6.3
Africa	2.5	0.0	0.4	2.4
TOTAL	100.0%	100.0%	100.0%	100.0%

	Destination[b]			
Hometown city size	United States (N = 466)	France (N = 662)	Europe (except France) (N = 67)	Africa (N = 19)
Less than 2,000	58.4%	43.4%	40.3%	78.9%
2,000–4,999	18.0	17.7	13.4	0.0
5,000–9,999	18.0	25.7	34.3	5.3
10,000 or more	5.6	13.3	11.9	15.8
TOTAL	100.0%	100.0%	100.0%	100.0%

[a] The total omits 2 emigrants who went to Canada and 39 of unknown destination or hometown city size.
[b] 4 emigrants went to Latin America, 1 from each city size.

ready established in France, the United States, Latin America, or Europe. Since not every applicant for an *Entlassungsurkunde* provided this information, the actual proportion may have been even higher. Before his own emigration, Edmond Uhry had an aunt and uncle who had moved to Galveston in 1888 and then to Cincinnati in 1900, an uncle in Brooklyn, a cousin in Louisiana, and two older brothers elsewhere in the United States, who had also departed in the 1880's.[15] Close family connections of course greatly facilitated the difficult process of resettlement, not only because better-off relatives abroad could often help out with the costs of transportation, but also because they were frequently willing to take the newly arrived into their businesses or to oversee their education. Occasionally, a childless relative welcomed the opportunity to take in one of a brother's or sister's numerous offspring.[16]

Fellow townspeople who had emigrated also were helpful, and the knowledge that Jewish institutions existed to provide a sense of community enhanced the attractiveness of a particular destination. As Uhry commented, "Wherever one from a town would settle, others from the same district would join him."[17] In other words, although emigration was predominantly an individual matter, the choice of destination was at least in part communally determined.

It is clear that, although economic motives may have been paramount, cultural and political factors still played an important role in propelling post-1872 emigration from the annexed provinces. Among non-Jews who presented motives for their emigration, a significant number cited cultural-religious considerations. Many said that they wanted to be educated in France or at least in the French language. A number of them intended to attend Catholic seminaries, usually in France, but also in Belgium, Luxembourg, or French-speaking Switzerland. And a good many Catholics who did not emigrate sent their daughters to convents in France. To some extent, of course, the motives were religious, but pro-French parents could also rest assured that their children's religious training would be conducted in French.

Of the Jewish emigrants, 13.4 percent attributed their migration to cultural considerations, chiefly, a lack of proficiency in German and a desire to obtain a French education.[18] When the Jewish broker Simon Kahn applied for an emigration permit for his son Nathan in 1877, he explained to the Haguenau Kreisdirector that his son had spent the last five years in France. After completing his education, Nathan had found a job in an important bookkeeping firm there. His son would never return to Germany, the broker said, "because he is not proficient in the German language."[19] Similarly, Léon Blum, a Jewish sawmill owner in Niederbronn, explained in 1878 that it would not be practical for his sixteen-year-old son, who had spent the last three years studying in a French lycée, to return to Alsace. Not only had the family already invested a considerable sum of money in his education, but the son, "who is not proficient in the German language, sees before his eyes, so to speak, earning his living in France. [He will otherwise] have his studies snatched from him and will be sent to a German elementary school at an age when he should be entering the university."[20]

Political motivations, although more difficult to discern owing to the impossibility of those applying for legal emigration permits to express such views openly, also continued to exert a strong influence, at least on young men of draft age, Jews and Gentiles alike. It may be argued that draft evasion was not essentially political in nature but rather an expression of a traditional hostility toward military service, and the fact that so many emigrants in general went to the United States, where there was no conscription, might tend to support this view. Yet several important factors lend credence to the political interpretation of draft evasion from the annexed territories. Certainly the emigrants heading toward France would have had to face rigorous regulations regarding military service, because, as noted in Chapter 3, the French conscription law of 1872 mandated up to five years of basic military service for all men between the ages of twenty and forty, as well as significant time in the reserves. Although the term of service was reduced to three years in 1889 (and to two years in 1905), the majority of Alsace-Lorraine emigrants left prior to 1889. It is also significant that draft evasion assumed greater proportions in Alsace-Lorraine than anywhere else in the Reich. In 1872 over 77 percent of those called up for active service in Alsace-Lorraine did not appear. This figure had tapered off to 25 percent by 1879, but it remained at this still relatively high level until about 1895.[21] Legal emigration of young males was also high: 6,850 male youths under seventeen years of age emigrated legally from the Reichsland between 1873 and 1882.[22] Ostensibly, emigration permits were not to be granted to those whose primary purpose was to evade the draft, but it was almost impossible for local officials to weed out these cases, and both the administration and the press were aware that, so far as motivation was concerned, legal emigration and illegal emigration were often identical. In both cases, as the Haguenau Kreisdirector noted, anti-German hostility was very much involved.[23]

There is no doubt, furthermore, that government authorities perceived draft evasion to be a distinctly political problem, linked to the broader dilemma of how to reconcile the native population to the annexation.[24] In 1879 the Lorraine Bezirkspräsident regretted the decision not to create a special military academy for Alsace-Lorrainers, since "the young people have not been inspired with confidence in the idea of military service."[25] The Kreisdirector of Mulhouse noted in 1880 that the sons of wealthy industrialists and merchants from Guebwiller (Haut-Rhin) and Mulhouse were continuing to emigrate to France, and that many went on to become French army reserve officers.[26] Four years later the High Military Command complained that the sons of these notables, after having served in the French army, often returned to Alsace and taunted their less well-to-do brethren, who remained behind to fulfill their military obligations in the Reich.[27] Under such circumstances, the Military Command remarked, "the consciousness that it is an honor to serve in the German army cannot develop at this time."[28] As late as 1894 the *Kölnische Zeitung* denounced prominent Alsace-Lorraine officials for continuing to send their sons to France before fulfilling their military service, thus setting a bad example for the rest of the population.[29]

Incidents of this sort forced the government to take stringent measures to curb emigration. One line of attack was to demonstrate the penalties of leaving the country. Emigrants who returned to visit their families were subjected to constant surveillance and even expulsion if they violated the terms of their visa. For example, the son of the rabbi of Sarreguemines, who had emigrated to Nancy in 1873, was expelled when he returned home for a visit the following year and overstayed his two-week limit.[30] During the Franco-German crisis of late 1887–88, still more severe steps were taken. With the introduction of Bismarck's "regime of passports," no one could enter the Reichsland from France without having obtained a special passport from the German embassy in Paris. French military personnel, both active and reserve, as well as former Alsace-Lorraine emigrants, were required not only to procure the passport but also to obtain special authorization from either the local Kreisdirector or the local chief of police.* As the Lorraine Bezirkspräsident noted in 1889, one favorable side effect of this legislation was that it effectively discouraged emigration.[31] In view of the unpleasant consequences of emigration, the progovernment *Courrier du Bas-Rhin* warned parents to reflect with great care before allowing their young sons to expatriate: "To remain ten or twenty years far from one's country, or if one does return earlier, to see oneself faced with the same necessity [conscription] that one had wanted to escape through emigration—

---

*The "passport regime" entirely prohibited suspect people from crossing the border. These laws remained in effect for civilians until the end of 1891, and for military personnel until 1900. See Silverman, *Reluctant Union*, pp. 57–59; Pfister, *Pages*, p. 273; Eccard, *Alsace*, pp. 141–43, 188; and Roth, *Lorraine*, p. 123.

that is the alternative!"[32] At least in terms of draft evasion, therefore, post-1872 emigration in general represented a continuation of option.

Substantial evidence indicates that these political considerations played an important role in the determination of many Jews to leave the Reichsland. If material considerations alone could account for emigration, we would expect a similar demographic decline in Jewish emigration from other regions in the Reich that closely resembled Alsace-Lorraine economically. But this is not the case. The proportion of Jews in the Alsace-Lorraine population sank from 2.7 percent to 1.9 percent between 1875 and 1900. By contrast, although the Jewish populations of both Baden and Bavaria declined in relative terms, the downward trend was not nearly so steep as in the Reichsland. Over that period, the proportion of Jews decreased from 1.8 percent to 1.4 percent in neighboring Baden, and from 1.0 percent to 0.9 percent in Bavaria. Clearly, other forces contributed to Jewish emigration from the annexed provinces.[33]

A glance at the age distribution of the Haguenau applicants for emigration permits indicates that Jewish minors were even more likely than their non-Jewish counterparts to file for emigration. As Table 4.13 shows, almost 81 percent of all Jewish applicants, in contrast to some 71 percent of all Gentile applicants, left before they reached their seventeenth year. Moreover, since only about 1 percent of Jewish emigrants were over twenty-eight years of age, compared with almost 6 percent of non-Jews, it is clear that proportionately greater numbers of Jews, whatever their real motives, were successfully evading military service. Can we conclude, then, that Jews were among the most persistent draft evaders?

Literary testimonies confirm this view. Edmond Uhry, who emi-

TABLE 4.13
Age Distribution of Jewish and Non-Jewish Emigrants

Age at emigration	Jews (N = 308)	Non-Jews (N = 1,214)	Total (N = 1,522)
17 and under	80.8%	70.8%	72.8%
18–27	17.9	23.3	22.2
28–37	0.6	3.1	2.6
Over 37	0.6	2.8	2.4

grated in 1891 just before he reached his seventeenth birthday, recorded three reasons behind his decision to leave: extremely limited economic possibilities, the threat of three years of military service, and the fear of another war. Speaking both as an Alsatian and as a Jew, Uhry wrote:

And yet (despite dangers) nearly every family in our town sent boys out into the world. Greater opportunity and more freedom in new lands were an inducement, but [were] taken less into account in making the decision than was the fact of compulsory military service.

Three years of this was looked upon with great dread. We lived in a frontier country in an atmosphere charged with Prussian militarism. We were a people resentful of the injustices of the Bismarckian system and continually fearful of the recurrence of war.[34]

When a Jewish youth named Alphons Blum submitted an application for an *Entlassungsurkunde* in 1890, the Kreisdirector of Erstein (Bas-Rhin) remarked that the young man's wish to emigrate was "without a doubt" solely for the purpose of evading his military service, "as is customary among the Jewish population."[35] The police commissioner of Bischwiller similarly noted in 1895 that of all the military-age men who had emigrated from the canton in the last few years, half belonged to Jewish families. Speculating on their motives, he added:

These young people are emigrating mostly to North America, allegedly to find a better living there. It is a plausible assumption, however, that these conspicuous and continuing attempts at emigration, which in general also have characterized previous years, are chiefly politically motivated. [This is] true especially of the Jewish families, who less because of the pressure of bad material circumstances than because of antipathy toward *Deutschtum* seek to have their sons emigrate early to avoid German military service.[36]

Desertion statistics further support the conclusion that Jews avoided German military service to a greater extent than did other groups in the population. Although the desertion rate in general was only about 2 to 3 percent, a significant proportion of those youths who did desert were Jews.[37] An 1882 police report, for example, notes that J. Roos, a twenty-two-year-old cantor from Bischheim, deserted "because he does not want to be a German soldier."[38] In 1883 the district of Molsheim (Bas-Rhin) brought charges against a Jewish merchant named Molling Lévy for encouraging his son Emmanuel to desert.[39] On the basis of data from Strasbourg-campagne, at least 7.5 percent of all deserters between 1874 and 1914 were Jews.[40] Extant data from the other Bas-Rhin districts suggests this proportion was about average throughout the province.[41]

Jewish antipathy toward the Reich is also reflected in the criminal statistics for Alsace-Lorraine in the late nineteenth and early twentieth centuries. According to figures presented by Schnurmann, nearly one-fifth (19.4%) of all "offenses against the state, public order, and religion"* committed by Jews in the years 1899, 1900, 1902, and 1904 were violations of prescriptions regarding military service. In terms of relative importance, these offenses ranked only behind violations of Sunday rest laws and defamation within this category of crimes.[42]

To sum up, distinctions between post-1872 Jewish emigration and Jewish option in 1871–72 reveal differences within the Alsace-Lorraine Jewish community's sense of French national identity. Although cultural and political motives were still an important part of the motivation in post-1872 Jewish emigration, the more frequent choice of the New World over France suggests that these essentially rural and lower-class Jews felt less integrated into the French national community than did the primarily urban and bourgeois Jews who had opted. Post-1872 Jewish emigrants were by no means politically naïve, and had to that extent achieved a certain level of national assimilation, but their political sentiments were articulated more as anti-German hostility than as pro-French patriotism.

Moreover, the social structure of post-1872 Jewish emigration, which parallels the model of economically motivated migrations, together with the preference for the New World as a destination, indicates the inadequacy of interpreting this population movement solely within a political framework. From a socioeconomic perspective, post-1872 Jewish emigration from Alsace-Lorraine appears to be not merely a continuation but indeed an acceleration of the Jewish emigration patterns that first became evident during the Second Empire, in sharp contrast to option, which had constituted a signifi-

*Such crimes included treason, offenses against public officials, violations of Sunday rest laws, violations of prescriptions of military service, fraudulent monetary practices, illegal marriages, defamation, and "crimes against public morality," such as bigamy, incest, and homosexuality.

cant break with those trends. Thus, although political and cultural reasons were part of the motivation in post-1872 Jewish emigration, the materialist interpretation is more persuasive in this case than it is for Jewish option. Finally, this comparison of long-range Jewish emigration tendencies after 1872 with Jewish option and emigration in 1871–72 demonstrates the fallacy of offering a single causal explanation for Jewish emigration in the postannexation era.

FIVE

The Persistence of French Loyalties

Pro-French sympathies, so deeply rooted in political, socioeconomic, and cultural conditions, could not be suddenly extinguished. The persistence of French patriotism in the Reichsland after 1872 was stimulated by the inherent contradiction of Bismarck's policy. Summing up this dilemma, Dan P. Silverman writes: "Hoping to win the sympathy of the people of Alsace-Lorraine, Bismarck nevertheless regarded the region as Germany's first line of defense. Many German officials felt that the military security of the empire could be achieved only by depriving the Alsace-Lorrainers of the basic rights enjoyed by other citizens. In denying these rights, the Germans blasted their own hopes for conciliation."[1] Whether, as Silverman argues, continued French nationalism in Alsace-Lorraine grew primarily out of a reaction to German policies rather than out of an innate love of France is not really the issue here. Political repression in the Reichsland, in response to Franco-German tensions and the very real threat of war until the 1890's, forced the nationality question to the forefront of regional political life.* Internal political and economic conflicts were relegated to the background.[2]

---

*A series of repressive measures, arising out of national security considerations, was introduced in Alsace-Lorraine in 1887–88. These included the dissolution of certain associations, restrictions on residency for Frenchmen, the expulsion of all agitators, the introduction of a political police, the abolition of municipal council elections for mayors, the redistribution of electoral districts, the suppression of dangerous newspapers and the banning of French newspapers, and the imposition of a passport system for all French citizens visiting Alsace-Lorraine. The last measure was the most controversial and the most difficult to enforce. For a discussion of these measures and Bismarck's motivation for instituting them, see Silverman, *Reluctant Union*, pp. 55–62.

Jews, who had shown themselves to be among the most francophile elements of the population immediately following annexation, did not remain untouched by these political forces. Although certain sectors manifested a readiness to accommodate, the majority of Jews, especially during the first twenty-five years, continued to harbor anti-German sentiments. Besides option and emigration, the most overt demonstrations of pro-French sympathies, Jews turned to new channels of expression more appropriate to the changed political situation. Alsace-Lorraine Jewish emigrés in both France and the United States still participated in French nationalist organizations and, unconstrained by fears of political reprisal, became leading spokesmen of revanche.

Jews who remained in the Reichsland and became German citizens of necessity adopted more subtle modes of expression. Although as a minority group, Jews felt unable to demonstrate their anti-German sentiments in as conspicuous a fashion as native Catholics and did not show open resistance to the new regime, the most vociferous among them embraced political activity as one avenue of protesting the annexation. The majority of Jews, however, felt more comfortable with various other forms of cultural resistance. Familial, economic, and religious ties to France helped cement these pro-French loyalties and ultimately slowed down the process of integration.

After 1871 Alsace-Lorraine became the focus of attention for all French patriotic organizations,[3] and a number of Alsace-Lorraine emigré associations sprang up in France that professed more or less revanchist aims and continued their activities until the First World War. Occasionally, Alsatian Jews formed their own patriotic organizations, such as the Union Alsacienne, founded in Paris in 1872;[4] but more often they joined general, nonsectarian Alsace-Lorraine societies. The membership lists that survive indicate that Jews often played a disproportionate role in these organizations. One of the largest was the staunchly republican Association Générale d'Alsace et de Lorraine, founded in 1871 to provide money and assistance to Alsace-Lorrainers who emigrated. Although primarily a charitable organization, the association also fostered political activities, including the indirect encouragement of emigration from the annexed territories and aid to Alsace-Lorraine youths who wanted to enlist in the French Foreign Legion in order to evade German military service.[5]

According to an 1889 list of the association's 1,295 members, approximately 13 percent were Jews. This is a strikingly high figure for a group that made up less than 1 percent of the total French population at that time and had been less than 3 percent of the total Alsace-Lorraine population in 1871; it may well reflect both the disproportionate number of Jews among the optants as well as the probable involvement of Alsace-Lorraine Jews who had been living in the French interior before the annexation. Jews were even more strikingly represented on the association's central committee—composing roughly 18 percent of its 111 members.[6] Among the most prominent Jewish families represented in the association were the Sées, Goudchauxs, Alcans, Dalsaces, Cerfs, Bambergers, Blins, and Blochs. At the association's annual Christmas celebrations in Paris, where as many as 14,000 people occasionally gathered, the Jewish poets Eugène Manuel and Louis Ratisbonne were among the most outspoken advocates of revanche.[7]

Jewish representation in other Alsace-Lorraine emigré societies in France was similarly high. In 1889 Jews constituted approximately 13 percent of the 1,163 members of the Société de Prévoyance et de Secours Mutuels des Alsaciens-Lorrains (Alsace-Lorrainer Society of Providence and Mutual Aid).[8] The Société de Protection des Alsaciens Demeurés Français (Society for the Protection of Alsatians Remaining French), founded in 1872, whose primary aims were to give material assistance to Alsace-Lorraine emigrants, to raise money to send Alsace-Lorraine students to schools in France, and to create special villages in Algeria to receive the emigrants, also counted a number of Jews among its most important leaders.[9] The Jewish banker Henri Aron, who later became the mayor of Paris's second arrondissement, belonged to this organization; also Jules Gougenheim, treasurer of the Nancy committee; Mme Worms, organizer of the Paris committee; and Captain Rouff, of the Rouff publishing house in Alger.[10] The Société de Réintégration des Alsaciens-Lorrains, working to ease the naturalization process of Alsace-Lorraine emigrants to France, had three Jewish presidents between 1884 and 1918.[11] In 1891 approximately 8 percent of the Ligue de Revanche of Nancy was Jewish, and Jews often constituted 15 percent to 20 percent of some of the smaller patriotic Alsace-Lorraine associations in France during the 1880's and 1890's.[12]

The most striking evidence of the Jews' continued French chauvinism was their participation in Paul Déroulède's Ligue des Patriotes, which was founded in 1882 as an ardently republican group with revanche as its primary goal.[13] Not all the league's members were Alsace-Lorraine emigrés, but many were, and indeed 53 of the 237 members in 1886–88 were still residing in the Reichsland. Approximately 22 percent of the 237 were Jewish.* Again, this was an amazingly high proportion, given the Jews' representation in the total population, and even their proportion among the optants.[14] The *Univers israélite* proudly boasted in 1887 that Georges Hirtz, a Sarrebourg Jew, had unanimously been elected secretary of the league's Lille branch.[15] In light of this evidence, it is not surprising that Jules Blin, son of the prominent Jewish textile manufacturer in Elbeuf, Théodore Blin, who had opted for French nationality in 1872, was president of the administrative council of the *Alsacien-Lorraine*, one of the most important revanchist newspapers in France.[16] Clearly, the ardently pro-French Jewish historian Georges Delahache was not merely spouting rhetoric when he wrote, refuting antisemitic jibes against Jewish patriotism, "Glance through the lists of the Alsace-Lorraine organizations constituted nearly everywhere after the war and ask Déroulède if they [Jews] were not enrolled in great numbers in his Ligue des Patriotes at the time of its foundation."[17]

Even in the United States, Jewish emigrés continued to lend strong support to Alsace-Lorraine organizations, and when circumstances demanded, they openly declared their pro-French patriotism.[18] The most outstanding example is the refusal of the prominent New York Jewish businessman Joseph Aron, a native of Phalsbourg, to accept the invitation of Mayor Grace in 1885 to join a fund-raising committee for a monument to General Grant. Explaining his refusal in his book *Alsace-Lorraine: Monument to Grant*, Aron declared: "I have declined to be a member of the said committee because during the Franco-German war of 1870–71, General Grant, in his quality of President of the United States, congratulated the German Emperor upon the victories which he had won over France. As a Frenchman, I cannot forget this insult offered to my country."[19] Aron's book created quite a stir in the American, French, and Alsace-Lorraine press and won him letters of thanks from other Alsace-Lorraine patriots.

*Although in the 1890's Déroulède occasionally employed antisemitic rhetoric for political purposes, antisemitism was not a central theme of the Ligue's ideology or propaganda.

In that same year, perhaps because of his pro-French sentiments, Aron, an associate of the New York firm Lazard Frères, returned to France.[20]

In the Reichsland as well, Jews often played a prominent role in pro-French organizations. In the years just before the First World War, the presidents of the Mulhouse and Rosheim veterans' associations were Jews. According to a newspaper account, at a 1912 ceremony to award French medals for service during the Franco-Prussian war, the Rosheim president declared, "Comrades, we have sworn loyalty to the French flag and we will remain loyal to our oath until death."[21] There were many Jews among the adherents of the pro-French, Paris-based veterans' organization Souvenir Français, including Sylvain Berr, the mayor of Sarrebourg, and the banker Alfred Cerf, assistant to the mayor of Wissembourg. The president of the organization's Molsheim branch was also a Jew.[22]

Republican-minded Jews were also actively involved in the Protest movement—a broad coalition of groups in Alsace-Lorraine that protested the annexation and called for the return of the conquered territories to France. Temporarily burying confessional rivalries, Jews and Catholics, along with some Protestants, united in the 1870's to back the pro-French cause in the annexed provinces.[23] It was in fact a Jewish banker of staunch republican, pro-Gambetta leanings, Edmond Goudchaux, who first nominated the Catholic bishop Dupont des Loges as Lorraine's Protest candidate in the 1874 Reichstag elections.[24] One contemporary observer noted that nearly all of Metz's 3,000 Jews supported the bishop; he related how, "several days before the election, an elderly Jewish woman was heard crying, to the applause of her coreligionists who surrounded her, 'I will make my husband vote for *our* bishop.'"[25]

Dupont des Loges's militantly pro-French successor to the Reichstag in 1882, Jules Antoine, also received enthusiastic support from Jewish emigrés in Paris. Once again Goudchaux, who had emigrated from Lorraine to Paris in 1879 and had become a deputy of the centrist Opportunist party, became one of Antoine's most devoted friends and supporters.[26] The extremely patriotic Masonic lodge in Paris, *Alsace-Lorraine*, which included such prominent Jews as Goudchaux, Edouard Bamberger, and Adolphe Crémieux, who served as Minister of Justice in the early Third Republic, offered Antoine a stepping-stone into politics.[27] Among Antoine's most generous financial supporters were the emigré Jewish bankers from Metz—Goudchaux, Schwartz, Worms, and Halphen. Furthermore, money raised in France for his political campaigns was discreetly deposited into his account at a bank in Metz, Mayer Frères et Cie, whose director, Isaac Mayer, was vice-president of the Metz Jewish Consistory.[28] Antoine's expulsion from Lorraine in 1887, however, together with the continued emigration of the most actively pro-French elements, led to a sharp decline in the strength of the Protest movement during the following decade.[29] Thereafter, links between local Alsace-Lorraine politics and the emigré community in France progressively weakened.

If consistorial notables were representative of urban upper- and upper middle-class Jews, it appears that this segment of the population nearly unanimously exhibited pro-French tendencies following the annexation. Government officials described the Strasbourg rentier Jacques Schwartz and the Bischwiller manufacturer Adolph Rueff, both elected to the Bas-Rhin Consistory in 1872, as "enragé French" ("*enragirter Franzose*").[30] In 1880 Louis Morhange, president of the Metz Consistory, owed his seat on the municipal council to Protest voters.[31] Indeed, local administrators considered nearly every lay member of the Bas-Rhin Consistory in the 1880's a sympathizer of the Protest party.[32] When the extremely wealthy and influential banker Léon Blum-Auscher was first elected to the Strasbourg Consistory in 1872, the police director predicted, "If he hasn't yet totally reconciled himself to the new circumstances, this will nevertheless come about."[33] But in 1887, when Blum-Auscher was reelected to the Consistory, the Bezirkspräsident conceded that although the banker had not played a prominent role in politics and had good relations with many Old German immigrants, "he desires, as most of the Jews here, not to fall out of favor with the Protesters and cultivates intimate relations with them as well."[34] As late as 1903 Ferdinand Wimphen, a wealthy businessman in Thionville and member of the Jewish Consistory in Metz from 1872 to 1896, was denied a German decoration because, the Bezirkspräsident wrote, "he is considered decidedly pro-French, has two married daughters in France, and according to a communication from the central police, was a member of the Ligue des Patriotes."[35] Despite these political leanings, however, consistorial members were generally described as "reserved" in their political deportment, and none participated actively in anti-German agitation, perhaps because they feared harmful repercussions for the Jewish community.[36]

Various forms of cultural resistance accompanied political protest after 1871. Language was one arena where conflicts occasionally arose. The enforced use of German was part of Bismarck's broad strategy of "germanizing" Alsace-Lorraine. At different stages the German government legislated its use in educational, religious, business, and administrative affairs.[37] Since the majority of Jews in the Reichsland spoke either German or their own variant form of Yiddish, Judaeo-Alsatian, the consistories generally found compliance with these decrees a relatively easy task and for the most part conformed to government demands.* But French remained the preferred language of the consistories and was used whenever allowed. The Bas-Rhin Consistory informed the government in 1874 that it had complied fully with a March 1872 regulation mandating the use of German in official reports, decrees, minutes, and the like, while acknowledging that French-speaking communities had been excepted, as permitted by law.[38] Accordingly, until 1876 the minutes of the meetings of the Bas-Rhin Consistory were kept in German. At the end of that year, however, the Consistory reverted to French, perhaps because it realized that the chances of government agents ever seeing these records were extremely slight.† Many more municipalities in Lorraine were predominantly French-speaking or bilingual, and they too were temporarily exempted from the German-language regulations.[39] The Consistory in Metz continued to use French exclusively until the mid-1880's, and only in 1889 began using German in official, governmental correspondence.[40] Although in Bas-Rhin and Haut-Rhin the government generally required synagogue sermons to be in German, in Lorraine Jews were allowed

---

*Some German officials did find fault with the German of Jewish clerical personnel. Of the rabbi nominated for a position in Lauterbourg in 1874, the Kreisdirector reported: "He certainly knows the language; he writes and preaches in German. However, with respect to the correctness of his usage of German, as is the case for the Jews generally, one mustn't apply too strict a standard." Kreisdirector, Wissembourg, to Bezirkspräsident, Bas-Rhin, Dec. 8, 1874, Archives départementales du Bas-Rhin, AL 133 119.

†The minutes of the meeting of Dec. 31, 1876, were the first recorded in French. The shift was not due simply to a change in secretaries, since the handwriting remained the same. In the 1880's the Consistory reverted to German.

to continue holding sermons in both French and German. The Kol Nidre sermon of Yom Kippur, the most important of the year, continued to be delivered in French in Metz until the First World War.[41]

In the late 1880's, as Franco-German tensions mounted, the Reichsland authorities strove to accelerate the germanization process. In 1887, in accordance with the Statthalter's intention to impose German on all ecclesiastical authorities throughout the annexed territories, the administration of Bas-Rhin conducted a survey of all religious personnel to ensure compliance with the 1872 laws.[42] In 1888 the Consistory of Haut-Rhin instructed its rabbis, cantors, and community presidents to use German exclusively in their official proceedings and correspondence.[43] Although there is no evidence of open resistance to these measures for either Haut- or Bas-Rhin, in Lorraine, perhaps because of the earlier linguistic liberalism there, compliance was slow to come. In 1891 the Bezirkspräsident of Lorraine addressed a circular to the presidents of the various Jewish communities within his jurisdiction inquiring whether they would be prepared to use German as the official language of correspondence after April 1, 1892, when new language regulations for the Reichsland were to be imposed. The majority of community leaders (33 of 55), even in predominantly German-speaking municipalities, responded that they would be able to conduct official correspondence only in French. The government was skeptical and had police agents carry out another investigation, which completely contradicted the results of the first inquiry. The new findings demonstrated that Jewish community leaders possessed a solid knowledge of German, even in predominantly French-speaking municipalities. As a result, with the exception of three communities that were granted a one-year exemption, Jewish communities throughout Lorraine, as well as the Consistory, were finally compelled to accept German as the official language.[44]

It was primarily the upper strata of the urban bourgeoisie that continued to use the French language in Alsace-Lorraine after the annexation. Well assimilated into French culture by 1870, the urban middle classes spoke French almost exclusively.[45] Jews were no exception. As historians have remarked, the most cultivated sector of the Jewish community remained loyal to France throughout the annexation period. Representative of this segment of the Jewish population was the prominent banker Marx Hannaux, who spoke German so poorly that he was forced to resign his office as president of the Metz Consistory during the First World War.[46]

It is not surprising, then, that these bourgeois Jews followed their non-Jewish class counterparts in endeavoring to provide their children with a French education. Girls were often sent to schools in Nancy; boys were placed in lycées in either French Lorraine or the Vosges.[47] The community of Remiremont in the Vosges even established a kosher kitchen to meet the needs of these students, and similar special arrangements were made at schools in Paris.[48] Even in such small towns as Rosheim in Alsace, it was not uncommon for Jewish middle-class families to send their daughters to Paris as pensionnaires for several years.[49] For Jews who could not afford to send their children to France, local Jewish communities occasionally offered supplementary courses in the French language, since the number of hours allowed for this subject in the primary schools had been sharply curtailed.[50] Furthermore, until the late 1880's, when exchanges across the border became more difficult, many Alsace-Lorraine rabbinical students continued to attend the Ecole Rabbinique in Paris. Several families also sent their sons to that seminary's Talmud Torah school, not to prepare for a rabbinical career, but only to receive religious instruction in French.[51]

The memoirs of Edmond Uhry from Ingwiller attest to the extreme anti-German sentiments held by many Jews, not simply of the urban bourgeoisie, after the annexation. Such animosities influenced not only Uhry's decision to emigrate to the United States in the 1890's, but also his choice of careers. Uhry wrote that, although he was naturally inclined toward the field of engineering, "my own instinctive apathy for anything so directly under German government dominion fortunately guided me into different channels."[52] Less weighty decisions were governed by similar considerations. Describing his uncle, "a patriotic Frenchman," Uhry recalled: "On one of my visits I brought him a Gorham silver match box. In hardly visible type this was engraved 'Made in Germany.' Uncle's eagle eye spied this mark of origin and he refused to touch or own this German 'dreck.'"[53]

The most remarkable testimony of the persistence of Jewish pro-French patriotism after the annexation is provided by several surviving Alsatian *mappot*, the decorated cloths that are wrapped around the Torah scrolls to keep them closed. Patriotic themes first began to appear on Alsatian *mappot* around 1830, probably as a response to an amelioration of Jewish life following the fall of the empire and the expiration in 1818 of the "Infamous Decree" of 1808, which had sharply curtailed Jewish moneylending in Alsace. Following the July Revolution, the red, white, and blue of the French flag, and sometimes even the flag itself, regularly decorated Alsatian *mappot*.[54] Commenting on this phenomenon, Robert Weyl notes, "The Jews of Alsace felt themselves profoundly French, and they showed it naïvely."[55]

Annexation to Germany did little to inhibit these practices. In January 1874 a three-year-old Alsatian child, Baroukh Bloch, wrapped his *mappa*, inscribed with the words "mazel tov" in red, white, and blue, around the Torah scrolls.[56] The most extraordinary patriotic *mappa*, that of Benjamin, son of Meier of Rosheim, dates from 1881. In poignant counterpoint to a pastoral marriage scene, two soldiers, one French, the other Prussian, cross swords in combat. Supporting these two puppet-like soldiers are the two shafts of the Hebrew letter *lamed* in the month *eloul*. Elsewhere on the *mappa*, a French officer stands at attention, carrying the tricolor, while another French soldier shoots at an invisible enemy. "The Jews of Alsace," Weyl remarks, "did not have a Hansi [the popular Alsatian artist who frequently depicted pro-French themes] to express their profound affection for France, but [they had] tens of obscure scribes who bore firm witness in close proximity to that which the Jews considered the most sacred, the holy scrolls of the Torah."[57]

Anti-German antipathy was further reflected in the strained relations between native Alsace-Lorraine Jews and the numerous German Jews who came to the Reichsland. After 1870 significant numbers of Germans immigrated into Alsace-Lorraine, partly compensating for the population decline resulting from option and emigration. According to one Jewish resident of Metz in 1890, "If German immigration had not come to attenuate the losses arising from the departure en masse of French Jews, this ancient *Kehilla* [community], formerly so flourishing, would have found itself absolutely disorganized."[58] Between 1871 and 1895 the number of Old German citizens in Alsace-Lorraine grew from 46,448 to 190,343 (12.5% of the total 1871 civil population).* Primarily attracted to the large urban commercial and industrial centers, German-born immigrants to Strasbourg in general numbered 44,577 in 1895, compared with 87,301 natives. In Metz by this date there were 27,311 immigrants and 28,690 natives. Colmar had roughly 5,500 immigrants and 26,000 natives.[59] Although the census figures do not break down the Jewish population according to nationality, the Lorraine Consistory claimed that by 1884 one-quarter of the Jews in Metz were Old German immigrants; another source states that as of 1895, 1,052 of Strasbourg's 2,012 Jews were of German origin.[60]

As the Lorraine Bezirkspräsident reported in 1872, many of the German newcomers were rich capitalists.[61] Some of them were Jews who came to play a prominent role in the economic life of Alsace-Lorraine. The two most prosperous industrial enterprises established in Alsace after 1871 were owned by German Jews: the large metallurgy firm of Wolf Netter and Jacobi in Koenigshoffen, a branch of their German company, and the tannery of Adler and Oppenheimer in Lingolsheim.[62] In 1898 small shopkeepers in Mulhouse complained of unfair competition from large department stores, which according to the Bezirkspräsident of Haut-Rhin, "without exception are branches of German business firms and are in the hands of Jews."[63] Men like Karl Kaufmann, member of the Bas-Rhin Consistory after 1906 and director of the Rheinische Kreditbank, came to Strasbourg from Baden in 1871 and played an important role in the expansion of German commerce into the Reichsland.[64] German Jewish investment in Alsace-Lorraine was considerable. In 1872 a consortium of German bankers and manufacturers, headed by the Berlin Jewish firm Beer and Hirzberg, bought up deserted textile factories in Bischwiller in an effort to reverse the economic decline that had set in with the emigration of the town's leading manufacturers.[65] Similarly, the large German Jewish textile houses of Berlin and Cologne—Levy Brothers, Reisenberg and Massbaum, and Edouard Siegel—bought up many of Lorraine's textile factories, particularly those that produced luxury goods.[66] The important glass works Trois Fontaines in Lorraine was sold in 1887 to two German

*Statistischen Bureau, *Statistisches Handbuch*, 1902, pp. 46–47; Reuss, *Histoire d'Alsace*, p. 390. As Reuss correctly points out, a child of immigrants who was born in the Reichsland automatically had Alsace-Lorraine state citizenship and was no longer counted in the census as a citizen of the parents' state of origin.

Jewish financiers, Leon Hirsch and Leon Hammel.[67] Still, in an 1876 appeal to the mayor of Strasbourg for a subsidy to build a new synagogue, the Bas-Rhin Consistory noted that despite the large German Jewish immigration into Strasbourg, the community's income had declined after 1871 "because many rich families opted for France, who have not been replaced by other rich families."[68]

Many German Jews who came to Alsace-Lorraine served the new government as civil servants. The administration made particularly strong efforts to recruit German Jewish teachers to assume the posts vacated by the large number of Jewish teachers who had opted for French citizenship and emigrated. German Jews filled positions even in smaller communities such as Schirrhofen, Ingwiller, Mutterholtz, St.-Avold, Grussenheim, and Mommenheim after 1871. Joseph Bloch of Haguenau recalls that although most of these German Jews were good teachers and were knowledgeable in Jewish matters, "at times they were overly zealous in patriotism. They made us sing with much spirit and conviction 'Deutschland über alles' and 'Was ist des Deutschen Vaterland?'"[69]

Despite their common religious and cultural background, relations between native Jews and the German Jewish immigrant community were severely strained. Paralleling the situation in the general society, all sources attest to the social gulf that separated the two groups.[70] Marriages between Alsatian Jews and German Jews became increasingly rare after 1871.[71] A comic play by the Alsatian Jewish dramatist Maier Woog that appeared in 1884 portrays the problems arising from this animosity. When an Alsatian Jew opposes the marriage of his daughter to a Jewish Prussian subofficer, the subofficer wonders, "Is it perhaps because I am Prussian and you Alsatian?" Attempting to win over the young woman against her father's will, he argues, "Love is tolerant, it knows no nationality."[72] Preceding the 1890 legislative elections, the French newspaper *Le Matin* insinuated that the German socialist candidate August Bebel was trying to win the Jewish vote in the district of Colmar by bringing the German Jewish socialist Paul Singer on his campaign trips. *Le Matin*'s correspondent argued that such ploys would never succeed: "Whatever the solidarity that is said to exist between Jews of all countries, our Alsatian Jews take a dim view of the German Jews. The reason? Because they are Germans. This reason is sufficient. The Alsatian Jews are passionately attached to France, 'the country of civil equality and religious liberty.'"[73] According to the Alsatian rabbi Honel Meiss, who served in France during this period, the Yiddish Alsatian term "Aschkeness," meaning German Jew, came to share the same pejorative overtones as the French slur "Boches."[74]

Economic rivalries aggravated the social tensions. The *Univers israélite* reported in 1901 that native Alsace-Lorraine commercial establishments in general were losing ground daily to their Old German competitors. The correspondent continued:

> On the two sides there are Jews, but the stores of the French [Alsace-Lorraine] Jews are scarcely better able to attract customers than those of the other Frenchmen [Alsace-Lorrainers]. We are obliged, therefore, to recognize that the success of the Jewish immigrant merchants is due not to alleged ethnic qualities but to innovations that they brought from Germany: to the relinquishing of certain bad commercial methods, and to the less routine business practices that they learned on the other side of the Rhine.[75]

The fears about German competition expressed by native Alsace-Lorraine Jewish merchants at the time of the annexation thus appear to have been confirmed.

At least until the turn of the century, Jewish organizational life remained rigidly divided along nationality lines.[76] German Jews, for example, attended only the German lectures of Metz's Jewish literary society, while Lorraine Jews attended only those delivered in French.[77] In 1893 the Société de Bienfaisance de la Jeunesse Israélite (Jewish Youth's Benevolent Society) in Metz did not have a single German member, and even as late as 1918, when the membership of this organization had risen to over 200, only half a dozen German Jewish immigrants had joined its ranks.[78] By the same token, Alsatian Jews were reluctant to join nationwide German Jewish associations. In 1909, for example, only 40 of the Reichsland's 260 Jewish communities were members of the Deutsch-Israelitischer Gemeindebund (German-Jewish Community League), an organization that supported the welfare and educational needs of Jewish communities throughout the Reich.[79] In response, German Jews occasionally formed their own organizations, such as the Verein Jüdischer Akademiker (Association of Jewish Academicians) of the University of Strasbourg, which was composed exclusively of Old German Jews.[80] Even within the ranks of the fledgling Zionist movement, which arose in the early years of the twentieth century, cooperation between the two communities was sharply circumscribed.[81]

National rivalries penetrated into the highest levels of Jewish communal life. In 1884 the German Jews in Metz, constituting approximately one-quarter of the city's Jewish population, petitioned the Lorraine Consistory to appoint one of their number to the administrative board of the Metz synagogue "in the interests of harmony."[82] At a Consistory meeting in 1890, a member of the Strasbourg Jewish community called for an end to conflicts between Old Alsatian and Old German Jews, advocating that in the future only the interests of the community as a whole should be taken into account.[83]

In 1900 a Strasbourg Jew wrote to the *Allgemeine Zeitung des Judentums*, disturbed because "until recently the parties in this community have hostilely opposed one another as enemy brothers." But this abyss, he noted, "arises not from religious causes and perceptions, but rather, if one must say so, from national [ones]."[84] In Strasbourg the first German Jew (Isaak Adler of the Adler and Oppenheimer tannery) was elected to the Consistory board in 1895, nearly a quarter of a century after the annexation.[85] It would be another five years before the first German Jew, the grain dealer August David, won a seat on the Lorraine Consistory.[86] Particularly bitter relations between Jewish natives and immigrants plagued the burgeoning industrial town of Thionville (Diedenhofen), where 20 of the 66 Jewish families were of Old German extraction in 1904. During the electoral contest for the administrative commission of the Jewish community that year, "many Prussian voters" complained to the *Strassburger Bürger Zeitung* of anti-German discrimination: "Electoral agitation was so lively that debates that began in the cafés were continued in the streets. Here one voter shouted into the ear of another: 'Don't give a single vote to the Prussians!'"[87] As late as 1914 a prominent German Jewish immigrant from Thionville notified the Bezirkspräsident in Metz that an opposition list for the Lorraine consistorial election was out of the question "because the majority of voters being native-born Lorrainers, will certainly not give their vote to an immigrant."[88] To some extent class tensions may have exacerbated this nationalistic discord, since most Old German Jewish immigrants in Thionville would have been wealthy merchants and industrialists.

Anti-German resentment was further reflected in the resistance of Alsace-Lorraine Jews to accepting German Jewish teachers, rabbis, and cantors. The *Courrier du Bas-Rhin* took notice in 1873 that after more than a year, the vacancy for the post of Jewish teacher in Mertzwiller had finally been filled by a German Jew. "Perhaps," the correspondent added, "this post would have been occupied long ago, if the population had not insisted on an Alsatian teacher."[89] Even as late as 1915 the government received complaints that the community of Delme in Lorraine had preferred to appoint a Pole as its cantor, despite applications from several well-qualified German candidates.[90] The *Jüdischer Sprechsaal*, a local Jewish paper edited by a German rabbi, Dr. Goldstein, admitted in 1883 that "German rabbinical candidates still find no sympathy in Alsace-Lorraine."[91] Indeed, at a meeting of the Bas-Rhin Consistory in 1900, strong sentiments were still expressed that Alsatian candidates be found for vacant rabbinical posts.[92] But the cutting-off of the provinces from the Ecole Rabbinique in Paris after the annexation had resulted in a serious shortage of rabbinical candidates, and many communities were obliged to accept German rabbis.[93]

A particularly bitter conflict erupted in Obernai in 1894, when the leaders of the Jewish community vehemently opposed the Consistory's appointment of the Old German rabbi from Munich, Dr. Staripolsky. Protesting directly to the Alsace-Lorraine Ministry of Interior in 1895, Staripolsky denounced the "national machinations" of the local synagogue commission, which was trying to force him to resign: "The so-called notables of the community find themselves extremely offended that they have been given a rabbi whose cradle did not stand in Alsace. As soon as they protested against the nomination of the rabbi, the notables supposedly declared: 'We will introduce an organ [a Reform innovation] into the synagogue, and by this means repel the German rabbi, who in religious respects belongs to the conservative tendency.'"[94] Although the Consistory eventually dissuaded the community from installing the organ,[95] it followed the police director's advice to transfer Staripolsky at the first suitable opportunity.[96] Taking into account such feelings, the German administration contented itself with finding pro-government Alsatian rabbis in the hope that they could reconcile the two distinct segments of the community.*

*Writing to the Kaiser on July 18, 1890, Statthalter Hohenlohe-Langenburg described the type of rabbi he wanted to replace Grand Rabbi Aron of Strasbourg, who had recently died. He should be an Alsace-Lorraine citizen "who has shown himself to be pro-German and pro-regime, someone who would be equally acceptable to both immigrant and native Jews and who would, by means of his personal

In order to train conservative Alsace-Lorraine rabbis of the French spirit, the three consistories succeeded by 1880 in establishing a rabbinical preparatory school, the Ecole Rabbinique, in Colmar.[97] The German government had granted subsidies to Alsace-Lorraine rabbinical candidates who wished to pursue their studies at the Berlin or Breslau seminaries ever since the annexation. But the consistories, arguing that "it is not possible to compare the German rabbinate with the French and Alsatian rabbinate," held out for forming their own institutions.[98] Students graduating from the preparatory school still had to attend courses at Breslau, Berlin, or the University of Strasbourg, where a modest rabbinical program was inaugurated in 1885.[99] Nevertheless, the creation of the Colmar seminary was regarded as a first step in preserving the particularist traditions of the Alsace-Lorraine rabbinate. Initially, the consistories insisted on the appointment of either a French or an Alsace-Lorraine rabbi as director, because "the administration of the school desires that the director be, at the same time, equal to teaching French, always indispensable for Alsace-Lorraine rabbis." They therefore advertised the post only in French and Alsace-Lorraine newspapers and solicited the recommendations of the Grand Rabbi of France for suitable candidates. Following his advice, the consistories chose a native Alsatian, Rabbi Bloch.[100] After Rabbi Bloch's sudden death in 1881, the shortage of native rabbis forced the consistories, against their original inclinations, to appoint an Old German rabbi in 1882, Dr. Zacharias Wolff.[101] Despite these initiatives, the consistories' efforts met with little success. The Colmar Ecole Rabbinique closed in 1900, and the rabbinical program at the University of Strasbourg virtually disintegrated after the death of Grand Rabbi Aron in 1890. Ultimately, rabbinical candidates had no choice but to pursue their studies in Germany.[102]

To some extent, the tension between the two national groups was a consequence of the different paths that German and French Judaism had taken during the nineteenth century. The sectarianism of German Jewry, which lacked any centralized authority and by the end of the century was clearly delineated into Liberal or Reform,

---

behavior, be suited to bring about a reconciliation between the two parts of the Jewish population." Archives départementales du Bas-Rhin, AL 71 277. On July 31, 1890, State Secretary Puttkamer recommended Grand Rabbi Weil of Metz to Hohenlohe-Langenburg as meeting these requirements. Ibid., AL 27 548.

Conservative, and Orthodox movements, was quite alien to the monolithic, consistorial-dominated French system.[103] Liberal German Jewish immigrants often criticized the consistorial system in the Reichsland for being too conservative; many German Orthodox Jews considered it too liberal.

There is no doubt that Liberal German Jews accelerated the progress of a reformed Judaism in Alsace-Lorraine, sometimes antagonizing their native-born coreligionists.[104] For example, organs had been allowed by the Consistory prior to 1871 but had encountered significant traditionalist resistance in the two provinces; during the German period they were increasingly accepted even by some of the smaller communities, "in spite of the opposition of conservatives."[105] In 1892 Rabbi Moock of Mulhouse solicited the opinion of the Grand Rabbi of France, Zadoc Kahn, on the question of introducing a sexually mixed choir into his community. Moock was opposed to the trend as repugnant to Alsatian Jewish traditions, and lamented: "This question will be the order of the day in Alsace sooner than one may think, since we are concerned with German communities, where mixed choirs are extolled. . . . Their introduction will have as an inevitable consequence an unfortunate and deplorable schism."[106] Liberal-minded German Jews in Strasbourg complained to the government in 1900 that Rabbi Adolph Uhry, recently appointed Grand Rabbi of Bas-Rhin, lacked skill in delivering sermons, a talent they highly esteemed. According to State Secretary Puttkamer, Strasbourg's German Jews had long expressed the desire for a second Grand Rabbi to be appointed—"a good preacher [and] if possible an 'Old German.'"[107]

Hostility also marred relations between native Jews and German orthodox immigrants like Rabbi Staripolsky, who refused to accept many of the reforms instituted by the Central Consistory during the course of the nineteenth century, particularly the introduction of the organ and the elimination of the *piyuttim* (liturgical poetry) from the prayer service.[108] Whereas in Metz the majority of German Jewish immigrants were Reform Jews, Strasbourg now housed, not only Liberals, but "the most fervent partisans of traditional Judaism, avoiding amalgamation with those who were not of strict observance."[109] In 1882 the Orthodox society Ez Chaim seceded from the community, and in 1888 it won formal recognition from the government, despite the vehement protestations of the Consistory.[110] Although there were several Alsatians among the society's forty-one members in 1883, the majority were Old German Jews who had immigrated to Strasbourg after 1871, including Dr. Staripolsky. Furthermore, nine of the society's ten-member executive committee in 1888 were German immigrants, and the tenth was of Swiss origin.[111] Modeling itself on separatist Orthodox communities in Germany, Ez Chaim established its own synagogue, rabbi, kosher butcher, school, and even cemetery.[112] In 1899 a similar Orthodox association was founded in Mulhouse.[113] The Liberal-Orthodox tension was certainly not alien to Alsace-Lorraine Jewry,[114] but the most serious sectarian rifts during this period seem to have been between German Jews of whatever bent and the native establishment.

Religious ties beween Alsace-Lorraine Jews and their coreligionists in France acted to sustain their pro-French sympathies. Alsatian rabbis continued to refer *Halachic* (Jewish legal) questions to the Grand Rabbi of France, and because the consistorial system persisted after the annexation, the Reichsland consistories also frequently turned to the Central Consistory in Paris for advice on technical matters such as salaries and nominations.[115] In 1906 the Consistory of Bas-Rhin presented the Association Culturelle Zadoc Kahn in Paris with a donation, noting that, "on political grounds, a certain reserve is necessary."[116] Moreover, many Alsace-Lorraine Jews who lived in Paris after 1871 continued to give generous financial support to community institutions and charities in their hometowns.[117]

Often, family bonds between Jews in the Reichsland and Jews in France cemented loyalties. Many families had been separated by option and emigration, and exchanges between relatives on the two sides of the border were regular.[118] Lazare Weiller, who was elected to the French Senate in 1919, and the historian Georges Delahache were but two of the many Jews who returned annually to visit relatives who had not opted.* A good many prominent members of the Alsace-Lorraine Jewish community even chose to emigrate to France on retirement in order to join their families there.[119] German au-

---

*Lazare Weiller wrote of his parents: "They sent me to France for my education, but not once during that long period between the two wars [1870 and 1914] did I fail to take my annual vacation at Sélestat." Weiller, "Alsace," p. 837. On Delahache, see Pfister, "Historien," p. 427. André Spire, who was born in Lorraine, also reports that he returned to his native province frequently throughout the period of the annexation. Spire, *Juifs*, avant propos.

thorities were sometimes suspicious of these family links. They chose to ignore slanderous innuendos against Grand Rabbi Adolph Uhry, who allegedly could not be trusted since his uncle had served as Grand Rabbi of France,[120] but were not so forgiving in other cases. In 1874 the police director of Molsheim (Bas-Rhin) assumed the pro-French sympathies of Rabbi Schwab of Mutzig to be a natural consequence of his having a brother who was a French citizen.[121] As noted earlier, the residence in France of the consistorial member Ferdinand Wimphen's two daughters contributed to the government's decision to refuse him a decoration. Similarly, some German officials in 1911 regarded the emigration to France of the three sons of Simon Cahen, also a member of the Metz Consistory, sufficient cause to consider Cahen politically objectionable.

Commercial relations between the Jews of Alsace-Lorraine and France also persisted and occasionally resulted in awkward political consequences. As we have seen, many Jewish-owned industrial and commercial firms moved to the French interior after 1871, often retaining a branch in the Reichsland, usually under the supervision of a family member. Even after 1871 prominent Jewish businessmen who continued to migrate to France frequently kept up the Alsace-Lorraine connection. Edmond Goudchaux, for example, despite his move to Paris in 1879, remained the director of the Bank of Metz until his death.[122] This bank, described by the Bezirkspräsident of Metz as "ultra-French," suffered severe losses during the French stock market crash of 1882 on account of its considerable French investments.[123]

The most unusual instance of this interconnection between politics and commerce is found in the case of the horse-dealing firm Sylvain Michel Lévy et Cie. It is an interesting example of the annexation's impact on a trade virtually monopolized by Jews. The two brothers who owned the firm, Solomon and Sylvain Lévy, born in Sarre-Union in Bas-Rhin around 1830, had lived in Strasbourg, where their business was located, until 1880. They then moved to Paris and eventually became French citizens, but they returned to Alsace periodically to buy and sell in the Alsatian horse markets and even maintained a dwelling in Kehl for that purpose. In 1887, as a result of suspicions that they were in the employ of the French War Ministry and had supplied the French army with as many as 6,000 horses, they were expelled from the Reichsland for carrying on activities inimical to German national security. After repeated petitions and disclaimers that they were involved primarily in importing French horses into Germany, rather than exporting German ones to France, the Lévy brothers succeeded in persuading the government in 1895 to cancel their expulsion.*

Many Alsace-Lorrainers annually crossed the border to participate in French national festivals.[124] Jews were prominent among them. In 1890, for example, they constituted approximately 27 percent of the 115 residents of Saverne who attended Bastille Day celebrations in France.[125] Ceremonies held in the Reichsland also not unfrequently assumed a pro-French hue, notably those that were held at Noisseville, Lorraine, in 1908 and at Wissembourg, Bas-Rhin, in 1909 in commemoration of the soldiers who had died at those sites during the Franco-Prussian War. Describing the popular motivations behind the ceremony at Noisseville, the native-born Bezirkspräsident of Lorraine, Count von Zeppelin, reported:

> It is natural that the population is not chauvinistically German. So long as the Dictator paragraph [the law of December 30, 1871, which invested the Statthalter with emergency powers, generally reserved to military authorities in a state of siege] and the old laws of associations remain in force, and the population remains subject to moral oppression, expressions of popular sentiment, now prominent, will be forcibly repressed. In this way "germanization" has been more harmful than useful. It is impossible to force an entire population to accept new ideas.[126]

Thus, even Alsatian officials were keenly aware that the contradictory character of German policies fanned the flames of such anti-German sentiments.

The Noisseville and Wissembourg ceremonies afforded opportunities for Jews to express not just anti-German feelings, but continued pro-French sentiments.[127] The monument for the fallen soldiers of Noisseville was the work of the Jewish emigré sculptor Emmanuel Hannaux, a brother of the banker Marx Hannaux, a

* Archives départementales du Bas-Rhin, D 98 206 (59–17¹). A curious sidelight on this affair is that it was other Alsatian-Jewish horse dealers who first accused the Lévy brothers of espionage. They were apparently motivated by economic grievances since they also claimed that the Lévys artificially held prices down by receiving French government subsidies.

member of the Metz Consistory.* And Jewish banker Alfred Cerf was instrumental in organizing the festival at Wissembourg.[128] The tricolor hung throughout the special synagogue-sponsored ceremonies on these occasions.[129] At a memorial service held at the Metz synagogue as part of the Wissembourg commemoration, Rabbi Nathan Netter, while praising Jewish patriotism in general terms, abstained from taking a partisan stand toward either France or Germany.[130] But Rabbi Koch of Wissembourg made his biases quite clear. Although commending the Kaiser for having maintained peace in the Reichsland, he criticized Germany for its informal administrative discrimination against Jews. Referring to the Jews who died in 1870, Rabbi Koch proclaimed, "They have shown that the Jew never forgets his duties toward his country, when the latter accords him the rights and advantages that citizens of other religions enjoy." Even more blatantly, he directly attacked the German annexation of Alsace-Lorraine, which had totally ignored public opinion: "Ah! Would that justice one day reign in this world; then all tyrannies and all oppressions will cease; then peoples will no longer be disposed of without consulting their will. Prejudices will disappear and barriers that separate men will fall and the whole of humanity will form only a single family."[131] Despite the growing acceptance of the new regime by the twentieth century and a gradual turn toward Alsatian-Jewish particularism, France continued to stand as the chief symbol of liberalism and universalism for many Jews.

That Jews came to play so prominent a role in pro-French patriotic organizations and activities belies the frequently made assumption that Jews were more conciliatory toward the new regime than other groups.[132] Jews in the annexed provinces suffered not only from general discrimination against Alsace-Lorrainers, who never fully won equal rights with other German citizens, but also from anti-Jewish prejudice.[133] Although the Reichsland regime was in many ways more liberal toward Jews than the imperial government

*Lipman, *Un Grand Rabbin français*, pp. 13–14. Emmanuel Hannaux, a graduate of the Ecole Israélite d'Arts et Métiers, was sixteen when he emigrated to Nancy from Metz. His other works include a statue of Dupont des Loges in the Cathedral of Metz, the *Poilu* in the esplanade in Metz, a monument to David Bloch in Guebwiller, and a monument to Erckmann-Chatrian in Phalsbourg. See Paul Wilmoth, "Un Sculpteur messin, Emmanuel Hannaux," in *Revue de Rhin et de la Moselle*, 11 (1922–23), pp. 28–32.

and eventually succeeded in winning the goodwill of most of its Jewish residents, the persistence of official anti-Jewish discrimination long encouraged an unfavorable comparison of Germany with France among many Reichsland Jews. Discussing the failure of the German army to allow Jews to become officers, one Jewish veteran asked, in a letter to the *Strassburger Neue Zeitung* in 1910, "Is the Alsace-Lorrainer reproached for *antipathy toward Prussia*? This antipathy is directed not against Prussia, but against the prevailing reactionary system in Prussia."[134] Anti-German hostility, Silverman argues, "could have been mitigated had the Germans treated the territorial population fairly and as equals of other German citizens."[135] Yet for reasons of national security, there was little likelihood of this for Alsace-Lorraine. Anti-Jewish prejudices, deeply embedded in the German political system, precluded the possibility even more for Alsace-Lorraine Jews.

SIX

The Failed Alliance: Jewish-Catholic Relations

The Franco-Prussian War and France's loss of Alsace-Lorraine to Germany provided an opportunity for Catholics and Jews to ally themselves in behalf of common pro-French interests. Despite the staunch resistance Catholics had exhibited toward the French government's "gallicization" efforts in the nineteenth century, they became, in reaction to the introduction of Bismarck's anti-Catholic legislation into Alsace-Lorraine in late 1871, the backbone of the pro-French movement. And Jews too, as we have seen, grateful to the nation that had granted them civil rights and had protected them from incidents of popular antisemitism, manifested their pro-French patriotism after the war. Not surprisingly, even the newly installed administration in 1871 targeted Jews and ultramontanes as two major reservoirs of potential anti-German subversion. As a result of these shared pro-French sensibilities, Jews became, for a time, the natural allies of those Catholic inhabitants of the Reichsland who remained unreconciled to the annexation.

The alliance was short-lived, however. The development and political use of antisemitism by Catholics in the two provinces in the following years, as well as the impact of the French antisemitism that erupted during the Dreyfus Affair of the late 1890's, inevitably split the two groups again. The conflict not only brought to the surface deep-seated religious, ideological, and social tensions, but illustrated that the two groups ultimately harbored diametrically opposed conceptions of nationalism and citizenship.

Before 1870 Alsace and Lorraine were considered the hotbed of French antisemitism. That prejudice stemmed primarily from the role of the Jew as moneylender and middleman in a predominantly agricultural economy that lacked adequate credit institutions until the second half of the nineteenth century.[1] Throughout the eighteenth and nineteenth centuries peasant unrest, especially in times of economic misery, manifested itself in antisemitic outbreaks. During the French Revolution, Alsace and Lorraine experienced serious anti-Jewish riots; the most vociferous opponent of Jewish emancipation at the National Assembly in 1791 was the Jacobin deputy from Alsace, Jean François Reubell. It was in fact anti-Jewish sentiment in Alsace that led Napoleon I to issue the "Infamous Decree" of 1808, which sharply restricted Jewish moneylending in Alsace and Lorraine. Every subsequent revolution was accompanied by antisemitic outbreaks. In 1832, following the July Revolution, armed peasants pillaged the Jewish communities of Bergheim and Itterswiller under the leadership of the local priest and forced many Jews to flee to neighboring towns.[2] The worst antisemitic riots occurred during the Revolution of 1848, when government troops had to be called in to quell the disorders. The Catholic clergy, when it did not actively take the lead in exciting these religious animosities, nearly always bestowed on them its tacit approval.[3]

The years immediately preceding the Franco-Prussian War were no exception to these patterns, and religious tensions seriously threatened the social stability of the two provinces. Antisemitism surfaced in the 1869 Haut-Rhin elections, when the Jews allied with the liberal Protestant candidate, Frederick Hartmann, against the Catholic, governmental candidate, Lefevre fils. The first president of the Colmar district court denounced Hartmann's "serious efforts . . . to detach the Jewish population," which he believed "would come to nothing." To his dismay, his prediction proved erroneous, even though "the Grand Rabbi and the principal members of the community [had given him] a formal assurance," since he had previously "striven to react in favor of the Jewish community against local prejudices." In the wake of Hartmann's victory, the prefect of Haut-Rhin wrote that the Jews, though generally devoted to the government of Napoleon III, had voted against the official candidate because "the Protestants, face to face with the fierceness of the clerical party, have joined together with the advanced party. In Colmar they have succeeded in getting the Jews to vote with them. Regrettable divisions have resulted and will leave profound traces."[4]

The prefect of Haut-Rhin attributed the turnabout of the Jewish vote in 1869 to the antigovernment stance of the president of the Jewish Consistory of Haut-Rhin and to Julien Sée, an influential Jewish editor of Hartmann's liberal paper, the *Courrier de Colmar*.[5] Militant Catholics in the province also blamed Sée for Hartmann's victory and for leading a campaign in favor of an anti-government vote in the impending May 1870 national plebiscite called by Napoleon III to win popular approval for the constitutional reforms of 1860, and, above all, to consolidate his dynastic position. Playing on popular antisemitism to stir up pro-government sentiment, their organ, the *Volksbote*, proclaimed on the eve of the plebiscite:

Formerly, the Jews were not considered citizens because it was thought that the Jewish element was not in its place within a Christian people. Now the Jews are called "Messieurs les Israélites"; they are citizens, buying and selling under the sole condition of respecting the laws of the land. And how, alas, are they respecting them? They can make business deals, [and] write newspapers in favor of M. Hartmann of Munster. . . . M. Hartmann has the right to insult and deride our Reverend Bishop, the Council, the Pope himself, in his *Courrier de Colmar* by means of Jewish pens.[6]

As a result of the opposition victory in 1869, the government launched a particularly strong propaganda campaign in Haut-Rhin in 1870 to rally popular support for the plebiscite, including special efforts by local officials to woo the Jewish electorate. In 1870 the prefect of Haut-Rhin won the assurances of Grand Rabbi Isaac Lévy that he would personally campaign in the Jewish communities for a "yes" vote. This time the prefect's precautions bore fruit, for Lévy did actually win over a number of influential Jewish leaders, in that way contributing to the government's victory.[7]

Religious tensions also erupted during the strikes of 1869–70, which saw Catholic workers in Alsace, led by ecclesiastical leaders, aligned against Protestant and republican industrialists.[8] Once again, the campaign on behalf of the workers, led by the *Volksbote*, was strongly tinged with antisemitism, pitting Protestant industrial and Jewish commercial interests against those of the Catholic working class.[9] These clashes between Protestants, Catholics, and Jews, aggravated by the fact that class divisions in Alsace and Lorraine to some degree mirrored religious differences, appeared to many in 1870 to constitute as serious a threat as that posed by the external enemy, Prussia.[10]

These rifts notwithstanding, the Franco-Prussian war and France's loss of Alsace-Lorraine to Germany provided a rallying point behind which all groups of the population could unite in behalf of common interests. Protestants in general, although attached to France, found it relatively easy to adapt to the new and predominantly Protestant regime. Catholics and Jews, however, each for their own particular reasons, greeted the new order with fear and hostility. Hoping for pro-Catholic concessions on the part of the German government, Catholics initially exhibited signs of a conciliatory attitude.[11] In late 1870 Civil Commissioner Kühlwetter, attempting to rally the clergy to the cause of "germanization," promised to reorganize the confessionally mixed normal schools of the two provinces on a confessional basis.[12] So pleased were some clergymen with this proposal that they openly proclaimed themselves in favor of accommodation to the new regime. Writing to the Abbé Marbach, professor at Strasbourg's Petit Seminaire and editor-in-chief of the Catholic biweekly *Volksfreund*, the priest Joseph Guerber declared, "Kühlwetter's measures in regard to the schools are excellent and of a nature to reconcile us to the inevitable, if our fate must completely depend on Germany."[13] Marbach responded in the *Volksfreund* that "to remain on the land where our cradles stood and where our coffins are buried, that is love of the *patrie*."[14] In November 1871, 797 members of the Catholic clergy signed a message to the Kaiser expressing the hope that the power of the Catholic church would be maintained intact, and that it would be allowed to exercise its influence freely through education, the press, and the numerous religious orders that existed in Alsace and Lorraine.[15] This message, according to Dan P. Silverman, amounted to a declaration of "Give to God what appertains to God; give to the Kaiser what appertains to the Kaiser."[16] Thus, the initial tendency of the Catholic leaders following the annexation was to accept and make the best of a given situation.

The introduction of Bismarck's anti-Catholic campaign, the Kulturkampf, into Alsace-Lorraine in late 1871 marked the end of these relatively good relations between native Catholics and the German government. By charging the ultramontanes in Alsace-Lorraine with attempting to undermine the authority of the new government, Bismarck contributed an anti-French coloring to the Kulturkampf in the annexed territories.[17] Among the most important Kulturkampf measures instituted in the two provinces were the expulsion of the Jesuits and related religious orders, the arrest of several priests for allegedly disturbing the peace with their inflammatory sermons, the reinstitution of divorce, the seizure of bishops' pastoral letters containing anti-German allusions, the refusal to pay Catholic priests salaries on a par with those of Protestant and Jewish clergy, and, most critical, changes in the educational system, which under Napoleon III had become increasingly dominated by the Church.[18] The new German government advocated state control over education and quickly imposed compulsory, government-supervised schooling.[19] Contrary to Kühlwetter's promises, Bismarck reestablished the normal schools on a nonconfessional basis.* German became the official language of the schools, and the teaching faculties of the colleges and lycées were reorganized so as to be almost entirely staffed by German personnel.[20]

It was the Kulturkampf that most exacerbated the already existing difficulties of administering the newly conquered territories and destroyed any possibility of assimilating Alsace-Lorraine. "To transform the population of Alsace-Lorraine into a loyal German citizenry," Silverman argues, "the new regime above all else had to win over the Catholics. For a Protestant power to have successfully integrated a predominantly Catholic territory would have been difficult in any case. In Bismarck's mind, 'Germanization' included the destruction of Roman Catholic political and 'cultural' opposition whether it be in Prussia, the Reich, or Alsace-Lorraine."[21] As a result of the Kulturkampf, political Catholics in Alsace-Lorraine emerged as the major force behind the Protest movement—the political party calling for the revocation of the annexation and a return of the territory to France.[22]

Since Jews also had specific reasons for greeting the annexation with anxiety, the political situation of Alsace-Lorraine in the early 1870's provided a potential groundwork on which a Catholic-Jewish coalition, based on a shared French patriotism and hostility to the

*In the early 1880's, after Bismarck abandoned the Kulturkampf, the secondary and normal schools were once again turned into confessional schools. In fact, in 1879 under the newly appointed Statthalter, Edwin von Manteuffel, clerical control over education was increased. See Silverman, *Reluctant Union*, p. 104; Roth, *Lorraine*, p. 154; *Univers israélite*, July 16, 1883, p. 674; and *Archives israélites*, March 22, 1883, p. 89, Oct. 4, 1883, pp. 320–21.

German government, might have been forged. Indeed, in the first years of the annexation, politically conscious Jews joined their Catholic counterparts in support of the pro-French cause. The cooperation between the two religious groups in the Protest movement was so extensive that one Lorraine journalist in 1881 even cited the "tight alliance of Jews and Catholics" as the chief source of continued French nationalism in the Reichsland.[23]

Even in the 1870's, however, underlying strains were not entirely absent from the Catholic-Jewish coalition. Although the delegation elected from Alsace-Lorraine to the German Reichstag in 1874 was composed totally of Protest candidates, the fact that nearly all of them were Catholics was not without significance. As a result of the option and emigration of many bourgeois republicans following the annexation, politics in the Reichsland became increasingly confessional and oriented toward the political right.[24] Consequently, the Protest movement gradually assumed a strongly Catholic hue, hostile to secular liberal and republican ideas.

Julien Sée, the liberal republican and strongly anticlerical Jewish journalist in Colmar, depicted the elections of 1874 not as a patriotic manifestation of pro-French sympathies in Alsace-Lorraine but as a clerical victory. Sée, a fervent French patriot, realized that it was religious antagonism toward Germany caused by the Kulturkampf more than pro-French sentiment that had transformed Catholicism in the provinces into the primary force behind the Protest movement.* Testifying to the veracity of Sée's observations is the fact that influential Catholic families shunned Jules Antoine, Lorraine's most prominent Protest deputy in the 1880's, because of his anticlerical views, while republican financiers in Paris, many of whom were post-1872 Jewish emigrés from Alsace-Lorraine, provided him with generous financial support.[25] Although Catholic-Jewish differences

---

*Sée, *Nos élections*, pp. 33–34. See also A. Wahl, *Confession*, 2:916. The liberal *Journal d'Alsace* also took note of this tendency. Regarding the 1874 elections, it declared: "This is no longer the electoral movement originally announced that had protest as its main slogan. It is now proclaimed that we are going to Berlin to defend the 'liberty of the Church.'" *Journal d'Alsace*, Jan. 27, 1874, cited in A. Wahl, *Confession*, 2:931. Wahl argues (p. 936) that in their voting behavior rural Jews, because of their fear of Catholic domination, favored Protestant liberal candidates who were conciliatory toward the annexation over Catholic Protest Party candidates. If true, this tendency stands in marked contrast to the political orientation of urban Jews. Wahl's method for arriving at this conclusion seems to me questionable, however.

never openly erupted over the character of the Protest movement, these tensions set the stage for a total breakdown with the advent of political antisemitism in the Reichsland. Traditional economic tensions between Jews and Catholics exacerbated growing political differences. Throughout the nineteenth century antisemitism in Alsace-Lorraine remained linked to the problem of agricultural credit. Notwithstanding polemics concerning the relative importance of Jewish to non-Jewish moneylending in the countryside, it is undeniable that Jews, owing to their important position as commercial intermediaries between urban and rural areas, frequently provided the major, and sometimes the only, source of ready loans.[26] Unfortunately, this economic role often exposed them to the wrath of their debtors, the peasantry, particularly during times of economic need and political unrest. Although the French government had made several attempts to deal with the problems of agricultural credit and usury in rural Alsace-Lorraine before 1870, these measures had not been successful. Several credit banks were created during the Second Empire, but owing to strict regulations on the repayment of loans, peasants continued to resort primarily to Jews for needed loans until the 1880's.[27] Consequently, it was left to the German regime to solve this long-standing problem.

In late 1878 the usury issue again came to the foreground with the introduction of the German penal code into Alsace-Lorraine. Unlike the French laws in effect until then, it left interest rates wholly unregulated. The result was a sudden upsurge of usury in the Reichsland, ultimately leading the Supreme Court at Leipzig to rule that "if the German penal code does not contain provisions on usury, it may not be inferred that usury is permitted in Alsace-Lorraine, where the pertinent French laws have not been formally abrogated by the law introducing the penal code and so are still in force there." Although for the moment interest rates continued to be regulated, increasingly vociferous demands from elsewhere in the German Reich for a definitive solution to the credit problem began to strike an ever more responsive chord in Alsace-Lorraine.[28]

Not surprisingly, this debate on usury in the two provinces soon assumed antisemitic overtones. The German newspaper *Augsburger Allgemeine Zeitung* carried an article in December 1878 on the problem of agricultural credit in the Reichsland in which it held the Jews collectively responsible for the evil of usury. The liberal *Journal d'Alsace* also denounced usury as "one of the plagues of our land," but it defended the Jewish population, arguing that the problem could not be blamed on any single religious group. It strongly censured the *Augsburger Allgemeine Zeitung* for

> rendering the entire Jewish population, that is to say, 40,000 citizens, responsible for certain usurious practices that take place in the countryside, and, moreover, are not the exclusive privilege of one certain religion or special class. The fact that this article was reprinted by the *Strassburger Zeitung* must inevitably have agitated the Jews of our town, inasmuch as one is accustomed to seek in the columns of that paper the opinion of the government itself. On the other hand, no one would deny that the nature of articles of this sort could be such as to provoke, under certain given conditions, real disorders and to create a dangerous situation for the Jews. What we are saying will appear fanciful only to those who have forgotten the events of which our land was the theater in the last years or who are not familiar with them.

According to the *Journal d'Alsace*, the Bas-Rhin Consistory even planned to protest the publication of such inflammatory articles to the government.[29] Under the circumstances, it is no wonder that when a number of trials against usurers were initiated late in 1878 the Jewish press felt it necessary to point out repeatedly that the overwhelming majority of those sentenced were not in fact Jews.[30]

In the 1880's measures were finally taken to deal with the problem of agricultural credit. The first Raiffeisen banks, named after their German founder, were established in Alsace in 1882. These were mutual credit associations modeled after those recently created in southern Germany, whose aim was to provide cheap credit to the peasantry.[31] The spread of these banks in the Reichsland was given a boost when the government's 1884 agricultural *enquête* attributed the worsening of the peasants' conditions since the last French survey of 1866 primarily to Jewish usury: "Many peasants groan under the yoke of indebtedness to the Jews; usury of land, homes, money, goods, grain, and cattle is sucking up all the wealth."[32] A number of deputies in the Alsace-Lorraine delegation, the Landesausschuss, promptly called for the creation of a network of credit banks and the imposition of strict legal measures against usury and cattle dealing, a Jewish monopoly in Alsace-Lorraine that served as an important vehicle for moneylending.[33] In response to the 1884 inquiry, the government helped subsidize the Raiffeisen banks.[34] Initially advocated and ultimately controlled by the Catholic clergy, these credit societies exhibited a marked confessional character and a strong antisemitic bias.[35] They spread rapidly throughout the Reichsland and came to wield tremendous political influence among the peasantry.[36] The religious hostilities stirred up by these associations did little to promote Jewish-Catholic relations.

Besides this traditional antisemitism, there arose a new indigenous political antisemitism in the early 1890's, which saw Catholicism and socialism emerge as the two major political contestants. With the Papal Bull *Rerum Novarum* in 1891, the Church stepped into the field of social reform to compete with the Social Democratic Party, which until 1890 had been illegal in all Germany, including Alsace-Lorraine.[37] Antisemitism proved to be the Catholics' most successful weapon in this competition. As the Catholic priest Victor Guerber pointed out in his book *Sozialismus der Erzfeind steht vor der Thüre* (Socialism, the Archenemy, Is Imminent), published in 1891, Christian socialists shared the Social Democrats' desire to eradicate the evils of capitalism: big industry, unrestrained free trade, and usury. For Guerber, however, this anticapitalist struggle needed to be executed in a "Christian" fashion. As opposed to the program of "atheistic" socialism, Guerber and other Christian socialists posited a return to medieval corporatism. They proposed the establishment of small-scale voluntary corporations resembling medieval guilds, which would rely on the Christian principles of charity and love to forge moral bonds between workers and owners. This form of corporatism was intended to halt the expansion of large-scale capitalist industry—*Judenindustrie* as Guerber called it—and bring about a new economic balance of industry, handicrafts, and agriculture. *Judenindustrie*, according to Guerber, was responsible for the economic displacement of the Christian artisanry:

> One Jew, who has money, begins a clothing factory. In a short time he has brought the community tailor to a standstill; he produces cheap goods, average or even worse, and the dumb people buy from him. And soon an honest tailor can exist no longer; he must request work from the Jews, and from a master [he] turns into a poor man, a dependent fellow. So it is with many artisans. They sink to the ground and fall victim to free trade.[38]

Jewish usury, which Guerber claimed had considerably worsened after the emancipation of the Jews by the French Revolution, was similarly causing a displacement of the peasantry from the countryside. The evil consequences of these trends were the destruction of the middle classes and the increasing polarization of society between the "small number of millionaires and big industrialists" and "the proletariat or the poor." Guerber hoped his brand of Christian socialism, which called for severe legal curtailments of free trade, big industry, and usury, would prevent these displaced artisans and peasants from flocking to the ranks of the Social Democratic Party (SPD).[39]

In his battle against Social Democracy, Guerber identified Jews not only with capitalism, but also with atheistic socialism. Socialists were anarchists, not Christians, and he blamed their irreligiosity on the fact that so many of them were Jews.[40] Responding to this antisocialist-antisemitism, the SPD in Alsace-Lorraine became an important defender of Jews, denouncing antisemitism and calling for the extension of Jewish civil rights.*

The additional strain on Jewish-Catholic relations caused by this politicization of antisemitism foreshadowed the final rupture that came with the Dreyfus Affair. The Affair, the most infamous political scandal of late-nineteenth-century France, began to erupt in late 1897 when it became increasingly apparent that the 1894 conviction of Alfred Dreyfus, a French Jewish army officer, on the charge of having sold military secrets to the Germans, was based on evidence that had been falsified by top-ranking members of the French General Staff. The ensuing battle between republicans, who rallied to Dreyfus's defense, and antirepublicans, who insisted that the honor

*Two of the most important Socialist leaders in Alsace-Lorraine during this period were in fact Jews—Georges Weill and Solomon Grumbach—and Socialists often tried to woo the Jewish vote. *Le Matin* claimed in 1890 ("En Alsace," Aug. 8) that the Socialist candidate for the Reichstag in Alsace, August Bebel, tried to win the local Jewish vote by having the Jewish Socialist Paul Singer accompany him on his campaign trips. Similarly, during the 1899 complementary elections in Mulhouse, a Jewish socialist candidate played up the clerical antisemitism of the Dreyfus Affair to win the Jewish vote. In 1912, the SPD candidate Peirotes was the leading proponent of improving the position of Jews at the University of Strasbourg. See L. Strauss, "Militants," pp. 468–73; Cetty, "Elections"; *Strassburger Israelitische Wochenschrift* (*SIW*), March 27, 1912, p. 7; and *Allgemeine Zeitung des Judentums*, April 12, 1912, suppl., p. 4. For Socialist denunciations of antisemitism, see "Von der Judenhetze," *Elsass-Lothringische Volkszeitung*, July 15, 1892; and *SIW*, Nov. 13, 1912, p. 7.

of the army must be upheld at all costs, quickly assumed the dimensions of a civil war and unleashed a domestic antisemitic campaign of unprecedented scope and violence in the postemancipation era.

That Dreyfus was both a Jew and an Alsatian added a significant dimension that had long-lasting repercussions on the attitudes toward France of both Jews and non-Jews in the annexed provinces. French antisemites attacked Dreyfus not only as a Jew, whose patriotism was therefore suspect, but also as an Alsatian. Their attacks fully exposed for the first time the ambivalent feelings of many in France toward the inhabitants of the annexed territories.[41] Even before 1870 it was not uncommon in France for doubts to be expressed concerning the "Frenchness" of Alsace-Lorraine, since both linguistically and culturally France's eastern provinces had retained a strong germanic character well into the nineteenth century. After the annexation, although the patriotism of those who had opted for French nationality was applauded, the loyalties of the remaining population, people who had necessarily become German citizens, increasingly became a matter of suspicion.* Dreyfus's father, an influential Mulhouse textile manufacturer, had opted for French nationality, emigrating in 1872, together with his wife and six of his seven children, including Alfred. But the fact that the eldest son continued to reside in Mulhouse until 1897 to oversee the family business, and that Alfred's brother Mathieu, his chief defender, had also lived in Alsace shortly before the outbreak of the Affair, cast a shadow of doubt over the family's real loyalties.[42] Even the patriotism of those Alsatians who had emigrated to France following the annexation was not to be trusted, according to the French antisemitic leader Edouard Drumont: many of them, especially the Jews, were actually German spies masquerading under a false Alsatian identity.[43] One of Dreyfus's most important supporters, Auguste Scheurer-Kestner, vice-president of the French Senate, who was himself a post-annexation emigré, was attacked in the antisemitic press as an "Old Pharisee" and a "Prussian." His Dreyfusard activities were condemned as "dirty Alsatian intrigues" and he was accused of

---

*Gauthier, "Les Alsaciens et l'Affaire Dreyfus," p. 58. Allan Mitchell has also argued that the Dreyfus Affair must be seen against the French military establishment's pervasive xenophobia after 1870, exemplified by a widespread paranoia about the infiltration of foreign, and particularly German, agents into France. See his "The Xenophobic Style."

having hired himself out as the agent of Israel in order to bring about France's ruin.[44]

Potentially, this anti-Alsatian element, which deeply offended the sensibilities of many pro-French Alsatians, might have rallied all groups of the Reichsland population to the Dreyfusard cause, and it is significant that no united front ever materialized.[45] Instead, the polarization that afflicted French society during the Affair was replicated in Alsace-Lorraine. The anti-Dreyfusard Right, led by ultramontanes, royalists, and antisemites, stood opposed to the pro-Dreyfus forces—liberal republicans, including most Jews, and eventually the socialists. The Catholic party in the provinces, ignoring the anti-Alsatian element of anti-Dreyfusard propaganda in France, made profession of belief in Dreyfus's guilt the basic credo of its pro-French patriotism.

The polemic between these two blocs of public opinion in Alsace-Lorraine fully exploded in mid-May 1898, when the *Siècle*, an important liberal Dreyfusard French newspaper, carried an article "Une Voix d'Alsace-Lorraine," signed by a certain X, allegedly a prominent deputy of the Landesausschuss.[46] Briefly, the writer explained that before 1898 the Landesausschuss had been almost equally divided into three camps. First, there were those parliamentary deputies representing Haut-Rhin who took the honorable reputation of the Dreyfus family in that region as sufficient proof of Dreyfus's innocence. A second group, to which X himself belonged, maintained that Dreyfus had sold secrets not to Germany, but to Russia, with the commendable intention of abetting the Franco-Russian alliance. The third group was the militant clerical party, which had never wavered in its firm conviction of Dreyfus's guilt.

Early in 1898, X continued, an event occurred that completely transformed public opinion in Alsace-Lorraine and caused these distinct views to merge into one unanimous affirmation of Dreyfus's innocence. This pivotal incident was German Chancellor von Bülow's public denial in January of 1898 of any dealings between the German government and the accused Dreyfus. Explaining how it was that von Bülow's proclamation could so completely sway public opinion in the Reichsland, X pointed out that even the most pro-French Alsatians considered the German government highly trustworthy and its word indisputable. The French patriotism of Alsace-Lorraine Jews surpassed that of all other groups in the population, he argued, and they were to be commended for preserving the French language and culture in the provinces. X warned that the French Right's continuing antisemitic campaign would have the pernicious effect of alienating a significant sector of the provinces' pro-French population. For if France were not in fact the country of justice and egalitarianism that the Protesters had imagined it to be, X concluded, perhaps it would be far simpler to accept finally the annexation as a fait accompli.

The *Siècle* article aroused a storm of protest among anti-Dreyfusards in Alsace-Lorraine, who responded by formulating the issue in rigid nationalistic and ideological terms. The Catholic press disclaimed X's contention that public opinion in the Reichsland unanimously agreed on Dreyfus's innocence, and the *Volksfreund*, the most viciously antisemitic Catholic paper, questioned the authenticity of the *Siècle* letter, claiming that not a single Alsatian deputy could possibly have expressed so outlandish an opinion.[47] Emile Keller, a former antirepublican Alsatian deputy then living in France and chief of the Catholic party, pointed out that the "true" Alsace-Lorraine, loyal to France and therefore unquestioning of the integrity of the French army, was of necessity anti-Dreyfusard. Only collaborators like X, who had accommodated to German rule and who placed more value on the word of German officials than on that of the highest circles in the French military, could possibly believe in Dreyfus's innocence. He added that the opinion of Alsatians like X, "for whom William was a God, and Dreyfus the best and most sacred of patriots," was unimportant anyway, since these Alsatians had been lost to the French cause long ago. As for X's glorification of Jewish patriotism, Keller retorted: "Our dear Alsatians have shrugged their shoulders in seeing themselves relegated to the background in the matter of patriotism, of hearing about the centuries of honorable poverty of these Jews, for whom they should have, as for the Emperor, a cult of adoration."[48]

Nevertheless, as the facts of the case were brought to light in 1898–99, the majority of the Reichsland population increasingly came to accept Dreyfus's innocence.[49] "Only the clerical organs," government reports noted, "still hold fast to their point of view and dutifully follow in the footsteps of their colleagues on the other side of the Vosges. Here, as there, at present, sympathy for the party of the French General Staff is accompanied by a pronounced anti-

The Failed Alliance

semitic tendency."[50] Indeed, a right-wing group in Mulhouse even sent a 1,500-franc donation to the Henry Memorial in France—the subscription for a monument to rehabilitate the name of Colonel Henry, the forger of the documents that were used to incriminate Dreyfus. The memorial was sponsored by Henry's widow and strongly supported by antisemites.[51] Thus, for the clerical Right, antisemitism and anti-German sentiment continued to go hand in hand.[52]

Jews and many liberals in Alsace-Lorraine could not accept this equation of anti-Dreyfusism and French patriotism. Their ideal of the French *patrie* was diametrically opposed to that of the clerical Right, and rested on a firm belief in the egalitarian and humanistic ideals of the French Revolution. Not even patriotism, apparently, could bridge this gulf between Jews and militant Catholics. As the *Metzer Zeitung* remarked, one of the most outstanding consequences of the Affair was "the noticeable breakdown of the hitherto extremely close union [between] enthusiastic Jews and like-minded clericals and chauvinists on behalf of 'la belle France.'"[53]

For the Jews of Alsace-Lorraine, many of whom had made great sacrifices to the French cause since 1871, the Dreyfus Affair proved to be a profoundly disillusioning experience. The prominent Jewish revanchist historian Georges Delahache, whose parents had emigrated from Alsace to Nancy in 1871, wrote two books during the Dreyfus Affair defending the patriotism of Jews and Alsatians, the dual targets of the French Right. The opening scene of his book *Juifs* depicts an Alsatian Jewish family who had opted for French nationality in 1872 preparing to depart from France in order to flee the antisemitic movement there. In his book *Plaidoyer pour les "annexés,"* Delahache argued that the anti-Alsatian sentiment that had surfaced during the Affair reflected a lack of sympathy for the vast majority of Alsatians who had not emigrated and was inconsistent with the expressed aim of French nationalists for revanche. Although Delahache continued to see France as a spokesman for liberal values, his hitherto undiminished patriotic faith had clearly suffered a blow.[54]

Michel Bréal, another French Jew of Alsatian origin and a professor at the Collège de France, also warned that the Dreyfus Affair was likely to alienate many Alsatians, both Jews and Christians, and would ultimately stimulate their rapprochement with Germany. In a long letter published in the *Siècle*, Bréal declared that a major cause of the pro-French patriotism of Alsace-Lorraine Jews since 1870 had been the persistence of anti-Jewish discrimination within the German army. Bréal therefore found it inconceivable that Dreyfus could have betrayed France "for the profit of that same Germany that would have . . . nothing to offer him except the disdain of all the officers, together with the contempt of all honest men." Deeply distressed by the antisemitic and anti-Alsatian attacks of the French press during the Affair, Bréal continued:

If one had wanted . . . to discourage, to deter Alsatian youth, what better ploy could have been found? I'm speaking here not of the Jews, whom certain newspapers cover with mud to such a degree that Germany in comparison must appear to them the country of tolerance, but of the Protestants of Alsace, who see how men such as Scheurer-Kestner and Picquart are treated,* of the sincere Catholics who do not want to allow the law to be made for them by journalists without conviction and without scruple. . . . These are not only good servants lost for France; sooner or later, they will be good servants gained by our neighbors. What remains to us of Alsace is on the verge of being lost.[55]

Such predictions were indeed already being realized in the Reichsland. The government noted a marked diminution of pro-French sympathies among the native population as a whole and forecast that it would not be long before the indigenous population would rally to the cause of *Deutschtum*.[56] The shift in sentiment among the Jewish population was even more remarkable. The Bezirkspräsident in Metz noted, "The sympathies of the native Jewish population for France, following the antisemitic incidents there, have experienced a marked cooling," and his counterpart in Strasbourg commented, "Alsatian Jewry, who formerly showed itself to be extremely engaged in French affairs, have had their confidence in the neighboring country severely shaken in this respect by the outbreak of the antisemitic movement."[57]

This disillusionment had several long-range consequences. While some Jews remained committed to a pro-French stance, others sought new answers. As Bréal had pointed out, Germany no longer compared so unfavorably with France in the treatment of its Jewish

---

*Georges Picquart, an Alsatian, was a lieutenant colonel in the French army who spoke out in Dreyfus's defense when he discovered the General Staff's cover-up. He was subsequently imprisoned.

minority. As a result, many Jews in Alsace-Lorraine found themselves increasingly willing to accommodate to the German regime in the years following the Affair. The birth of a local Zionist movement, although it was not very strong until after the First World War, was another outcome of the turmoil of these years.* In the past, the Jews of the two provinces had always looked to France as the land of civil liberties, but by 1900 Dr. Alfred Elias, a Zionist leader from Mulhouse, was ready to conclude that the recent antisemitic campaign showed this to be a false illusion. "After all," Elias said, "Alsatian Jews must gradually come to realize that likewise in France the ideal conditions they dream of do not prevail [and] they perceive that despite all the sacrifices they have made for their fatherland [France], they remain strangers there." The outbreak of an indigenous antisemitic movement during the Affair proved to Elias that antisemitism was endemic everywhere and hopes of ultimate assimilation futile.[58] Accordingly, for some, Zionism now offered the only reasonable solution.

Alsace-Lorraine Catholics also became disillusioned with France, but the fact that their alienation stemmed not so much from the Dreyfus Affair as from its consequences, that is, the triumph of anti-clericalism in France and ultimately, the 1905 separation of church and state, further proves that the French patriotism of Catholics had been based on religion and conservatism.[59] Although the clerical party did make several attempts to win back Jewish support after 1900, especially against Protestant candidates,[60] political cooperation between the two groups was in reality no longer possible because of the persistence of antisemitism.† When Daniel Blumenthal, a liberal

---

*The first Zionist group in Alsace-Lorraine was established in Mulhouse in 1899. According to the Bezirkspräsident in Colmar, it was headed by doctors and businessmen. Bezirkspräsident, Haut-Rhin, Administrative report, April 6, 1899, Archives départementales du Bas-Rhin, AL 71 277. The first Zionist association in Strasbourg, composed mainly of students and professors from the university, was created in 1902. See Raphael and Weyl, *Juifs en Alsace*, p. 389; Raphael and Weyl, *Regards*, pp. 268–69; and *Univers israélite*, April 10, 1903, p. 89.

†When antisemites in Germany began to attack the Jewish method of butchering meat as "inhumane" to animals, it was the Catholics in Alsace who came to their defense. To be sure, in championing religious tolerance for Jews, they had their own rights in mind: "If today under the pretext of protecting animals they shackle the religious liberty of Jews, tomorrow a hygienic society will insist on the prohibition of baptism because immersion in water might cause poor babies to get colds." Abbé N.

and anticlerical candidate of Jewish origin, was elected to the Reichstag from the rural district of Strasbourg in 1903, Catholics in the region rioted against Jews and Protestants.[61] An extremely hostile antisemitic campaign during the municipal elections of 1908-9 ended in defeat for a number of previously successful Jewish candidates. One Jewish correspondent remarked, "One would believe oneself transplanted directly back to the year 1848," and the *Strassburger Israelitische Wochenschrift* warned Jews never to support clerical candidates because "the clericals recently have attempted unmistakably to introduce Jew-hatred into our land."[62] The local clerical press cast further aspersions on the Jews of Alsace-Lorraine by exploiting the Bernstein Affair of 1911, in which a Jewish playwright was forced to withdraw his play from production by the Comédie Française in Paris because he had deserted from the French army in his youth.[63] During the 1912 Landtag elections, the clerical party, in accordance with its traditional policy, excoriated Jews throughout the Reichsland for supporting socialist candidates.*

Although Jews and Catholics in Alsace-Lorraine to some degree traveled parallel paths in the years between 1871 and 1914—from revanchism to disillusionment with France and a tentative accommodation to the German regime—they were not drawn together by their mutual political evolution.[64] On the contrary, the ideological, religious, and class divisions characteristic of Catholic-Jewish relations before 1870 persisted and proved far more durable than initially shared pro-French sentiments. As a predominantly middle-class element that owed its emancipation to the French Revolution,

---

Delsor, "Revue du mois," *Revue catholique d'Alsace*, April 1899, p. 297. In the 1908 municipal election in Strasbourg, the Center party played on these fears of government interference in religious practice to try to win the Jewish vote away from the Liberal candidate who supported regulations against Jewish *schechita*. See "Aus dem Strassburger Gemeinderat," *Strassburger Israelitische Wochenschrift*, Nov. 5, 1908, pp. 3-4.

Strassburger Israelitische Wochenschrift, March 6, 1912, p. 7, May 1, 1912, p. 6; *Archives israélites*, Oct. 31, 1912, p. 351. A group of Colmar Jews, in a published circular, appealed to their coreligionists not to vote for the clerical candidate Preiss who, although a Protestant, had supported the election of an antisemitic candidate in Paris. Responding to this call, another group of Colmar Jews defended Preiss and publicly declared their support for his election. Ultimately, however, most Jews as well as Protestants voted for the SPD. See *Le Nouvelliste*, Nov. 3, 1911; and Mayeur, *Autonomie et politique en Alsace*, pp. 31, 176.

the Jews of Alsace-Lorraine embraced a social vision encompassing liberalism, democracy, and, occasionally, socialism. The France to which they warmly professed their allegiance was the France of 1789. The France to which the Catholic parties in Alsace-Lorraine gave their loyalties was the socially conservative, Catholic France of the ancien régime.* Moreover, whereas Jews were unequivocably committed to defining citizenship in terms of legal membership in the nation-state, political Catholics fervently adhered to an ethnic-cultural definition of nationality, typical of the emerging integral nationalist movements of the late nineteenth century.[65] For these fundamental reasons, the temporary revival of a *union sacrée* between pro-French Jews and Catholics in the Reichsland during the First World War was also doomed to failure. Since the nationalistic visions of political Catholics and Jews were ultimately antithetical, despite initial outward similarities, it became evident that patriotism could serve as a unifying factor only when there was a clearly defined external threat. Otherwise, the essentially diverse liberal and conservative world views of political Jews and Catholics overwhelmed any hopes of a successful Jewish-Catholic alliance.

*As one Catholic paper put it in 1870, "If we, as Frenchmen, do not want to know anything about him [the King of Prussia], all the more reason for us, as Catholics, not to want to have anything to do with him." *Volksfreund*, Aug. 7, 1870, cited in A. Wahl, *Confession*, 2:906–7; see also pp. 912–13, 915–16. Exemplifying this brand of Catholic nationalism in France at the time of the Dreyfus Affair, Father Bailly, a leading Assumptionist priest, argued, "True patriotism is that of the baptized. To be Catholic and to be French are one and the same thing." Cited in Bredin, *The Affair*, pp. 289–90. Not all Catholics, of course, supported the clerical political parties. The majority of the working class was Catholic, and many of its members supported the Social Democrats.

SEVEN

The Politics of Accommodation

With the realization that the annexation of Alsace-Lorraine was not the temporary phenomenon many anticipated immediately after the war, some form of modus vivendi between the Jewish population and the new government became inevitable. French Jewish historians, perhaps for political reasons, generally ignore this process of accommodation, focusing only on the unwavering pro-French loyalties of Alsace-Lorraine Jewry throughout these forty-seven years.[1] A different interpretation has recently been posited by François Roth, who argues that once the most ardently pro-French republican Jews had emigrated after the war, the remaining Jewish population, with the exception of the most cultivated sector, adapted easily to the new regime.[2] Both these views are correct to a certain degree, but they are far too limited and one-sided. Accommodation did occur, as Roth correctly points out, but it developed gradually, and it was not always the smooth process he describes. Although before the 1890's, conciliatory overtures to the government were made primarily by certain traditionalist Jews and, to a certain extent, by the consistories themselves, it was only after the Dreyfus Affair that avenues toward fuller integration were opened. One segment, at least, of Alsace-Lorraine Jewry, profoundly disillusioned by the outbreak of antisemitism in France, responded by formulating a particularist identity, signaling an acceptance of annexation as a fait accompli and an increased willingness to strive, together with German Jews, for equality within the German empire. Had the world war not broken out, some form of rapprochement between Jews and Germans in the Reichsland might have been achieved.

For all that francophile sentiments predominated among the Jews in Alsace-Lorraine in the 1870's, certain elements actively sought reconciliation with the new regime. These groups consisted mainly of those religious traditionalists who, having long resented the reformist domination of the Central Consistory in Paris, hoped to profit from the annexation by reimposing more orthodox standards on the local consistories. In December 1871 an anonymous article appeared in the *Courrier du Bas-Rhin* entitled "On the Reorganization of the Jewish Religion in Alsace-Lorraine," in which the writer called for numerous religious reforms, the most important being the augmentation of rabbinical prerogative and a diminution of lay authority in the local consistories.[3] Speaking of earlier attempts to inaugurate these changes in 1862, the article said: "The communities had hoped to emerge finally from the too thorough tutelage of the consistories. The Rabbinate flattered itself on seeing the spiritual element introduced a little more into the councils and consistories, which, entirely laic as they are, sometimes assume a quasi-dogmatic character." Owing to the failure of these attempts under the French regime, the article went on, young rabbis, who had devoted the best years of their lives to study, were still being forced to have their appointments confirmed by "six persons for whom wealth perhaps is the only talent." To end this intolerable situation, the writer appealed to the imperial government to convoke a provincial assembly in Strasbourg to institute his proposed reforms. This assembly would be composed of all the rabbis in the province and a certain number of lay officials elected by the communities. In return for convening this assembly, "Alsace-Lorraine Judaism, which forms the most lively and certainly not the least loyal and honest sector of the annexed populations, would be infinitely grateful to the government that would thus have bestowed upon it a reorganization as radical as [it is] generous."

This article elicited strong reactions in both French and German Jewish circles. The *Revue israélite* in Paris, while acknowledging the validity of certain of the writer's criticisms, condemned his apparent lack of pro-French sympathies.[4] In the same paper, a German immigrant from Sarrebourg, declaring that the proposed reforms did not go far enough, called for a total dissolution, not just a mere reform of the consistorial system. Any reorganization of Jewish institutions in Alsace-Lorraine would have to take into account the interests of the immigrant community, he warned, and only complete communal autonomy, as it existed in Germany, would be acceptable.[5]

Caught in the cross fire of these conflicting demands, the author of the *Courrier* article formulated what might be called a localist identity. He responded that it was the needs of Alsatian Jews, rather than those of the ten or twenty Old German Jewish immigrants, that needed to be met: "In a word, we are *Israélites* and *Alsatians*. That is a declaration of fact that our present masters will never obfuscate, since we are firmly persuaded that in every Jewish question, the German government will always walk in the path, so noble and so generous, of the former French administration, the memory of which will never be effaced from our grateful hearts."[6]

The government never responded to this appeal. No assembly was convoked, and the consistorial system, dominated by lay elements, was maintained intact. Traditionalist Jews reiterated their demands for reform at the end of the decade, once again with no result.[7] Yet the willingness of these groups to turn to the new government for concessions signaled an important advance in the road toward accommodation. Furthermore, the articulation of a particularist Judaeo-Alsatian identity that depended on acceptance of the new political status quo, although for the moment cloaked only in religious terminology, foreshadowed later trends.

The consistories, more by virtue of their function as intermediaries between the Jewish community and the government than by any overt expression of political ideology, also acted as agents of accommodation. The emigration of many consistorial members after the annexation had thrown the consistories, especially in Colmar and Metz, into a state of profound disarray.[8] They were quickly reconstituted, however, by Jewish community leaders who, bound by a sense of duty, felt it imperative to remain in Alsace-Lorraine to assume the task of guidance.[9] Although consistorial nominees from the three departments were consistently described in official reports as ardently pro-French, with close connections to the Protest Party,[10] their steadfast avoidance of active political involvement made cooperation with the administration possible. Day-to-day affairs took precedence over long-range political aspirations, and in spite of their pro-French sentiments, the new consistorial leaders never failed to treat the German authorities respectfully in return for governmental tolerance.[11]

The consistories may still have preferred the French language, but for the most part they complied with government regulations on the introduction of prayers for the Kaiser into the synagogue service and the use of German in official correspondence and sermons.[12] For example, when the Sarrebourg school inspector accused Rabbi Isaac Bigart of Phalsbourg of resisting the use of German in schools and synagogues in Phalsbourg and Sarrebourg in 1872,[13] the Lorraine Consistory, prodded by the government, instantly directed Bigart to begin using German or submit to a transfer.[14] Bigart vehemently protested the school inspector's accusations, maintaining that only in exceptional circumstances had he used French. He added that now, better informed on the letter of the law, he would comply immediately with the government's demand.[15] Bigart and the Consistory succeeded in dispelling the administration's doubts. By 1874, when Bigart was nominated to become Grand Rabbi of Lorraine, his thorough knowledge of German and his political reserve in the midst of an extremely pro-French Jewish population made him a particularly suitable candidate in the eyes of the government.[16]

Disagreements occasionally did arise between the Consistory and the government, as for example when the Lorraine Consistory attempted to obtain a dispensation for a large number of French-speaking communities from the 1892 law requiring German as the official language, but these conflicts never erupted into open rebellion. When push came to shove, the Consistory always bowed to official orders. In large measure the conciliatory attitude of the Consistory and of the Jewish population generally arose in response to the new administration's considerable tolerance.[17] Having initially perceived the Jews as an extremely anti-German element within the local population, the German government made strong overtures to appease them.[18] Significant salary raises for rabbis, cantors, teachers, and other religious personnel supplemented official assurances that Jewish civil rights in Alsace-Lorraine would be protected.[19] Generous subsidies for the building of new schools and synagogues similarly characterized the new administration's policy.[20] Jews, in fact, received proportionately more in state expenditures than any other religious group after 1871.[21]

Politically, the government also exhibited a lenient attitude. Although the Consistory was expected to conform to all official regulations on "germanization," the administration manifested a willingness to tolerate consistorial members harboring extremely pro-French views as long as they did not engage openly in political activity.* In its political attempts to appease the Jewish community, the government even recommended in 1872 that in Haut-Rhin, because of potentially inflammatory conditions following the option for France of Grand Rabbi Lévy and several other Consistory members, the newly elected Consistory should be exempted from taking the legally mandated loyalty oath to the Emperor.[22]

The new regime's firm stand against antisemitism further helped win it the goodwill of Alsace-Lorraine Jewry. Sensitive to Jewish fears, the government repeatedly promised the Jewish community that antisemitism would be suppressed. In 1874 the *Metzer Zeitung*, considered a mouthpiece for official views, declared that the antisemitism that had prevailed in Metz before 1870 would now be rigorously combated.[23] The Alsace-Lorraine government was generally responsive to consistorial requests to suppress the circulation of antisemitic literature. It confiscated August Rohling's infamous tract on the Jewish blood libel in 1883,[24] halted the distribution of the German antisemitic papers the *Geldmonopol* and the *Wucherspille* in 1884,[25] and banned Theodor Fritsch's antisemitic pamphlet "Brennende Fragen" ("Burning Questions") in 1886.[26] Even though a rather vulgar official antisemitism continued to characterize the treatment of East European immigrants, who were beginning to arrive in Alsace-Lorraine in great numbers during this period, the attitude toward the indigenous Jewish population was quite favorable.†

Popular antisemitism, to be sure, continued to thrive. Liebermann von Sonnenburg, a leader of the antisemitic German Reform Party, ran for the 1893 Reichstag elections as a candidate from Lorraine. Although he was unsuccessful, he rallied a good deal of support, particularly from Old German non-Jewish immigrant and military circles.[27] Native Catholic antisemitism, as already shown, also aroused significant popular sympathy. Yet the government in

---

*No candidate elected to any of the three consistories was rejected by the government until 1915. See Archives départementales du Bas-Rhin, AL 133 paq. 27 102–4; and Roth, *La Lorraine annexée*.

†Eastern European Jewish immigrants were regarded as "undesirable" elements by the government authorities in Alsace-Lorraine, as they were throughout the entire Reich. They generally were denied naturalization and were frequently subject to expulsion.

Alsace-Lorraine never sanctioned such antisemitism, and indeed took strong measures to suppress it.[28] This attitude may account for the absence of serious antisemitic outbreaks during this period, and the Consistory more than once expressed gratitude to the regime for pursuing a policy that it believed had prevented antisemitism from taking root in Alsace-Lorraine.[29]

The state's fight against antisemitism was paralleled, at least until the twentieth century, by its consistent treatment of Jews on a level of parity with non-Jews. Jewish leaders in the Reichsland, in contrast to their German counterparts, received invitations to official functions, and high-ranking state officials frequently honored Jewish synagogues with their visits.[30] Furthermore, although German administrative discrimination against Jews holding high-level civil service posts extended into Alsace-Lorraine, Reichsland Jews came to regard their status as substantially better than that of Jews elsewhere in Germany.[31] Jewish leaders saw the appointment of many German Jews to official positions in the years immediately following the annexation as an omen of the forthcoming liberalism of the new regime. Not only did the government stipulate that each of the three normal schools in the Reichsland would have a professor of Judaism, but it even appointed several German Jews to the prominent position of lycée professors in 1871–72.[32]

According to the *Archives israélites*, the only reason native Jews were not recruited was that none could be found who were willing to accept jobs in a German administration.[33] Even more significantly, two German Jewish lawyers succeeded in winning promotions to judgeships in Metz and Saverne in 1871, making them the first German Jews in all the Reich to attain posts of such stature.[34] Although one French-Jewish correspondent speculated that this tolerance was due "perhaps less to the sentiment of equity than to the difficulty of recruiting officials for the conquered provinces," others were less cynical.[35] Commenting on these appointments, the *Israelit* of Mayence declared: "These nominations prove to us that the Chancellor of the Confederation seriously intends to grant equality of rights to our coreligionists. The Jews of the annexed provinces can therefore free themselves of their worries on this subject."[36] The non-Jewish liberal *Kölnische Zeitung* added: "It must be hoped that the same procedure will be followed in the Old German provinces. It is a question of knowing whether this measure will have an effect on the organization of justice in the motherland, and will contribute to lifting the barriers confronting the Jews that have until now barred them access to the magistracy, and that have remained in force in spite of all the declarations of the law in favor of the equality of their rights to public office."[37]

Alsace-Lorraine's Jews continued to benefit from this policy of toleration. The appointment of G. Levi as president of the Regional Tribunal of Strasbourg in 1907 signaled another landmark for German Jewry since, as the *Allgemeine Zeitung des Judentums* pointed out, "In Prussia such a case has not yet occurred. . . . In Prussia an unconverted Jew has not yet become president of the Regional Tribunal."[38] Dr. Marx, writing in the *Strassburger Israelitische Wochenschrift*, similarly praised the government's appointment of an unconverted Jew, adding, "[While] the complaint of Justice councilor Breslauer in his memoir *Discrimination Against Jews in the Judicial Service* is above all valid for Prussia, it can no longer apply to local circumstances."[39]

Still more of a stir was created in 1910 when Levi, despite the opposition of Berlin, was promoted to the presidency of the Chamber of the Colmar Court of Appeals, an even more prestigious judicial rank. The *Archives israélites* reported, "The nomination of M. Levi as President of the Chamber was not effected without difficulty on the part of the Bundesrat, but the government of Alsace-Lorraine held firm and ultimately triumphed."[40] The clerical press was apparently correct when it commented, "The Alsace-Lorraine Judicial authority, which is not in the least antisemitic, has sought to compensate for the antisemitism of the Imperial Government by nominating the Director of the Regional Tribunal, Levi, to be the Senate-President of the Court of Appeals in Colmar."[41] The Bundesrat in Berlin got its revenge, however, by rejecting Levi's nomination to the Supreme Court of Justice in Leipzig.[42] The Levi case thus demonstrates that at least as far as Jews were concerned, the regime in Alsace-Lorraine was indeed quite liberal. Whether because of French traditions or resistance to Prussian domination, or both, administrative antisemitism seemed far less entrenched there than in other parts of Germany.

As frequently pointed out, the Kaiser Wilhelm University in Strasbourg was also notably less tainted by antisemitism than its "Old German" counterparts.[43] One contemporary observer noted in

1898, "The University of Strasbourg has until now resisted the current antisemitism, of which in many German towns, more than one scholar has been the victim."[44] Professor Otto Michaelis, at the twenty-fifth anniversary of the university, similarly observed:

> The University of Strasbourg . . . has been able to protect itself from antisemitism. A rather considerable number of professors are Jews; they study and teach their science with the same zeal, the same authority, the same success as their Christian colleagues, and they enjoy the same esteem. The students, on their part, have not allowed themselves to be engaged by this aberration. At least, it doesn't seem so, since they do not exhibit any of the coarseness of customs and language that antisemitism carries with it.[45]

This liberal atmosphere enabled Jews to receive professorial appointments in Strasbourg far more easily than elsewhere in the Reich. One deputy even complained in the Landesausschuss, the Alsace-Lorraine provincial assembly, of the disproportionate number of Jewish professors.[46] The most prominent example of Strasbourg's less restrictive climate is the case of the eminent sociologist Georg Simmel. Born in Germany of converted parents in 1858, Simmel received his first German university appointment at the Kaiser Wilhelm University in Strasbourg only in 1911, after years of delay owing to his Jewish origin and nonconfessional stance. Three years later he was appointed full professor on the university's faculty of Philosophy, only to have his career instantly interrupted by the war.[47]

Ironically, the toleration of Jews at the university owed more to the policy of the regime than to the enlightened attitude of the faculty. When the issue of antisemitism in university appointments was raised in the Landesausschuss in 1906, the government disclaimed any responsibility for discrimination, declaring that appointments were wholly in the hands of the faculty.[48] This proved not entirely true, however, for in 1911 the administration actually forced the university, against its will, to appoint a Jewish professor. In January of that year the directorship of the university's Institute of Bacteriology and Hygiene became vacant and the most qualified candidate for the office was an Old Alsatian Jew, Dr. Ernest Levy. When Levy's name failed to appear on the initial list of candidates, both the Jewish press and certain deputies in the Landesausschuss charged that "this scholar has, in the eyes of the German government, a double defect: he is Alsatian and Jewish."[49] But it soon became known that the Statthalter had in fact been ready to confirm Levy's nomination, and it was the Faculty of Medicine, composed primarily of Old German professors, that had vetoed the appointment. Ultimately, the government pressured the faculty into accepting Levy, leading the *Strassburger Israelitische Wochenschrift* to remark: "This case should once again serve as a warning to Jewish newspapers that in the future if they intend to reprove our Alsace-Lorraine government with prejudice against Jews, they should exercise a bit more caution. It does not deserve this reproach."[50] Thus the regime once again demonstrated its firm commitment to fighting anti-Jewish discrimination.

To be sure, antisemitism did not disappear entirely from the university. A number of student organizations, including the Zionist Verein jüdischer Studenten, were founded specifically to combat antisemitism.[51] Several faculties, notably Jurisprudence and Philosophy, had no Jewish professors at all, and the question of anti-Jewish discrimination in professional appointments was debated several times in the Landesausschuss.[52] Commenting on Justice Councilor Breslauer's memoir, which claimed that conditions for Jews were better at Strasbourg than at other German universities, the *Wochenschrift* cautioned, "Certainly, this does not yet mean that there remains nothing more for us to wish for."[53] Yet no one would have denied the essential correctness of Breslauer's observations.

On a local level the ambiguities inherent in the tension between accommodation and the persistence of pro-French sentiments came to light in the course of a dispute over the Consistory's appointment in 1885 of Simon Blum to head the synagogue commission in Dettwiller, a small town near Saverne, in Bas-Rhin.[54] Blum's appointment created a schism in the community, with the opposition complaining to the local government that as a former optant who maintained a legal residence in Nancy and continued to receive a military pension from the French government, Blum should be regarded as a foreigner and therefore be declared ineligible for the post.[55] Later on, the opposition accused Blum of openly manifesting pro-French sentiments by attempting to thwart the recitation of prayers for the Kaiser and the Crown Prince in the synagogue.[56] The Consistory vigorously defended the appointment, arguing that Blum, a reputable man, could not be considered a foreigner, since he had relinquished his French citizenship and residence upon his return to Alsace. It also argued that although Blum continued to receive his 1,200-franc pension from the French government, this in no way reflected on his political activities, which it described as absolutely correct.[57] The matter was finally resolved when the government had to dismiss the opposition's complaint because of an 1844 consistorial ordinance that disallowed administrative intervention in the affairs of communities not receiving state funds, including Dettwiller.[58] To some extent the controversy over Blum's appointment may have grown out of personal jealousy on the part of certain members of the community or out of a sense of anger against the Consistory for having made the appointment without the community's consent.[59] Nonetheless, the way in which the dispute developed into a conflict over Blum's nationality, and the obvious resentment against what may have been perceived as the privileged position of former optants, indicate that certain elements in the Jewish population were eager to make peace with the new government even before the Dreyfus Affair.

Historians have universally noted that it was in the 1890's that the population of Alsace-Lorraine as a whole began increasingly to come to terms with the German regime. This was the decade that witnessed the coming of age of a new generation, (one "which knew France only through remembrance, traditions, or trips").[62] It was only natural that this generation, which had studied in German schools, served in the German army, and benefited from the economic prosperity of the German regime, would come to accept the annexation as a fait accompli.[61] The Protest movement declined as a political force, and new political issues, primarily autonomism and the contest between the socialists and the clericals, increasingly supplanted nationalism.[62] A growing emphasis on Alsatian cultural particularism and an acceptance of autonomism by nearly all groups of the native population signaled a recognition that the time had come to strive for equality within, rather than against, the Reich.* Jews

*Despite the general acceptance of autonomism after 1900, it continued to have different meanings for different groups. To the most pro-German elements of the population, autonomism implied a "desirable condition in the empire." For those who harbored an Alsatian particularist identity, autonomism meant "the only acceptable solution for Alsace-Lorraine so long as the 'faits accomplis' are not brought back into question." And to those whose sympathies continued to lie with France, autonomism connoted "the Protest Movement's last line of defense." Mayeur, *Autonomie et politique en Alsace*, p. 69.

were certainly not immune from these trends, and it was in this same decade that they first began to attend German universities across the Rhine.[63] As Armand Lipman, son of the former Grand Rabbi of Lorraine, Benjamin Lipman, noted: "A new generation [had grown up] under foreign domination, trained in [German] schools. It sought to adapt to the new regime and submitted itself loyally to the laws and exigencies of the Constitution."[64]

Particularly for the Jewish population of the Reichsland, the Dreyfus Affair provided an additional stimulus in effecting the rapprochement between native Jews and the German administration. As Georges Delahache, Michel Bréal, and government officials had predicted, the profound disillusionment with France experienced by Alsace-Lorraine Jews during the Affair led to a significant cooling of pro-French sympathies and to the emergence of more favorable attitudes toward Germany. Illustrative of this changing attitude was the schism that erupted in the Strasbourg Jewish community in 1900. At a ceremony celebrating the appointment of a new Grand Rabbi, an effusively pro-German patriotic speech by the president of the Strasbourg Consistory, Dr. Gustav Lévy, elicited sharply mixed reactions. One group of native Jews, remaining firm in their pro-French stance, sent Lévy a threatening anonymous letter, written in French, in which they accused him, a former Protester, of being "untrue to his conviction and his duty as a French patriot." But as the police commissioner noted with satisfaction, Lévy's speech was generally well received, even by "Old Alsatian" Jews, "upon whose political disposition the Dreyfus Affair, with its accompanying malicious antisemitic symptoms, has had a good influence."[65]

In the following years Alsace-Lorraine Jews gradually came to see their problems as those of German Jews as a whole, although they remained aware of the distinctness of their situation. Instead of revolving around the nationality issue, the major focus was now on the drive for equal rights within the Reich and the fight against antisemitism. In the early years of the twentieth century, the problems of anti-Jewish discrimination at the University of Strasbourg, in the civil service, and in the army became the major preoccupations of Jews in the Reichsland. Native Jews became increasingly outspoken in their demands for equal treatment and for an extension of their civil rights.

When, in 1905, the government failed to invite the Grand Rabbi of Metz to the memorial service for the soldiers who died at Gravelotte during the Franco-Prussian War, the Consistory protested to the Bezirkspräsident in Lorraine, Count von Zeppelin. Catholic and Protestant clergy had been included, the Consistory pointed out, and it complained that this was only one of a series of slights suffered by the Consistory at the hands of the government over the past few years. Maintaining that these acts stood in sharp contrast to the former administration's policy of absolute equality, the Consistory added, "This is even stranger, since we have lived here in a country, where for *more than one hundred years*, the Jewish religion has been placed on the same footing as the other religious confessions."[66] Consistorial complaints about official neglect in the matters of invitations to state dinners, public ceremonies, and visits of high officials to synagogues were reiterated throughout 1906 and 1907.[67] Bruno Weil, a noted liberal Jewish journalist and jurist who later became deputy chairman of the Centralverein, together with the French Jewish press, attributed this shift in government policy to the increasing influence of the militant Catholic party in Alsace-Lorraine.[68] But if local officials were not always receptive to consistorial complaints, as illustrated by Count von Zeppelin's astonishing assertion that he had been completely unaware of Judaism's officially recognized status in Alsace-Lorraine,* the higher levels of government generally responded favorably. Soon after the Consistory protests, Jewish representatives were invited not only to banquets honoring the Statthalter but even to those for the Kaiser.[69]

The other major issue that stirred demands for equality among Alsace-Lorraine Jews was that of representation in the newly created Landtag, or parliament, in 1911. After years of persistent demands on the part of the native population for a greater degree of political autonomy, the imperial government finally agreed in 1910–11 to the creation of a new constitution and parliament for Alsace-Lorraine.[70] Jews fully supported this development, but they vehemently protested the fact that the constitutional plan drawn up by the Landes-

*Bezirkspräsident, Lorraine, Count von Zeppelin, to the Statthalter, June 17, 1906, Archives départementales du Bas-Rhin, AL 27 545. That Count von Zeppelin was a native of Lorraine may suggest that Jews indeed had more to fear from indigenous officials than from Old German immigrant representatives of the Reich.

ausschuss in 1910 designated only Protestant and Catholic representatives to sit in the first chamber of this new representative body.[71] Non-Jewish liberals joined them in their protests. The *Journal d'Alsace*, a prominent liberal paper with pro-French leanings, wrote:

> The ostracism that has struck Alsace-Lorraine Judaism, to whom a representative in the first chamber has been refused without a single authorized voice being raised to protest against this blow to our rights, is a sign of the times; it proves that our land is not as refractory to germanization as people have striven to proclaim.... The implanting of Prussian customs here... will not contribute to raising the prestige of our land in the eyes of the civilized world.[72]

As a result of these protests, and in spite of conservative opposition, the constitutional plan was amended to include a Jewish representative in the first chamber, the Grand Rabbi of Strasbourg, Adolph Uhry.[73] Although Catholic and Protestant representatives were appointed for life whereas the Jewish representative was to be elected for only a five-year term,[74] this disparity was due more to the absence of any central Jewish authority than to anti-Jewish discrimination, and on the whole, the Jewish community considered this case a victory for Jewish rights.

The articulation of an increasingly pro-German loyalty on the part of Reichsland Jews is best illustrated by the *Strassburger Israelitische Wochenschrift*, the major Jewish newspaper in Alsace-Lorraine, which began publication in the decade after the Dreyfus Affair erupted. Responding to a portrayal of Alsatian Jews as one of the most pro-French and anti-German segments of the native population in H. Ruland's book *Deutschtum und Franzosentum in Elsass-Lothringen* (1908), the *Wochenschrift* declared: "The Jewish population and the Jewish clergy in Alsace-Lorraine ... express to our provincial government undiminished recognition of its commitment to justice.... The younger generation of Jewish clergy and of the Jewish population belongs to that segment of the Alsatian inhabitants who express the greatest sympathy to *Deutschtum*."[75]

The *Univers israélite* carried an article in 1910, signed by a certain R.M., allegedly a former Grand Rabbi of Alsace (probably Isaac Lévy, who died in 1912), that portrayed the German regime as extremely repressive. R.M. went on to offer strong support to the autonomist aspirations of the Alsatian deputy Abbé Wetterlé, which he interpreted as an expression of pro-French sentiments.[76] Dismayed, the *Wochenschrift* felt obliged once again to offer a sharp rebuttal to dispel suspicions that Alsace-Lorraine Jews shared these opinions. While affirming its gratitude to France, the *Wochenschrift*, having appointed itself spokesman for all Reichsland Jewry, pointed out: "We also recognize the Treaty of Frankfurt as a thoroughly valid agreement according to the statutes of international law, and consequently we consider ourselves dutiful and loyal citizens of the German Reich. For us there can be no talk of struggle between the spirit of conquest and the spirit of justice. More and more we are of the opinion that our provincial and imperial government is guided only by the spirit of justice." The *Wochenschrift* was committed to greater autonomy for Alsace-Lorraine, but stressed that autonomy in its eyes meant equality within the Reich rather than independence, an equality that would ultimately rest on the Treaty of Frankfurt. As for Abbé Wetterlé's brand of autonomism, the *Wochenschrift* declared: "We are as thankful for the Republic of Herr Wetterlé and his political friends as M. "R.M." would be for a Republic of MM. Drumont, Meyer, Lemaître, Barrès *e tutti quanti*."* Clearly, the *Wochenschrift* preferred a German administration to an independent, Catholic-dominated Alsace-Lorraine, which it feared would be prone to antisemitism.

Similarly, when Zionists accused Alsace-Lorraine Jews in 1913 of being untrue to their French heritage by creating a local chapter of the self-defense organization the Centralverein, the *Wochenschrift* retorted: "And if the Alsace-Lorraine Jews have confirmed a true remembrance of their former membership in the French cultural community, this in no way prevents them from fulfilling in thoroughly loyal and sincere ways their duties as German citizens and fighting shoulder to shoulder with the Centralverein."[77] Accompanying this new attitude was an increased criticism of French Jews for their assimilationist tendencies and blindness to antisemitism.[78] When the French Ecole Rabbinique itself came under the *Wochenschrift*'s attack for its religious laxity, the *Univers israélite* lamented, "One can see, alas, that Alsace is becoming Germanic."[79]

*That is, Edouard Drumont, Arthur Meyer, Jules Lemaître, and Maurice Barrès—all French right-wing nationalists and antisemites. *Strassburger Israelitische Wochenschrift*, Feb. 17, 1910, p. 2. See also *Allgemeine Zeitung des Judentums*, Feb. 25, 1910, p. 87.

This new acceptance of a local version of *Deutschtum* was reflected in improved relations between indigenous Jews and their German immigrant coreligionists. Although the two communities still remained socially segregated, there was a marked improvement in cooperation at the institutional level.[80] Not only were German Jews increasingly represented in the consistorial administration,[81] but the perception that German antisemitism was spreading into the Reichsland served to ally the two groups in defense activities. As Bruno Weil observed in a series of newspaper articles in 1905, antisemitism was becoming increasingly prevalent in the Strasbourg student movement, in local satirical magazines, and on the music hall stage.[82] Another concern was the creation of a regional branch of the Wandervogel, the strongly *völkisch* German youth movement with apparent antisemitic tendencies.* Alsatian and German Jews together lobbied for the acceptance of Jews into the army officer corps, contesting views espoused even by the Old German liberal press in Strasbourg that the sons of wealthy Jews would introduce into the corps a "spirit of materialism," that Jews already controlled "our entire public life," and that "Gentile soldiers would not have the necessary respect for a Jewish officer."[83] Consequently, Alsace-Lorraine Jews manifested a greater willingness to participate in German Jewish organizations, especially those devoted to defense such as the Centralverein and the Verband der deutschen Juden (Union of German Jews).[84]

Reichsland Jews, though they recognized that they shared many common concerns with German Jews, still felt their situation to be distinct. Significantly, the *Wochenschrift* made a claim for a degree of autonomy for Alsace-Lorraine Jewry within the Centralverein:

> Relations in our narrow homeland are of an entirely different nature from the rest of Germany. Our religious organization, dating from French times, is a different one, our relation to the government and to the non-Jewish population, our entire political constellation, shows, in comparison with Germany, the greatest differences. Therefore, it would be a mistake for

---

**Strassburger Israelitische Wochenschrift*, April 30, 1914, p. 5. The term *völkisch* refers to the nationalistic and romantic ideology that began to emerge during the last quarter of the nineteenth century and sought to define membership in the German nation in narrowly cultural, ethnic, or most significantly, racial terms. For an excellent discussion of the rise and institutionalization of the *völkisch* ideology, see Mosse, *Crisis of German Ideology*.

those in Berlin to prescribe to the representatives of the Centralverein in Alsace-Lorraine what they should and shouldn't do about the attainment of civic equality for Alsace-Lorraine Jewry.[85]

Thus, the Jews of the Reichsland, just as the general population did, came to develop a particularist identity. As their predecessor, the author of the *Courrier du Bas-Rhin* article of the early 1870's had already shown, this localism, while maintaining a separate identity, was not in the least antithetical to integration into the Reich.

More than anyone, Nathan Netter, who became Grand Rabbi of Lorraine in 1900, embodied the anomalies inherent in this new situation. Born in a small Alsatian village in 1866, the son of a cattle dealer, Netter grew up and was educated almost entirely during the German period.[86] Confronted by the problem of nationalism, he solved it in an unprecedented manner: he elevated patriotism into a universal ideal, divorcing it from nationalism. This paradoxical solution enabled Netter, and the Jews of Alsace-Lorraine in general, to express loyalties to both France and Germany simultaneously. In his sermon at the 1908 Noisseville commemoration to erect a monument for the fallen soldiers of 1870, Netter declared, "In honoring today their beautiful spirit, we have made a resolution . . . to be inspired by their example, whatever the country to which we belong, since the cult of the *patrie* is international, to give in our turn our heart and our soul to the *patrie* the day when it will have need of us."[87] This seemingly contradictory point of view was in many ways a natural outgrowth of the peculiar situation of Alsace-Lorraine generally and of Alsace-Lorraine Jewry especially. By the twentieth century, though Jews in the Reichsland continued to live under the constant pressure to prove their patriotism, they were no longer sure which country they should turn to. At Noisseville, Netter glorified *"le culte du souvenir"* ("the cult of remembrance"); but only a few years later he published an effusively patriotic pro-German sermon, and during the First World War he encouraged Jewish loyalty to the German war effort.* As a result, French officials in Alsace-Lorraine after the

---

*Netter, *Die Vaterlandsidee; Allgemeine Zeitung des Judentums*, Feb. 12, 1915, pp. 3-4. The only parallel I have ever seen to Netter's peculiar distinction between patriotism and nationalism was articulated in 1906 by a Jew from Posen, an area similarly torn by a nationality conflict. Max Kollenscher, a leading Posen Zionist, argued that although Jews might never achieve integration into the German nation, it was entirely possible for them to express patriotism toward the German state. As

war regarded Netter as pro-German, in spite of his ardently pro-French sermons and speeches throughout 1918 and 1919.[88] When, in 1919, Netter offered to conduct a propaganda campaign on behalf of the Jewish population of the Sarre basin, the Director of Services of the Interior wrote that even if there were a need for such a campaign, Rabbi Netter was not in the least qualified to take charge of it, "first of all because he has clearly given evidence of German sympathies (because he received several years ago the Cross of the Red Eagle in recompense for his germanizing zeal)."[89] Netter himself explained the acceptance of German decorations as not an intrinsically pro-German act, "since to refuse the decoration and continue to remain in the country was to expose oneself to the greatest vexations."[90] In time, Netter's pro-French activities brought about a change of heart among French officials, so great a change in fact that he received the Legion of Honor in 1931.[91]

Netter's oscillations between France and Germany might appear at first glance to have been motivated by sheer opportunism. However, since his views were echoed by other Alsace-Lorraine Jews and by the Alsatian Jewish press, it is probably more just to see him as an expression of the inherent tensions afflicting Alsace-Lorraine Jewry. Like the author of the 1871 *Courrier du Bas-Rhin* article, Netter perceived his first duty as the defense of the interests of native Jewry. In order to carry out this obligation, the link to France during the period of the annexation, and especially after the Dreyfus Affair, was increasingly relegated to the "culte du souvenir" while the more immediate issues of improving Jewish status in the Reichsland took precedence. As a spokesman for Jewish civil rights in the Reichsland, Netter was an active member of the Metz Centralverein and an outspoken proponent of Jewish equality in the army officer corps.[92] Thanks to his efforts as the Jewish representative in the first chamber of the Landtag, Jews finally won the right to be named full professors at the University of Strasbourg in 1917.[93] Netter's peculiar divorcing of patriotism from nationalism thus facilitated Jewish in-

---

Kollenscher succinctly put it: "We [Zionists] do not repudiate German patriotism. Nationality has nothing in common with patriotism. [Patriotism] fixes itself upon the state, and the state is not the exclusive possession of one nation alone." Cited in Hagen, *Germans, Poles, and Jews*, pp. 314–15. This universalization of patriotism appears to have been a particularly Jewish way of reconciling what appeared on the surface to be conflicting national identities.

tegration into the Reich before the First World War and into France afterward.

The process of accommodation began to encounter obstacles only when, under the strain of the political tensions marking the prewar years, the increasingly repressive German authorities stepped up their efforts at "germanization."[94] In spite of the well-known pro-French sympathies of certain consistorial members, their elections had always received government confirmation without difficulty. Suddenly in 1910, on the recommendation of the police president in Metz, the Lorraine Bezirkspräsident counseled for the first time that two of the three elected candidates to the Lorraine Jewish Consistory should not be confirmed for political reasons. Although the two men in question had previously served on the Consistory, given the new political climate, the Bezirkspräsident now felt it wise to reconsider their confirmation. One of the nominees, the lawyer and Justice councilor Dr. August Ernest Müller, was the co-owner of the anti-German paper *Le Messin* and had earlier been a contributor to that paper. Furthermore, "in spite of the fact that formerly he [Müller] had often frequented circles of 'Old German' immigrants, he still [could not] be considered pro-German."[95] As for the other nominee, the merchant Solomon Cahen, his three sons had emigrated from Lorraine, supposedly with his consent. True, two of the three had returned to Lorraine and had been renaturalized, but the third, although he had never received a valid emigration permit, had emigrated anyway before his military service and was therefore considered a draft evader. As the police president saw it, "These facts must throw sufficient light on the political convictions of the father, Cahen, whether or not he is politically active in public."[96]

The more liberal state secretary suggested to Statthalter von Wedel that the government should reject the recommendations of the Lorraine provincial authorities. He argued that neither Müller nor Cahen, the former a member of the Consistory for twenty years and the latter for two, had ever played an active role in politics. Furthermore, he maintained that Müller's politics since his appointment as Justice councilor in 1900 had consistently been described as "constantly correct." Nor had he ever been suspected of harboring anti-German sentiments. As for Müller's collaboration with the *Messin*, he "had doubtless participated in this newspaper enterprise at a time when the *Messin* exhibited an entirely different political orientation from that of today. It is to be assumed on the basis of Justice councilor Müller's hitherto observable political reserve that he is not implicated in the transformation of the *Messin*." In the case of Cahen, the return of two of his sons spoke in his favor; and the action of the third son was unclear: "It has not been established that the son emigrated with the father's knowledge and wishes." The state secretary felt it unjust to refuse Cahen an appointment, since he had been confirmed in previous years. Ultimately, the appointments of both Müller and Cahen were approved.[97]

In this case, the highest government authority showed itself to be more liberal than the local authorities regarding "germanization." Certain administrative changes were made following the Saverne (Zabern) Affair, however, when tensions erupted between the local population and German military troops stationed in Alsace, and from then on, the government was increasingly repressive toward the Lorraine Consistory.[98] At the end of 1914 Marx Hannaux, president of the Metz bank Mayer et Cie., was reelected to the Lorraine Consistory along with the two other lay members. Hannaux had been a member of the Consistory since 1902 and had served as president since 1909, always receiving government confirmation.[99] Nevertheless, the fact that Hannaux, who neither spoke nor wrote German, was sure to be reelected as president of the Consistory in 1915 now posed a serious problem for the government. Language had always been considered a political tool, and the public use of French was frowned on as a manifestation of germanophobia.[100] During the war it became a crime and even a pretext for arrest. In December 1914 a member of the Jewish community of Thionville, Adolph Levy, apparently a German Jew, denounced Hannaux to the government: "It lies in the interest of *Deutschtum* to see a man at the head of this religious authority who is competent in the German language in speech and in writing, which is not at all the case for Herr Hannaux. This man speaks not one word of German, and therefore he can never conduct a German discussion at the meeting [of the Consistory] without having a make use of a translator." Levy added that since Alsace-Lorraine had been annexed to the Reich for forty-four years, there was no excuse for any native Lorrainer not to have learned German. He strongly advised the government against approving the appointments of any consistorial members not fluent in German.[101]

The Bezirkspräsident of Lorraine fully concurred with Levy's opinion and wrote to the Minister of the Interior that he considered it "undesirable for the interest of *Deutschtum* as well as for the interest of the Jewish population of the province that Hannaux be president any longer." He requested that Hannaux's appointment be rejected and suggested that the Old German manufacturer Felix Tuteur replace Hannaux as president.[102] This time the recommendation fell on more receptive ears. The Minister of the Interior, now serving a far more reactionary regime and responding to new conditions engendered by the bitter war against France, responded positively to the Bezirkpräsident's recommendations. The matter was of the utmost seriousness, the minister noted, since according to a law of May 31, 1911, the Lorraine Consistory was required to use German exclusively as its official language.[103]

At the end of September 1915, after almost a year of negotiations, the government and the Consistory finally worked out a compromise. The administration agreed to confirm the three elected candidates, including Hannaux, but the election of a president was postponed until the end of the war. Furthermore, at that time and thenceforth the Consistory, contrary to precedent, would have to submit its presidential candidates to governmental approval. In the interim, the administration designated Grand Rabbi Netter to take over the functions of president.* These consistorial appointments were finally confirmed in November 1915.[104]

The period 1871–1914 was one of considerable political change for the Jewish community of Alsace-Lorraine. Adherence to the pro-French Protest movement in the 1870's and 1880's gradually gave way, especially after the Dreyfus Affair, to an increased willingness to accept the status quo. This new and more conciliatory attitude was accompanied by two important trends. On the one hand, Alsace-Lorraine Jewry showed a greater readiness to strive, together with the German immigrant community, for an expansion of Jewish civil rights within the Reichsland. On the other, Alsatian Jewish particularism, first narrowly articulated in religious terms in the 1870's, found fuller expression as a political and cultural ideology in the prewar years. Complementing one another, these two trends stimulated the integration of Alsace-Lorraine Jews into imperial Germany

---

*After the war Hannaux resumed his position as president of the Metz Consistory. He was hailed as a great French patriot, and his refusal to learn German was applauded as an act of resistance to German domination. See *Univers israélite*, March 13, 1925, p. 585, April 3, 1925, p. 658, and 1924–25, suppl., "La Famille israélite," p. 308.

and increasingly pushed the nationality issue into the background. Chances for rapprochement between the government and Reichsland Jewry were not ruined, therefore, by internal pro-French resistance from within the Jewish community. Rather, as the cases of Müller, Cahen, and especially Hannaux illustrate, it was external political obstacles and ultimately the outbreak of the war that brought an abrupt end to this process of accommodation.

EIGHT

Social Transformations

Social transformations, in addition to political developments, laid the groundwork for the integration of Alsace-Lorraine Jewry into the German Reich following the annexation. The predominance of urban middle- and upper middle-class Jews among those who opted for French citizenship and emigrated to France in 1871–72 indicates that urbanization and embourgeoisement were critical ingredients in the parallel processes of acculturation and the development of a sense of national identity. Certainly, the departure of those Jews who had forged the closest political, cultural, and economic links to France made a difference in the "germanization" of the remaining Jewish population. A second, no less significant, trend that could have encouraged this same result was the lateness of social change in Alsace-Lorraine. Substantial evidence indicates that for those Jews who stayed behind in the Reichsland, large-scale urbanization and embourgeoisement occurred only after 1871. Eugen Weber, in his social history of late-nineteenth-century rural France, suggests that concrete economic changes resulting from the Industrial Revolution and the expansion of national communication and transportation systems may be essential prerequisites for the internalization of a sense of national identity among rural populations. These transformations did not occur in the annexed provinces until the last quarter of the nineteenth century.[1] Although Weber's argument pertains specifically to peasants, it holds true also for Jews in Alsace-Lorraine, the majority of whom still resided in rural villages and engaged in petty commerce on the eve of the annexation. In other words, the social setting in which a national consciousness could arise among the rural population as a whole developed not during the French period, as is often assumed, but only during the German period, and it was this delay that set the stage for the assimilation of Alsace-Lorraine Jewry to German rather than to French culture.

Perhaps the most striking social transformations undergone by Alsace-Lorraine Jewry during the post-annexation period are evidenced in the community's changing demographic contours. Two trends are readily discernible: population loss and urbanization. The Jewish population of Alsace-Lorraine experienced a steady and rapid diminution, plummeting from 40,938 in 1871 to 30,483 by 1910—a precipitous drop of 25 percent. Over that period the Jewish representation in the total population fell from 2.6 percent (the 1871 total population includes military personnel) to 1.6 percent.[2] Second, those Jews who remained were becoming increasingly concentrated in the largest urban centers of the Reichsland. Both these trends were perceptible long before 1871, but they continued at a far more accelerated pace throughout the German period.

Although both French and German Jews agreed that emigration was the principal cause of the constant diminution of the Jewish population, declining fertility played an important role and became a matter of grave concern to Alsace-Lorraine Jewish leaders during the annexation period. In the early nineteenth century the birthrate of Alsatian Jewry was extremely high, in some regions amounting to between 35 and 42 per 1,000 of the total Jewish population.[3] The figures available for the city of Strasbourg beginning in 1895 and published by Erwin Schnurmann in his book *La Population juive en Alsace* indicate a tremendous decline in Jewish fertility during the course of the century. Despite the limitations of these statistics, they still permit a rough comparison of trends in Jewish and non-Jewish fertility.[4]

Schnurmann's crude birthrates for Strasbourg reveal that Jewish fertility was significantly lower than that of the total population. In 1896 there were 18.7 births per 1,000 Jews in Strasbourg, compared with 31 per 1,000 inhabitants of the city as a whole. By 1905 the gap had narrowed somewhat—to 17.5 births per 1,000 Jews and 28.3 per 1,000 for the total population. Five years later, the gap was all but closed: the birthrate of the total population steadily declined, to stand at 23.8 per 1,000 for all Strasbourg inhabitants in 1910, while the Jewish rate increased to 21.3 per 1,000, perhaps owing to the influx of young Eastern European Jews. Still, the crude Jewish birthrate remained slightly lower than that of the total population, and Schnurmann rightly describes Jews as "the precursors of the low birthrate of the total population."[5]

The statistics on household size from the 1910 census, which group families according to the number of children living in a household, similarly suggest a lower birthrate for Jews (Table 8.1). In municipalities with over 2,000 inhabitants, 67.1 percent of all Catholic households had two or fewer resident children, compared with 72.7 percent and 76.2 percent for Protestant and Jewish households, respectively. In municipalities numbering fewer than 2,000 inhabitants, the respective figures for Catholic, Protestant, and Jewish households were 58.8 percent, 68.1 percent, and 73.6 percent. For the city of Strasbourg the figures were 72.8 percent, 76.1 percent, and 82.9 percent. Thus, while the mean percentage of small Jewish households was 75.3 percent, the figure for the general population was only 64.2 percent. In all religious groups the family size decreased as the population density increased, strongly suggesting that declining fertility was related to urbanization.[6] Consequently, although it appears that the Jewish birthrate in both rural and urban areas was comparatively lower than that of Catholics and Protestants, it is also clear that the fertility of urban Jews was markedly less than that of their rural counterparts.*

Not only was the crude Jewish birthrate in Alsace-Lorraine low in comparison with the general Reichsland population, it was also lower than general birthrates elsewhere in Europe. Strasbourg's

---

*It should be stressed here that household size is only an approximate measure of fertility. Other factors differentiating Jews and non-Jews—mortality rates, age of marriage, emigration rates, etc.—may also have played a role in determining household size. Nevertheless, the evidence strongly suggests that declining fertility was the major factor. First, as Hyman, "Jewish Fertility," p. 82, points out, the overall mean family size of Jews in Alsace-Lorraine had been declining throughout the nineteenth century. Second, the significantly lower rates of infant mortality, as well as the late age of marriage, among Alsace-Lorraine Jewry may have served to increase household size. (On the lower infant mortality rates among Jews, see Schnurmann, *La Population juive*, pp. 125–34.) Finally, there is substantial evidence indicating significantly lower fertility rates among southwest German Jews, even in villages, compared with both Catholics and Protestants. We would expect to find a similar pattern of low fertility among Alsace-Lorraine Jews. See two works by Goldstein: "Aspects of Change," and *Determinants of Change*, pp. 24–27.

TABLE 8.1
Distribution of Households with Two or Fewer Resident Children by City Size and Religion, 1910
(Percent of households in group)

Category	Number of children resident in household:			
	0	1	2	Combined total
Towns[a]				
Jews	21.3%	28.0%	24.3%	73.6%
Protestants	18.2	25.9	24.0	68.1
Catholics	15.5	22.2	21.1	58.8
Cities[b]				
Jews	24.4	27.8	24.0	76.2
Protestants	22.8	27.6	22.3	72.7
Catholics	20.4	24.9	21.8	67.1
Strasbourg only				
Jews	25.5	31.5	25.9	82.9
Protestants	25.2	28.6	22.3	76.1
Catholics	24.2	26.3	22.3	72.8
Alsace-Lorraine				
Jews	23.3	27.9	24.1	75.3
Protestants	20.5	26.7	23.2	70.4
Catholics	17.7	23.4	21.4	62.5
Combined total	18.3	24.1	21.8	64.2

SOURCE: Erwin Schnurmann, *La Population juive en Alsace* (Paris, 1936), p. 165. I have adjusted the figure for Strasbourg Jewish households with 2 children from 35.9%, presumably a typographical error.

[a] Fewer than 2,000 inhabitants.
[b] 2,000 or more inhabitants.

Jewish population had an even lower crude birthrate than the total population of France, the nation claiming the lowest birthrate at that time.[7]

The low Jewish birthrate in Alsace-Lorraine was to some extent a consequence of the low marriage rate for Jews. In the ten years 1872–82, the rate of purely Jewish marriages fell from 10.4 per 1,000 to 5.2 per 1,000. By 1910 it showed a slight increase, but at 6.1 per 1,000 it was still low. The trend was most pronounced in the large cities. In Strasbourg the marriage rate of the total population was 9.0 per 1,000 in 1896, double the 4.1 rate of the Jewish population.[8] Schnurmann attributes this lower marriage rate to the fact that Jews generally married later than non-Jews, partly because it took a long time for young Jews to attain the status of independent merchant or businessman, the career to which they mostly aspired.⁹ Owing to the long period of capital accumulation for such careers—unlike the occupations of peasants and artisans—it was not uncommon for Jews to marry in their thirties, waiting until they became financially independent and could adequately provide for a family.* The large-scale emigration of young Jewish males and the propensity of some bourgeois Jewish families to send their daughters to France to marry may also have contributed to the low marriage rate.[10]

The primary cause of declining fertility and the related phenomenon of declining marriage rates among Jews was the process of embourgeoisement that occurred during this period. As Schnurmann notes, Alsace-Lorraine Jewry in general, and Strasbourg Jewry in particular, was significantly more middle class than the general population. It is not surprising that prosperity should have played a role in the changing structure of the family. As Jews increasingly rose into the ranks of the urban bourgeoisie, children became far less important as revenue earners than they had been in rural areas. Significantly greater portions of income were now allocated to providing fewer children with better educations and higher standards of living than to the proliferation of large families. With respect to embourgeoisement, Schnurmann notes an interesting fact—Jewish fertility corresponded to that of Strasbourg's bourgeois population in general. The reason for the higher birthrate of Strasbourg's total population was that it included a significant proletarian population not found among the city's Jewish community. Isolating Strasbourg's two bourgeois districts in 1910, the Place de la République and the Université, we find that they had birthrates of 18.6 and 20.6 per 1,000, respectively. Such figures accord closely with the 21.3 per 1,000 figure for the Jewish community. On the other hand, the birthrate of Strasbourg's working-class districts was over 40 per 1,000. Low Jewish fertility, therefore, was primarily an indicator of the relatively high degree of Jewish urbanization and embourgeoisement.[11]

*According to Eugen Weber, the situation among the French peasantry was the reverse: as the marriage rate increased, the birthrate decreased *Peasants into Frenchmen*, pp. 178, 184. Alice Goldstein and Steven Lowenstein have similarly noted the late age of marriage among nineteenth-century village Jews in Baden and in Bavaria. See Goldstein, *Determinants of Change*, pp. 19–20; and Lowenstein, "Voluntary and Involuntary Limitation," pp. 97–98. Although Schnurmann's observations refer specifically to men, we can infer that women too were deciding to marry at a later age.

Declining Jewish fertility may also have been due to the loosening hold of religious traditionalism. As women became more urban and middle class, and wanted greater educational and economic opportunities for themselves and their children, they too came to reject traditional Judaism's injunctions encouraging large families. Moreover, it is probable that the migration of Jewish youths from rural to urban areas also tended to alter traditional views of the family, since it was precisely those uprooted migrants who became most receptive to modern ideas.[12]

Like population decline, urbanization—the second major demographic trend characterizing Alsace-Lorraine Jewry during the annexation period—was underway before 1871. But again, the most important change occurred during the German era. Between 1871 and 1910 the Jewish population of Alsace-Lorraine shed its essentially rural character and became highly concentrated in the largest cities of the Reichsland.[13] Emigration was one aspect of the urbanization process—it was the large cities of France, the United States, Latin America, and Switzerland that attracted the Jews of Alsace-Lorraine—but internal migrations within the Reichsland and the influx of Jewish immigrants from Germany and eastern Europe to the major cities were no less significant. In 1871 only 21.7 percent of Alsace-Lorraine Jews resided in cities with populations of over 10,000 inhabitants; by 1910 the figure jumped to 45.7 percent. Similarly, 28.9 percent of Reichsland Jews lived in cities of over 5,000 inhabitants in 1871; by 1910 the figure had risen to 54.9 percent. Thus the proportion of Jews living in the largest urban centers doubled during these thirty-nine years, and continued to exceed considerably the level of urbanization of the total population (Table 8.2).

The most remarkable increase occurred in Strasbourg. In 1871 only 15.3 percent of all Bas-Rhin Jewry (military population included) resided in the capital city of the province. By 1910 the figure had shot up to 36.6 percent. During this same period, the Jewish population of Strasbourg grew by 87.2 percent (Table 8.3). In Metz, the capital of Lorraine, although the increase was less drastic, the Jewish population grew 27.7 percent in the same period: in 1871, some 17.5 percent of all Lorraine Jews were concentrated here, compared with 27.2 percent in 1910. This pattern was repeated in Haut-Rhin: 26.0 percent of all the Jews of Haut-Rhin lived in Mulhouse and Colmar in 1871, and by 1910 the figure had climbed to 45.4

TABLE 8.2

Growth of the Urban Jewish and Total Populations of Alsace-Lorraine by Province, 1871–1910

Province	Cities of over 5,000 inhabitants		Cities of over 10,000 inhabitants	
	Jewish population	Total population	Jewish population	Total population
Bas-Rhin				
1871	26.2%	21.7%	18.4%	14.1%
1910	51.8	39.6	42.3	32.1
Haut-Rhin				
1871	34.4	25.7	30.0	21.5
1910	59.9	40.5	49.2	29.3
Lorraine				
1871	27.3	13.2	17.5	8.4
1910	56.4	49.5	49.4	23.6
Total				
1871	28.9	20.2	21.7	14.5
1910	54.9	43.3	45.7	28.3

SOURCES: Statistischen Bureau des Kaiserlichen Ministeriums für Elsass-Lothringen, *Statistische Mitteilungen über Elsass-Lothringen, 1871; Statistisches Jahrbuch für Elsass-Lothringen, 1912*, p. 295.

NOTE: In this table and Table 8.3 the 1871 figures are based on the civil population only; the 1910 figures include the military.

TABLE 8.3

Size of the Jewish Population in the Major Cities of Alsace-Lorraine, 1871 and 1910

City	1871	1910	Percent change
Strasbourg (Bas-Rhin)	3,088	5,780	+87.2%
Mulhouse (Haut-Rhin)	1,997	2,287	+14.5
Metz (Lorraine)	1,496	1,911	+27.7
Colmar (Haut-Rhin)	1,139	1,202	+5.5
Haguenau (Bas-Rhin)	630	611	−3.0
Bischheim (Bas-Rhin)	493	294	−40.4
Sarreguemines (Lorraine)	364	436	+19.8
Sarrebourg (Lorraine)	374	371	−0.8
Wissembourg (Bas-Rhin)	267	173	−35.2
Saverne (Bas-Rhin)	245	322	+31.4
Sélestat (Bas-Rhin)	244	248	+1.6
Thionville (Lorraine)	187	332	+77.5

SOURCES: Same as Table 8.2.

percent. The Jewish population of both these cities remained considerably more stable than that of Strasbourg, however. Mulhouse's Jewish population grew 14.5 percent and Colmar's only 5.5 percent over the period. The second most striking increase took place in Thionville (Diedenhofen) in Lorraine. There the Jewish population increased 77.5 percent as Eastern Europeans and migrants from other parts of Alsace-Lorraine and Germany flooded in to take advantage of the region's growing commercial opportunities sparked by the rapidly expanding mining industry.

Internal migrations were responsible for much of the increased urbanization that occurred during this period. The *Landflucht*, or rural flight, of the Jews became a major preoccupation of the local Jewish press in the early twentieth century.[14] As Table 8.4 shows, the only districts registering increases in the Jewish population for the period 1871–1910 were Strasbourg-ville, Metz-ville, and Thionville. Strasbourg-campagne, Haguenau, Molsheim, Saverne, Colmar, Metz-campagne, and Boulay lost approximately one-third of their Jewish populations; Erstein, Sélestat, Altkirch, Guebwiller, Thann, and Sarrebourg over two-fifths; and Wissembourg, Ribeauvillé, and Château-Salins over one-half. In 1931, when the Jewish population of Wissembourg had shrunk to 19 percent of its 1871 total, Paul Lévy wrote, "We have the impression that there are as many if not more Jewish natives from the arrondissement of Wissembourg in Strasbourg than there are in the arrondissement itself."[15] Demographic trends in villages with large Jewish concentrations offer additional evidence of the rural flight (Table 8.5). Some villages lost 60 percent or more of their Jewish populations between 1871 and 1905, and numerous Jewish schools throughout the provinces were forced to close because of rapidly diminishing student populations.[16] Taking into account these dramatic demographic shifts, the Landesausschuss in 1908 decided to reduce from forty to twenty-eight the number of rabbinical seats in the Reichsland, excluding those of the three Grand Rabbis. This redistribution reflected not only the decline of the rural Jewish population, but also the process of urbanization, since three new rabbinical posts were created in Lorraine, including one in Thionville.[17] Although urbanization was to some extent a general trend, the total population remained strikingly more constant: thirteen of Alsace-Lorraine's twenty-two districts actually registered population increases during this period. Jews were

TABLE 8.4
Size of the Jewish and Total Populations of Alsace-Lorraine by District,
1871 and 1910

District	Jewish population			Total population		
	1871[a]	1910	Percent change	1871[a]	1910	Percent change
Bas-Rhin						
Strasbourg-ville	3,088	5,780	+87.2%	85,654	178,891	+108.9%
Strasbourg-campagne	3,133	1,959	−37.5	75,037	97,795	+30.3
Erstein	2,522	1,348	−46.6	63,187	65,159	+3.1
Haguenau	2,970	1,911	−35.7	73,593	80,292	+9.1
Molsheim	1,619	993	−38.7	74,910	67,069	−10.5
Sélestat	1,906	1,030	−46.0	78,162	67,581	−13.5
Wissembourg	2,163	971	−55.1	62,333	56,579	−9.2
Saverne	2,760	1,787	−35.3	87,530	87,572	+.05
TOTAL	20,161	15,779	−21.7%	600,406	700,938	+16.7%
Haut-Rhin						
Altkirch	1,052	551	−47.6%	55,603	51,748	−6.9%
Colmar	3,330	2,221	−33.3	81,046	97,736	+20.6
Guebwiller	1,678	879	−47.6	64,181	61,659	−3.9
Mulhouse	4,466	3,248	−27.3	126,343	188,988	+49.6
Ribeauvillé	693	339	−51.1	67,102	58,151	−13.3
Thann	861	451	−47.6	64,598	59,583	−7.8
TOTAL	12,080	7,689	−36.3%	458,873	517,865	+12.9%
Lorraine						
Metz-ville	1,496	1,911	+27.7%	53,623	68,598	+27.9%
Metz-campagne	857	542	−36.8	69,323	113,674	+64.0
Boulay	832	579	−30.4	47,735	41,825	−12.4
Château-Salins	1,018	494	−51.5	52,801	45,303	−14.2
Thionville	1,070	1,085	+1.4	76,591	151,212	+97.4
Forbach	924	773	−16.3	64,141	94,191	+46.8
Sarrebourg	1,429	803	−43.8	62,457	66,222	+6.0
Sarreguemines	945	828	−12.4	63,788	74,186	+16.3
TOTAL	8,571	7,015	−18.2%	490,459	655,211	+33.6%

SOURCES: Statistischen Bureau des Kaiserlichen Ministeriums für Elsass-Lothringen, *Statistisches Handbuch für Elsass-Lothringen, 1885*, p. 39; *Statistisches Jahrbuch für Elsass-Lothringen, 1912*, p. 3, 1913/14, p. 16.
[a] Civil population only.

therefore deserting the countryside at a far quicker pace than their non-Jewish compatriots.

Economic factors lay at the root of urbanization. Both Jews and non-Jews were attracted by the expanding industrial, commercial, and educational opportunities offered by large cities in the wake of the Industrial Revolution. Industrialization also brought the means

TABLE 8.5
Decline of the Rural Jewish Population of Alsace, 1871–1905

Village	1871	1905	Percent decrease
Hegenheim (Haut-Rhin)	413	110	−73.4%
Marmoutier (Bas-Rhin)	351	140	−60.1
Brumath (Bas-Rhin)	478	352	−26.4
Sarre-Union (Bas-Rhin)	327	201	−38.5
Durmenach (Haut-Rhin)	373	138	−63.0
Grussenheim (Haut-Rhin)	347	193	−44.4
Schirrhofen (Bas-Rhin)	407	140	−65.6
Lauterbourg (Bas-Rhin)	225	65	−71.1
Ingwiller (Bas-Rhin)	367	322	−12.3
Mommenheim (Bas-Rhin)	261	167	−36.0
Niederhagenthal (Haut-Rhin)	321	93	−71.0
Mutzig (Bas-Rhin)	154	135	−12.3
Obernai (Bas-Rhin)	205	171	−16.6
Hochfelden (Bas-Rhin)	300	168	−44.0
Dambach (Bas-Rhin)	295	98	−66.8
Niederrödern (Bas-Rhin)	229	121	−47.2

SOURCES: Statistischen Bureau des Kaiserlichen Ministeriums für Elsass-Lothringen, *Statistische Mitteilungen über Elsass-Lothringen, 1871; 1905*, vol. 31, part B.

to facilitate these urban-bound migrations. Edmond Uhry vividly describes in his memoirs how the completion of the railroad linking Ingwiller to Strasbourg in 1888 revolutionized life in that town; few young men remained there and even many of the young women left to take jobs in the larger cities or to marry men from other locales. Uhry, born in the early 1870's, first visited Strasbourg only in the 1890's after he returned from the United States. By then the railroad had reduced the time of the journey from Ingwiller to Strasbourg from between four and six hours to a mere thirty-five minutes.[18]

Several economic developments in this period had a negative impact on the commercial role of Jews in particular, and encouraged not only urbanization, but emigration as well. As we have seen, new types of banking facilities—state-initiated branch banks, joint stock companies, and mutual loan associations (*Raiffeisen* banks)—gradually displaced the Jewish moneylender as the main source of agricultural credit. Similarly, the development of agricultural cooperatives and consumer societies brought about the ruin of a large segment of rural commerce dominated by Jews. The virtual Jewish monopolies on trading in cattle, grain, and other agricultural products were gradually broken by the agricultural cooperatives, which proclaimed one of their primary goals to be the elimination of the Jewish commercial intermediary.[19] The increased governmental regulation of cattle and horse dealing to safeguard against the spread of disease seriously threatened one of the most vital of Jewish rural livelihoods. Conditions became so precarious that by 1912 the cattle dealers of Alsace-Lorraine organized a union to protect their interests.[20] Government laws against peddling, regarded as an economic scourge, accelerated the disappearance of this frequently Jewish trade.[21] Small commerce gradually gave way to large-scale commerce, even in rural districts: "The chain stores, home delivery organized by the stores of the towns," Schnurmann notes, "shook up commerce in the villages to such a degree that many Jews could no longer subsist if they did not decide to leave."[22]

Internal migrations alone did not account for the increased urbanization during this period. Jewish immigrants, both from Germany and from Eastern Europe, also streamed into the large cities of Alsace-Lorraine after the annexation. Since the immigration of German Jews has already been discussed at some length, only Eastern European Jews need be dealt with here. Although the largest wave of Eastern European Jewish immigrants did not arrive in Alsace-Lorraine until after the First World War, people fleeing persecution and economic hardship began to seek refuge there in the 1880's, as they did elsewhere in the West. In 1895, according to Schnurmann's statistics, there were 42 Jews of Russian (including Polish, Estonian, and Lithuanian) origin and 44 of Austrian origin residing in Strasbourg, accounting for 2.1 percent of the city's 4,012 Jews.[23] However, these figures may underrepresent the East European element, since an 1895–96 list of charity recipients in another Jewish community, that of Wissembourg district, shows 96 Alsatians, 215 Russians, 45 Rumanians, 184 Hungarians, 156 Germans, and 72 people of unstated origin.[24] At any rate, by the First World War the numbers of East European immigrants had grown substantially, although no precise statistics exist.[25] Most of these Jews were extremely poor, commonly finding employment as peddlers or artisans; some made their way as beggars.[26] A significant number of students at the University of Strasbourg were also of Eastern European provenance.

The official policy of antisemitism carried out by the German administration against these immigrants added misery to their already difficult existence. The government treated the native Jewish population in the Reichsland with considerable respect and tolerance, but it regarded Eastern European Jews as "undesirable" and "disagreeable" elements. As early as the winter of 1870, the new German prefect in Metz issued an order expelling all Poles—the majority of whom were Jews—from the city. When Grand Rabbi Benjamin Lipman interceded on the Poles' behalf, the prefect explained that the government's aim was to "germanize Lorraine" and remove "those elements that were contrary to the German spirit. And . . . nobody was more opposed to that spirit than the Poles."[27]

Although Lipman succeeded in getting the German order revoked in 1872, the situation for Eastern European Jews in the provinces remained precarious. They were nearly always refused naturalization, and as elsewhere in the Reich, even temporary residency papers and work permits were frequently denied. Since employment was impossible without such papers, immigrants often became public charges, and therefore at risk of expulsion. In 1887 the *Univers israélite* reported, "A certain number of Jewish families coming from Russian Poland have recently been expelled from Alsace-Lorraine since they had no means of existence and because several among them lacked papers."[28] In 1900 the Bezirkspräsident of Haut-Rhin reported: "In Mulhouse there has been an intense immigration of Russian, Polish, and Galician Jews. The increase of these undesirable elements will be countered by the expulsion of several persons who have made themselves exceptionally unpleasant."[29] Such expulsions became increasingly common in the twentieth century, and the consequences were often tragic. The immigrants usually fled to some neighboring German state where they were tolerated, since expulsion remained a state rather than a national policy, but they were frequently separated from their families, and in some cases spent ten to fifteen years petitioning for readmission to the Reichsland.[30]

For the most part, native Jews strove to aid their Eastern European coreligionists, sponsoring subscriptions to provide relief, but relations between the two communities were not altogether unstrained.[31] Here, as elsewhere in Western Europe and the United States, native Jews who desired to assimilate often perceived the Eastern European immigrants as a threat, and they feared that the newcomers' visible Jewishness, together with their poverty, would draw increased attention to "the Jewish problem."[32] Those same charges leveled by non-Jews against Alsatian Jewry during the French Revolution, that is, that Jews were in dire need of regeneration, were now reiterated by Alsace-Lorraine Jews against the Eastern Europeans.[33] Furthermore, many native Jews adopted the same views held by the authorities on the immigrants' economic practices, excoriating them as parasitical and degenerate. In consequence, massive campaigns were launched to eliminate the problem of wandering beggars and peddlers.[34] Religious conflicts further aggravated the relationship. As the *Strassburger Israelitische Wochenschrift* pointed out, although the majority of Russian Jews were "Jews only in name" and therefore able to assimilate with relative ease into the native liberal Jewish community, the Galician Jews were extremely traditional and found the local prayer service unacceptable. After initial confrontation with the consistories, Galician Jews in Strasbourg and Metz were permitted to hold their own prayer services, on condition that they recognize the Consistory's authority.[35] Thus, the immigration of the Eastern European Jews had begun to transform significantly the social and cultural physiognomy of Alsace-Lorraine Jewry even before the First World War.

Despite the breakdown of the rural Jewish economy, the broad occupational outlines of the Alsace-Lorraine Jewish community remained relatively stable during this period.[36] As in the years before 1871, Alsace-Lorraine Jews remained most heavily concentrated in commerce. A 245-member electoral list of the Lorraine Jewish community in 1890 indicates that 73.5 percent of those named were involved in commercial activity, a figure slightly higher than the 64 percent for Strasbourg Jews in 1846.[37] Some of them were quite wealthy wholesale merchants, small industrialists, and bankers. The Fürst brothers, for example, owned a prosperous cigar and cigarette factory, made possible by the elimination of the French tobacco monopoly; and Isaac Mayer, president of the Lorraine Jewish Consistory and the Metz Chamber of Commerce, was the director of the bank Mayer et Cie. Furthermore, this list illustrates that Jews continued to be important commercial intermediaries in rural Lorraine. Twenty of thirty-two heads of Jewish households in Ennery, twenty of twenty-six in Buding, eighteen of forty in Delme, and seven of fifteen in Morhange were cattle and horse dealers.[38] There is no doubt that the absolute numbers of Jews in these trades were shrinking during this period, but their proportion relative to total rural

TABLE 8.6
Occupational Distribution of Alsace-Lorrainers by Religion, 1907

Sector	Jews		Catholics		Protestants	
	Number	Percent	Number	Percent	Number	Percent
Agriculture	200	0.1%	275,197	81.1%	62,906	18.5%
Industry	2,699	0.8	286,239	81.7	60,923	17.4
Trade, commerce	8,428	8.6	65,240	66.9	23,701	24.3
Military service	309	0.4	35,039	47.0	39,143	52.5
Civil service, liberal professions	618	1.8	24,504	70.3	9,630	27.6
Other (including no occupation)	2,284	2.5	70,221	76.1	19,754	21.4
TOTAL	14,538	1.5%	756,440	76.5%	216,057	21.9%

SOURCE: Statistischen Bureau, *Statistisches Jahrbuch für Elsass-Lothringen, 1909*, p. 34.
NOTE: Only the major religious groups are shown. The percentages are calculated on the basis of the total active population.

Jewish population probably remained constant. Indeed, the same socioeconomic changes in the countryside that propelled Jewish emigration and urbanization simultaneously served to keep the traditional structure of rural Jewish society intact, albeit on a much smaller scale, by alleviating the pressures of surplus population.[39]

In 1907, 8,428 people, or 8.6 percent of the total Alsace-Lorraine population involved in trade and commerce, were Jews (Table 8.6).[40] Put another way, 58.0 percent of the active Jewish population was employed in trade and commerce. This compares with only 8.6 percent and 11.0 percent, respectively, for the active Catholic and Protestant populations. Furthermore, if we isolate the sector "commerce" from other aspects of trade (figures not given in Table 8.6) Jews accounted for 8,150 of the 44,603 people employed in this category, or some 18.3 percent.

According to 1907 manuscript census data, the majority of Jewish businessmen were in sedentary commerce, and the next largest percentage were active as commercial agents.[41] Schnurmann points out that only 1.1 percent of the active Jewish population in trade and commerce were involved in banking and credit. He attributes this low participation to the inability of local Jewish banks to compete with the larger national banks that began to penetrate the region by the middle of the nineteenth century. Furthermore, the development of credit cooperatives (*Raiffeisen* banks) gradually eliminated the Jewish moneylender from the countryside. Since Schnurmann presents no figures by which to calculate the proportion of Jewish to non-Jewish bankers, it is difficult to assess the role of Jewish banking in the entire economy.[42] Until the First World War a number of influential local banks in Alsace continued to be Jewish-owned; some observers argue that it was only in the 1920's and 1930's that the small banks in Alsace—almost entirely in Jewish hands in the nineteenth century—began to be absorbed by the large national banks.[43]

A significantly higher percentage of Jews in trade and commerce in 1907 were self-employed (57.2%) than either Catholics (27.2%) or Protestants (25.5%). In all three cases, however, this represented a substantial decline since 1895, when 67.1 percent of Jews, 39.6 percent of Catholics, and 32.7 percent of Protestants were self-employed businessmen. Schnurmann attributes this trend to the progressive economic concentration under capitalism, which drove people away from ownership into salaried work.[44]

Jews were barely represented at all in agriculture, but they were to be found in significant numbers in the ranks of industry and artisanry. Although Jews represented only 0.8 percent of the total employed in this category, they accounted for 18.6 percent of the active Jewish labor force—a sizable proportion considering the small number of Jews employed in such trades earlier in the nineteenth century. Schnurmann attributes this development to the efforts of the *écoles de travail* established in Metz in 1820, Strasbourg in 1824, and Mulhouse in 1842 with the specific aim of creating a Jewish artisan class.[45] Jews were active in every branch of industry and artisanry, but the largest numbers were employed in five categories: foodstuffs (1,027), clothing (764), textiles (220), the leather industry (111), and the manufacture of machines and instruments (102). The extremely high figure in the foodstuffs category, which embraces both the production and the distribution of food products, is due primarily to the large number of Jewish butchers, necessitated by the requirements of Jewish dietary laws. Jewish tailors, as elsewhere in Europe and the United States, played a disproportionate role in the clothing industry. The proclivity of Jews for self-employment is once again striking: 48.7 percent of all Jews in industry and artisanry were independent owners, compared with just 14.3 percent of Catholics and 19.9 percent of Protestants.[46]

Surprisingly few Jews held positions in the civil and military services and liberal professions during this period. In 1907 Jews accounted for 0.8 percent of the total in this category—6.4 percent of the active Jewish population. A study of mid-nineteenth-century Alsatian Jews indicates 6 percent of the Jews in Strasbourg and 4 percent of those in rural areas were in these occupations. Electoral lists from the mostly rural district of Strasbourg-campagne in 1874 similarly show only 4 percent in these professions. Thus, there was relatively little change in this category over a period of 50 years or so.[47] A survey of current public officeholders in Alsace-Lorraine conducted by the Catholic paper *Der Elsässer* in 1897 showed that many government administrations did not include a single Jew. Schnurmann attributes this phenomenon to the antisemitic policies of the German bureaucracy that barred Jews from entering these careers and points out that as soon as the obstacles were removed after the First World War, the number of Alsace-Lorraine Jews in public services increased considerably.[48]

But in fact this low percentage cannot be attributed solely to the exclusion of Jews from high-level civil and military posts. As we have seen, Reichsland Jews were a good deal better off in this respect than Jews elsewhere in imperial Germany. Moreover, even during the French period few Alsatian Jews were represented in the civil service.[49] The number of Jews in liberal professions, where antisemitism was not a decisive factor, also remained relatively low, at a time when Jews were flocking to these careers in other European countries. Commenting on the occupational distribution of the 1890 electoral lists of the Lorraine Jewish Consistory, François Roth writes, "The Jews had nearly disappeared from the liberal professions, where they had been so brilliantly represented before 1870."[50] Although a significant number of Alsace-Lorraine Jews continued to become lawyers and doctors, there is little doubt that the option and emigration of many middle-class Jews following the annexation drained the provinces of a good many Jewish public servants and potential professionals.

Despite the relative stability, in broadest outline, of the occupational distribution of Alsace-Lorraine Jewry, the community as a whole gives the impression of steady upward mobility. Freddy Raphael, concurring with André Neher's assessment of the slow ascendancy of the Jews of Alsace-Lorraine into the ranks of the bourgeoisie,[51] believes that their real embourgeoisement occurred in the German period:

If the peddlers and ragpickers of Alsace, transplanted to Paris, were progressively transforming themselves into free artisans in the second half of the nineteenth century, it was only with the German occupation after the war of 1870, the progressive emigration of the rural population to the urban centers, and the fact that a proletariat of foreign origin supplanted the native proletariat on its way to disappearance, that one segment of the Jews of Alsace ascended to the ranks of the bourgeoisie.[52]

The fact that Jews remained heavily concentrated in commerce by no means implies that there was no upward mobility within this broad category. Even before 1870, as the percentage of Jews active in peddling and secondhand dealing began to diminish, the number of Jewish shopkeepers, merchants, and wholesalers increased.[53] Urbanization and industrialization served as powerful motors of social change, driving small rural Jewish merchants into urban commerce, industry, and artisanry. It was not unusual for rural Jewish grain traders to become directors of the grain industry, or for Jewish property merchants in the countryside to become real estate agents.[54] Immigration also accelerated the pace of embourgeoisement. German Jews who immigrated into the Reichsland came to share in the region's economic prosperity. The Eastern European immigrants, though poor at first, were able to better themselves economically once they established more secure roots, so that, as Simon Schwarzfuchs points out, "It was a very *embourgeoisée* population that was returned to France."[55]

In education, another indicator of mobility and integration, Alsace-Lorraine Jews played a role disproportionate to their numbers in the total population. In 1883 9.7 percent of all students attending public and private higher schools (*Gymnasium, Lyzeum, Realschule*, and *Oberrealschule*) were Jews.[56] By 1910 this figure had fallen slightly, to 7.8 percent, owing partly, no doubt, to the decline of the total Jewish population (especially of the younger generation of Jews on account of emigration) and partly also to the growth of the non-Jewish student body. Nevertheless, the relative proportion of Jews remained significant.[57]

Jewish attendance at Kaiser Wilhelm University in Strasbourg was similarly high (Table 8.7). In 1898 Jews accounted for 8.7 percent of all students; reflecting the economic role of the Jews, 61.1 percent of these native and immigrant students came from families involved in commercial occupations.[58] The faculties with the highest Jewish representation in 1898 were Medicine (15.9%) and Mathematics and

TABLE 8.7
Composition of the Student Body of Kaiser Wilhelm University,
Mid-December 1898

Faculty	Jews	Catholics	Protestants	Other	Without	Total
Theology						
Natives[a]			41			41
Immigrants			14			14
Old Germans			18			18
Foreigners						0
TOTAL	0	0	73	0	0	73
Law and political science						
Natives[a]	9	41	33			83
Immigrants	1	43	99			143
Old Germans	2	24	66			92
Foreigners		8	3	3		14
TOTAL	12	116	201	3	0	332
Medicine						
Natives[a]	13	53	43			109
Immigrants	6	16	36			58
Old Germans	23	29	64	1	2	119
Foreigners	10	15	10	4	2	41
TOTAL	52	113	153	5	4	327
Philology						
Natives[a]	2	22	9			33
Immigrants	1	14	17			32
Old Germans	5	20	42			67
Foreigners	3	1	6		2	12
TOTAL	11	57	74	0	2	144
Mathematics and natural sciences						
Natives[a]	7	31	28			66
Immigrants	3	14	30			47
Old Germans	7	26	38			71
Foreigners	2	3	10	1	2	18
TOTAL	19	74	106	1	2	202
Combined total						
Natives[a]	31	147	154			332
Immigrants	11	87	196			294
Old Germans	37	99	228	1	2	367
Foreigners	15	27	29	8	6	85
TOTAL	94	360	607	9	8	1,078

SOURCE: Statistischen Bureau des Kaiserlichen Ministeriums für Elsass-Lothringen, *Statistisches Handbuch für Elsass-Lothringen, 1902*, p. 468.
[a] Students whose fathers were born in Alsace-Lorraine.

Natural Sciences (9.4%). Since official antisemitism often deterred Jews from entering careers in law or public service, the more apolitical medical and scientific professions were particularly attractive to German Jews in general. Also, the political situation after the annexation encouraged many Alsace-Lorrainers, non-Jews as well as Jews, to choose careers in medicine and science, which involved little contact with the government.[59]

A look at the distribution of Jewish students by nationality in 1898 reveals some interesting facts. For one thing, we find that the Alsatians were well in the minority: 39.4 percent of the Jewish students were Old Germans, and if immigrants are included (most would have been Old Germans who had assumed Alsace-Lorraine state citizenship), 51.1 percent. The same pattern applies to the student body as a whole, which was 34.0 percent Old German without immigrants and 61.3 percent with them. Another interesting point is the large proportion of foreign Jewish students in the total foreign student body—17.6 percent—most of whom were Russian. By 1909 it was the Russians, not the Old Germans, who predominated, accounting for nearly half the Jewish students, while the number of native Alsace-Lorraine Jews remained low.[60] Continuing the trend already apparent in the 1898 statistics, most of the Russian students, including a large number of women, were in the Faculty of Medicine.[61] It is not surprising, then, that by 1913 the Jewish students' share in the Faculty of Medicine had risen to 27.0 percent, or an astounding 71.3 percent of the total Jewish enrollment.[62]

In post-emancipation Europe, conversion and intermarriage were the most extreme forms of social assimilation. Conversion in nineteenth-century France, including Alsace-Lorraine, was never the widespread phenomenon that it was in Germany and Austria-Hungary, where formal conversion was a prerequisite for attaining high positions in the civil and military administrations.[63] It is noteworthy, therefore, that even with the advent of a German administration, the number of conversions to Christianity in Alsace-Lorraine remained significantly lower than elsewhere in the Reich or in Austria. Although the statistics on conversion are incomplete, it appears that the proportion of converts fell short of 1.0 per 1,000 and was probably closer to 0.5 per 1,000. (By way of comparison, the annual mean for Hamburg between 1885 and 1910 was 1.9 per 1,000, and for Vienna between 1871 and 1919, 2.8 per 1,000.)[64] Protestant-

TABLE 8.8
Jewish Converts to Protestantism in Alsace-Lorraine, 1889–1907

Year	Number	Year	Number	Year	Number
1889	7	1896	5	1903	7
1890	1	1897	2	1904	2
1891	1	1898	10	1905	5
1892	4	1899	7	1906	6
1893	3	1900	2	1907	4
1894	2	1901	6		
1895	6	1902	4		

SOURCE: Erwin Schnurmann, *La Population juive en Alsace* (Paris, 1936), p. 18.

ism attracted far more converts than Catholicism. Schnurmann found only 13 recorded instances of Jews joining the Catholic Church in the years 1906–7, 1913, and 1915–18, against 84 conversions to Protestantism between 1889 and 1907 (Table 8.8).

Intermarriage, on the other hand, increased markedly after the annexation. Mixed marriages remained an extremely rare phenomenon in the years immediately following the Franco-Prussian War (Table 8.9). The proportion of Alsace-Lorraine Jews intermarrying between 1871 and 1876 averaged only 0.3 percent. Over the years 1881–99 the average rose to 1.9 percent. After 1900 the figure increased significantly, to 3.7 percent in 1900–1904, 5.4 percent in 1905–9, and 8.5 percent in 1910–14. The extremely high figure for the years 1915–19 reflects the abnormal situation created by the war. Also, the percentages were higher by a good deal in the large cities than in the Reichsland as a whole. In 1910–14 an average of 15.3 percent of Mulhouse Jews intermarried, and in Strasbourg the figure surpassed 20 percent. From the point of view of the Jewish community, assimilation by intermarriage, a rare event before 1870, had indeed become a grave threat by 1914. This tendency can perhaps be attributed to the fact that traditional Alsace-Lorraine Judaism had always been deeply rooted in the family and the community. The rupturing of these bonds by mass urbanization may well have led to a break with religion as well.

The above analysis of various social indicators associated with assimilation—urbanization, declining fertility, emigration, embourgeoisement, education, conversion, and intermarriage—reveals that the annexation period was one of profound social change for

TABLE 8.9
Jewish Marriages and Mixed Marriages in Strasbourg,
Mulhouse, and Alsace-Lorraine as a Whole, 1872–1919

Period	Number of Jews marrying Jews	Number of Jews marrying non-Jews	Ratio Jews–non-Jews to Jews–Jews
Strasbourg			
1895–1899	254	15	5.9
1900–1904	330	46	13.9
1905–1909	286	55	19.2
1910–1914	326	78	23.9
1915–1919	154	45	29.2
Mulhouse			
1891–1894[a]	76	6	7.9
1895–1899	168	12	7.1
1900–1904	178	9	5.1
1905–1909	182	13	7.1
1910–1914	118	18	15.3
Alsace-Lorraine			
1872–1876	3,466	9	0.3
1881–1884[a]	1,698	29	1.7
1885–1889	1,976	42	2.1
1890–1894	1,994	36	1.8
1895–1899	2,156	44	2.0
1900–1904	2,156	80	3.7
1905–1909	2,126	115	5.4
1910–1914	1,686	144	8.5
1915–1919	672	98	14.6

SOURCE: Calculated from data in Erwin Schnurmann, *La Population juive en Alsace* (Paris, 1936), pp. 88–90.
[a] 4-year totals.

Alsace-Lorraine Jewry. As we have seen, the transition from French to German authority did not provide the impetus for each and every one of these trends. Nonetheless, there is little doubt that the annexation served as an important catalyst of social change among Alsace-Lorraine Jews. Certainly, it can be said that the large-scale industrialization and capitalist expansion that occurred during the decades of German hegemony in the provinces created the social context in which Alsace-Lorraine Jewry could have begun to develop a sense of German national identity. Political events and particularly the outbreak of the First World War, however, brought an abrupt end to this process of national integration.

NINE

Resurrected Conflicts: The First World War

The advent of war in 1914 marked a particularly tragic event for the Jewish inhabitants of Alsace-Lorraine, whatever their political loyalties. The specter of fratricide no longer seemed to trouble most French and German Jews, for whom the experience was not new. The situation in the Reichsland, however, was far more complex. Sylvain Halff poignantly describes the painful dilemma facing the Jews who remained in the provinces: "As German subjects . . . they ran the danger of shooting their kin in the trenches before them."[1] This worry was by no means unique to the area's Jews, but since the majority of them had relatives in France, the problem was especially acute in their case.

A secondary problem, at least from the point of view of the German authorities, was the lack of enthusiasm on the part of the local population for the German cause. At best the allegiances of most Reichsland inhabitants could be described as mixed. Writing in her diary in August 1914, one Colmar Jew, Elisabeth Esther Lévy, summed up these sentiments:

> It is to be noted that the Colmarians did their duty entirely vis-à-vis the Germans and even treated them as friends. That they equally helped the French, that's understandable! . . . Many had served in the French army and the sight of a Frenchman awakened their love for their former *Patrie*. Many have family in France. Others imagine that if they do a good deed for a prisoner, their sons may well find themselves at the front. However, it was clandestinely that one gave to the French.[2]

The German authorities greeted such views with grave suspicion and immediately following the outbreak of war, arrested hundreds of Alsace-Lorrainers on charges of being anti-German (*deutschfeindlich*).³ Above all the government lacked confidence in the loyalty of troops from the provinces. Rather than open the door to betrayal by pitting Reichsland soldiers against friends and relatives in France, the German government generally sent them either to the German interior or, more often, to the eastern front, where, according to some commentators, many allowed themselves to be captured and ended up working in French armaments factories.⁴

The Jewish population of Alsace-Lorraine shared the mixed allegiances described by Elisabeth Esther Lévy. There is even some evidence that they exceeded their Christian compatriots in expressing their pro-French loyalties. In part this francophile proclivity may have been due to their tight personal and institutional bonds with the Jews of France, but more important, perhaps, was the fact that in the eyes of Reichsland Jewry, France continued to symbolize the country of emancipation par excellence. Although Jews and many other politically liberal Alsace-Lorrainers had experienced profound disillusionment with France during the antisemitic and anti-Alsatian campaigns of the Dreyfus Affair, the favorable outcome of the Affair, together with the French laicization program of the early twentieth century, reinforced their faith that the French government, if not all Frenchmen, still upheld the enlightenment ideal of civic equality.* It was above all the Reich's ruthless "germanization" campaign during the war, as well as its obvious mistrust of the Reichsland population, that transformed this nostalgia into open French patriotism. "Before the war," Elisabeth Esther Lévy wrote in her diary in late 1914, "many people said, 'in order to avoid combat, we prefer to remain Germans.' Now everyone aspires to be French." Shortly after she had been denounced to the police for distributing refreshments to French troops, Lévy added: "It's a joy for me to come to the aid of the sons of France. That country proclaimed to the entire world liberty, equality, and fraternity; it gave the Jews civil rights. I felt I was

---

*On the common tendency among French Jews to read the antisemitism of the Dreyfus Affair merely as a temporary aberration, see Schnapper, *Juifs et israélites*, pp. 192–93. Even in 1899, as the Dreyfus Affair was winding down, Emile Durkheim remarked, "There is reason, I believe, to distinguish between French antisemitism and foreign antisemitism, which seem to me to be two phenomena of very different significance. . . . Ours constitutes an acute crisis, caused by temporary circumstances." Cited in Schnapper, pp. 192–93 n. 3.

performing a humanitarian act, regardless of differences of nationality or belief."[5] The experience of war thus reversed whatever progress had been made toward integrating Alsace-Lorraine into the German Reich. Inevitably, the same nationalistic divisions that had prevailed in 1870–71 resurfaced almost unchanged in 1914–15.

Jews in the Reichsland found themselves confronted with several choices when the war broke out. Many, especially from the districts of Haut-Rhin, fled to Switzerland and remained there for the duration.[6] In the view of the German war ministry, the majority of Alsace-Lorrainers who did so—both Jews and Gentiles—were collaborating with French organizations on military matters in the Reichsland.[7] Among the most prominent Jews who spent the war years in Switzerland were Grand Rabbi Isidore Weil of Haut-Rhin, Armand Bernheim, a Mulhouse textile manufacturer and a member of the Haut-Rhin Consistory, and Eugène Meyer, the director of the Bank of Alsace-Lorraine in Mulhouse. The case of Bernheim was particularly embarrassing for the German government, for it had awarded a decoration in 1909 to a man now accused of having helped two nephews evade military service. Court proceedings were initiated against Bernheim in November 1915 and his property in Mulhouse was seized.[8] After the war Bernheim returned to Mulhouse and assumed the presidency of the Haut-Rhin Consistory.[9]

Perhaps even greater numbers of Alsace-Lorraine Jews crossed the border into France in 1914. The decision to leave must have been a painful one. A prominent Jewish judge from Metz, Alfred Weil, left his post illegally and fled to France on the gamble of an eventual French victory.[10] Another not atypical example, reported by police, is that of Alexandre Kahn and his family, who were the first to flee from their native village in Strasbourg-campagne to France in 1915. Kahn, a prosperous Jewish merchant, left behind significant property holdings and a thriving business. The Kahns had a married daughter in France and two sons in the French army, but they also had a son fighting for the Germans on the eastern front.[11]

Many of those who fled to France offered their services to the French army. The Sainte-Marie-aux-Mines Jewish industrialist Schuhl served as an interpreter-officer for its anti-enemy propaganda branch and carried out several perilous missions in Germany for which he later received the Grand Cross of the Legion of Honor. Halff has recorded numerous examples of Alsace-Lorraine Jews who enlisted in the French army, including the prominent socialist deputy and journalist Georges Weill and Léon Auguste Uhry, son of the Grand Rabbi of Strasbourg.[12]

The story that perhaps more than any other became part of the legend of the unfailing pro-French patriotism of Alsace-Lorraine Jewry is that of David Bloch. Bloch was born in the Haut-Rhin town of Guebwiller in 1895 and had spent several years working in France before the outbreak of war. In 1914 he refused to return to fulfill his military obligations in Alsace, where his parents still resided, and instead enlisted in the French infantry. Physically too weak to be sent to the front, he volunteered for a special reconnaissance mission that took him back to Alsace. Shortly after he arrived there he was captured by the Germans, tried for high treason, and condemned to death. On pronouncement of the sentence, Bloch proudly proclaimed, "I am a French soldier, I have done my duty," and warned, "my country [*patrie*] will revenge me." After the war the French government commissioned the Lorraine sculptor Emmanuel Hannaux to erect a monument in honor of the young Bloch, who became a folk hero not only to Jews but to all pro-French Alsatians.[13]

A significant number of Jews who decided to stay in the Reichsland and weather the war were arrested and condemned for anti-German activities.[14] The bravery of one Mulhouse Jew, Naphtalie Wallach, was hailed in the French as well as the Jewish press after the war. For four years, while serving in the German army, Wallach clandestinely distributed meat to French border areas.[15] Another Jew, a resident of Barr, in Bas-Rhin, died in a German prison camp for having aided France. In 1919 the French army recognized his service and posthumously awarded him the military cross, praising him as an "Alsatian who paid for his life by his devotion to France."[16] One story, perhaps biased, concerns the "Old German" Professor Gneisse, director of the Colmar Gymnasium until 1918, who claimed that "many gaily-dressed Colmarians—among whom Jewish girls were especially strongly represented—threw horse turds" at him and his group as they were being driven from the city after the war.[17] Even the Zionists in Alsace-Lorraine seemed inclined to favor France. Following the war, the French government honored one of their leaders, Dr. Alfred Elias, with a medal in recognition of his generous aid to French troops on maneuvers in Alsace during 1914. Such individual illustrations could be repeated ad infinitum.[18]

Statistics prove that these were not isolated cases. From officially published lists of crimes committed by Alsace-Lorrainers against the state during the war, Jews were clearly disproportionately represented in every category. They constituted at least 6 percent of all Alsace-Lorrainers condemned for high treason, approximately 7 percent of those charged with anti-German offenses, and about 10 percent of those stripped of their citizenship in 1915 and 1916 for not responding to the imperial government's appeal to Germans abroad to return home.[19] Many of these people, especially in the third category, were thus guilty of not fulfilling their military obligations. Figures from the district of Saverne in early 1915 similarly show that somewhere between 11 percent and 16 percent of the 630 draft evaders were Jewish.[20] Absolutely, as well as relatively, the number of Jewish evaders and deserters was high, since evasion of military service was widespread among all elements of the population. As many as 5,656 men failed to return to Alsace-Lorraine from abroad after war was declared.[21] In 1917 one councilor testified before the chamber of deputies in the Reichsland that 18,426 Alsace-Lorrainers had deserted, not including those who were AWOL or draft evaders.[22]

Alsace-Lorraine Jews who spent much of the annexation living abroad could afford to be more vocal in expressing their pro-French patriotism. For those exiles who had grown up in France, the war provided the long-awaited opportunity for revanche. The wartime letters of Captain Raoul Bloch, who was born in Auxerre (Yonne) in 1872 just after the emigration of his family from Lauterbourg in Alsace, typify this attitude. Raoul Bloch had two brothers who had fought in the Franco-Prussian war: Robert, who died of a disease contracted during the war, and Richard, who was decorated and later became the father of the well-known writer Jean-Richard Bloch.[23] At the age of forty-four, Raoul Bloch enlisted in the French army and volunteered to take command of a front-line unit. He wrote to his wife in January 1915.

With what joy will I head toward Alsace and with what memories on entering in uniform that country of our dreams! Our poor fathers there would be aquiver in their tombs! Finally the revanche that they talked of so much, that overwhelmed their hearts! To be among those who will have contributed directly to restoring to you the cradle of your birth will be for me so sweet a joy and a complement to our life so united and so tender. What a beautiful anniversary of our twenty years of married life together, the "rue de la Mésange" to become once again French! What more beautiful present could I dream of bringing you! And Lauterbourg, Niederbronn, Bionville, all that under our three colors! You can understand why I wanted to and had to leave; isn't the entire family tradition with me? To be able to take you and our dear ones to Alsace-Lorraine and to say to them: "Papa has done all in his power to return this lovely country to France," what finer recompense for me?[24]

Later that year, only a matter of months before his death in combat, Bloch wrote that his only regret was "of not having gone to war on the soil of Alsace."[25] Such revanchist sentiments were voiced as far away as the United States and even Latin America, where Alsace-Lorraine Jews stood in the forefront of rallying support for the French cause.[26] After the war, Sylvain Halff relates, several young Alsace-Lorraine Jews visited their parents' tombs to deposit such inscriptions as "Papa, they have returned!" and "It is done!"[27]

In light of these attitudes, it is not surprising that the majority of Reichsland Jews shared the emotions of "the Alsatian side" of Edmond Uhry's family, who were "hilariously happy at the outcome of the war and its return to French citizenship."[28] Synagogues throughout Alsace and Lorraine sponsored patriotic festivals in November and December of 1918 to celebrate the French victory and to express their enthusiastic willingness to rejoin the Franco-Jewish community. In a letter to the president of the Central Consistory in Paris, Georges Schmoll, president of the Bas-Rhin Consistory, passionately declared:

> After forty-seven years of an odious serfdom and four years of a tragic war, delivered by the glorious armies of France from the brutal vise that was gripping us, we begin, ravished, a new life. We are thirsty for the ideal; we are eager to take our part in the intellectual and religious life of the communities of France; we are coming to you animated by the most ardent filial love for the recovered *Patrie*, and we rejoice with you at working under your auspices for the well-being of both Alsatian Judaism and France.[29]

Representatives from Lorraine echoed these emotional sentiments.[30] The Central Consistory warmly received these declarations of loyalty and wired back to its newly regained constituencies: "If France never was consoled for the loss of two provinces in the East that were her pride, what is there to say of French Judaism of which the immense majority of faithful are descended from Alsace and Lorraine! . . . 'Blessed be the Lord who has allowed us to live so long in order to see this fine day!'"[31] The Central Consistory also sent letters of thanks to General Foch and the French premier, Georges Clemenceau, "hailing with a pious enthusiasm the return to the *Patrie* of the beloved provinces of Alsace and Lorraine delivered from a long martyrdom."[32]

For all the jubilant rhetoric of Franco-Jewish patriotism in 1918 and 1919, the transition back to French rule was not entirely without obstacles. French authorities suspected the loyalties of several members of the Alsace-Lorraine consistories. The case of Nathan Netter, Grand Rabbi of Metz, has already been discussed (Chapter 7). As for Lucien Mannheimer, president of the Haut-Rhin Consistory, a French official in Colmar wrote: "It is certain that, from a national point of view, . . . M. Lucien Mannheimer is absolutely undesirable. His attitude, his remarks during the war, profoundly offended the French Alsatians and are now earning him public insults in Colmar."[33] Ultimately, the French government decided to dissolve the Haut-Rhin Consistory entirely, most of whose members had been appointed by the Statthalter after 1914, and to appoint an interim body until elections could be held in the spring of 1919. The revised list of members excluded Mannheimer and included Armand Bernheim, who was overtly pro-French in his sympathies and had spent the war in Switzerland.[34]

Conflicts surfaced in Strasbourg as well. The city's wartime Grand Rabbi, Dr. Emile Levy, had openly expressed his support of the German cause. Though a native of Alsace, Levy had received his religious education at the Orthodox seminary in Berlin and his doctoral degree from the University of Berlin. Early in his career he had served as the rabbi of Charlottenburg, near Berlin; then, with the outbreak of war, he had become a chaplain in the German army. For his outstanding dedication in this post, the German government awarded him the Iron Cross. When the Grand Rabbi of Bas-Rhin, Adolph Uhry, died in 1916, Levy, a fervent Zionist, was elected as a compromise candidate. His flexibility on religious matters, as illustrated by his willingness to allow an organ in the synagogue despite his own religious leanings, helped bridge the gap between religiously liberal and conservative Jews. More important, as a native-born Alsatian and the son of a rabbi from Haguenau, he was acceptable to the Old Alsatian community, which, as the *Univers israélite* noted, "until now has known how to be self-sufficient, to the exclusion of foreign elements." At the same time, the Old German Jews favored him because of his pro-German outlook and his patriotic services as army chaplain.³⁵ But the very qualities that had made Levy an excellent compromise candidate during the war made it impossible for him to accept the new French regime. Following the armistice, he refused to hail the "liberation" of Strasbourg. Several Old Alsatian members of the Strasbourg Jewish community even complained directly to the president of the Central Consistory in December 1918 about Levy's pro-German sentiments. Under pressure from the French government, Levy resigned his post and opted to return to Germany in order to retain his German citizenship.³⁶

Aside from the issue of clerical officials, the most serious potential conflict that could have hindered the process of reintegrating Alsace and Lorraine to France concerned laicization. Like their Catholic and Protestant compatriots, Jews from the formerly annexed provinces strongly opposed the introduction of the 1905 French legislation that completely separated church and state and thus negated the principle by which all religious officials received state salaries. Sensitive to this issue, Israel Lévy, assistant Grand Rabbi of the Central Consistory, declared in an interview:

> From the religious point of view, one cannot forget that religions are still administered by the system in force before 1870, and that our enemies sought to cultivate the sympathy of those pious populations by the raising of salaries of ministers of religion and by all sorts of acts of generosity in favor of churches, temples, and synagogues. To apply today in Alsace the system of separation of Church and State, that would be to risk engendering regrets [about the return to French rule], and France would certainly not wish that.³⁷

Heeding such warnings, the French authorities to this day have not introduced the separation of church and state into the two provinces. Some Jews in Alsace-Lorraine had also feared that rabbis might become too secular, and that the extensive network of Jewish social and charitable institutions, which had thrived under the patronage of the German Jewish immigrants, might be reduced. Such apprehensions proved unwarranted, however, and the process of postwar reassimilation proceeded relatively smoothly.³⁸

It is perhaps ironic that, although the institutional framework of the Alsace-Lorraine Jewish community survived largely intact, the communal relations that had given life to those institutions were ripped asunder by nationalistic enmities. Those Old Alsatian Jews from Strasbourg who complained to the Central Consistory about the loyalties of Grand Rabbi Levy alleged that he had excoriated the Alsatian Jews for denouncing and even mistreating their German coreligionists following the armistice, but they believed that their behavior was only just retribution for the way the German Jewish immigrant community had treated them during the war. They even went so far as to criticize Grand Rabbi Levy's French accent, which was "far from being that eloquent Alsatian accent, upon which many of our compatriot rabbis deservedly pride themselves, and to listen to him preach or pray in French is offensive to our ears."[39]

In a reversal of option the majority of German Jewish immigrants who had lived in the Reichsland, together with their Gentile compatriots, returned to Germany after the war to retain their German citizenship. Only a very few native Alsace-Lorraine Jews, including Grand Rabbi Levy, followed the Germans in making this choice.[40] In the next few years this emigration was partially compensated for by the return of many former Alsace-Lorraine Jews as well as the growing immigration of East European Jews.

To many observers in 1919, it appeared that little had changed in the provinces during the forty-seven years of the annexation. The commonly shared antagonism toward Germany engendered a sort of *union sacrée* in Alsace-Lorraine similar to the one that existed in France. Once again nationalism provided the instrument through which diverse religious as well as political groups could unite in common cause. Because politics in the Reichsland had retained a profoundly confessional character, these alliances frequently overlapped. All contemporary sources attest to dramatically improved relations among Alsace-Lorraine Catholics, Protestants, and Jews, closely resembling the temporary coalition that had been forged during the Franco-Prussian war.[41] Once again the population found itself split between the pro-French indigenous inhabitants on the one side, and the German intruders on the other. All internal rivalries and dissensions thus appeared to be obliterated, at least for the moment.

TEN

Reflections on Jews and National Identity

To see the resurgence of pro-French patriotism among Alsace-Lorrainers in 1919 as merely a throwback to 1871 is a gross oversimplification. Such a view belies the profound changes experienced by the Reichsland population in general and by Jews in particular during the nearly half century of German rule. Dan P. Silverman is right to point out the significant forces that could have resulted in accommodation and the eventual integration of the annexed territories into the Reich. By the 1890's and early twentieth century rising economic prosperity, the emergence of a new generation educated in German schools, and disillusionment with France, caused either by the Dreyfus Affair itself in the case of Jews and liberals or by its aftermath, in the case of political Catholics, had prepared the ground for a new relationship between the Reichsland and Germany. With clamors for revanche dying down, Jewish and Gentile Alsace-Lorrainers alike were beginning to recognize the annexation as a fait accompli and to strive for political equality within that new frame of reference.

All the same, the fact that significant pro-French sympathies persisted for at least two decades following the annexation, only to resurface again during the First World War, indicates that French national identity had not disappeared entirely from the political scene, as Silverman, who adopts a Marxist perspective on nationalism, attempts to argue. Although I agree with him that the polemical concentration on nationalism as the single most important political factor in the provinces has been vastly overemphasized, that emphasis, nevertheless, is based in a very real historical truth. For the population of the Reichsland in general, two conditions continued to fuel the flames of pro-French nationalism: first, the ever-present possibility, at least until the late 1880's, of a renewed Franco-German war; and second, the anomalous political position of Alsace-Lorraine within the German Reich, owing to the national security fears of Bismarck and his successors. French nationalism remained an important political force primarily because the Germans would not allow it to die.

For Jews in Alsace-Lorraine, there was a third element at work in keeping French nationalism alive—the persistence of official antisemitism in the Reich. In the eyes of the predominantly commercial and increasingly bourgeois Jewish citizenry of the annexed provinces, nationalism remained closely linked to a liberal vision of the state. Initial Jewish reactions to the annexation prove beyond a doubt that Jews indeed perceived France as the emancipator and protector of their civil rights, and for that reason they harbored very real fears about the institution of a less liberal German regime. To be sure, the civil status of Jews in Alsace-Lorraine turned out to be considerably better than elsewhere in the German empire, perhaps because of the greater bureaucratic fluidity in this newly conquered frontier region. The opportunity of Jews to rise to civil positions that were closed to them in other German states, together with the vigorous official suppression of antisemitism, earned the regime the gratitude of native and immigrant Jews alike. Nevertheless, at least until the Dreyfus Affair, Germany could not but compare unfavorably with France on the issue of Jewish civil rights. And although the antisemitic excesses of the Dreyfus Affair proved to be a shocking disillusionment to Jews, the subsequent victory of liberal and republican forces renewed the bond of sympathy between France and its former Jewish subjects. For Jews, therefore, the Nation represented far more than an abstract idea; it symbolized concrete and pragmatic advances that they had made in the realm of civil rights.[1]

The foundation of Jewish patriotism in a liberal faith highlights an important aspect of Jewish political behavior popularized by Hannah Arendt: the alliance of Jews with the state.* Although Jews

---

*Illustrating this firm faith in the state, Ludwig Philippson, editor of the *Allgemeine Zeitung des Judentums*, commented in 1854: "All in all, we Jews recognize with gratitude that among all elements of the modern age it is the State, and above all and in particular, the bureaucratic State, that has been and still is most openminded toward us, since in every period of storm and stress, the people rose up against us, and in every period of reaction it was the nobility and the upper bourgeoisie who did the same; thus, it is only the State, developing a steady pace, that

in Germany and Central Europe also looked to the central authorities as guardians against local antisemitism and guarantors of Jewish civil rights, the view of the state as the repository of liberal values seemed most natural in France, the first nation to have granted legal emancipation to the Jews. While Arendt, and more recently Michael Marrus, have condemned this trust in the state as Jewish political naïveté,[2] a strong case can be made that it evidenced, on the contrary, a considerable political sophistication in the case of the French Jews in general and the Alsace-Lorraine Jews in particular. It was the French government that had granted emancipation, despite an extensive ground swell of local anti-Jewish pressure. Furthermore, those rights, firmly embedded in the French legal tradition during the Revolution, successfully weathered every change of regime, and would continue to do so until the emergence of Vichy. Those same Jewish assimilationists who are condemned by Arendt and Marrus lobbied for the retention of Jewish emancipation in Alsace-Lorraine under German rule, actively participated in liberal and republican politics both within the Reichsland and in France, vigorously protested any infringement of Jewish rights earlier granted by France, and successfully demanded the suppression of all popular antisemitism. Jews in Alsace-Lorraine viewed their participation in liberal politics, not as an effacement of their Jewish identity, but as a means of reconciling their Jewish interests with their desire for acculturation. The late-nineteenth-century nation-state—including both France and Germany—never reached the level of disintegration that Arendt describes. For all these reasons, I maintain that it was political perspicacity, not naïveté or passivity, that propelled Alsace-Lorraine Jews to look to the central government of France, and later Germany, for protection.*

Paradoxically, the Jews' distinctively liberal brand of patriotism often isolated them politically from the majority of the population,

---

grants us tranquility, justice and freedom, and in it alone lie our hopes for the future." Cited in Rürup, "European Revolutions."

*Ismar Schorsch has recently put forward the argument for the political sagacity of assimilationist Jews, but locates this perspicacity in the points of conflict between the Jewish community and the state. I believe, as Arendt argues, that the commitment of Jews to political liberalism in post-emancipation Germany necessarily implied cooperation with the state, although Schorsch is right to point out that differences between Jews and the central government continued over specific points of policy. See Schorsch, *On the History*, passim.

despite initial hopes that patriotism would serve as an all-embracing and unifying issue. The case of Alsace-Lorraine suggests that only when there was a common antagonist, as in 1871 or 1914–18, could patriotism forge links across divergent political and confessional lines dividing the native population. At other times, class and confessional rivalries surfaced, preempting the national question.

There is only one way, in my view, to explain why patriotism failed to serve as a permanent unifying factor: the fact that nationalism had more than one face. As the splintering of the Catholic-Jewish alliance in the Reichsland during the Dreyfus Affair illustrates, liberal nationalism, so cherished by Jews and republicans, possessed an illiberal underside—integral nationalism—closely identified with the forces of the emerging radical Right. While Jews and liberals continued to define citizenship as legal membership in the state, political Catholics and the new French Right in general perceived citizenship within the far more constrictive boundaries of belonging to a particular cultural or even racial group.[3]

The particularity of their patriotism separated Jews in the Reichsland not only from political Catholics attracted to integral nationalism, but also from those Protestants who were beginning to envision some sort of autonomous status for Alsace and Lorraine after the turn of the century. Committed as they were to the state, Jews of the Reichsland found it as difficult to support autonomism as it was for their coreligionists in the multi-ethnic empires of Central Europe, where the issue was far more urgent.[4] Although autonomism became a major political force only after 1919, it had already recruited many followers in the years before the First World War.[5]

There is much to be learned about the nature of patriotism in these differences between Catholics, Protestants, and Jews in Alsace-Lorraine. Patriotism appears as an independent political factor only when an external political threat unites all groups in the population. At other times it is only one ingredient of a much larger *Weltanschauung* that encompasses a wide variety of civic values. For Jews, that vision embraced the liberal ideology of the French Revolution, which they associated with their emancipation. For political Catholics it meant a return to the traditional Christian social values of the ancien régime. Although the Protestants' world view resembled the Jews' in its essentially liberal character, they sought closer affiliations with Germany and advocated a greater degree of local autonomy than would have been possible under any French government.

In refusing to accept the distinction being made by the early twentieth century between a "patriotism" that equated the Nation and the State and a "nationalism" that increasingly connoted a *völkisch* or cultural conception of Nation highly antithetical to liberalism, Jews not just in Alsace-Lorraine, but in Western and Central Europe as a whole, became alienated from important currents in European politics. Indeed, as Hannah Arendt has argued, such political isolation often had dire consequences. Jews, who in the popular mind had become the most visible symbol of the democratic state, easily fell victim to every political faction challenging the state's legitimacy. Yet, apart from the Zionist solution proffered by Arendt and Marrus, it is difficult to see what alternatives were open to Jews who strongly believed in the viability of life in the diaspora.*

Although all Reichsland Jews shared to some extent a certain view of what patriotism was all about, this study clearly shows that the Jewish community was by no means the monolithic entity portrayed by the Franco-Jewish polemicists. As the analyses of option and emigration illustrate, it was above all the urban middle-class Jewish elite who most visibly manifested their pro-French sentiments immediately following the annexation. Not only did they emigrate to France in disproportionately high numbers in 1871–72, but they actively participated in pro-French organizations and worked to maintain French culture throughout the entire period of German sovereignty. Integrated into France both culturally and economically by 1870, it was natural that this class of the Jewish population should have felt most threatened by the transition to German rule. The rural masses of Jews, who were less assimilated to France culturally, linguistically, and economically, expressed their nationalistic sentiments primarily by antipathy to Germany, usually in the form of draft evasion, rather than by a positive preference for France. Statistics on Jewish emigration support the hypothesis that a strong correlation existed between acculturation, including the development of a sense of French national identity, and other aspects of socioeconomic integration.

*Arendt was committed to a Zionism in the tradition of the late-nineteenth-century French publicist and political activist Bernard Lazare, who envisioned Zionism less as a territorial solution for antisemitism than as the awakening of a new sense of Jewish peoplehood. She was hostile to Theodor Herzl's brand of political Zionism and eventually broke with the Zionist movement in the 1940's over the Arab question. See Sharon Muller, "Origins of Eichmann," pp. 245–50.

Further proof that the ideology of Patrie/Religion had indeed penetrated substantial segments of the Alsace-Lorraine Jewish population by 1871 was the persistence of social separateness, which tarnished the interaction between Old German Jewish immigrants to the Reichsland and the Old Alsatian Jewish population. Although relations between the two Jewish communities improved substantially following the Dreyfus Affair, as evidenced by increasing institutional cooperation, these new bonds proved insufficiently resilient to survive the political strains of the First World War. The often bitter patriotic polemics that entangled Alsace-Lorraine and German Jews were traceable to very tangible national rivalries, despite a shared religious, cultural, and linguistic heritage up to the time of the French Revolution. This same national divisiveness poisoned relations between Alsace-Lorraine Jews and the growing numbers of Eastern European immigrants, and ultimately resulted in communal fragmentation in the 1930's, just when cooperation between natives and immigrants became crucial.[6] It perhaps should come as no surprise that sizable numbers of Alsatian Jews were active participants in the chauvinistic, right-wing Franco-Jewish organizations in Paris that sprang up in the 1930's.[7]

Yet even with the very real national distinctions that had arisen among Jews, there was a remarkable similarity in the ideology and rhetoric of Jewish patriotism not only in Alsace-Lorraine, France, and Germany, but throughout Europe and even in the United States. Ironically, this patriotism, much more so than religion, came to constitute a new transnational Jewish identity, the identity of Jewish assimilationism, what Deborah Dash Moore has recently termed Jewish "civil religion."[8] The truth behind the frequently made observation that Jews are more German than the Germans or more French than the French grows out of the experience of emancipation. Regardless of country of residence, Jews throughout Western and Central Europe were confronted with similar pressures to prove themselves worthy of citizenship. Patriotism became the chief way in which they hoped to accomplish that task, and it provided the unifying link between the various denominations of Western and Central European Judaism.

Although the Holocaust delivered a shattering blow to the liberal variety of patriotism embraced by German Jews, and their coreligionists to the east as well, in France that ideology emerged relatively unscathed and persists today. Alternative political ideologies that have voiced greater skepticism about the alliance between Jews and the state, including Zionism, socialism, communism, and even democratic pluralism, have been advocated within the French Jewish community almost exclusively by immigrants, first from Eastern Europe and more recently from North Africa.

Although these ideologies have indeed begun to influence native Jews in the last several decades, as evidenced by their growing receptiveness to diaspora Zionism and to a more pluralistic vision of French society, both of which allow greater room for the articulation of Jewish political concerns, the amazing endurance of liberal nationalism among French Jews in general and Alsace-Lorraine Jews in particular begs for explanation. One important element is the strength of pro-French sentiments in family traditions, which kept alive the legacy of France even among a whole generation of Jews born and educated under German rule. Political developments, such as the French victory in the First World War, the French state's protection of Jewish civil rights until the fall of the Third Republic, the restitution of democratic government after Vichy, and possibly even the distinctions in policy that the Vichy government made between native and foreign Jews—all these may also have been important in the survival of liberal nationalism among native French Jews.[9]

Perhaps the most fundamental explanation can be found in the social fabric of France itself. Until the recent influx of North Africans and Blacks to France, Jews were the single most prominent ethnic minority in a society marked by an extremely high degree of homogeneity. Consequently, they were under far greater pressure to conform than they would have been in a land of immigrants like the United States. The rise of political antisemitism in the late nineteenth century, which ultimately exploded forth with renewed fury during the Holocaust, by no means alienated French Jews from the nation-state. Indeed, it often had the opposite effect, exacerbating the already heavy pressures on them to demonstrate even further their worthiness for membership in the body politic. One way of doing this was to reaffirm their faith in liberal nationalism, at a time—the 1930's—when many others in France were rapidly abandoning it in favor of alternatives on the extreme Left or Right. Nor was it at all unusual that many native French Jews should have eagerly desired to reclaim their liberal faith after the Second World War, when liberalism as a political ideology emerged reinvigorated among important sectors of the general population. It is therefore only against this extensive background of what we have termed the task of becoming citizens that we can begin to comprehend the centrality of patriotism not only in the ideology but also in the reality of the modern Jewish experience.

Reference Material

APPENDIX A

Option and Emigration, 1871-1872

For the data on Jewish option and emigration in 1871–72, I have drawn on the original dossiers and lists of optants in the departmental archives of Strasbourg, Colmar, and Metz. These dossiers include information on the declarant's age, gender, occupation, marital status, place of birth, current domicile, number of dependents involved, and their ages and places of birth, and occasionally the intended destination. The population consists of all the Jews who opted for French nationality from (1) every district in Bas-Rhin for which there are data on individual optants; (2) the list of optants from the district of Sarreguemines in Lorraine; and (3) the individual dossiers of optants from the city of Colmar and from three municipalities in the district of Altkirch in Haut-Rhin.[1] Data from these disparate sources are highly likely to represent characteristics shared by the Jewish optant group as a whole. Moreover, they also allow us to estimate the number of Jews who opted from particular localities, information that is important in determining the ratio of Jewish to non-Jewish optants. Since religion was not registered on the option declarations, onomastic criteria were used to determine which optants were Jewish. Obviously there is a degree of uncertainty in relying on this method since some patronyms in Alsace and Lorraine were shared by Jews and non-Jews. The population therefore ranges from a maximum number of possible Jewish optants (727) to a minimum number (517) whose Jewish identity is in little doubt.[2] The statistical calculations are based on the smaller number.

Two major qualifications should be made about these data. First, option and emigration are, strictly speaking, two distinct phenomena. Many Alsace-Lorrainers emigrated in 1871–72 without ever filing a declaration of option.[3] On the other hand, not everyone who filed a declaration of option actually emigrated, and many of those who did emigrate returned within a short time.[4] Consequently, many declarations of option were subsequently annulled by the German authorities. Nevertheless, option probably reflects real (in contrast to legal) emigration to a far greater extent than the number of annulled option declarations might indicate. The nullification of options frequently just signified that the head of household had failed to emigrate; it says nothing about family members. Officially, minors under 20 years of age could opt independently only if accompanied by a parent or legal guardian. Male minors, however, often had their parents file option declarations and then emigrated alone, hoping that eventually the German authorities would recognize their emigration as legal and not consider them draft evaders.[5] Although the German government did eventually publish the tallies of valid and invalid option declarations made in Alsace-Lorraine, it would be extremely difficult to trace the fate of individual Jewish optants to determine whether or not they actually emigrated.[6] Consequently, even though the data presented here accurately reflect option, they only imprecisely indicate the magnitude of emigration. It is possible, however, to work on the assumption of a correlation between option and emigration.

Another difficulty in studying option is that declarations were required not only from inhabitants who actually resided in the annexed provinces in 1871–72, but from all those born in Alsace-Lorraine, regardless of residence at the time of the annexation. Approximately 388,150 option declarations were thus filed from outside the annexed territories.[7] The overwhelming majority of these optants had left their native provinces long before 1871 and are not dealt with in this study.

APPENDIX B

Emigration, 1872-1914

The population of post-1872 Jewish emigrants was drawn from the dossiers of all Jewish men applying for emigration permits from the Bas-Rhin district of Haguenau between 1873 and 1898 (N = 316). To provide a basis for comparison, information was also collected on all non-Jewish applicants for emigration permits from the district (N = 1,259).[1] These dossiers contain data on age, place of birth, domicile, father's or son's occupation, religion,[2] civil status, total number of people involved, and usually intended destination. Frequently, the dossiers also contain letters indicating whether the applicant had relatives abroad as well as the declared motive for emigration. The stated motive cannot of course be taken at face value, particularly for youths who had reached the age of 17 and were required to register for the draft. Nevertheless, these letters afford valuable information on the cultural and economic backgrounds of the petitioners for *Entlassungsurkunde*, or emigration permits.

Haguenau was the only Bas-Rhin district for which I was able to locate a complete file of individual applications for emigration permits. Since it had a sizable Jewish population (2,748 people, or 3.9% of the district's total civil population of 69,975 in 1875), the availability of the data was fortuitous. Jews in this district were dispersed between both commercial and industrial urban centers, including the important cities of Haguenau (with a 6.2% Jewish minority in 1875) and Bischwiller (with a 2.4% Jewish minority in 1875), as well as a number of rural villages. It was therefore a district that in many ways was highly representative of late 19th-century Alsatian Jewry in general, although the 35.6% decline in its Jewish population between 1871 and 1910 was slightly less than the 42.1% decline for the Jewish population of Bas-Rhin as a whole.

It is important to point out that the actual number of emigrants was probably higher than this data set indicates. According to the German law of nationality, introduced into the Reichsland on January 28, 1873, only men who had either (1) already completed their military service or (2) not yet reached the age of 17 and been legally emancipated by their parents were eligible to apply for *Entlassungsurkunde*. (Women did not require permits to emigrate.) To validate an *Entlassungsurkunde*, the applicant had to depart within six months of the date it was issued. Otherwise, the permit was rescinded. A boy whose permit was rescinded was reinscribed on the list of men eligible for conscription on reaching the age of 20. Those who validated their permits could not return to the Reichsland until they had turned 31. The government granted males between 17 and 25 years of age emigration permits only under exceptional circumstances.[3]

On the other hand, these dossiers probably reflect real (in contrast to legal) emigration far more accurately than other statistics compiled by the German authorities since they include all applications for *Entlassungsurkunde*, regardless of whether the government finally accepted the petitions. Men whose applications for *Entlassungsurkunde* were rejected frequently emigrated anyway. They were then considered draft evaders and were subject to criminal penalties and expulsions on returning to the Reichsland. This illegal emigration reached considerable proportions. François Roth estimates that only one of six emigrés left Lorraine legally.[4] The group under study here, therefore, represents an important contingent of all male emigrants, legal and illegal.

Notes

For full authors' names, titles, and publication data on the works cited in short form in these Notes, see the Bibliography, pp. 248–69. Except where otherwise indicated, governmental officials and institutions cited in the correspondence are from Alsace-Lorraine. The following abbreviations are used in the Notes:

ADBR	Archives Départementales du Bas-Rhin
ADHR	Archives Départementales du Haut-Rhin
ADM	Archives Départementales de la Moselle
AE	Archives du Ministère des Affaires Étrangères
AI	*Archives israélites*
AMS	Archives Municipales de Strasbourg
AZJ	*Allgemeine Zeitung des Judentums*
CBR	Archives du Consistoire du Bas-Rhin
CC	Archives du Consistoire Central
CP	Archives du Consistoire de Paris
LBIYB	*Leo Baeck Institute Yearbook*
RI	*Revue israélite*
SIW	*Strassburger Israelitische Wochenschrift*
UI	*Univers israélite*

BOOK EPIGRAPH: M. Bloch, *Vertus*, p. 14.

CHAPTER ONE

1. Katz, *Out of the Ghetto*, p. 1.
2. On the inseparability of the religious and national components of medieval Judaism see Baron, "Newer Approaches"; and Baron, *Modern Nationalism*, pp. 213–21. On the medieval Jewish community, see Baron, *Jewish Community*, vols. 3 and 4; Ben-Sasson, pp. 385–723; and Katz, *Exclusiveness*.

3. Katz, *Out of the Ghetto*, pp. 9-27. Although this threat receded by the early modern period, several major Jewish communities, including those of Hamburg and Vienna, experienced expulsions as late as the second half of the 17th century.
4. Ibid., pp. 5-6; Baron, *Modern Nationalism*, p. 216.
5. Baron, "Newer Approaches," p. 65; Baron, "Ghetto." On the Jewish community during the centuries of transition from the Middle Ages to the modern period see Katz, *Tradition*; Katz, *Out of the Ghetto*, chaps. 2, 3; and Hertzberg, *French Enlightenment*.
6. National Assembly, Dec. 23, 1789, in *Réimpression de l'Ancien-Moniteur ("Gazette nationale" ou le "Moniteur universel")*, vol. 2. (Paris, 1859), p. 456. See also Hertzberg, *French Enlightenment*, pp. 360-61.
7. Baron, *Modern Nationalism*, p. 217.
8. Dohm, pp. 75-80. See also Katz, *Out of the Ghetto*, pp. 57-64.
9. Grégoire, pp. 100, 109.
10. Cited in Katz, *Out of the Ghetto*, p. 91. I have slightly rephrased Katz's translation.
11. Mendelssohn, p. 90.
12. Cited in Katz, *Out of the Ghetto*, p. 92.
13. Grégoire, pp. 83-85, 99, 111-12.
14. Katz, *Out of the Ghetto*, pp. 99-100.
15. On the expectations of the Enlightenment, see Hertzberg, *French Enlightenment*, chaps. 8-10. On the implicitly contractual nature of the emancipation, see Baron, *Modern Nationalism*, pp. 219-20; and Baron, "Newer Approaches."
16. Hertzberg, *French Enlightenment*, chap. 10.
17. For an excellent analysis of these two paths toward emancipation and their relationship to socioeconomic conditions within various countries, see Rürup, "Jewish Emancipation." On emancipation in Germany see the works by Schmidt, Kohler, and Herbert Strauss.
18. Tama, pp. 11, 24, 72; Maslin, p. 9.
19. On the "Infamous Decree," see Maslin, pp. 26ff. The provision prohibiting Jews from buying military replacements was lifted in 1812. On Napoleon and the Jews in general, see Robert Anchel, *Napoléon et les juifs* (Paris, 1928); Baruch Mevorach, *Napoleon and His Era* (in Hebrew; Jerusalem, 1968); François Pietri, *Napoléon et les israélites* (Paris, 1965); Simon Schwarzfuchs, *Napoleon, the Jews and the Sanhedrin* (London, 1979); Bernhard Blumenkranz and Albert Soboul, eds., *Le Grand Sanhedrin de Napoléon* (Paris, 1979); L'Huillier, *Recherches*, pp. 519-49; André Neher, "Bourgeoisie," p. 437; "Alsace," in *Encyclopedia Judaica*, 1972 ed.; and "L'Antisémitisme dans le département du Bas-Rhin au temps de Napoléon," *Tribune juive*, suppl. to no. 230, Nov. 24, 1972.

20. Patrick Girard, p. 61; Albert, *Modernization*, pp. 61, 152; Helfand, "French Jewry," pp. 84–86, 228–31.

21. On Geiger, see Wiener. On the question of messianism in the German Reform movement, see Philipson, especially pp. 246–55. On Hirsch, see his *Nineteen Letters of Ben Uziel*; and Liberles, especially pp. 113–230. On ethical monotheism as an aspect of the Wissenschaft des Judentums (Science of Judaism) movement, see also Immanuel Wolf, "On the Concept of a Science of Judaism," LBIYB, 2 (1957): 194–204; Heinrich Graetz, *History of the Jews*, vol. 5 (Philadelphia, 1946), pp. 705–31; Ismar Schorsch, Introduction to Heinrich Graetz, *The Structure of Judaism and Other Essays* (New York, 1975); and Meyer, pp. 144–82.

22. Philipson, p. 254.

23. Rabbi Lazare Isidore (1814–88), cited in Patrick Girard, p. 146. On the reinterpretation of Jewish messianism in France, see also Helfand, "French Jewry," pp. 303–4. For discussions of Franco-Judaism, see Marrus, pp. 85–121; Hyman, "Joseph Salvador"; and Patrick Girard, pp. 138–53.

24. Rabbi David Berman, "Juifs de France," UI, April 5, 1935, pp. 470–71; J.-H. Dreyfuss, p. 357.

25. Patrick Girard, pp. 140–42, 249.

26. Cited in Wiener, pp. 88–90.

27. Cited in ibid., p. 71.

28. On German-Jewish self-defense activities, see Schorsch, *Jewish Reactions*; Lamberti; and Sanford Ragins, *Jewish Responses to Anti-Semitism in Germany, 1870–1914: A Study in the History of Ideas* (Cincinnati, 1980). On the attitude of French Jews prior to and during the Dreyfus Affair, see Marrus; and Wilson, pp. 692–730. On their position in the 20th century, see Hyman, *From Dreyfus*, especially chaps. 1, 2, 8.

29. For this theory, see especially Arendt; and Marrus.

30. On the Reform movement in Germany, see Philipson; and Plaut. On France, see the three works by Albert: *Modernization*, especially chaps. 7, 9, 10; "Rôle des consistoires"; and "Non-Orthodox Attitudes." On the Reform movement that arose in Metz, see Plaut, pp. 44–47, 104–6; AI, 2 (1841): 468–70, 531–35; and Contamine, 1:45–46; 2:355.

31. Bauer; Albert, *Modernization*, chap. 9.

32. Treschan, pp. 75–79; M. Bloch, *Oeuvre*, pp. 6–9. On Germany, see Kober.

33. Chouraqui; Joan Gardner Roland, "The Alliance Israélite Universelle and French Foreign Policy in North Africa, 1860–1918," Ph.D. dissertation, Columbia University, 1965. On the Alliance's refusal to protest antisemitism in France, see Marrus, pp. 140–41.

34. See Szajkowski, "Growth," p. 304; Albert, *Modernization*, p. 19.

35. On the 18th-century Alsatian Jewish community, see Hertzberg,

French Enlightenment; and Szajkowski, *Jews*, pp. 151-219, 297-335. On Reubell and antisemitism during the French Revolution, see Hertzberg, *French Enlightenment*, pp. 354-68; Szajkowski, "Anti-Jewish Riots During the Revolutions"; Szajkowski, *Jews*, pp. 336-57; and R. Marx, "Opinion."

36. Cited in Hertzberg, *French Enlightenment*, p. 355.

37. Ibid., pp. 179-87, 314-68. For a history of the Sephardim during this era, see Frances Malino, *The Sephardic Jews of Bordeaux: Assimilation and Emancipation in Revolutionary and Napoleonic France* (University, Ala., 1978).

38. Cited in Ben Ammi, "Un Siècle de judaïsme alsacien," UI, March 6, 1908, pp. 76-77.

39. M. Bloch, *Oeuvre*, p. 3.

40. Albert, *Modernization*, p. 143.

41. M. Bloch, *Oeuvre*, pp. 6-7; M. Bloch, *Alsace*, pp. 8-9. On the battle against Alsatian Yiddish, see Treschan, pp. 77-78; and P. Lévy, "Parler."

42. Michel Lévy, passim.

43. Lowenstein, "Pace"; Toury, "Deutsche Juden"; Richarz, *Jüdisches Leben*, pp. 19-63; Rürup, "European Revolutions," pp. 13-15; Albert, *Modernization*, p. vii; Hyman, "Migration."

44. Katz, *Out of the Ghetto*, pp. 176-90; Kuznets, "Economic Structure"; Cohen, *Promotion*, 1:37, 2:373; R. Marx, "Régénération." On the problem of apprentices, see Cahnman, pp. 112-13.

45. D. Cohen, *Promotion*, 2:381; Cahnman, pp. 116-17.

46. Hyman, "Migration"; Raphael and Weyl, *Juifs en Alsace*, p. 369; Bensimon-Donath, p. 360; D. Cohen, *Promotion*, 2:373-74; André Neher, "Bourgeoisie."

47. Contamine, 1:45-46; Delpech, pp. 312-13; Roth, *Lorraine*, p. 413; André Neher, "Bourgeoisie," p. 435; Szajkowski, "Growth," pp. 306-7; Raphael and Weyl, *Juifs en Alsace*, pp. 372-73.

48. A. Weil, *Sittengemälde*, 2:209.

49. Julien Weill, p. 4.

50. Szajkowski, "Growth," pp. 306-7; Delpech, p. 312; *Das Jüdische Blatt*, June 8, 1911, p. 3.

51. P. Lévy, "Parler," pp. 274-75; P. Lévy, *Histoire*, 2:260; P. Lévy, "Ecoles."

52. Posener, "Immediate Effects," p. 310. On the Guizot law and Jewish schools, see Joseph Bloch, *Historique*, pp. 37-38; and Raphael and Weyl, *Juifs en Alsace*, p. 354.

53. P. Lévy, *Histoire*, 2:91.

54. Riegert, *Quelques idées sur l'usure des juifs dans les départements du Haut- et du Bas-Rhin* (Paris, 1918), p. 205.

55. AI, 9 (1848):553-54, cited in Helfand, "French Jewry," p. 126.

56. Stauben, pp. 112-13, 225.

57. Stenne, p. 28. See also Scheid, p. 24. Scheid (1841-1922) was an administrator and historian of Alsatian Jews. He was born in Haguenau and served on that city's municipal council prior to the annexation. In 1883 he left Alsace for Palestine to work as an inspector for Baron Edmond de Rothschild's settlement project, a post he held until 1899. The portions of his memoirs dealing with the transition from French to German rule provide an interesting first-hand account.
58. On the use of German in Alsace-Lorraine during the French period, see P. Lévy, *Histoire*, 2:80-134.
59. "Testament Isaac Auscher," ADBR, D 240-197 (39.10).
60. Julien Weill, p. 3.
61. Stenne, p. 83.
62. I. Lévy, *Isaïe*, pp. 109, 139.
63. J.-J. Wahl, p. 91. On the more conservative nature of 19th-century French Judaism generally, see Helfand, "Symbiotic Relationship."
64. Albert, *Modernization*, pp. 171, 254-55, 295-96, 301-2; Helfand, "French Jewry," pp. 181-82, 190-91. On the rift between traditionalist and reformist Jews generally, see Albert, *Modernization*, pp. 50-55, 66-68, 197-98, 298-99, 314; Szajkowski, *Jews*, pp. 1058-75; and Helfand, "French Jewry," pp. 94-97, 153-95.
65. Cited in M. Liber, "Napoléon Ier et les juifs: La Question juive devant le conseil d'état en 1806," *Revue des études juives*, 71 (1920): 130.
66. Cited in D. Cohen, *Promotion*, 1:3-4.
67. Eugène Coquebert de Monbret, *Notice sur l'état des israélites en France* (Paris, 1821), p. 81, cited in Raphael and Weyl, *Juifs en Alsace*, p. 383.
68. Erckmann-Chatrian, pp. 2-4, 314-15. See also Raphael, "Présence," pp. 138-40.
69. I. Lévy, *Isaïe*, pp. 74-75.
70. Raphael, "Juifs d'Alsace," p. 139. Elie Scheid, in his memoirs, similarly mentions his joy on being exempted from military service in the 1860's.
71. On attitudes toward intermarriage, see Raphael and Weyl, *Juifs en Alsace*, p. 411; and Bailly. On conversion, see Raphael and Weyl, *Juifs en Alsace*, p. 411; Patrick Girard, p. 156; Treschan, pp. 155-56; and Schwarzfuchs, *Juifs*, pp. 245-46.
72. Cited in D. Cohen, "Image," pp. 72-74.
73. Cited in ibid., p. 73. See also Contamine, 2:352-53.
74. D. Cohen, *Promotion*, 1:37; M. Bloch, *Alsace*, pp. 21-22; Patrick Girard, pp. 164-65; Anchel, *Review*.
75. Mossmann, pp. 261-62. See also Spach.
76. Contamine, 1:46. See also Albert, *Modernization*, p. 38; and Patrick Girard, p. 252.

77. All cited in D. Cohen, "Image," p. 75. See also Contamine, 2:352-53.

78. On the antisemitic riots of 1848 in Alsace, see Szajkowski, "Anti-Jewish Riots During the Revolutions"; Szajkowski, "Anti-Jewish Riots in Alsace"; Ginsburger, "Troubles"; Delpech, pp. 319-22; Albert, *Modernization*, pp. 159-60; Eduard Stadtler, "Die Judenkrawalle von 1848 im Elsass," in *Elsässische Monatschrift für Geschichte und Volkskunde*, 2 (1911):673-86; Paul Muller, *La Révolution de 1848 en Alsace* (Paris, 1912), pp. 28, 31; D. Cohen, *Promotion*, 1:44; Raphael and Weyl, *Juifs en Alsace*, pp. 373-74; Gehler, pp. 27-28; Kiechel, "Documents"; and Jacob Toury, *Turmoil and Confusion in the Revolution of 1848: The Anti-Jewish Riots in the "Year of Freedom" and Their Influence on Modern Antisemitism* (in Hebrew; Tel Aviv, 1968).

79. Cahnman, p. 108. See also Raphael and Weyl, *Juifs en Alsace*, pp. 386, 419.

80. On the village economy in Alsace, see Uhry, 1:1, 41. On the persistence of a regional versus a national economy in France until the last quarter of the 19th century, see E. Weber, *Peasants*.

81. Roth, *Lorraine*, p. 46.

82. "Un Couple bien assorti," pp. 89-90, in Albert Neher.

83. On German Jewish immigration into Alsace and Lorraine during the early 19th century, see Leuilliot, *Alsace*, 3:233-35; and Posener, "Immigration."

84. See Halff, *Fidélité*; Halff, "Jews"; Delahache, *Juifs*; and Raphael and Weyl, "Juifs d'Alsace." For a collection of primary sources on Alsace-Lorraine's central role in the development of French nationalism, see Girardet, pp. 37-84.

85. Zeldin, 2:3-28, discusses the necessity of distinguishing between the rhetoric and the reality of nationalism in France and argues that French nationalism was a multifaceted phenomenon that developed at an uneven pace among diverse sectors of the population.

86. See especially Silverman, *Reluctant Union*.

87. Ibid.; Schoenbaum.

CHAPTER TWO

1. A. Wahl, *Option*, pp. 50-51; A. Wahl, *Confession*, 2:905-16, 930-49.

2. Population statistics are based on Statistischen Bureau, *Statistische Mitteilungen (vom. 1. Dez. 1871)*. On Catholic as well as Protestant opposition to the central government's policy of imposing the French language in the schools and churches, see Craig, "Mission," pp. 23, 32-33, 100; Craig, *Scholarship*, pp. 25-28. P. Lévy, *Histoire*, 2:37, 106, 161-63; Igersheim,

"Politique," pp. 249-50; Georges Weill, pp. 116-17; and Rossé et al., 3:47-52, 359, 395.

3. Lichtenberger, pp. 3, 31-33; AI, June 15, 1873, p. 365.

4. See n. 1 above.

5. Roth, *Lorraine*, pp. 142, 664; A. Wahl, *Confession*, 2:905-16, 935; Rossé et al., 3:355, 357; *Journal des débats*, Dec. 25, 1875; Fleurent, p. 332; L'Huillier, "En guise," p. 381; Bezirkspräsident, Bas-Rhin, administrative reports, May 1, 1872, May 6, 1874, ADBR, AL 71 277.

6. Silverman, *Reluctant Union*, p. 23; Hartmut Dieter Soell, "La Question nationale et les débuts du mouvement ouvrier en Alsace pendant les vingt premières années de l'annexion allemande (1871-1890)," in *Artisans et Ouvriers d'Alsace*, vol. 9 (1965), p. 395; *Journal des débats*, Dec. 25, 1875.

7. *Journal des débats*, Dec. 25, 1875.

8. *Siècle*, Jan. 14, 1871, cited in UI, Feb. 15, 1871, p. 234. Several years later *The Times* carried an article on Jewish patriotism in Alsace, which was duly reported in the *Archives israélites* (Oct. 15, 1874, p. 614): "Likewise the Jews attest to a profound aversion for German domination. A sentiment of gratitude . . . closely binds them to France. Since 1871, they have rivaled Catholics and Protestants in manifesting their repugnance for German domination."

9. See *République française*, Feb. 26, 1872; UI, Sept. 15, 1871, pp. 43-50, March 15, 1872, pp. 169-172; and AI, Dec. 15, 1871, pp. 464-65.

10. Police director, Strasbourg, supplemental report, Aug. 14, 1871, ADBR, AL 71 277.

11. RI, June 23, 1871, p. 489.

12. Asch, entry for Sept. 29, 1870, p. 21.

13. Cited in UI, Feb. 15, 1872, pp. 359-60.

14. Cited in AZJ, Sept. 26, 1871, p. 781; RI, Oct. 6, 1871, p. 734.

15. *Courrier du Bas-Rhin*, March 5, 1872.

16. UI, April 1, 1872, p. 457.

17. Cited in AZJ, Sept. 26, 1871, p. 781.

18. RI, June 23, 1871, p. 489.

19. *Procès-verbal de la séance tenue à la mairie de Colmar le 24 mars 1871 (pour délibérer sur les mesures à prendre en vue de sauvegarder les intérêts alsaciens au point de vue des conséquences de l'annexion* (Strasbourg, 1871), pp. 5-6. Also cited in Igersheim, "Politique," p. 256.

20. AZJ, June 20, 1871, p. 498.

21. Cahun, p. 92.

22. Lipman to Baron Baude, March 3, 1871, cited in A. Lipman, pp. 42-43; minutes, Lorraine Consistory, March 1871, ADM, 17 J 41.

23. Minutes, Central Consistory, March 6, 1871, CC, 1 B 5, pp. 453-58.

24. RI, June 23, 1871, p. 491.

25. "Was hatten die Juden in Elsass und Deutsch-Lothringen zu tun?," AZJ, April 4, 1871, p. 272.
26. "Bamberger, Edouard," in *Dictionnaire de biographie française*; Salomon, pp. 223–34 passim; Halff, *Fidélité*, pp. 1–2; *La Guerre*, pp. 103–4.
27. Hiegel, "Protestations." See also Hiegel, "Option," 74:109; and *Journal d'Alsace*, Aug. 26, 1880, p. 3.
28. For Weill's biography, see "Alexandre Weill," UI, April 28, 1899, pp. 184–86; Blumenkranz, p. 329; and M. Bloch, *Alexandre Weill*, pp. 2–3. On Weill as a cultural intermediary between France and Germany, see especially his *Briefe*.
29. A. Weill, *Ma jeunesse*, 1:22–23; A. Weill, *Briefe*, p. 227.
30. A. Weill, *Briefe*, p. 217; M. Bloch, *Alexandre Weill*, p. 1.
31. A. Weill, *Lettres d'amour*, "note explicative." See also A. Weill, *Lettres de vengeance*, pp. 8–9, 47, 62.
32. A. Weill, *Lettres d'amour*, p. 193.
33. A. Weill, *Lettres de vengeance*, pp. 4, 62; A. Weill, *Epopée*, p. 87; A. Weill, *Rimes*, pp. 58–59.
34. A. Weill, *Lettres de vengeance*, pp. 30–31; A. Weill, *Epopée*, pp. 7–8.
35. A. Weill, *Lettres de vengeance*, pp. 48–49.
36. A. Weill, *Epopée*, pp. 7–8. In *Rimes*, p. 4, Weill offers another verse in the same vein: "Alsaciens, nous étions toujours un peuple libre. / Nous buvions notre vin et plantions notre bière. / Nos villes étaient des villes francs. / A la France nous sommes attachés comme des bardanes / Nous parlons allemand quand cela nous plaît, / Mais jamais Moltke ne sera notre héros! / Tous les cieux tomberont plutôt sur la terre / Que de nous voir devenir Prussiens!" (We Alsatians have always been a free people. / We drink our own wine and make our own beer / Our towns were free cities / We are attached to France like cockleburs / We speak German when we wish / But Moltke will never be our hero! / The heavens would sooner crash down to earth / Than see us become Prussians!)
37. See especially A. Weill's *Rimes*, passim, *Lettres de vengeance*, pp. 32, 37–39, 50–51, 62, and *Briefe*, p. 227.
38. Cahun, pp. 31–32.
39. Ibid., pp. 92–93. See also Meiss, *Choses*, passim.
40. For Isaac Lévy's biography, see "Un Patriote alsacien: Le Grand Rabbin Isaac Lévy," UI, Sept. 22, 1916, pp. 693–94; and *La Guerre*, pp. 108–10.
41. I. Lévy, "Allocution prononcée au Temple de Metz," June 9, 1871, in his *Alsatiana*, pp. 31–32. See also "Exorde d'un sermon—prononcé la veille de Kipour (Kol Nidre) 1871, au Temple de Colmar," in ibid., pp. 14–15.
42. I. Lévy, "Passé," p. 180; I. Lévy, *Adieu*, p. 7. This sermon can also be found in Girardet, pp. 38–41.

43. I. Lévy, "Allocution prononcée au Temple de Metz," Sept. 7, 1871, in his *Alsatiana*, pp. 27–28.
44. AI, June 1, 1875, p. 342; I. Lévy, "Passé," p. 181; I. Lévy, *Nathan*, pp. 14, 44–51.
45. I. Lévy, "Passé," p. 184. See also his *Alsatiana*, pp. 15, 21–22, 31, 62–63, "Sermon, Belfort," p. 194, and *Adieu*, p. 9.
46. I. Lévy, *Adieu*, p. 8. On Benjamin Lipman's refusal to take the loyalty oath, see Lipman, *Un Grand Rabbin*, pp. 19, 45.
47. I. Lévy, *Adieu*; UI, Sept. 30, 1873, p. 88; RI, June 7, 1872, p. 392. On the fervent French patriotism of another Alsatian rabbi, see J.-H. Dreyfuss.
48. "Juden im Elsass." On the reaction of the German press in general to the annexation, see Mitchell, *Bismarck*, pp. 55–72.
49. "An unsere Glaubensgenossen im Elsass und Deutsch Lothringen," AZJ, March 14, 1871, pp. 209–11. All citations are from this article. On Philippson's chauvinism, see Stern, p. 473.
50. AI, Oct. 15, 1871, p. 332, April–June, 1871, p. 92.
51. *La Presse israélite*, April 5, 1871, p. 52.
52. Italics in the original. UI, April 1, 1871, p. 296.
53. *La Presse israélite*, April 5, 1871, p. 53.
54. UI, April 1, 1871, p. 295.
55. See, for example, AZJ, Oct. 10, 1871, pp. 843–44, Oct. 31, 1871, p. 883, June 16, 1885, p. 402; and AI, Nov. 15, 1871, pp. 403–4, Aug. 15, 1872, p. 483, Nov. 15, 1875, p. 678.
56. *La Presse israélite*, April 5, 1871, p. 51.
57. AI, Oct. 15, 1871, p. 333.
58. AZJ, Oct. 10, 1871, p. 843.
59. "Die Israeliten im Elsass," *Strassburger Zeitung*, Sept. 30, 1871, p. 2.
60. *Strassburger Zeitung*, Sept. 14, 1871. Portions of this article are translated into French in RI, Sept. 22, 1871, p. 691. They are also summarized in AI, Oct. 15, 1871, pp. 333–34.
61. AI, Nov. 1, 1871, p. 364, Dec. 12, 1918, p. 197; Netter, *Vingt siècles*, p. 450.
62. *Courrier du Bas-Rhin*, July 26, 1872; UI, July 1, 1885, pp. 627–30; Netter, *Vingt siècles*, p. 451.
63. *Courrier du Bas-Rhin*, Sept. 2, 1872; Netter, *Vingt siècles*, p. 450.
64. RI, Oct. 27, 1871, p. 780.

CHAPTER THREE

1. Halff, *Fidélité*, passim; for a slightly revised English translation of this article, see Halff, "Jews." See also Delahache, *Juifs*; Isidore Cahen, "Les exilés volontaires," in AI, 1872, pp. 332–38, 439–40, 722–24, 754–56; AI, June 15, 1874, p. 358; and UI, Feb. 15, 1901, pp. 692–94.

2. Emile Cahen, pp. 8-9, 14-15.
3. Szajkowski, "Growth," pp. 308-9. See also Szajkowski, "Some Facts," p. 314.
4. Raphael, "Stéréotype," pp. 146-47.
5. Wallerstein, "Die jüdische Bevölkerung." For a discussion of the debate between French and German patriots in general, see A. Wahl, *Option*, pp. 9-10, 191; and Barry, p. 134. The French point of view is specifically expressed in Delahache, *L'Exode*; and Eccard. For the German perspective, see Kloss, "Auswanderung"; and Kloss, "Die Elsass-Lothringer."
6. On pre-1870 Jewish migration from Alsace-Lorraine to other places in France, see Szajkowski, "Growth," pp. 304, 306; Szajkowski, *Poverty*, p. 31; Bensimon-Donath, p. 98, 106; P. Lévy, *Langue*, 1:13; D. Cohen, *Promotion*, 1:90-92; Roth, *Lorraine*, p. 108; Roblin, p. 53; and Patrick Girard, pp. 104-12. On pre-1870 Jewish emigration to the United States, see D. Cohen, *Promotion*, pp. 100-104; Roth, *Lorraine*, pp. 112-13; Szajkowski, "Some Facts," pp. 312-14; and Albert, *Modernization*, p. 34.
7. Szajkowski, "Growth," p. 304; Albert, *Modernization*, p. 19. According to Szajkowski, Alsace-Lorraine Jewry constituted 62.2% of all French Jewry in 1861 and 56.9% in 1866. Albert claims they constituted 56.5% in 1861. Neither author presents the raw figures.
8. Delahache, *Juifs*, pp. 17-18; AI, April 1, 1872, p. 210.
9. Bensimon-Donath, pp. 117-18.
10. On antisemitism as a stimulus to emigration, see "Zur Geschichte der Juden im Sundgau," *Annuaire de la Société d'Histoire Sundgovienne*, 1960, p. 48; Roblin, p. 52.
11. Hvidt, p. 8. On this subject, see also ibid., pp. 6-7, 31, 199-200; Köllman; and Thomas, pp. 88, 166-69. For the Jewish perspective, see Kuznets, "Immigration," pp. 85-86, 88, 121; Hersch, pp. 428-29; and Lestschinsky, pp. 1207-8, 1213.
12. Hvidt, p. 200; Lestchinsky, p. 1213; Peterson.
13. Schnurmann, p. 9; D. Cohen, *Promotion*, 1:100-105; Weinberg, p. 2.
14. D. Cohen, *Promotion*, 1:100-105; Patrick Girard, p. 104. This organization never took any action, however.
15. Kuznets, "Immigration," p. 83. See also Peterson, p. 53; and Lestschinsky, p. 1207.
16. George, pp. 39-42; Kuznets, "Immigration," pp. 93, 99, 122.
17. The best statistical survey of option and emigration in the general population is A. Wahl, *Option*. See also statistics amassed by the German authorities, ADBR, AL 69 604, and AL D 34 paq. 1. For local studies, see A. Wahl, "Metz," and Hiegel, "Option."
18. For press reports making this claim, see UI, Aug. 1, 1872, p. 266; and AI, Aug. 25, 1910, p. 266, Nov. 21, 1918, p. 185. Historians who make

this assertion include André Neher, "Présentation," p. 5; Szajkowski, "Growth," pp. 179-96, 297-315; and Halff, *Fidélité*, passim.

19. A. Wahl, *Option*, pp. 76-77, 214; Barry, p. 140; François Dreyfus, p. 9.

20. A. Wahl, *Option*, p. 214; A. Wahl, *Confession*, 2:910-11; François Dreyfus, p. 9.

21. On Lévy's option, see AI, Nov. 1, 1871, p. 364; UI, Sept. 30, 1873, p. 88; and RI, June 7, 1872, p. 392. On Lipman's option, see Netter, *Vingt siècles*, pp. 445, 448-49; and Lipman, pp. ix, 19, 45. For I. Lévy's farewell address, see his *Adieu à l'Alsace, Le Passé et le présent*, pp. 173-86, and *Alsatiana*. On Lipman's farewell address, see Lipman, pp. 77-78; and Netter, *Vingt siècles*, pp. 448-49.

22. *La Guerre*, p. 107. On Isidore's patriotism, see UI, March 1, 1872, p. 389. In the same vein, see also the speech by the Alsatian rabbi J.-H. Dreyfuss, "Allocution prononcée à la cérémonie commémorative de la bataille de Sedan, 1 septembre, 1872," in *Sermons de guerre*, p. 9.

23. AE 88[II], cited in A. Wahl, *Option*, p. 112.

24. Kreisdirector, Molsheim, to Bezirkspräsident, Bas-Rhin, supplemental report, Aug. 22, 1872, ADBR, AL 71 277; A. Wahl, *Option*, p. 78.

25. *Courrier du Bas-Rhin*, Oct. 1, 1872.

26. In an antisemitic vein the paper added that those Jews who left "purchased everything possible from their neighbors—the baker, the cobbler, the butcher—on credit, but never gave a thought to paying for anything." Cited in *Strassburger Tageblatt*, Oct. 1, 1872.

27. Hiegel, "Option," 74:109, states that only 15 Jews opted from the district of Sarreguemines, but I count at least 27.

28. On the Ligue d'Alsace in general, see Eccard, pp. 58-76; Silverman, *Reluctant Union*, pp. 68, 172-75; and Reuss, p. 377. On the League's pro-option propaganda, see Silverman, *Reluctant Union*, p. 68; and A. Wahl, *Option*, p. 131.

29. A. Wahl, *Option*, pp. 115, 118-19. Solomon Herzog's option declaration can be found in ADBR, D 384, paq. 30.

30. AI, Dec. 1, 1873, p. 714.

31. Szajkowski, "Growth," pp. 308-9; Albert, *Modernization*, p. 406, n. 10. The total number of Jewish optants and emigrants from the annexed provinces is unknown; there are discrete data on option only for some districts. See Appendix A.

32. AI, Aug. 30, 1872, p. 553, Oct. 1, 1873, p. 162, Dec. 1, 1873, p. 714.

33. Statistischen Bureau, *Statistische Mitteilungen, 1871, 1875*; Szajkowski, "Growth," p. 308. Szajkowski's calculations for 1875 are slightly inaccurate. This trend was true for non-Jews as well. See A. Wahl, *Option*, p. 158.

34. Bensimon-Donath, p. 100. On the variability of gender selectivity in emigration, see Thomas, pp. 68, 163; and Hvidt, pp. 81-89.

35. Hvidt, pp. 71-72. See also Szajkowski, "Growth," p. 308.

36. On the desire to evade German military service in general, see extract from *La Liberté*, Nov. 21, 1871, in ADBR, AL 69 604; Hiegel, "Option," 74:94; Roth, *Lorraine*, p. 96; D'Elstein, p. 93; Silverman, *Reluctant Union*, p. 68; Barry, pp. 139-40; A. Wahl, *Option*, pp. 55, 112, 159, 182-84; and Bezirkspräsident, Bas-Rhin, to Oberpräsident, Alsace-Lorraine, administrative report, Aug. 31, 1872, ADBR, AL 71 277. On draft evasion as a stimulant to emigration from another annexed German territory, Schleswig-Holstein, see Hvidt, pp. 17, 138-40.

37. Florent-Matter, p. 45; Hiegel, "Option," 74:107.

38. Delahache, *Alsace-Lorraine*, p. 123.

39. Florent-Matter, p. 45. Of these, 795 were exempted for previously having served in the French army.

40. A. Wahl, *Option*, p. 45.

41. *Courrier du Bas-Rhin*, Aug. 17, Sept. 1, 1872.

42. AE 88[II], "Option de nationalité, lettres."

43. On draft evasion in Alsace-Lorraine during the French period, see Reuss, p. 392; A. Wahl, *Option*, pp. 78-79, 191; *Courrier du Bas-Rhin*, Sept. 6, 1872; and Raphael and Weyl, *Regards*, pp. 235-41.

44. On the new conscription laws in France following the Franco-Prussian War, see Ralston, pp. 139-40; Thomson, pp. 147-48, 152, n. 2; and Mitchell, *Victors*, pp. 15-48. On Alsace-Lorrainers in general who joined the French army in 1871-72, see Bezirkspräsident, Bas-Rhin, to Oberpräsident, Alsace-Lorraine, administrative report, Aug. 3, 1872, ADBR, AL 71 277. On the Foreign Legion, see *L'Alsace française*, 19 (1930):125; and Silverman, *Reluctant Union*, p. 71. On Alsace-Lorraine Jews who entered the French army, see "Alsace," in *Encyclopedia Judaica*, 1972 ed., p. 755.

45. D. Cohen, *Promotion*, 2:415.

46. Uhry, 1:7-8.

47. "Zur Erinnerung an den Krieg von 1870/71," *Das Jüdische Blatt*, Dec. 20, 1912, p. 4.

48. ADBR, 3 M 703, "Emigration en Amérique d'habitants du Bas-Rhin, 1828-37." Onomastic criteria were used to determine which emigrants were Jewish.

49. A. Wahl, *Option*, p. 174, points out that over 75% of the optants who emigrated came from large cities (+5,000 inhabitants) in which only 20.2% of the general 1871 population lived. See also ibid., pp. 56, 121, 130-31, 156, 190-91; and Roth, *Lorraine*, pp. 98-99.

50. On the economic repercussions of the annexation, see Silverman, *Reluctant Union*, pp. 163-89; Rossé et al., 2:365; and Camus, p. 60.

51. Cited in UI, Nov. 15, 1874, pp. 184–85. On the bourgeois character of option in general, see A. Wahl, *Option*, p. 174; Hiegel, "Option," 74:112; and Roth, *Lorraine*, p. 221. On the impression that many Jewish optants came from bourgeois backgrounds, see G. Cahen, "Juifs dans la région Lorraine," p. 78; RI, Oct. 20, 1871, p. 757; Roth, *Lorraine*, p. 419; André Neher, "Bourgeoisie," p. 439; UI, July 5, 1871, p. 423; and AI, June 1, 1872, p. 342.
52. A. Wahl, *Option*, p. 159.
53. RI, Oct. 20, 1871, pp. 757–58.
54. Bernheim, pp. 5–6, 17–18. See also Delabrousse, p. 61.
55. On Aronssohn, see Strauss, *Le Docteur Paul Aronssohn: Ancien professeur agrégé à la faculté de médecine de Strasbourg, Chevalier de la Légion d'Honneur. (Paroles prononcées sur sa tombe) 30 mai, 1887* (Paris, 1887), p. 5. On Hirtz, see *Journal d'Alsace*, Jan. 31, 1878, p. 3; Kahn, *Souvenirs*, p. 69; AI, Feb. 15, 1878, p. 115; and Halff, *Fidélité*, p. 3.
56. On the migration of lawyers in general, see Civil Commissioner Kühlwetter's report, March 17, 1871, ADBR, AL 71 277.
57. On Maase, see minutes, Bas-Rhin Consistory, June 26, 1899, April 12, 1905, CBR; AI, March 30, 1905, p. 103; and UI, June 18, 1920, pp. 298–99.
58. On the option and emigration of teachers in general, see Roth, *Lorraine*, p. 158; A. Wahl, *Option*, p. 56; and Bezirkspräsident, Bas-Rhin, supplemental report, Dec. 31, 1871, ADBR, AL 71 277.
59. RI, Oct. 20, 1871, pp. 757–58; Craig, *Scholarship*, pp. 22–23.
60. Roth, *Lorraine*, p. 418. The Jewish bailiff from Mulhouse, Solomon Wahl, also claimed that practical problems arising from the transition to German motivated his emigration. See von Klöcker to Oberpräsident, Alsace-Lorraine, Feb. 18, 1871, ADBR, AL 87 5(17).
61. Asch, entry for Sept. 29, 1870, pp. 21–22.
62. AI, April 15–June 16, 1871, p. 92, Sept. 1, 1871, p. 230, Oct. 15, 1871, p. 325, Oct. 15, 1875, p. 622.
63. Delahache, *Alsace-Lorraine*, pp. 100–103, 116–17; Roth, *Lorraine*, p. 52; A. Wahl, *Option*, p. 159.
64. A. Wahl, *Option*, pp. 78, 159; Hiegel, "Option," 74:103.
65. Mull, p. 320. Elie Scheid's memoirs provide some interesting first-hand observations on the hops trade in Haguenau. See Scheid, pp. 41–49, 77, 91.
66. The Jewish hops merchants from Haguenau who opted were Ephraim Abraham, Alphons, Jacques and Léon Eisenmann, Isidore Gugenheim, Julius Gugenheim, Jacques Heimann, Isaac Hirsch, Alfred Lantzenberg, Benjamin Liebschutz, Arthur Wolfgang Moch, Jacob Weill, Simon Weill, and Abraham Weyl. One hops broker from the city of Bischwiller also opted—Michel Bloch. On the fate of the hops trade following

the annexation, see Rinckenberger, pp. 7–8; Camus, p. 77; and Barry, p. 140. On the bad harvests, see *Courrier du Bas-Rhin*, June 11, 1872.

67. Hiegel, "Option," 74:105; Voilliard, p. 89.

68. AI, Feb. 27, 1890, p. 71; UI, April 20, 1923, p. 117; Lipman, p. 17; "Dupont, Pierre Mayer," in *Dictionnaire de biographie française*; Kahn, *Souvenirs*, p. 263.

69. On the impact of the annexation on the Alsatian textile industry, see Fritsch, p. 137; Camus, pp. 60–61, 69–74; A. Wahl, *Option*, p. 164; Delahache, "De Bischwiller," pp. 566–67; and Laufenburger, pp. 140–41. On the creation of branch companies across the border in France, see Silverman, *Reluctant Union*, p. 173; and A. Wahl, *Option*, p. 173. On the important role of Jews in the building up of the Alsatian textile industry earlier in the 19th century, see Szajkowski, "Notes," pp. 536–38. On the similarly influential role of Jews in the German textile industry, see Jacob Toury, *Jüdische Textilunternehmer in Baden-Württemberg, 1683–1938* (Tübingen, 1984).

70. Laufenburger and Pflimlin, pp. 120, 372; Silverman, *Reluctant Union*, p. 20; Schnurmann, p. 48.

71. On the Langs, see A. Wahl, *Option*, pp. 122, 173, 200; Livet and Oberlé, p. 264; *La Guerre*, pp. 22–23; Voilliard, pp. 88–89; AI, June 1, 1882, p. 177; and UI, April 25, 1902, pp. 183–84.

72. On the Dreyfus family in Mulhouse and its response to the Franco-Prussian War, see Alfred Dreyfus, pp. 40–42; Bredin, pp. 11–12; Laufenburger, pp. 443–44; and Gauthier, pp. 58–59. The emigration of a number of Mulhouse textile manufacturers to Switzerland was also due in part to the close connection with Swiss finance. See Landes, p. 168.

73. Camus, p. 36.

74. On the rise of the Bischwiller Jewish community, see Fritsch, p. 127; Camus, pp. 42–43; and "Histoire des communautés: Bischwiller." On Bischwiller's economic boom in the 1840's and 1850's, see Fritsch, p. 96; and Camus, pp. 35–36.

75. On the economic decline of Bischwiller following the annexation, see A. Wahl, *Option*, pp. 187–88; Laufenburger and Pflimlin, p. 129; Delahache, "De Bischwiller," pp. 567–71; "Industries"; Fritsch, p. 99; and Camus, pp. xii–xiii, 61, 66–69. On the favored destinations of the industrialists, see Delahache, "De Bischwiller," p. 567; "Industries"; Camus, pp. 61–64; Fritsch, p. 98; Szajkowski, "Growth," p. 308; and AI, June 1, 1872, pp. 334–35, July 15, 1872, p. 440, Dec. 1, 1872, p. 722, Dec. 15, 1872, p. 755. The destinations of the Jewish optants from Bischwiller were Elbeuf 15; Sedan 14; Paris 4; Lunéville, Nancy, Vienne, Vire, 2 each; and Montbéliard, Roubaix, and the United States, 1 each. These figures refer to heads of households only.

76. On the demographic decline of Bischwiller in general, see also

A. Wahl, *Option*, p. 115; Camus, p. 67; Fritsch, pp. 98, 136; Delahache, "De Bischwiller," p. 567; and "Industries." On the decline of the Jewish population in particular, see Camus, p. 43; "Histoire des communautés: Bischwiller," p. 13; *Courrier du Bas-Rhin*, Dec. 15, 1873; and AI, June 1, 1872, p. 334.

77. The Fraenkels were not included in the option list and therefore must have opted only in France. Ernst Herzog was a minor at the time; his father, Solomon, actually filed the option declaration. The Jewish textile manufacturers who opted from Bischwiller were Léon Auscher; Léon Weill Auscher; Maurice and Théodore Blin; David, Edgar, and Isidore Bloch; Samuel Cahen; Samuel Hirsch; Léopold Levy; and Julius Weill. Frédéric Picard, a manufacturer of textile machinery, also opted.

78. On the emigration of the Jewish textile manufacturers, see A. Wahl, *Option*, p. 165; Camus, pp. 61–64; Halff, *Fidélité*, pp. 2–3; Maurois, p. 13; RI, May 24, 1872, p. 361; UI, June 1, 1872, p. 607, Aug. 1, 1872, p. 699; and AI, June 1, 1872, pp. 333–35. On Nathan Fraenkel, see Raphael and Weyl, *Juifs en Alsace*, p. 437. On Maurice Blin, see *Journal d'Alsace*, Nov. 5, 1873, p. 3, Nov. 23, 1879, p. 2; *L'Alsace-Lorraine Israélite*, June 1879, p. 2; and AI, May 22, 1879, p. 168. On Théodore Blin, see *Journal d'Alsace*, March 11, 1897, p. 85.

79. J.-R. Bloch, pp. 32–33.

80. Ibid., pp. 45–46. On the material hardships of emigration, see also AI, June 1, 1872, p. 333.

81. Maurois, p. 7. On the family relationship between Bloch and Maurois, see Sommer, p. 1.

82. Maurois, p. 149.

83. J.-R. Bloch, p. 230.

84. Camus, pp. 61–62.

85. J.-R. Bloch, pp. 86–87.

86. *Courrier du Bas-Rhin*, Oct. 17, 1872.

87. Bourguignon, p. 357. See also Camus, pp. 70–74.

88. J.-R. Bloch, pp. 70, 229.

89. Report of the Bischwiller police commissioner, Dec. 7, 1875, ADBR, D 383 paq. 26, cited in A. Wahl, *Option*, p. 164.

90. Jewish community, Saint-Dié, to Minister of Public Education and Religion, 1872, CP, I CC23 (1872–1905).

91. Bensimon-Donath, p. 152. On transportation subsidies, see AI, June 1, 1872, p. 335; and J.-R. Bloch, p. 78.

92. AI, June 1, 1872, pp. 342–43.

93. UI, July 5, 1871, p. 423. See also UI, April 1, 1880, p. 434; and AI, June 1, 1872, pp. 332–33, Sept. 15, 1872, p. 561, July 20, 1882, p. 235.

94. On influential people who opted from Metz, see the list in ADBR, AL 69 604; Delahache, *L'Exode*, p. 123; Netter, *Vingt siècles*, pp. 448, 457;

Roth, *Lorraine*, pp. 187, 418; and AI, April 15–June 15, 1871, pp. 90–91. On Terquem, see AI, July 14, 1887, p. 223; on Mayer, see AI, Jan. 30, 1890; and on Bamberger, see Chap. 2.

95. Jewish Consistory, Bas-Rhin, to Mayor of Strasbourg, Oct. 31, 1876, AMS, 375/2101 (Neubau einer Synagog 1880–1900).

96. Minutes, Lorraine Consistory, Oct. 19, 1873, ADM, 17 J 41, pp. 60–61. See also Roth, *Lorraine*, p. 419; Israelitische Gemeinde zu Metz, *Synagogen Verwaltungsbericht über die Rechnungsjahre 1886–1891 (Israelitisches Konsistorium, Lothringen)* (Metz, 1892), p. 7.

97. On the socioeconomic status of Alsace-Lorraine Jews in Paris in 1872, see Bensimon-Donath, pp. 133, 136, 149, 151, 192, 227–28, 232, 235.

98. Wallerstein.

99. G. Cahen, "Juifs dans la région Lorraine," p. 77; Netter, *Vingt siècles*, p. 448; Lipman, p. 344; RI, Sept. 29, 1871, p. 715, Dec. 13, 1872, p. 780.

100. "Historique de la *Société de bienfaisance de la jeunesse israélite de Metz*" (1886), ADM, 11 AL 25; Bezirkspräsident, Lorraine, to Ministry of Interior, Bas-Rhin, July 12, 1894, ADBR, AL 69 462.

101. Minutes, Central Consistory, March 19, 1872, CC 4 B2. On rabbis who opted from the provinces, see UI, Oct. 25, 1901, p. 170, May 13, 1910, p. 114, Feb. 2, 1923, p. 464, Feb. 20, 1925, p. 10; and minutes, Bas-Rhin Consistory, Oct. 3–Nov. 13, 1884, CBR.

102. Bensimon-Donath, pp. 95–96; Sylvain Halff, untitled article, *Paix et droit*, Nov. 1934, p. 4; Weinberg, p. 2.

103. Paris Consistory to Central Consistory, Sept. 14, 1872; to Ministry of Religion, March 24, 1873; and minutes, Sept. 30, 1872, CP I CC$_{35}$.

104. On the destinations in general, see "Alsace," in *Encyclopedia Judaica*, 1972 ed., p. 756; Schnurmann, p. 10; Bensimon-Donath, p. 71; G. Cahen, "Juifs dans la région Lorraine," p. 77; Szajkowski, "Growth," p. 302; Marrus, p. 33; minutes, Central Consistory, July 1, 1871, p. 459, CC I B 5; minutes, Central Consistory, July 13, 1871, CC I B 6; Lévy, *Langue*, 1:153–54; A. Wahl, *Option*, p. 180; D. Cohen, *Promotion*, 1:86–89; Schwarzfuchs, *Juifs*, p. 269; and AI, July 15, 1872, p. 440, Jan. 1, 1873, pp. 17–18.

105. RI, Feb. 2, 1872, p. 116, Nov. 17, 1871, pp. 817–18, March 29, 1872, p. 242; minutes, Central Consistory, Nov. 7, 1871, March 12, 1872, CC I B 6; Lipman, pp. xv, 20–21; AI, Dec. 1, 1872, p. 722, Dec. 15, 1872, p. 755, Jan. 1, 1873, pp. 17–18; UI, March 1, 1872, p. 410.

106. AI, April 1, 1873, p. 211. See also AI, Nov. 1, 1872, p. 652, Dec. 15, 1872, pp. 750–51; UI, April 15, 1874, p. 488; and M. Bloch, *Alsace*, p. 24. On the efforts of the French government and Alsace-Lorraine organizations to recruit emigrants to Algeria, see A. Wahl, *Option*, p. 212; *Courrier du Bas-Rhin*, Jan. 26, March 1, March 10, and July 28, 1872; Delahache, *L'Exode*,

p. 139; Delahache, *Alsace-Lorraine*, p. 124; Jaeger, "Alsaciens," pp. 624–25; and *Société de protection*, *1873*, pp. 23, 27, *1874*, pp. 24, 28.

107. Minutes, Central Consistory, July 1, 1871, pp. 459–61, CC I B 5, July 13, 1871, CC I B 6; Delpech, p. 324; Schwarzfuchs, *Juifs*, p. 269; RI, Jan. 12, 1872, p. 65. The seat at Vesoul was later transferred to Besançon. See Jewish community of Besançon to Central Consistory, March 1876, June 26, 1877; to the Consistory of Lyons, Jan. 15, 1877; and to the Ministry of Justice and Religion, Dec. 10, 1879, CC I A 6(C).

108. AI, Nov. 1, 1871, p. 358, July 1, 1879, p. 101, Feb. 27, 1879, pp. 69–70; RI, Jan. 12, 1872, p. 69; Roblin, p. 139.

109. AI, Feb. 27, 1879, pp. 69–70; Lipman, pp. 19–21.

110. Minutes, Central Consistory, March 16, 1871, p. 453, CC I B 5.

CHAPTER FOUR

1. Silverman, *Reluctant Union*, p. 69. See also Rossé et al., 3:365; Jules Koch, p. 587; P. Lévy, *Histoire*, pp. 342–43; P. Lévy, *Langue*, p. 153; Reuss, pp. 389–90; Delahache, *Alsace-Lorraine*, p. 158; Gaston Moch, p. 27; and Roth, *Lorraine*, pp. 115–16. A good case study on emigration in general during this period is Hiegel, "Option," part 2 (1975).

2. See, for example, AI, Oct. 15, 1875, p. 623, May 19, 1898, p. 159, June 6, 1907, p. 183, Aug. 25, 1918, p. 266; AZJ, Nov. 10, 1885, p. 739; and Wallerstein.

3. Delpech, pp. 309–10.

4. George, pp. 39–42; Kuznets, "Immigration," pp. 85–86, 88, 121; Kessner, p. 30; Bensimon-Donath, p. 100.

5. Roth, *Lorraine*, p. 109; Bensimon-Donath, p. 119. Although the individual dossiers after 1898 were closed to me, a typewritten list of the names of all applicants for emigration permits through 1914 shows a decline.

6. Based on Statistischen Bureau, *Statistische Mitteilungen*, *1871*.

7. Bensimon-Donath, p. 111.

8. On Jewish emigration from Schirrhofen, see also SIW, July 16, 1911, p. 8; and "Communauté israélite de Schirrhofen," p. 14.

9. The electoral lists for Haguenau were not available. For the Strasbourg-campagne (Bas-Rhin) electoral lists, see ADBR, D 384 34(108).

10. See letters to Kreisdirector, Haguenau, from Joseph Kahn, Oct. 10, 1878, Aron Kahn, Nov. 1889, Moritz Lévy, April 24, 1875, and Judith Lévy, June 7, 1876, ADBR, D 384 38; and from Valentin Herzog, June 30, 1889, ADBR, D 384 42.

11. Uhry, 1:45. On Jewish emigration to the United States from Ingwiller, see also L. W., "Histoire de nos communautés: Ingwiller (Bas-Rhin)," *Bulletin de nos communautés*, 12, no. 22 (1956), p. 12; and SIW, Feb. 18, 1908, p. 9.

12. Aron Kahn to Kreisdirector, Haguenau, Nov. 1889, ADBR, D 384 38.

13. SIW, May 21, 1908, pp. 6–7. On the basis of impressionistic evidence, Steven Lowenstein and Avraham Barkai also see the general pattern of rural Jewish out-migration in 19th-century Germany as "poor to America—rich to the cities," a pattern that stands in marked contrast to Christian rural out-migration. Lowenstein, "Rural Community," p. 226; Barkai, "German Jews," pp. 135–36; Barkai, "German-Jewish Migrations," p. 311.

14. On the importance of kinship and friendship relationships as an influence on the choice of destination in general, see Hvidt, pp. 172–90; Kuznets, "Immigration," p. 112; Lestschinsky, pp. 1207–8, 1213; Jansen, *Social Aspects*, pp. 19–20; Peterson, p. 62; Brown et al., pp. 100–101; A. Girard et al., p. 218; Chevalier, pp. 161–62; and Leslie Moch, pp. 23–26, 159–63. With specific reference to Jews, see Barkai, "German-Jewish Migrations," p. 312.

15. Uhry, 1:11, 12, 17, 24, 145.

16. See various letters, ADBR, D 384 37–44. Although there are few statistics, Jewish emigrants appear to have had large families. Of the 20 cases in which the number of children is known, only one family had 2 children; 6 families had 3–5, 8 had 6–8, 4 had 9–11, and 1 had 12.

17. Uhry, 1:146.

18. I noted 40 non-Jews who claimed they wanted to receive an education in the French language.

19. Simon Kahn to Kreisdirector, Haguenau, March 1, 1877, ADBR, D 384 38.

20. Léon Blum to Kreisdirector, Haguenau, Aug. 8, 1878, ibid.

21. Reuss, pp. 392–93; Silverman, *Reluctant Union*, p. 72; Pfister, *Pages*, p. 260. According to Silverman, p. 72, by 1904 the draft evasion rate was only about 8%.

22. *Kölnische Zeitung*, July 24, 1894, clipping in ADBR, AL 27 329.

23. Kreisdirector, Haguenau, to Bezirkspräsident, Bas-Rhin, Feb. 1, 1882, ADBR, D 68 4-IV ∫ 21; *Kölnische Zeitung*, July 24, 1894, ADBR, AL 27 329; Hiegel, 75:94.

24. See, for example, State Secretary to Statthalter, Manteuffel, April 14, 1882, ADBR, AL 27 318; Kreisdirector, Haguenau, to Bezirkspräsident, Bas-Rhin, Feb. 1, 1882, ADBR, D 68 4-IV ∫ 21; Kreisdirector, Strasbourg, to Bezirkspräsident, Bas-Rhin, Jan. 4, 1888, ADBR, D 388 78(474); Bezirkspräsident, Bas-Rhin, administrative reports, April 8, July 6, 1884, Jan. 4, 1888, ADBR, AL 71 277; "En Alsace," *Le Matin*, May 20, 1898; and *Courrier du Bas-Rhin*, June 1, June 5, 1873.

25. Bezirkspräsident, Lorraine to Oberpräsident, Alsace-Lorraine, supplemental report, July 5, 1879, ADBR, AL 71 277.

26. Bezirkspräsident, Haut-Rhin, administrative report, March 4, 1880,

Kreisdirector, Mulhouse, administrative report, Dec. 26, 1880, Bezirkspräsident, Haut-Rhin, administrative report for Jan.–March 1884, ADBR, AL 71 277.
27. Bezirkspräsident, Bas-Rhin, administrative report, July 6, 1884, ibid.
28. Bezirkspräsident, Bas-Rhin, administrative report, April 6, 1884, ibid.
29. *Kölnische Zeitung*, July 24, 1894, in ADBR, AL 27 329. For a list of government officials from the Reichsland who sent their sons to France before they reached military age, see the report of Oct. 1, 1894, in ibid.
30. Hiegel, "Option," 75:97–98. On expulsions, see also *Journal d'Alsace*, Sept. 13, 1876, p. 3.
31. Bezirkspräsident, Lorraine, administrative report, July 4, 1889, ADBR, AL 71 277.
32. *Courrier du Bas-Rhin*, July 18, 1874. See also June 1, June 5, 1873.
33. Wallerstein, p. 581.
34. Uhry, 1:146.
35. Kreisdirector, Erstein, to Bezirkspräsident, Bas-Rhin, July 29, 1890, ADBR, D 49–61.
36. Police Commissioner of Bischwiller's report, Dec. 13, 1895, ADBR, D 384 444. According to Hiegel, "Option," 75:94–95, 9.9% of legal emigrants from Sarreguemines were Jews of military age. He attributes the disdain Lorraine Jews held for German military service to their "traditional germanophobia."
37. ADBR, D 46 645.
38. Police report, Nov. 30, 1882, ADBR, D 46 645.
39. Kreisdirector, Molsheim, to Bezirkspräsident, Bas-Rhin, Feb. 9, April 24, 1883, Oberpräsident, Alsace-Lorraine, to Ministry of Interior, May 17, 1883, ADBR, D 46 645.
40. ADBR, D 398 130 (78.4). There are no data for the years 1877, 1880, and 1881, possibly because there were no desertions during those years.
41. ADBR, D 46 645.
42. Schnurmann, pp. 61–63.

CHAPTER FIVE

1. Silverman, *Reluctant Union*, p. 35.
2. On the persistence of pro-French nationalism in Alsace-Lorraine throughout the annexation period, see Morrison. For the opposing view that these internal conflicts were actually more important than the issue of nationalism, see Silverman, *Reluctant Union*, especially p. 2.
3. Girardet, p. 14. On the role of the Alsace-Lorraine question in French foreign policy and public opinion after 1871, see Mitchell, *Bismarck*, pp. 111–12; and Seager. Both authors argue convincingly that, even though

the rhetoric of revanche continued to play a symbolic role in French public life, there was nearly unanimous consensus from the start that the recovery of the lost provinces was not worth the risk of another war.

4. Szajkowski, "Yidn in di Pariser Commune," p. 115.
5. Jules Koch, pp. 588, 592.
6. Ministry of Interior to Kreisdirectors, Jan. 30, 1890, ADBR, D 68 paq. 2 IV ∫ 14. Figures are estimates, based on presumed Jewish names.
7. Jules Koch, p. 589; Manuel, *Dernier délai*; Manuel, *Anniversaire*; Ratisbonne.
8. Ministry of Interior to Police Director, Feb. 22, 1890, ADBR, D 68 paq. 2 IV ∫ 14.
9. Ibid., May 15, 1891; *Société de protection, 1873*, pp. 12–13.
10. Halff, *Fidélité*, pp. 7–8; RI, March 29, 1872, p. 249.
11. Halff, *Fidélité*, p. 7.
12. Ministry of Interior to Kreisdirectors, June 4, 1891, ADBR, D 68 paq. 2 IV ∫ 14.
13. Cobban, p. 34; Girardet, pp. 58–62, 267–78; Rémond, pp. 229n; Brogan, p. 344; Bader, pp. 39–60.
14. Ministry of Interior to Kreisdirectors and Police Directors, July 12, 1889, ADBR, D 68 paq. 2 IV ∫ 14.
15. UI, March 16, 1887, p. 410.
16. ADBR, D 68 paq. 2 IV ∫ 14.
17. Delahache, *Juifs*, p. 32, n. 1. For a general discussion of the role of these organizations in keeping alive the idea of revanche in France throughout the period of the annexation, see Zeldin, 2:79.
18. "Alsaciens."
19. Aron, p. 7. "Alsaciens," p. 407.
20. Szajkowski, "Some Facts," p. 316. In the 1890's Aron sponsored a journal to fight antisemitism. On these activities, see Marrus, pp. 149–53, 162, 213.
21. SIW, July 11, 1914, p. 7; Halff, *Fidélité*, p. 20.
22. Halff, *Fidélité*, p. 19; ADBR, D 388 paq. 112(697). For a general discussion of the role of these organizations in sustaining pro-French sentiments, see Morrison, pp. 258–322. On the Souvenir Français in particular, see p. 266.
23. Roth, *Lorraine*, pp. 132, 664–65; Eccard, pp. 79–81; Delahache, *Alsace-Lorraine*, p. 142; Reuss, p. 398; François Dreyfus, p. 10; Silverman, "Political Catholicism," p. 42; Morrison, pp. 36–43.
24. Silverman, "Political Catholicism," p. 44; Delahache, *L'Exode*, p. 127; Halff, *Fidélité*, p. 6; Lipman, p. 13; Netter, *Vingt siècles*, pp. 449, 457; D'Elstein, p. 157; Delabrousse, pp. 44–45.
25. D'Elstein, p. 157.
26. Roth, "Antoine," pp. 366, 384–85, 391; Roth, *Lorraine*, p. 196.

27. Roth, *Lorraine*, p. 188; Roth, "Antoine," p. 366. On the patriotism of the Jewish members of the Masonic lodge, see I. Lévy, "La Maçonnerie et l'Alsace-Lorraine," AI, Sept. 1, 1873, pp. 523–25.
28. Roth, *Lorraine*, p. 197; Roth, "Antoine," p. 371.
29. Roth, "Antoine," p. 389.
30. Kreisdirector, Haguenau, to Bezirkspräsident, Bas-Rhin, June 21, 1872, Police Director, Back, to Bezirkspräsident, Bas-Rhin, July 25, 1872, ADBR, AL 133 paq. 27 103.
31. AI, May 24, 1888, p. 160.
32. ADBR, AL 133 paq. 27 103.
33. Police Director, Back, to Bezirkspräsident, Bas-Rhin, July 25, 1872, ibid.
34. Bezirkspräsident, Bas-Rhin, to Ministry of Justice and Religion, Dec. 16, 1887, ibid.
35. Bezirkspräsident, Lorraine, to Ministry of Justice and Religion, April 30, 1903, ADBR, AL 133 paq. 27 104.
36. See various confirmation reports in ADBR, AL 133 paq. 27 103.
37. On "germanization," see P. Lévy, *Histoire*, 2:321, 341–42, 365–69, 372–73, 378, 464; Silverman, *Reluctant Union*, pp. 74–80; Eccard, pp. 24, 33–34; Roth, *Lorraine*, pp. 11, 54, 82–85, 158–72; Blumenthal, "Revanche," p. 206; and Craig, *Scholarship*, pp. 1–225.
38. Minutes, Bas-Rhin Consistory, Nov. 19, 1874, CBR.
39. Roth, *Lorraine*, p. 86.
40. ADBR, AL 133 paq. 27 104; ADM, 7 AL 4.
41. Netter, *Vingt siècles*, p. 469.
42. Bezirkspräsident, Bas-Rhin, to Kreisdirector, Saverne, Nov. 4, 1887, ADBR, D 387 53/314.
43. UI, April 16, 1888, p. 472; AI, April 19, 1888, p. 127; AZJ, May 3, 1888, p. 280.
44. P. Lévy, *Histoire*, 2:433; P. Lévy, "Parler," p. 275; minutes, Lorraine Consistory, May 11, Nov. 23, 1891, March 10, 1892, ADM 17 J 41.
45. Imbs, pp. 309–11; Dollinger, "Bourgeoisies," p. 439; P. Lévy, *Histoire*, 2:340–41; Rossé et al., 3:52–53, 67; François Dreyfus, p. 23; Craig, "Mission," pp. 401–3; Craig, *Scholarship*, pp. 102–4.
46. Roth, *Lorraine*, pp. 34, 144.
47. Raphael and Weyl, *Juifs en Alsace*, p. 438 n. 22; Halff, *Fidélité*, p. 5. Henri Wahl, member of the Haut-Rhin Consistory, sent his son to the Ecole Polytechnique in Paris. *Jüdischer Sprechsaal*, Sept. 13, 1883, p. 207. The parents of Lazare Weiller likewise sent him to school in France. Weiller, "Alsace," p. 837. On the general phenomenon of Alsace-Lorraine youths being sent to France to receive an education, see Craig, *Scholarship*, pp. 110, 112.
48. Raphael and Weyl, *Juifs en Alsace*, p. 438 n. 22.

49. Weyl, "Juifs," p. 112. According to Wallerstein, p. 582, many wealthy families sent their daughters to marry in France.
50. Imbert, p. 38. On similar activities by Catholic priests in the provinces, see Roth, *Lorraine*, p. 172.
51. Bauer, p. 144.
52. Uhry, 1:158. On the distaste of many Alsace-Lorrainers for these careers, see Craig, *Scholarship*, pp. 117–21.
53. Uhry, 1:9.
54. Weyl and Weyl, p. 132; Raphael and Weyl, *Juifs en Alsace*, p. 192.
55. Raphael and Weyl, *Juifs en Alsace*, p. 192.
56. Weyl and Weyl, p. 132.
57. Ibid., pp. 132–33; Raphael and Weyl, *Juifs en Alsace*, pp. 192–93; Weyl, "Juifs," p. 112.
58. AI, March 6, 1890, p. 79.
59. Statistischen Bureau, *Das Reichsland*, 1:2–3; Statistischen Bureau, *Statistische Mitteilungen über Elsass-Lothringen*, *1890*, p. xxiv.
60. Minutes, Lorraine Consistory, Dec. 7, 1884, ADM, 17 J 41; Schnurmann, p. 20.
61. Bezirkspräsident, Lorraine, to von Möller, Oberpräsident, Alsace-Lorraine, Sept. 8, 1872, ADBR, AL 71 277.
62. Sayous, part 1:16, part 2:122. For a brief history of the Wolf Netter and Jacobi firm, see *Festschrift zum 25 jährigen*.
63. Bezirkspräsident, Haut-Rhin, administrative report, June 29, 1898, ADBR, AL 71 277.
64. *Das Jüdische Blatt*, Aug. 25, 1911, p. 7.
65. "Bischwiller," *Courrier du Bas-Rhin*, Aug. 17, 1872.
66. Roth, *Lorraine*, pp. 235–36.
67. ADM, 8 AL 244, 8 AL 419, and 14 AL 92, all cited in Roth, *Lorraine*, p. 309. On the considerable economic expansion of Alsace-Lorraine in general during the period of the annexation, see Schoenbaum, pp. 80–81.
68. Bas-Rhin Consistory to Mayor of Strasbourg, Oct. 31, 1876, AMS, 375/2101.
69. Joseph Bloch, "Histoire," 13.4:10; Joseph Bloch, *Historique*, p. 40.
70. Netter, *Vingt siècles*, p. 469. On strained relations between the Alsace-Lorraine bourgeoisie and the Germans, see Redslob; Morrison, pp. 73–74; and Craig, *Scholarship*, pp. 77–78, 104.
71. Raphael and Weyl, *Juifs en Alsace*, pp. 193–94, 437 n. 9.
72. Woog, p. 29.
73. "En Alsace," *Le Matin*, Aug. 8, 1890. See also UI, Aug. 16, 1890, pp. 744–45.
74. Meiss, *Traditions*, p. 9. See also Matzen, p. 191.
75. UI, Sept. 6, 1901, p. 786.

76. G. Cahen, "Juifs dans la région Lorraine," p. 78; Bailly.
77. UI, Jan. 10, 1919, p. 424.
78. For the 93 members in 1893, the citizenship breakdown was as follows: Alsace-Lorraine, 61; France, 25; Russia, 3; Luxembourg, 2; Austria, 1; without, 1. Société de Bienfaisance de la Jeunesse Israélite to Bezirkspräsident, Lorraine, Dec. 19, 1893, ADM, 11 AL 25. See also UI, Jan. 10, 1919, p. 424.
79. UI, July 30, 1909, p. 633.
80. Das Jüdische Blatt, April 12, 1911, p. 9, June 11, 1911. On the social segregation between Alsatian and Old German students at the University of Strasbourg in general, see Craig, *Scholarship*, pp. 122–23, 128–35.
81. For details on the rise of the Zionist movement in Alsace-Lorraine, see footnote p. 133.
82. Minutes, Lorraine Consistory, Dec. 7, 1884, ADM, 17 J 41.
83. Minutes, Bas-Rhin Consistory, May 21, 1890, ADBR, AL 133 paq. 27 103.
84. AZJ, Jan. 12, 1900, suppl., pp. 3–4.
85. Statthalter, administrative report for third quarter 1895, ADBR, AL 71 277; ADBR, AL 133 paq. 27 103. In 1900 Ferdinand Oppenheimer, also of the Adler and Oppenheimer tannery, was elected to the Bas-Rhin Consistory. Schraut, State Secretary for the Ministry of Alsace-Lorraine, to Statthalter, Hohenlohe-Langenburg, ADBR, AL 27 548.
86. ADM, 7 AL 4; Roth, *Lorraine*, p. 144; Netter, *Vingt siècles*, p. 458. Soon after, another German immigrant, Felix Tuteur, a prominent soap manufacturer, also won a seat on the Lorraine Consistory. According to Roth, August Ernest Müller was the first immigrant elected to the Lorraine Consistory (1890). However, he was a native of Luxembourg, not Germany.
87. Letter of Nov. 19, 1904, signed "Many Prussian voters," in *Strassburger Bürger Zeitung*, clipped in ADM, 17 Z 228 (X6 no. 1).
88. Adolph Levy to Bezirkspräsident, Lorraine, Dec. 4, 1914, ADM 7 AL 4; Roth, *Lorraine*, p. 420.
89. *Courrier du Bas-Rhin*, June 5, 1873, p. 3.
90. S. Weil to Ministry of Religion, March 15, 1915, ADM, 7 AL 43.
91. *Jüdischer Sprechsaal*, Feb. 1, 1883, p. 7.
92. Minutes, Bas-Rhin Consistory, June 21, 1900, CBR.
93. On the shortage of native rabbis, see UI, March 1, 1873, p. 412; AI, May 3, 1883, p. 139; Bezirkspräsident, Haut-Rhin, to von Möller, Oberpräsident, Alsace-Lorraine, Nov. 14, 1873, AL 133 paq. 15 61; and *Jüdischer Sprechsaal*, Feb. 1, 1883, p. 7. To my knowledge, the following communities received German rabbis after 1870: Durmenach, Lauterbourg, Marmoutier, Niedersept, Obernai, Saverne, and Wintzenheim. There are probably several more.

94. Dr. Staripolsky to Ministry of Justice and Religion, June 4, 1895, ADBR, AL 133 paq. 15 62.
95. Bas-Rhin Consistory to von Freyberg, Bezirkspräsident, Bas-Rhin, Sept. 2, 1895, to Dr. Staripolsky, June 23, 1895, ADBR, AL 133 paq. 15 62.
96. Police Director to Bezirkspräsident, Bas-Rhin, Aug. 9, 1895, ibid. The police director recommended that Staripolsky replace the elderly rabbi of Saverne. In 1900 Staripolsky was appointed to that position. Minutes, Bas-Rhin Consistory, Feb. 11, 1900, in ADBR, AL 133 paq. 27 103. On the conflict over Staripolsky's appointment, see also Bezirkspräsident, Bas-Rhin, administrative reports for third quarter 1894, Oct. 1, 1894, for the first quarter 1895, and for the second quarter 1895, June 4, 1895, ADBR, AL 71 277; abstract from the administrative report of Kreisdirector, Erstein, for second quarter of 1895, ADBR, AL 133 paq. 15 62.
97. Minutes, Bas-Rhin Consistory, July 16, 1876, June 3, 1877, Feb. 29, Nov. 14, 1880; Delpech, pp. 324–25; Netter, *Vingt siècles*, p. 463.
98. Minutes, extraordinary meeting, Bas-Rhin Consistory, July 16, 1876, CBR; "Rabbiner-Seminar Colmar, Bericht über den moralischen und financiellen Stand desselben seit seiner Gründung (1880/1) bis Juli 1892" (Alsace, 1893), ADBR, AL 27 544.
99. Minutes, plenary meeting of the three Consistories, Nov. 1885, CBR; Netter, *Vingt siècles*, pp. 462–63, 465; Glaser, p. 60.
100. Minutes, Bas-Rhin Consistory, June 3, 1877, Sept. 21, 1879, Nov. 14, 1880, April 5, 1881, CBR.
101. Ibid., July 17, 1882, CBR; Netter, *Vingt siècles*, p. 464; AI, July 27, 1882, p. 244; Ch. Friedmann, "Le Rabbin Zacharias Wolf (1840–1915)," *Bulletin de nos communautés*, 21.19 (1965): 10.
102. Netter, *Vingt siècles*, p. 466; UI, March 24, 1899, p. 26; UI, "La Famille israélite," suppl. 1924–25, p. 108.
103. On the consistorial system, see Albert, *Modernization*.
104. Netter, *Vingt siècles*, pp. 458–59; Delpech, p. 324; Hertz, p. 32; UI, July 5, 1871, p. 423.
105. Joseph Bloch, *Historique*, p. 11; AZJ, June 14, 1907, suppl., p. 3; Netter, *Vingt siècles*, p. 459.
106. S. Moock to Z. Kahn, Nov. 21, 1892, Zadoc Kahn Papers, Correspondence, Jewish Theological Seminary Collection, New York.
107. State Secretary, Ministry for Alsace-Lorraine, to Statthalter, Hohenlohe-Langenburg, Jan. 18, 1900, ADBR, AL 27 548. On the comparatively slow development of the practice of delivering sermons in France, and in particular in Alsace, during the 19th century, see Helfand, "French Jewry," pp. 125–26.
108. Minutes, Bas-Rhin Consistory meeting to discuss affairs between June 26 and Sept. 7, 1881, CBR; David Levy, Ez Chaim, to Bezirkspräsident, Bas-Rhin, July 24, 1885; Police Director to Bezirkspräsident, Bas-Rhin,

Jan. 31, 1888, ADBR, D 240 198; AI, May 1, 1884, pp. 139-40, May 8, 1884, pp. 148-49, May 26, 1892, pp. 163-64.

109. Netter, *Vingt siècles*, p. 459.

110. Bezirkspräsident, Bas-Rhin, administrative report, Oct. 6, 1882, ADBR, AL 71 277; Bezirkspräsident, Bas-Rhin, to David Levy, Nov. 12, 1882, Police Director, Strasbourg, to Bezirkspräsident, Bas-Rhin, Nov. 27, 1882, Bas-Rhin Consistory to Bezirkspräsident, Bas-Rhin, Oct. 16, Dec. 15, 1882, Board of Directors, Ez Chaim, to Bezirkspräsident, Bas-Rhin, March 12, 1906, all in ADBR, D 240 198; minutes, extraordinary meetings, Bas-Rhin Consistory, July 17, Sept. 9, 1882, Nov. 8, 1883, CBR; Bezirkspräsident, Bas-Rhin, to Rabbi Buttenweiser, March 8, 1888, and to Mayor of Strasbourg, March 23, 1888, both in AMS, 375/2103; AI, Oct. 19, 1882, p. 399, Oct. 10, 1889, p. 331; UI, Nov. 8, 1895, p. 218.

111. From the 1883 membership list of Ez Chaim, and Police Director to Bezirkspräsident, Bas-Rhin, Jan. 31, 1888, ADBR, D 240 198. See also AI, May 12, 1892, p. 148.

112. Members, Ez Chaim, to Bezirkspräsident, Bas-Rhin, July 24, 1885, Nov. 29, 1887, ADBR, D 240 195; Netter, *Vingt siècles*, p. 459; UI, Nov. 8, 1895, p. 218; AI, May 22, 1884, pp. 168-69; minutes, Bas-Rhin Consistory, June 18, Nov. 27, 1885, CBR. On modern Orthodoxy in Germany, see Liberles.

113. Rabbi D. E. Struck to Statthalter, Hohenlohe-Langenburg, Nov. 9, 1899, ADBR, AL 133 dossier 81.

114. See Albert, *Modernization*, pp. 50-55, 66-68, 197-98, 298-99, 314; and Szajkowski, *Jews*, pp. 1058-75.

115. H. Wallach to Z. Kahn, Nov. 1892, S. Moock to Z. Kahn, Nov. 21, 1892, Nov. 3, 1897, Zadoc Kahn Papers, Correspondence, Jewish Theological Seminary collection, New York; Lorraine Consistory to Bezirkspräsident, Lorraine, Nov. 18, 1878, ADM, 7 AL 3.

116. Minutes, Bas-Rhin Consistory, Dec. 31, 1906, CBR.

117. ADBR, D 240 197. A wealthy Jewish rentier in Paris, M. Bloque, for example, continued to support communal institutions, both Jewish and non-Jewish, in his native town, Mertzwiller. *Courrier du Bas-Rhin*, March 24, July 26, 1872.

118. Halff, *Fidélité*, pp. 7-8; Delahache, "Juifs d'Alsace," p. 9.

119. In 1908 the rentier Sylvain Lévy, a member of the Lorraine Consistory, resigned and emigrated to Nancy to join his family there. Lorraine Consistory to Bezirkspräsident, Lorraine, Dec. 20, 1908, ADM, 7 AL 4; SIW, April 30, 1908, p. 7. There are many other examples.

120. Aron Durlach to Statthalter, Hohenlohe-Langenburg, Jan. 22, 1900, ADBR, AL 27 548.

121. Police Director, Molsheim, to Kreisdirector, Molsheim, April 3, 1874, ADM, 7 AL 4.

122. Delabrousse, p. 48.
123. Bezirkspräsident, Lorraine, administrative report, April 6, 1882, ADBR, AL 71 277.
124. Bezirkspräsident, Bas-Rhin, administrative reports, Nov. 11, 1878, Sept. 10, 1879, Oct. 4, 1897, ibid. For a general discussion of the role of these festivals and the clubs and organizations that sponsored them, see Morrison, pp. 258–82.
125. Police Councilor, Zahn, to Alsace-Lorraine Ministry—Central Police Headquarters, on Alsace-Lorraine citizens attending French festivals, two reports of July 31, 1890, ADBR D 388 58(353). See also police report on the Gymnastic festival in Nancy, March 26, 1892, in ibid.
126. Count von Zeppelin to Ministry of Interior, Sept. 17, 1909, ADBR, AL 69 462(46).
127. G. Cahen, "Juifs dans la région Lorraine," p. 78.
128. Hermann, list of sponsors.
129. G. Cahen, "Juifs dans la région Lorraine," p. 78; Collin, p. 42; SIW, Oct. 21, 1909, p. 9.
130. Collin, pp. 43–49.
131. Hermann, pp. 38, 40–41. According to Morrison, Rabbi Koch was exceptional among the clergymen present at the Wissembourg ceremony because he had not previously exhibited anti-German tendencies. Morrison, p. 314 n. 5.
132. For works supporting this assumption, see Roth, *Lorraine*, pp. 34, 144; and Sayous, part 2:126.
133. On the 1911 Constitution, see especially Mayeur.
134. His emphasis. Cited in "Strassburg," SIW, March 3, 1910.
135. Silverman, *Reluctant Union*, p. 66. On general discrimination against Alsace-Lorrainers in the civil service, see Redslob, pp. 443–44.

CHAPTER SIX

1. On the problem of agricultural credit and Jewish moneylending in Alsace-Lorraine, see R. Marx, "Juifs"; G. Cahen, "Juifs et la vie économique"; Szajkowski, *Jews*, pp. 914–70; Juillard, *Vie rurale*, pp. 487–88; L'Huillier, *Recherches*, pp. 519–49; and Leuilliot, *Alsace*, 2:176–93. On the problem during the Second Empire, see D. Cohen, *Promotion*, 2:676–702.
2. Szajkowski, *Jews*, pp. 1028–32; Delpech, p. 318; D. Cohen, *Promotion*, 1:24; Leuilliot, *Alsace*, 3:245.
3. The well-known Jewish polemicist, Alexandre Weill, blamed the clergy for the resurgence of antisemitism during the Restoration. He argued that though the peasantry, having gained *biens nationaux* during the Revolution, remained for the most part enemies of the ancien régime, many rural youths had nevertheless succumbed to clerical incitement. According

to Weill, around 1820 the Jews of Schirrhoffen and Sufflenheim barely escaped a Catholic-led pogrom. Weill added, "Nowhere was the Catholic clergy less enlightened than in Alsace." Weill, *Ma jeunesse*, 1:56-58. See also Joë-Yehoshua Friedmann, "Un Témoin de la vie juive en Alsace au xixe siècle: Alexandre Weill," p. 106.

In 1874 a Jew commenting on the attendance of Protestant clergy at the inauguration of a synagogue in Beueswiller wrote: "The lively part that our fellow Protestant citizens have taken in our glorious celebration offers additional proof of the union and concord between the two religions reigning here. It's up to the clergy, to the teachers, to further secure those bonds, and we must regretfully say that it is, unfortunately, precisely from those very quarters that the excitation toward hatred and animosity frequently issues forth." *Courrier du Bas-Rhin*, Sept. 16, 1874, p. 3. Léon Cahun has described how Jews in Alsace during the 19th century awaited Christmas night with terror. Cited in Raphael and Weyl, *Juifs en Alsace*, p. 410.

4. ADHR, I M 42(4), cited in Leuilliot, "Politique," p. 80; L. Strauss, "Plébiscite," pp. 105-6, 149-50; D. Cohen, *Promotion*, 2:613; A. Wahl, *Confession*, 2:896.

5. Prefect, July and Aug. 1869, ADHR, cited in L. Strauss, "Plébiscite," pp. 149-50. See also D. Cohen, *Promotion*, 2:613.

6. *Volksbote*, May 1, 1870, cited in L. Strauss, "Plébiscite," p. 119.

7. Purg. ADHR, 6606, Grand Rabbi, Colmar, May 6, 1870, cited in L. Strauss, "Plébiscite," pp. 123-25, 150. See also D. Cohen, *Promotion*, 2:613.

8. On Catholic-Protestant friction in the 1870 strikes in Alsace, see Silverman, *Reluctant Union*, pp. 19-20; A. Wahl, *Option*, p. 214; Eccard, p. 17; and Rossé et al., 3:358. On Catholic antisemitism during these strikes, see Szajkowski, "Yidn in di Pariser Commune," p. 104.

9. Szajkowski, "Yidn in di Pariser Commune," p. 104.

10. Silverman, *Reluctant Union*, p. 22; A. Wahl, *Confession*, 2:905-6.

11. Silverman, *Reluctant Union*, pp. 91-92; Silverman, "Political Catholicism," p. 40; Eccard, p. 79; A. Wahl, *Option*, p. 214.

12. Igersheim, "Politique," pp. 250-57; Silverman, *Reluctant Union*, p. 102; Rossé et al., 3:396; Reuss, p. 379; RI, Oct. 20, 1871, p. 764. Jewish students could attend either the Catholic college in Strasbourg or the Protestant one in Colmar.

13. Joseph Guerber to Ch. Marbach, cited in Igersheim, "Politique," pp. 256-57. Shortly after the annexation, Guerber counseled Alsatian Catholics against clinging "with narrow-minded obstinancy" to dreams of an early return to France. Cited in Silverman, *Reluctant Union*, p. 92.

14. *Volksfreund*, Jan. 1, 1871, cited in Igersheim, "Politique," pp. 256-57. Similarly, Griser, a Catholic priest for Lixheim in Lorraine, wrote: "We

have been detached from France by a definitive treaty. One must for better or for worse accept the situation and try to make the best of it. Do we cease to be Alsatians and Lorrainers because we have been annexed to Germany? Never! The more we miss France, the more we must devote ourselves to the interests of Alsace-Lorraine." Bishop Dupont des Loges of Metz also initially advised devotion to religious duties and abstinence from politics. Both cited in Silverman, "Political Catholicism," pp. 40–41, and in *Reluctant Union*, p. 92.

15. Eccard, pp. 79–80.
16. Silverman, *Reluctant Union*, p. 92; Silverman, "Political Catholicism," p. 40.
17. Roth, *Lorraine*, pp. 131–32, 137; Silverman, *Reluctant Union*, pp. 93–94; Eccard, p. 80; Duhem, p. 13.
18. Silverman, *Reluctant Union*, pp. 96–97; L'Huillier, *Histoire*, p. 94; Rossé et al., 3:348; Reuss, p. 396.
19. Silverman, *Reluctant Union*, p. 102; Reuss, pp. 378–79; Roth, *Lorraine*, pp. 53, 148. Rossé et al., 3:396–97, argues that the aim of increasing state control of education was to root out French influence in the schools.
20. Silverman, *Reluctant Union*, pp. 38, 102; Igersheim, "Politique," p. 287; Reuss, pp. 378–79; AZJ, Sept. 26, 1871, p. 781; Eccard, p. 67.
21. Silverman, *Reluctant Union*, p. 91. On the impact of the Kulturkampf in determining the patriotic loyalties of Alsace-Lorraine Catholics, see ibid., pp. 91–93, 190; Silverman, "Political Catholicism," pp. 40–41; Roth, *Lorraine*, pp. 126, 131–32, 664–65; Eccard, pp. 79–80; Rossé et al., 3:348; *Journal des débats*, Dec. 25, 1875; Reuss, p. 378; and L'Huillier, *Histoire*, p. 94.
22. Roth, *Lorraine*, pp. 132, 664–65; Eccard, pp. 79–81; Delahache, *Alsace-Lorraine*, p. 142; Reuss, p. 398; François Dreyfus, p. 10; Silverman, "Political Catholicism," p. 42; A. Wahl, *Confession*, 2:930.
23. AI, Sept. 1, 1881, pp. 291–92.
24. Roth, *Lorraine*, pp. 187, 664–65; Eccard, pp. 79–81; Delahache, *Alsace-Lorraine*, p. 142; Reuss, p. 398; François Dreyfus, p. 10; Silverman, "Political Catholicism," p. 42; Zeldin, 2:79; Morrison, pp. 36–43.
25. Roth, *Lorraine*, pp. 196–97; Roth, "Antoine," pp. 366, 370–71, 384; Delabrousse, p. 50.
26. Nearly all the antisemitic diatribes in Alsace-Lorraine attacked Jews as usurers. See Béchaux, p. 409; Hemerdinger, p. 103; Riegert, pp. 21–22; D. Cohen, *Promotion*, 2:676; Heilmann, pp. 16, 21; Hertzog; Ginsburger, "Der Wucher"; and Cetty, "Paysan."
27. On the inadequacy of the agricultural credit banks established under the Second Empire, see G. Cahen, "Juifs et la vie économique," p. 146; Raphael and Weyl, *Juifs en Alsace*, p. 370; and Klein, p. 147. Some argue that these banks succeeded in solving the usury problem and reduc-

ing popular antisemitism during the Second Empire. See Patrick Girard, p. 124; and Delpech, pp. 319-20. According to an 1884 governmental *enquête* into agricultural problems, however, indebtedness, primarily to Jews, was still considered the major cause of the peasants' troubles. See Ministerium für Elsass-Lothringen, pp. 193-97, 272; and Roth, *Lorraine*, p. 253.

28. "Les usuriers en Alsace," *Journal d'Alsace*, Nov. 6, 1878, p. 3, Jan. 10, 1879, p. 2; AI, April 17, 1879, p. 126; *Strassburger Zeitung*, Nov. 1, 1878; A. Wahl, *Confession*, 1:546-63.

29. *Journal d'Alsace*, Dec. 5, 1878, p. 3, March 6, 1879, p. 3. See also, AI, Dec. 15, 1878, p. 756; and AZJ, Dec. 24, 1878, p. 824.

30. AI, April 17, 1879, p. 126, Feb. 27, 1879, pp. 69-70, June 5, 1879, pp. 182-83; *L'Alsace-Lorraine israélite*, July 1879, pp. 1-2; AZJ, Feb. 18, 1879, pp. 116-17. Inevitably, several Jews were ultimately convicted. On Jan. 22, 1880, the *Journal d'Alsace* (p. 3) reported that a certain Isaac Lévy from Marmoutier had been sentenced for charging up to 60% interest. See also *Journal d'Alsace*, March 13, 1881, p. 3; *Jüdischer Sprechsaal*, Feb. 1, 1883, p. 7; and A. Wahl, *Confession*, 1:454-55. On the whole, however, it seems that very few Jews were among those tried and condemned.

31. Juillard, *Vie rurale*, p. 255; Klein, p. 147; d'Andlau, pp. 142, 147; Dollinger, p. 60; Baechler, pp. 37-39; A. Wahl, *Confession*, 1:464-588.

32. Rossé et al., 2:263-64; Ministerium für Elsass-Lothringen, pp. xxiii, 30-31, 193-202, 272; Landesausschuss debates on the problems of agricultural credit, ADBR, AL 87 1188; Gerdolle, p. 636.

33. *Die landwirtschaftliche Enquête in Elsass-Lothringen 1884*, Landesausschuss session, Feb. 26, 1885, pp. 286, 390, 397-98, 400, in ADBR, AL 87 1188; Ministerium für Elsass-Lothringen, pp. xxiii, 31, 195; Roth, *Lorraine*, pp. 351-52.

34. Dollinger, *Alsace*, p. 60.

35. Bezirkspräsident, Bas-Rhin, administrative report, Jan. 3, March 31, 1896, ADBR, AL 71 277; Cetty, "Paysan," pp. 224-25, 294, 345-46, 350-52, 354; R. Marx, "Juifs," p. 62; Klein, p. 147; "Viehwucher und seine Bekämpfung durch Raiffeisenvereine," *Der Elsässer*, Aug. 22, 1899; A. Wahl, *Confession*, 1:574-75, 843-46.

36. According to the Bezirkspräsident in Strasbourg, "The Raiffeisen societies, which are mostly under clerical control, apparently have influenced peasant voters." Bezirkspräsident, Bas-Rhin, administrative report, July 4, 1898, ADBR, AL 71 277.

37. On the development of political Catholicism and Catholic socialism in Alsace-Lorraine, see Silverman, "Political Catholicism"; Silverman, *Reluctant Union*, pp. 111, 123-24; Baechler, pp. 42-48; Mayeur, p. 26; Dollinger, *Alsace*, pp. 41-44; and Reuss, p. 442. On the growth of the Socialist Party, see Igersheim, *Recherches*; Eccard, p. 149; Rossé et al., 2:78; Mayeur, pp. 29-31; and Silverman, *Reluctant Union*, p. 120.

38. Guerber, pp. 17-18.
39. Ibid., pp. 15-20, 32, 35, 52-55. See also Silverman, "Political Catholicism," p. 59 n. 60; and Silverman, *Reluctant Union*, pp. 123-24.
40. Guerber, pp. 20-21.
41. On the anti-Alsatian element of the Dreyfus Affair, see Gauthier; Delahache, *Plaidoyer*; *Strassburger Post*, Nov. 10, 17, 24, 1897; AI, Oct. 5, 1889, p. 321; and Bredin, pp. 22-23, 115, 533. On the continuance of anti-Alsatian sentiments until the First World War, see Daudet, pp. 33-56. Bredin's book provides the best and most comprehensive analysis of the Dreyfus Affair to date.
42. Alfred Dreyfus, pp. 40-42; Gauthier, pp. 58-59; UI, July 19, 1935, p. 699; Delpech, p. 352.
43. Delpech, p. 352.
44. Delahache, *Plaidoyer*, p. 5; *Strassburger Post*, Nov. 10, 18, 1897.
45. On the wounded sensibilities of Alsatians during the Dreyfus Affair, see *Strassburger Post*, Nov. 24, 1897; and *Der Elsässer*, Feb. 22, 1898. The Bezirkspräsident in Strasbourg wrote: "The whole development of the matter and especially the progress of the judicial hearings has caused profound grievances among Old Alsatian circles. The perception of the corruption that has extended as far as the highest ranks of the army and even into the judicial administration has painfully offended even those elements of the native population who formerly made no secret of their pro-French sympathies." Bezirkspräsident, Bas-Rhin, administrative report, April 1, 1898, ADBR, AL 71 277. See also Bezirkspräsident, Haut-Rhin, administrative report, April 2, 1898, ibid.
46. *Le Siècle*, May 13, 1898. This article is summarized in "Une Voix d'Alsace-Lorraine," *Strassburger Post*, May 14, 1898.
47. "La Correspondance du *Siècle*," *Journal de Colmar*, May 19, 1898; "Der 'Ewige' Jude," *Volksfreund*, June 5, 1898, pp. 178-79.
48. Emile Keller, "Une Voix d'Alsace-Lorraine," *La Vérité*, May 27, 1898; "Fin de siècle: La voix de *la Vérité*," *Der Elsässer*, May 28, 1898. On the refusal of the clerical right-wing press to accept von Bülow's declaration, see Bezirkspräsident, Bas-Rhin, administrative report, April 1, 1898, ADBR, AL 71 277.
49. Early in 1899 the Bezirkspräsident in Colmar reported, "The number of those who had approved of the French government's conduct in the matter decreases day by day." Bezirkspräsident, Haut-Rhin, administrative report, Jan. 7, 1899, ADBR, AL 71 277. Similarly, the Bezirkspräsident of Metz wrote late in 1898, "Even the fanatical opponents of a revision of the Dreyfus case must now feel ashamed by the revelations and will begin a retreat." Bezirkspräsident, Lorraine, administrative report, Sept. 30, 1898, ibid. See also Bezirkspräsident, Lorraine, administrative reports, Dec. 31, 1898, July 2, 1899, ibid.

50. Bezirkspräsident, Haut-Rhin, administrative report, Oct. 8, 1899, ibid.
51. Bezirkspräsident, Haut-Rhin, administrative report, April 6, 1899, ibid. Elias, *Assimilations*, p. 8, claims they sent 1,200 francs. On the Henry Memorial, see Snyder, pp. 224–26; and Wilson, pp. 125–26.
52. On the link between antisemitism and Germanophobia in Alsace-Lorraine, the Bezirkspräsident in Strasbourg wrote, "With regard to the conduct of the press, the clerical papers *Volksfreund* and *Elsässer* have made use of a good opportunity to give themselves up wholeheartedly to their antisemitism and accompanying anti-German inclinations." Bezirkspräsident, Bas-Rhin, administrative report, April 1, 1898, ADBR, AL 71 277.
53. *Metzer Zeitung*, cited in *Der Elsässer*, Feb. 17, 1898.
54. See Delahache, *Plaidoyer*, especially pp. 8–9; and Delahache, *Juifs*, especially pp. 1–4, 44–45. Delahache continued to write prolifically on the subject of Alsace-Lorraine and after the First World War became the archivist of the Bibliothèque and Archives de Strasbourg. For his biography, see "Delahache," in *Dictionnaire de biographie française*; and "A la mémoire de Georges Delahache," *L'Alsace française*, 17.436, n.s. 9.20 (May 19, 1929), pp. 425–28.
55. Michel Bréal, "Encore un témoignage," *Le Siècle*, Aug. 20, 1898. See also *Der Elsässer*, Aug. 23, 1898; and Gauthier, p. 60.
56. Of the Dreyfus Affair, the Bezirkspräsident in Metz noted in 1898, "The development of the case in France has had a positive impact on the public's attitude toward Germany." In 1899 he added, "These circumstances [engendered by the Affair] certainly encourage the rapprochement of the Lorraine population to *Deutschtum*. Likewise, interest in French national festivals is constantly declining." Bezirkspräsident, Lorraine, administrative reports, Sept. 30, 1898, Sept. 30, 1899, ADBR, AL 71 277. See also Bezirkspräsident, Lorraine, administrative reports, Dec. 31, 1898, July 2, 1899, Bezirkspräsident, Bas-Rhin, administrative report, Oct. 3, 1898, Bezirkspräsident, Haut-Rhin, administrative reports, Jan. 7, April 6, 1899, and Statthalter Hohenlohe-Langenburg, administrative report, Oct. 25, 1899, all in ADBR, AL 71 277.

At the same time, however, the Bezirkspräsident in Colmar cautioned: "The [Dreyfus] Case, by delivering a severe blow to the prestige of the French officer corps, has certainly had an impact on the pro-French sympathies of the majority of the population. It would be a mistake, however, to expect any immediate upsurge or strengthening of pro-German sentiments. Those who thought and felt themselves to be French will not all of a sudden think and feel themselves to be German just because of an unjust sentence passed by a French military court." Bezirkspräsident, Haut-Rhin, administrative report, Oct. 8, 1899, ibid. See also his administrative report of April 2, 1898, ibid.

57. Bezirkspräsident, Lorraine, administrative report, March 30, 1898, Statthalter Hohenlohe-Langenburg, administrative report, April 26, 1898, Bezirkspräsident, Bas-Rhin, administrative report, April 1, 1898, ibid.

58. Elias, *Assimilations*, p. 8.

59. As early as 1901 the Bezirkspräsident in Metz wrote, "France's stringent measures against the clerical orders have not failed to engender criticism of the present French regime amongst the clerical newspapers here. As a result of the native Catholic press's enormous circulation and great influence, this trend may well cause a further turning away from France." Bezirkspräsident, Lorraine, administrative report, Oct. 4, 1901, ADBR, AL 71 277. See also Silverman, *Reluctant Union*, pp. 108–9; and Baechler, pp. 135–38. On the separation of church and state and its repercussions in general, see Adrien Dansette, *Religious History of Modern France*, tr. John Dingle (New York, 1961).

60. In the 1901 Landesausschuss elections, the clericals supported the Jewish banker Lucien Mannheimer, later president of the Colmar Consistory, rather than a Protestant candidate. The Bezirkspräsident in Colmar commented: "It would not be a mistake to suppose that the local clerical party, in the aftermath of its defeat in the provincial elections, felt it necessary to work toward a reconciliation with the Jews, who have not yet forgotten the clerical press's campaign against Dreyfus and Jewry. In so doing it will once again attempt to promote its program. The clerical members of the municipal council have succeeded in winning over their colleague Mannheimer in this game. But it is highly doubtful that this ploy will win over the Jewish electorate for future elections. Supposedly, after the elections, Mr. Mannheimer's mother greeted him with the words: 'Lucien, you've committed a grave blunder.' This verdict seems not unfounded." Bezirkspräsident, Haut-Rhin, administrative report, Jan. 1, 1901, ADBR, AL 71 277.

61. AI, July 16, 1903, p. 23; UI, July 10, 1903, p. 505; A. Wahl, *Confession*, 2:1042–44. For a brief biographical sketch of Blumenthal, who had in fact converted to Protestantism, see Morrison, p. 139.

62. This was the case particularly in Quatzenheim and Marmoutier (Maurmunster). See SIW, July 2, 1908, p. 4, July 16, 1908, p. 5, Oct. 21, 1909, p. 9; and AZJ, July 17, 1908, suppl., p. 3. On warnings to Jews not to vote for the Center party, see also SIW, Nov. 5, 1908, pp. 3–4, and March 6, 1912, p. 7.

63. On the Bernstein Affair, see E. Weber, *Action Française*, p. 83. On repercussions in Alsace, see SIW, March 16, 1911, p. 1.

64. For a fine study of the growing acceptance of German rule in the Reichsland, see Silverman, *Reluctant Union*.

65. On the distinction between these two types of nationalism, see Girardet, pp. 12–13; Wehler, p. 432; and Zeldin, 2:24–25. On the rise of

the several varieties of integral nationalism in France, see Girardet, pp. 8, 17–18, 28; E. Weber, *Action Française*; and the volumes by Sternhell, Curtis, Soucy, and Rémond. An excellent discussion of the liberal-socialist variety of patriotism is Ozouf and Ozouf, "Thème du patriotisme."

CHAPTER SEVEN

1. See, for example, Halff, *Fidélité*; Anchel, "Sentiment"; and three works by Raphael and Weyl: *Juifs en Alsace*, p. 387, "Juifs d'Alsace," and *Regards*, pp. 248–49.
2. Roth, *Lorraine*, pp. 34, 144.
3. "De la réorganisation du culte israélite en Alsace-Lorraine," *Courrier du Bas-Rhin*, suppl. no. 275, Nov. 25, 1871. See also UI, Jan. 15, 1872, pp. 299–303; and *L'Alsace-Lorraine israélite*, Sept. 7, 1877, pp. 9–11. The RI claimed that the author of the article was a former French civil servant. RI, Jan. 19, 1872, p. 8.
4. RI, Jan. 12, 1872, pp. 69–70.
5. RI, Dec. 22, 1871, p. 42.
6. *Courrier du Bas-Rhin*, Jan. 26, 1872.
7. *L'Alsace-Lorraine israélite*, Sept. 7, 1877, pp. 9–11, Oct. 19, 1877, pp. 3–4.
8. AZJ, Oct. 9, 1871, p. 883; minutes, Lorraine Consistory, March 12, 1871, ADM, 17 J 41; Lorraine Consistory to Bezirkspräsident, Lorraine, March 23, 1874, ADM, 7 AL 4.
9. Minutes, Lorraine Consistory, March 12, 1871, ADM, 17 J 41.
10. See various government reports confirming elections of Consistory officials in ADBR, AL 133 paq. 27 102–104.
11. Roth, *Lorraine*, p. 144.
12. Minutes, Lorraine Consistory, July 25, 1875, p. 100, ADM, 17 J 41; minutes, Bas-Rhin Consistory, March 1, 1887, ADBR, D 240 195(39-6); *Jüdischer Sprechsaal*, March 15, 1883, p. 17; SIW, Jan. 16, 1908, p. 5.
13. Inquiry, District School Inspector to Kreisdirector, Sarrebourg, Aug. 29, 1873, ADM, 7 AL 3; Kreisdirector, Sarrebourg, to Bezirkspräsident, Lorraine, Aug. 30, 1873, ibid.
14. Minutes, Lorraine Consistory, Oct. 19, 1873, p. 60, ADM, 17 J 41.
15. Ibid.; Lorraine Consistory to Bezirkspräsident, Lorraine, Oct. 10, 1873, ADBR, AL 133 paq. 27 104.
16. Kreisdirector, Sarrebourg, to Count von Arnim, Bezirkspräsident, Lorraine, March 21, 1874, ADBR, AL 133 paq. 27 104, and ADM, 7 AL 4; Bezirkspräsident, Lorraine, to von Möller, Oberpräsident, Alsace-Lorraine, May 20, 1874, ADBR, AL 133 paq. 27 104.
17. Roth, *Lorraine*, pp. 143–44.
18. Police Director, Strasbourg, supplemental reports, Aug. 14, Sept. 30,

1871, ADBR, AL 71 277; Bezirkspräsident, Lorraine, to von Möller, Oberpräsident, Alsace-Lorraine, May 20, 1874, ADBR, AL 133 paq. 27 104.

19. On promises to protect Jewish civil rights, see the *Strassburger Zeitung*, Sept. 13, Sept. 30, 1871; RI, Sept. 8, 1871, p. 661, Sept. 22, 1871, p. 691, Oct. 27, 1871, p. 78; AI, Oct. 15, 1871, pp. 333–34, Nov. 1, 1871, p. 364; Roth, *Lorraine*, p. 22; and AZJ, Sept. 25, 1871, p. 781. On salary increases, see Oberpräsident, Alsace-Lorraine, to Jewish Consistories, ADBR, D 11 10 109/1; *L'Alsace-Lorraine israélite*, Dec. 31, 1877, p. 12; *Courrier du Bas-Rhin*, May 25, 1872; and "Histoire de nos communautés— Sarre-Union-Bouquenom," p. 28.

20. UI, July 15, 1872, p. 678, April 1, 1874, p. 474, Nov. 8, 1895, p. 217; AI, Oct. 15, 1874, p. 622, Sept. 14, 1905, p. 289.

21. Rossé et al., 3 : 358.

22. Bezirkspräsident, Haut-Rhin, to von Möller, Oberpräsident, Alsace-Lorraine, Dec. 15, 1872, ADBR, AL 133 paq. 27 102.

23. Cited in UI, Sept. 15, 1874, p. 55. When Prince von Hohenlohe-Langenburg became the Statthalter of Alsace-Lorraine in 1885, he promised to follow in Manteuffel's footsteps and fight antisemitism. AZJ, Dec. 1, 1885, p. 785.

24. August Rohling, *Response to the Rabbis: The Jewish Blood Ritual*. On Rohling, see G. Mosse, pp. 129–30. On the suppression of Rohling's pamphlet in Alsace-Lorraine, see minutes, extraordinary meeting, Consistories of Metz, Strasbourg, and Colmar, March 25, 1883, CBR; UI, May 1, 1883; and *L'Alsace-Lorraine israélite*, April 5, 1883, p. 33. Ginsburger, "Elsässische Juden," p. 28, also notes that antisemitic literature in Alsace-Lorraine was not tolerated by the government.

25. Police Director, Metz, to Bezirkspräsident, Lorraine, Jan. 12, Feb. 29, 1884, ADM, 2 AL 90; Roth, *Lorraine*, pp. 419–20. On the Bas-Rhin Consistory's success in persuading the government to ban antisemitic literature, see AI, Aug. 2, 1883, pp. 247–48.

26. Grand Rabbi Aron of Strasbourg requested that the pamphlet be banned on Oct. 25, 1886. The government banned it on Nov. 4, 1886. ADBR, D 98 191. On Fritsch, who in this case went under the name Thomas Frey, see G. Mosse, p. 112.

27. On Liebermann von Sonnenberg's career in Alsace-Lorraine, see AI, Jan. 4, 1894; Roth, *Lorraine*, p. 507; UI, March 26, 1897, Sept. 9, 1904; and *Journal d'Alsace*, Sept. 10, 1897, March 9, 1898, p. 3. On von Sonnenberg in general, see Richard Levy.

28. More than once, the government of Alsace-Lorraine warned local officials not to indulge in antisemitism. See Under State Secretary, Ministry of Religion and Education, to Bezirkspräsident, Bas-Rhin, April 4, 1881, and Kreisdirector, Saverne, to Bezirkspräsident, Bas-Rhin, Dec. 29, 1886, Jan. 6, 1887, ADBR, D 98 191.

29. In 1885 the Bezirkspräsident in Strasbourg noted, "The Jewish communities have repeatedly expressed their satisfaction that, thanks to the conduct of the state authorities, antisemitic agitation has not been able to take root in the Reichsland." Bezirkspräsident, Bas-Rhin, administrative report, July 6, 1885, ADBR, AL 71 277. See also *L'Alsace-Lorraine israélite*, Sept. 7, 1877, p. 5; and *Jüdischer Sprechsaal*, Feb. 1, 1883, p. 3. Even the French Jewish press praised the firm stand of the Alsace-Lorraine regime against antisemitism. AI, Oct. 9, 1879, p. 336, Oct. 4, 1883, p. 320.

30. AI, March 22, 1883, p. 93, June 14, 1883, p. 195, June 4, 1885, p. 197; UI, June 1, 1877, p. 600, Nov. 16, 1885, p. 151.

31. A speaker for the Strasbourg chapter of the Centralverein claimed, "Although the Jews are much better off in Alsace than in other German states, even here we have to endure social antisemitism." "Unsere Kämpfe und unsere Pflichten," SIW, Nov. 13, 1913, p. 7.

32. AI, Nov. 15, 1871, p. 402; AZJ, Oct. 10, 1871, pp. 843–44; RI, Oct. 20, 1871, p. 758.

33. AI, June 1, 1872, p. 343.

34. RI, Oct. 5, 1871, pp. 734–35.

35. RI, Oct. 10, 1871, p. 758.

36. Cited in RI, Sept. 29, 1871, p. 715.

37. Cited in RI, Oct. 5, 1871, pp. 734–35.

38. AZJ, May 31, 1907, p. 3.

39. SIW, Jan. 2, 1908, p. 2.

40. AI, Dec. 22, 1910, p. 407. The *Wochenschrift* wrote, "The liberal press has shown that this nomination has succeeded despite the opposition of the Berlin authorities, who were forced to yield to the energetic determination of the Reichsland regime." Dec. 22, 1910, p. 6.

41. SIW, Nov. 24, 1910, p. 7.

42. AI, Dec. 22, 1910, p. 407; UI, Dec. 23, 1910, p. 744.

43. Craig, "Mission," pp. 390–91; Craig, *Scholarship*, p. 84.

44. Huisman, p. 149.

45. UI, May 14, 1897, p. 250. A letter from another University of Strasbourg professor testifying to the absence of antisemitism at the university appeared in the *Strassburger Post*, July 1, 1898, and in UI, Jan. 14, 1898, p. 538.

46. The Landesausschuss deputy in question was Spiess. The State Secretary, von Puttkamer, defended the appointments. UI, March 4, 1898, p. 764.

47. See "Simmel," in *Encyclopedia Judaica*, 1972 ed.; Craig, *Scholarship*, pp. 187, 192; and Gay, pp. 98, 120–21.

48. AZJ, March 30, 1906, suppl., p. 3.

49. UI, Jan. 13, 1911, p. 566; AZJ, Jan. 27, 1911, suppl., p. 3; AI, Feb. 9, 1911, p. 43; SIW, Feb. 16, 1911, p. 5.

50. SIW, Feb. 16, 1911, p. 5, June 15, 1911, p. 6; UI, March 3, 1911, p. 791.
51. SIW, Jan. 30, 1908, p. 6, Feb. 13, 1908, p. 4, May 7, 1908, p. 3, Feb. 25, 1909, p. 9.
52. *Das Jüdische Blatt*, April 28, 1911, p. 9; AZJ, March 30, 1906, suppl., p. 3; SIW, March 27, 1912, p. 7, March 5, 1914, p. 7; UI, March 4, 1898, p. 764.
53. SIW, March 27, 1912, p. 7.
54. For Simon Blum's biography, see SIW, Aug. 6, 1908, p. 6, and Aug. 18, 1908, p. 25.
55. Members of the Dettwiller Jewish community to Kreisdirector, Saverne, July 25, 1885, ADBR, D 240 195(39-6).
56. Members of the Dettwiller Jewish community to Kreisdirector, Saverne, Dec. 14, 1887, Police officer to Kreisdirector, Saverne, April 13, 1887, and Mayor, Dettwiller, to Kreisdirector, Saverne, Dec. 26, 1887, ibid.
57. Minutes, Bas-Rhin Consistory, Sept. 22, 1885, CBR; Bas-Rhin Consistory to Bezirkspräsident, Bas-Rhin, Sept. 28, 1885, Jan. 30, 1888, ADBR, D 240 195(39-6).
58. Kreisdirector, Saverne, to Bezirkspräsident, Bas-Rhin, Dec. 16, 1887, Bezirkspräsident, Bas-Rhin, to Kreisdirector, Saverne, Feb. 17, 1888, ADBR, D 240 195(39-6).
59. The Consistory actually claimed that the dispute over Blum's appointment grew out of a feud between two families in the community. Consistory, Bas-Rhin, to Bezirkspräsident, Bas-Rhin, Jan. 30, 1888, ibid.
60. Mayeur, p. 16.
61. See, for example, Fleurent, pp. 325-27; Roth, *Lorraine*, p. 12; Reuss, pp. 421, 429-30; Eccard, pp. 133, 152-53; Rossé et al., 2:23-24; and L'Huillier, *Histoire*, pp. 99-100.
62. On autonomism, see Mayeur, pp. 17, 69, 149, 188-89; Silverman, "Political Catholicism," p. 57; Reuss, pp. 429-32; Craig, *Scholarship*, pp. 136, 168-75; Roth, *Lorraine*, pp. 91, 668-70; and Braun, pp. 370-71.
63. Raphael and Weyl, *Juifs en Alsace*, p. 437.
64. A. Lipman, foreword to Netter, *Patrie*.
65. Police President, Strasbourg, to Bezirkspräsident, Bas-Rhin, March 12, 1900, ADBR, AL 27 548. On Lévy's earlier French patriotism, see AI, Dec. 15, 1871, pp. 464-65.
66. Emphasis in original. Cited in AZJ, Sept. 15, 1905, suppl., p. 3; and UI, Sept. 8, 1905, p. 794. See also AI, July 27, 1905, p. 239; Bezirkspräsident, Lorraine, to Lorraine Consistory, June 22, 1905, ADBR, AL 27 545.
67. Lorraine Consistory to Statthalter, June 17, 1906, ADM, 7 AL 3; Count von Zeppelin, Bezirkspräsident, Lorraine, to Statthalter, June 17, 1906, Lorraine Consistory to Statthalter, June 8, 1906, ADBR, AL 27 545;

AI, Dec. 26, 1907, p. 411; SIW, Jan. 2, 1908, p. 1, Jan. 3, 1908, p. 5; UI, March 6, 1908, p. 773.

68. "Metzer Brief," *Strassburger Burgerzeitung*, May 18, 1905, in the Bruno Weil Collection, Leo Baeck Institute, New York, AR-C 3055 7108; AI, Sept. 14, 1905, pp. 289–90.

69. UI, March 27, 1908, p. 55, May 13, 1910, p. 280; AI, June 18, 1908, p. 199, Sept. 10, 1908, p. 294; SIW, May 19, 1910, pp. 1–2, Nov. 16, 1911, p. 8.

70. On the 1911 Constitution, see Mayeur; François Dreyfus, pp. 12–13; and Dollinger, *Alsace*, pp. 33–34.

71. UI, Dec. 9, 1910, p. 405; AI, April 20, 1911, p. 123; SIW, June 15, 1911, pp. 3–4.

72. Cited in AI, April 20, 1911, p. 123. See also SIW, April 6, 1911, suppl.

73. *Das Jüdische Blatt*, June 1, 1911, p. 7, June 8, 1911, p. 8; SIW, June 1, 1911, p. 13; Netter, *Vingt siècles*, p. 488; Reuss, p. 440.

74. SIW, June 15, 1911, pp. 3–4.

75. SIW, Nov. 26, 1908, p. 4. See Ruland, pp. 79–83.

76. R.M., "En Alsace-Lorraine," UI, Feb. 11, 1910, pp. 677–83.

77. "Der Zentralverein im Elsass," SIW, July 10, 1913, p. 2. For the first generation of Western European Zionists, patriotism and Zionism were not necessarily antithetical. Many viewed their movement mainly as a remedy for their Eastern European coreligionists. See Schorsch, *Jewish Reactions*, pp. 179–202; Reinharz; Poppel; and Hertzberg, *Zionist Idea*, pp. 84–85.

78. SIW, Feb. 2, 1911, pp. 1–2; *Das Jüdische Blatt*, Feb. 28, 1913, p. 2; Elias, *Assimilations*, p. 4.

79. UI, Oct. 17, 1907, p. 138.

80. Netter, *Vingt siècles*, p. 469.

81. No German Jew was elected to the Consistorial board of Strasbourg until 1895, and it was 1900 before the first was elected in Metz. See notes 85 and 86, Chap. 5.

82. Articles by Bruno Weil of Jan. 25, Feb. 22, March 25, and Aug. 16, 1905, clipped in the Bruno Weil Collection, Leo Baeck Institute, New York, AR-C 3055 7108.

83. Cited in SIW, Nov. 24, 1910, p. 102. One of the primary debates with the German government over the matter of Jewish reserve officers revolved around the 1912 case of an Alsatian Jewish soldier, Arthur Lieber. For a brief account of this contest, see Angress, pp. 36–37.

84. SIW, Nov. 4, 1909, pp. 1–2; "Strasbourg," SIW, March 3, 1910; "Der Zentralverein im Elsass," SIW, July 10, 1913, pp. 1–2. For excellent histories of these organizations, see Schorsch, *Jewish Reactions*, and Ragins.

85. "Der Zentralverein im Elsass," SIW, July 10, 1913, p. 1.

86. Bezirkspräsident, Lorraine, to Ministry of Justice and Religion, May 4, 1900, State Secretary to Statthalter Hohenlohe-Langenburg, May 14, 1900, ADBR, AL 27 548.
87. Quoted in Collin, p. 48.
88. For Netter's pro-French speeches, see his *Patrie*. See also UI, Nov. 21, 1918, p. 199, Dec. 16, 1918, pp. 301-4, April 18, 1919, p. 153.
89. Director, Services of the Interior, to Commissioner General of the Republic, May 23, 1919, and to Rabbi Netter, May 27, 1919, ADBR, AL 133 119.
90. Netter, *Vingt siècles*, pp. 471-72.
91. ADBR, AL 133 120.
92. SIW, May 14, 1914; AI, Nov. 20, 1913, p. 375.
93. "La Page de Metz: Un chef spirituel du judaïsme, Le Grand Rabbin Nathan Netter," *Tribune Juive*, no. 29, 1933, p. 469.
94. See Dollinger, *Alsace*, pp. 34, 52-53.
95. Police President, Metz, to Bezirkspräsident, Lorraine, Dec. 16, 1910, ADM, 7 AL 4.
96. Ibid. The Bezirkspräsident forwarded these recommendations to the Ministry of Justice and Religion, Dec. 31, 1910, ADBR, AL 133 paq. 27 104.
97. State Secretary, Ministry of Justice and Religion, to Statthalter von Wedel, Jan. 13, 1911, ADBR, AL 27 548.
98. See Silverman, *Reluctant Union*, pp. 195-97; and Morrison, pp. 425-36. For a full discussion of the Zabern (Saverne) Affair and its far-reaching political consequences, see Schoenbaum.
99. State Secretary, Ministry of Justice and Religion, to Statthalter Hohenlohe-Langenburg, July 17, 1901, ADBR, AL 27 548; Bezirkspräsident, Lorraine, to Ministry of Justice and Religion, Feb. 1, 1915, ADBR, AL 133 paq. 27 104.
100. P. Lévy, *Histoire*, p. 481.
101. Adolph Levy, Diedenhofen (Thionville), to Bezirkspräsident, Metz, Dec. 4, 1914, ADM, 7 AL 4; Roth, *Lorraine*, p. 601.
102. Bezirkspräsident, Lorraine, to Ministry of Justice and Religion, Feb. 1, 1915, ADBR, AL 133 paq. 27 104; ADM, 7 AL 4.
103. Under State Secretary, Ministry of Justice and Religion, to Bezirkspräsident, Lorraine, Feb. 17, 1915, ADBR, AL 133 paq. 27 104; ADM, 7 AL 4.
104. Lorraine Consistory to Bezirkspräsident, Lorraine, Sept. 22, Oct. 31, Nov. 3, Nov. 17, 1915, Bezirkspräsident, Lorraine, to Ministry of Justice and Religion, official confirmation notice, Nov. 19, 1915, ADBR, AL 133 paq. 27 104; State Secretary, Ministry of Justice and Religion, to Statthalter von Dallwitz, Nov. 17, 1915, ADBR, AL 27 548; Under State Secretary,

Ministry of Justice and Religion, to Bezirkspräsident, Lorraine, Oct. 16, 1915, ADM, 7 AL 4.

CHAPTER EIGHT

1. E. Weber, *Peasants*, especially pp. 115-29, 195-220. For an excellent study of the socioeconomic transformation of the Jews in the modern period, see Goldscheider and Zuckerman.
2. See Tables 4.1 and 4.2.
3. Hyman, "Jewish Fertility," p. 84.
4. Schnurmann, pp. 99-106. Schnurmann's figures, derived from the *Bulletin statistique mensuel de la ville de Strasbourg*, vols. 1-26, have their limitations: birthrates are based on the total population, male and female, not on the population of childbearing age; with respect to some births, the mothers were not actually residing in Strasbourg; and there is no differentiation between natives and foreigners. For an excellent collection of essays on this subject in general, see Ritterband.
5. Schnurmann, p. 106. See also Wallerstein; and Hammel.
6. Schnurmann, pp. 112-13; A. Wahl, *Confession*, 1: 109-10, 130-39. On the rural-urban differential, see Lowenstein, "Voluntary and Involuntary Limitation," p. 100; and Hyman, "Jewish Fertility," p. 86. Hyman shows that for Alsace-Lorraine Jewry this rural-urban differential became evident only after 1851. For a general discussion of the impact of urbanization on Jews, see Ritterband, pp. 8-12.
7. Schnurmann, p. 109.
8. Ibid., pp. 74-76.
9. Ibid., p. 82.
10. Wallerstein, p. 582.
11. Schnurmann, pp. 114-15. Schnurmann's source of information for these figures is *Statistique de Strasbourg* (1923). For a discussion of the influence of secularization on fertility patterns, see Ritterband, pp. 12-15. On the influence of economic change on family structure in general, see E. Weber, *Peasants*, pp. 167-94; and Tilly and Scott.
12. Schnurmann, pp. 115-16.
13. Ibid., pp. 11-17; Bensimon-Donath, p. 111.
14. See especially Moïse Ginsburger, "Die Landflucht in Elsass-Lothringen," SIW, Aug. 17, 1911, pp. 1-2. On similar processes occurring in Baden, see Goldstein, "Urbanization in Baden."
15. P. Lévy, "Démographie," p. 363.
16. Arthur Weil, p. 109; "Auszug aus dem Register der Beratungen des Gemeinderats Buchsweiler, Unter-Elsass," Feb. 26, 1895, ADBR, D 388 98 (624).
17. UI, April 14, 1905, p. 119, May 28, 1909, p. 343; Under State Secre-

tary, Ministry of Justice and Religion, to Bezirkspräsident, Lorraine, and to Lorraine Consistory, April 17, 1909, Bezirkspräsident, Lorraine, to Kreisdirector, Diedenhofen-Ost (Thionville-Est), April 5, 1910, ADM, 17 Z 228(X64).

18. Uhry, 1:20, 2:249–50; *Das Jüdische Blatt*, Dec. 22, 1911, p. 2. On the impact of improved communications and transportation on social change in general, see E. Weber, *Peasants*, pp. 195–220; and Thabault, pp. 42–44, 68–76, 94–95, 114–15, 133–35, 164–65, 194, 229–30.

19. Schnurmann, p. 11; Raphael, "Stéréotype," p. 144; Juillard, *Vie rurale*, p. 448; "Les Juifs en Alsace," *L'Ami du Peuple*, no. 16, 1966, p. 10; Mangold, p. 36; André Neher, "Bourgeoisie," p. 438; Rossé et al., 3:353; Wallerstein, p. 582; A. Wahl, *Confession*, 1:587. For antisemitic tendencies in the Raiffeisen banks, see Chap. 6.

20. On government restrictions on cattle and horse dealing, see SIW, Feb. 4, 1909, p. 2, Nov. 4, 1909, p. 7, April 7, 1910, p. 4, June 8, 1911, p. 6, Jan. 4, 1912, pp. 2–3; Elias, *Assimilations*, p. 6; and Elias, *Die jüdische Handwerksschule*, pp. 11–12. On the organization of the cattle dealers, see SIW, Feb. 6, 1909, p. 6, Feb. 16, 1909, p. 9, Dec. 30, 1909, p. 10, Jan. 27, 1911, p. 7, and March 6, 1912, p. 7.

21. *Der Elsässer*, Dec. 20, 1898.

22. Schnurmann, p. 11. See also Elias, *Die jüdische Handwerksschule*, p. 12; and Hammel. On parallel socioeconomic developments elsewhere in Central Europe at the turn of the century, see Goldstein, "Urbanization," pp. 48–49; Goldstein, "Aspects of Change"; and Robert S. Wistrich, "Austrian Social Democracy and Galician Jewry, 1890–1914," *Leo Baeck Institute Year Book*, 26 (1981), pp. 94–96.

23. Schnurmann, p. 21.

24. Register of Income and expenses for the Wissembourg Jewish community's poor and charity fund, Jan. 1, 1895–Jan. 1, 1896, ADBR, D 240 197.

25. SIW, Feb. 20, 1908, p. 4; Raphael and Weyl, *Juifs en Alsace*, p. 364; P. Lévy, "Démographie," p. 364.

26. G. Cahen, "Juifs dans la région Lorraine," p. 78; Raphael and Weyl, *Juifs en Alsace*, p. 364; SIW, Feb. 20, 1908, p. 4.

27. Netter, *Vingt siècles*, p. 44; Lipman, pp. 17, 37–38, 41–42, 47; Stern, p. 147.

28. UI, April 1, 1887, p. 442. See also SIW, June 2, 1910, p. 8, Aug. 31, 1911, p. 10, July 14, 1914, p. 7.

29. Bezirkspräsident, Haut-Rhin, administrative report, Jan. 8, 1900, ADBR, AL 71 277.

30. See files on the Eastern European immigrants Abraham Silber, ADBR, D 98 36(29-8), J. Katz, ADBR, D 98 208, and Wolf Liebermann, ADBR, D 98 207. See also SIW, June 2, 1910, p. 8. On German

administrative policies toward Eastern European Jewish immigrants, see Wertheimer, "Unwanted Element."

31. On efforts of Alsace-Lorraine Jews to aid their Eastern European coreligionists, see AI, July 2, 1891, p. 213; and UI, Dec. 29, 1905, p. 482.

32. Raphael, "Rencontre," pp. 207, 211, 215, 220; Raphael and Weyl, *Regards*, pp. 255–59.

33. Raphael, "Rencontre," p. 217.

34. See the numerous articles on the *Wanderarmen* in the SIW throughout 1909.

35. Bas-Rhin Consistory to Bezirkspräsident, Bas-Rhin, Aug. 30, 1900, ADBR, D 240 198; Lorraine Consistory to Police President, Metz, Sept. 20, 1908, ADM, 7 AL 4; SIW, Jan. 7, 1908, p. 3, Feb. 20, 1908, p. 4, June 23, 1910, p. 8; Roth, *Lorraine*, p. 144. For works dealing with the friction between native Western Jews and Eastern European immigrants in other contexts, see Wertheimer, "German Policy"; Wertheimer, "Unwanted Element," pp. 37–39; Hyman, *From Dreyfus*, especially pp. 115–52; Weinberg; and Gartner, pp. 49–56.

36. Sources for an analysis of the occupational structure of Alsace-Lorraine Jewry in this period include an 1890 electoral list for the Jewish Consistory of Lorraine, ADM, 7 AL 3; Statistischen Bureau, *Statistisches Handbuch*, 1902, p. 81; *Statistisches Jahrbuch*, 1909, p. 34; and Schnurmann, pp. 23–59, based on manuscript censuses of the Office Régional de Statistique d'Alsace et de Lorraine. Unfortunately, more than a few cursory comments on social mobility in this period would be unwarranted, since most of the sources employed in such studies—manuscript censuses and birth, marriage, and death records—no longer exist for the years 1871–1914. (A study could perhaps be done of Strasbourg, since most of the *état civil* records are extant.) Furthermore, although several studies of Jewish social mobility in Alsace prior to 1870 have recently been completed, it is difficult to compare them with the data in the 1895 and 1907 censuses, since the occupational categories are different. See, for example, Hyman, "Migration and Social Mobility"; and D. Cohen, *Promotion*, 1:344–77.

37. Hyman, "Migration," Table 4.

38. "Final List of Jewish Voters in the Province of Lorraine," Oct. 24, 1890, ADM, 7 AL 3; Roth, *Lorraine*, pp. 227, 419, 440.

39. On the relationship between migration and the persistence of traditional socioeconomic structures in rural villages, see Köllman, p. 70; and Lowenstein, "Rural Community."

40. Schnurmann, pp. 45, 154–60.

41. Ibid., p. 46. This manuscript census has been destroyed.

42. Ibid., pp. 46–47.

43. Klein, pp. 142–44; Rossé et al, 2:337; Sayous, p. 5.

44. Schnurmann, p. 56. On the rising number of Jews in white-collar professions elsewhere in Europe at this time, see Rozenblit, pp. 47–70.
45. Schnurmann, p. 30. See also footnote, p. 11.
46. Ibid., pp. 30–42.
47. Hyman, "Migration," Table 4. For the Strasbourg-campagne figures, see my Table 4.8.
48. Schnurmann, pp. 49–51.
49. According to Hyman's sample of Jews in 1846, only 1% of Strasbourg Jews and less than 0.5% of village Jews were involved in civil service professions. See "Migration," Table 4.
50. Roth, *Lorraine*, p. 419.
51. André Neher, "Bourgeoisie," pp. 435–36, 439–41.
52. Raphael and Weyl, *Juifs en Alsace*, p. 381.
53. Hyman, "Migration," pp. 18, 20; Albert, *Modernization*, p. 26.
54. André Neher, "Bourgeoisie," pp. 438–39.
55. Schwarzfuchs, *Juifs*, p. 284.
56. Statistischen Bureau, *Statistisches Handbuch, 1885*, pp. 157–58.
57. Ibid., *Statistisches Jahrbuch, 1911*, p. 238.
58. Ibid., *Statistisches Handbuch, 1902*, p. 469.
59. Craig, "Mission," p. 424; Craig, *Scholarship*, p. 120.
60. SIW, June 17, 1909, p. 9. On the continuing low enrollment rates of native Alsace-Lorraine Jews at the University of Strasbourg in comparison with Jewish enrollment at other German universities, see Craig, *Scholarship*, pp. 114, 360.
61. SIW, Nov. 26, 1908, p. 6.
62. Statistischen Bureau, *Statistisches Jahrbuch, 1913/14*, p. 224.
63. Marrus, pp. 60–62.
64. Schnurmann, pp. 18–19. The figures for Alsace-Lorraine are based on manuscript documents from the Bishopric of Strasbourg. The statistics on other European cities are from A. Ruppin, *Soziologie der Juden* (Berlin, 1930), 1: 305–6.

CHAPTER NINE

1. Halff, "Jews," p. 61. See also Halff, *Fidélité*, pp. 9–10; Schwarzfuchs, *Juifs*, p. 283; Esther Lévy, entry of Oct. 24, 1915, p. 139; UI, Dec. 20, 1918, p. 346; and *La Guerre*, p. 4.
2. Esther Lévy, entry of Aug. 11, 1914, p. 36. See also L'Huillier, *Histoire*, p. 109; and Raphael and Weyl, *Juifs en Alsace*, p. 438.
3. Dollinger, *Alsace*, pp. 73–74; Netter, *Vingt siècles*, pp. 449–50, 489; Morrison, pp. 436–39.
4. Raphael and Weyl, *Juifs en Alsace*, p. 438; Florent-Matter, pp. 65–66; UI, Feb. 9, 1917, p. 481; Halff, *Fidélité*, p. 12; Halff, "Jews," pp. 61–62.
5. Esther Lévy, entries of Aug. 13, 1914, p. 39, Oct. 25, 1915, p. 139. For

the Franco-Jewish view of the impact of the "germanization" campaign during the war, see UI, Dec. 20, 1918, p. 347.

6. AZJ, Sept. 8, 1914, suppl., p. 4.

7. Minister of War, Berlin, to Minister of Interior, Sept. 2, 1916, ADBR, D 68 paq. 2 ∫ 14.

8. Bezirkspräsident, Haut-Rhin, to Ministry of Justice and Religion, Jan. 10, 1916, ADBR, AL 133 102; *Jahrbuch der Gesellschaft*, pp. 44-45. On Meyer, see Supreme Court of Justice, Mulhouse, to Bezirkspräsident, Haut-Rhin, Aug. 19, 1916, and reply of Aug. 23, 1916, ADBR, D 68 paq. 2 ∫ 14.

9. Councilor of State, Commissioner of French Republic in Colmar, to Under Secretary of State, President of the Council, Jan. 2, 1918, Commissioner of French Republic to High Commissioner of French Republic, Strasbourg, March 27, 1919, ADBR, AL 133 102; UI, April 4, 1919, p. 197; Camille Dreyfus, ed., *Le Juif* (Strasbourg), Oct. 9, 1919, p. 2.

10. Halff, *Fidélité*, pp. 10, 26-28; Halff, "Jews," pp. 61, 74-78.

11. Chief of Police, Breuschwickersheim, to Kreisdirector, Strasbourg-campagne, April 18, 1915, ADBR, D 398 130(78.7).

12. Halff, *Fidélité*, p. 10; Halff, "Jews," p. 65. For a brief biographical sketch of Weill, see Morrison, pp. 162-63.

13. Halff, *Fidélité*, pp. 14-17; Halff, "Jews," pp. 65-66; Blum; UI, Oct. 4, 1935, p. 19; Netter, *Patrie*, p. 83.

14. Netter, *Vingt siècles*, p. 439.

15. *Le Matin*, Jan. 28, 1919, cited in UI, Feb. 21, 1919, pp. 578-79; Halff, *Fidélité*, pp. 11-12; Halff, "Jews," pp. 62-63.

16. UI, Dec. 12, 1919, p. 274.

17. Heinrich Class, *Wider den Strom*, cited in Morrison, p. 472. The reliability of Class's account might be colored by his strong antisemitic bias.

18. Halff, *Fidélité*, p. 11; see also Halff's other works.

19. Florent-Matter, pp. 165-239; Halff, *Fidélité*, pp. 10-11; Halff, "Jews," pp. 61-62.

20. Evidence on Military Defectors from the District of Saverne," Jan. 11, 1915, ADBR, D 388 paq. 78(474). See also police reports on draft evaders from Strasbourg-campagne, 1915, ADBR, D 398 130(78.7).

21. Florent-Matter, pp. 165-239.

22. Reuss, p. 451; Blumenthal, *Alsace-Lorraine*, p. 55. For partial lists of deserters at the end of 1915, see Florent-Matter, pp. 143-64, who asserts that the Germans themselves estimated the number of deserters at more than 30,000 at the end of 1915.

23. UI, Aug. 4, 1916, cited in Spire, p. 22; Sylvain Lévy, Introduction, and letter from the Archives and Library of Strasbourg, March 1918.

24. Sylvain Lévy, Raoul Bloch to his family, Jan. 6, 1915, pp. 19-20. See also *La Guerre*, pp. 49-50; Halff, *Fidélité*, p. 9; and Halff, "Jews," pp. 60-61.

25. Sylvain Lévy, Raoul Bloch to his family, Sept. 10, 1915, p. 22.
26. Jaeger, "Alsaciens," pp. 636, 639.
27. Halff, *Fidélité*, p. 18.
28. Uhry, 2:290.
29. UI, Dec. 21, 1918; Consistoire israélite du Bas-Rhin, *Souvenirs des services solennels célébrés en novembre et décembre 1917 à l'occasion du retour de l'Alsace et de la Lorraine à la France*, pp. 20-21, in AMS, 371/2104; CC, I E-IV, Dec. 2, 1918.
30. UI, Dec. 27, 1918, p. 373, Jan. 13, 1919, p. 396; Metz Consistory to Central Consistory, Dec. 1918, CC, I E-IV; UI, Dec. 27, 1918, pp. 372-73, in CC, I A 8f.
31. Berg, p. 10; *Souvenirs des services*, (as cited in n. 29, above), pp. 19-20; AI, Nov. 21, 1918, p. 198.
32. Central Consistory to Clemenceau and Foch, Nov. 11, 1918, CC, I E-IV and CP B 105.
33. Councilor of State, Commissioner of French Republic in Colmar, to Under Secretary of State, President of the Council, Strasbourg, Jan. 2, 1918, ADBR, AL 133 102.
34. Ibid.; Commissioner of French Republic to High Commissioner of French Republic, Strasbourg, March 27, 1919, ADBR, AL 133 102; UI, April 4, 1919; C. Dreyfus, ed., *Le Juif*, (Strasbourg), Oct. 9, 1919, p. 2.
35. UI, June 23, 1916, pp. 394-95; State Secretary, Alsace-Lorraine, report, May 10, 1916, ADBR, AL 27 548; Joseph Bloch, *Historique*, p. 31.
36. Altorffer, p. 664; *Im Deutschen Reich*, 25 (1919): 167, cited in Niewyk, p. 110.
37. UI, Dec. 6, 1917, pp. 309-12, in CC, I A 8f.
38. Lucien Dreyfus, pp. 201-8.
39. Alsatian taxpayers to President of Central Consistory, Dec. 8, 1918, CC, 3 G 2.
40. Schwarzfuchs, p. 284; Netter, *Vingt siècles*, p. 511.
41. UI, Feb. 6, 1919, p. 527; Rossé et al., 3:359.

CHAPTER TEN

1. For debates on whether patriotism is grounded in practical benefits or is an abstract idea, see E. Weber, *Peasants*, pp. 95-114. On the commitment of Jews to political liberalism, see Niewyk, *Jews*; and Schorsch, "On History," pp. 14-16. Schorsch points out that in countries where Jews were not granted civil rights, they generally supported the opposition to the central government.
2. See Arendt, *Antisemitism*; and Marrus, *Politics of Assimilation*. For an excellent critical discussion of Arendt's thesis on Jewish political behavior, see Sharon Muller.

3. On the way nationalism paradoxically became a divisive rather than an integrative force in late-19th-century France in general, see Zeldin, 2:24-25.

4. On the nationalistic sentiments of Jews in Central Europe and their allegiance to liberalism and the state, see G. Cohen, *Politics*; G. Cohen, "Jews"; McCagg; Kann, "German-Speaking Jewry"; Kann, "Hungarian Jewry"; Baron, "Revolution"; Barany; and *Jews of Czechoslovakia*.

5. On the growth of the autonomist movement during the interwar years, see Bankwitz; Zeldin, 2:29-85; and Rothenberger, *Die elsasslothringische*.

6. Raphael and Weyl, *Juifs en Alsace*, p. 401; Raphael, "Rencontre." On this problem in France in general, see Hyman, *From Dreyfus*, pp. 115-52; and Weinberg, pp. 72-170.

7. Weinberg, p. 27.

8. See Deborah Dash Moore, *At Home in America: Second-Generation New York Jews* (New York, 1961).

9. On Vichy's Jewish policy, see Marrus and Paxton.

APPENDIX A

1. The sources are as follows. *Bas-Rhin*: (1) district of Strasbourg-ville, AMS, série administrative et contemporaine, RSEM, chemise 531; (2) district of Strasbourg-campagne, ADBR, D 398 paq. 9; (3) district of Haguenau, individual declarations, ADBR, D 384 paq. 30; listed by municipality, ADBR, D 383 paq. 23; (4) district of Wissembourg, ADBR, D 414 paq. 321; (5) district of Saverne, ADBR, D 388 paq. 60 and 61. *Haut-Rhin*: (1) district of Colmar, ADHR série purgatoire 25372 to 25377; (2) three municipalities in the district of Altkirch: (a) ADHR, Altkirch 7381; (b) ADHR, Durmenach 7404; (c) ADHR, Wittersdorf 7481. *Lorraine*: district of Sarreguemines, ADM, 16 Z 191. The communities in Haut-Rhin and Lorraine were selected because they included sizable Jewish populations.

2. For onomastic guides to Jewish names, see Heimerdinger, "Les Noms des israélites d'Alsace (1784)," UI, Dec. 27, 1901, pp. 467-71; A. Gain, "Population"; and Mendel. In doubtful cases, I checked birth certificates when possible.

3. A. Wahl, *Option*, pp. 78, 180-81, 190. Wahl claims that although the German government estimated the number of emigrants at between 2,000 and 3,000, the more likely range was 10,000-15,000. On the general regulations regarding option and controversies between the French and German governments over specific points of Article Two of the Treaty of Frankfurt, see ibid., pp. 44-46, 60; A. Wahl, "Metz," p. 83; Hiegel, "Option," 1974: 90-91; Silverman, *Reluctant Union*, p. 68; Reuss, p. 385; and *Journal des débats*, Feb. 25, 1875.

4. A. Wahl, *Option*, pp. 69–70, 78.

5. Hiegel, "Option," 1974:91; A. Wahl, *Option*, pp. 151, 213–14; *Journal des débats*, Dec. 25, 1875.

6. There are approximately 110,000 invalid options. See Reuss, p. 389; Pfister, *Pages*, p. 259; and Eccard, p. 62. Emigrés can be traced only by checking the lists of valid and invalid options against either the manuscript censuses or electoral rolls, and only a few of those records have survived. For sources, see A. Wahl, *Option*, "Aperçu des sources, méthodologie," sec. D-b.

7. Alfred Wahl claims that the gross total of options filed in France and abroad was 388,150, rather than the traditionally cited figure of 378,777, but estimates that once all the multiple-option declarations are subtracted, the net figure is about 372,000. Wahl, *Option*, pp. 131, 144. For options declared in France, see the printed *Bulletin des lois*, 1872–76. These volumes are available in most French libraries. They are also available on the Mormons' microfilm collection "France, Bas-Rhin, Citizenship, Ministre de Justice, *Bulletin des lois*, Option, 787154 and ff" (available from Salt Lake City at local Mormon churches). For options declared outside France, see Wahl, *Option*, "Aperçu des sources, méthodologie," sec. C.

APPENDIX B

1. ADBR, D 384 37–44. For several reasons, I have preferred to work with the individual dossiers of applicants rather than with unpublished emigration statistics compiled by local and provincial authorities. First, the individual dossiers date back to the early 1870's, whereas the government did not begin to tabulate emigration statistics until 1883. Furthermore, I was able to find tables only for the years 1883–92 and 1903–10. Second, although the official tables are broken down according to age, gender, religion, occupation, and destination, this information is not given for individual applicants. Finally, there are some inaccuracies in these tables, since the district figures do not always add up to the total for the province as a whole. Statistics on emigration from Bas-Rhin, broken down by district, are in ADBR, D 49 49, and ADBR, D 98-16a. Additional information on Strasbourg-campagne is in ADBR, D 398 paq. 7(35); on Strasbourg-ville, ADBR, D 49 68; on Saverne, ADBR, D 388 76; and on Haguenau, ADBR, D 384 37.

2. In the case of emigration, in contrast to option, there is less uncertainty about people's religion since birth certificates, which bore this information after 1871 when Alsace-Lorraine became German, were generally included in the applicant's file. For those born before 1871, when religion was not stated on French birth certificates, religion can usually be inferred from the parents' names.

3. On regulations regarding emigration permits, see Uhry, 1:145; Hiegel, "Option," 1975:93–94; Roth, *Lorraine*, pp. 108–9; *Journal d'Alsace*, Feb. 19, 1879, pp. 2–3; *Courrier du Bas-Rhin*, Sept. 4, 1872, July 18, 1874; and Silverman, *Reluctant Union*, pp. 219–20.

4. Illegal emigrants could not return to the Reichsland until they had passed the age of 55, and they were required to pay a fine. On illegal emigration see Roth, *Lorraine*, pp. 113–16; Hiegel, "Option," 1975:pp. 85–88; Silverman, *Reluctant Union*, p. 72; Reuss, pp. 392–93; Redslob, pp. 443–44.

Bibliography

The following abbreviations are used in the Bibliography: BNC, *Bulletin de Nos Communautés*; JSS, *Jewish Social Studies*; LBIYB, *Leo Baeck Institute Year Book*; and UI, *Univers Israélite*.

"Adresse présentée à l'Assemblée Nationale le 31 aôut 1789 par les députés des juifs." In vol. 5 of *La Révolution française et l'émancipation des juifs*. Paris, 1968.

Albert, Phyllis Cohen. *The Modernization of French Jewry: Consistory and Community in the Nineteenth Century*. Hanover, N.H., 1977.

———. "Non-Orthodox Attitudes in Nineteenth-Century French Judaism." In Albert and Frances Malino, eds., *Essays in Modern Jewish History*. East Brunswick, N.J., 1982, pp. 121–41.

———. "Le Rôle des consistoires israélites vers le milieu de xixe siècle," *Revue des Etudes Juives*, 130. 2–4 (April–Dec. 1971): 231–54.

Allgemeine Zeitung des Judentums. Gedenkbuch an den deutsch-französischen Krieg von 1870–1871 für die deutschen Israeliten. Bonn, 1871.

"Alsaciens et Lorrains aux Etats-Unis d'Amérique," *L'Alsace Française*, 13.21 (May 21, 1927): 401–22.

Altman, Georges. "Alexandre Weill, familier de Victor Hugo," *Evidences*, Jan. 1952, pp. 27–32.

Altorffer, Charles. "Le Recrutement des ministres des cultes." In Comité Alsacien d'Etudes, listed below, vol. 1, pp. 59–65.

Anchel, Robert. "L'Alsace juive depuis l'armistice," UI, 87 (1932): 360–61.

———. "L'Histoire des juifs en France." In *La Question juive vue par vingt-six éminentes personnalités*. Paris, 1934, pp. 19–33.

———. Review of Félix Ponteil, *L'Opposition politique à Strasbourg sous la monarchie de juillet, 1830–1848*, UI, 88 (Nov. 4, 1932): 180–81.

———. "Le Sentiment français des israélites d'Alsace," UI, 91 (Sept. 27, 1935): 11.

Angress, Werner T. "Prussia's Army and the Jewish Reserve Officer Controversy Before World War I," LBIYB, 17 (1972): 19–42.
Arendt, Hannah. *The Origins of Totalitarianism*, part 1: *Antisemitism*. New York, 1951.
Aron, Joseph. *Alsace-Lorraine: Monument to Grant (Refusal of Mayor Grace's invitation by a native of Phalsbourg, and his explanation)*. New York, 1885.
Asch, A. *Journal de la guerre, 1870–1871*. Strasbourg, 1937.
Aschkanaze, M. *Fest-Predigt zum neunzigsten Geburtstage Sr. Majestät des Kaisers und Königs Wilhelm I, 19 März, 1887*. Strassburg, 1887.
"L'Autonomie Alsacienne-Lorraine," *L'Europe Nouvelle*, 7.171 (Nov. 1908): 3–4.
Baas, Emile. "Notes pour une sociologie de la bourgeoisie alsacienne contemporaine." In *La Bourgeoisie alsacienne*, listed below, pp. 333–41.
Bader, Jeffrey A. "The Nationalist Leagues in France after Dreyfus, 1898–1906." Ph.D. dissertation, Columbia University, 1975.
Baechler, Christian. *Le Parti catholique alsacien, 1890–1939: Du Reichsland à la république jacobine*. Paris, 1982.
Bailly, Louis. "Die Juden in Hinsicht der elsässische Bevölkerungsgeschichte," *Nouvel Alsacien* (2 parts), Aug. 20, Sept. 31, 1952.
Bankwitz, Philip C. F. *Alsatian Autonomist Leaders, 1919–1947*. Lawrence, Kans., 1978.
Barany, George. "'Magyar Jew or Jewish Magyar?' (To the Question of Jewish Assimilation in Hungary)," *Canadian-American Slavic Studies*, 8.1 (Spring 1974): 1–44.
Barkai, Avraham. "German-Jewish Migrations in the Nineteenth Century, 1830–1910," LBIYB, 30 (1985): 301–18.
———. "The German Jews at the Start of Industrialization: Structural Change and Mobility, 1835–1860." In Werner Mosse et al., eds., *Revolution and Evolution: 1848 in German-Jewish History*. Tübingen, 1981, pp. 123–49.
Baron, Salo W. "Ghetto and Emancipation," *Menorah Journal*, 14 (June 1928): 515–26.
———. *The Jewish Community*. 3 vols. Philadelphia, 1942.
———. *Modern Nationalism and Religion*. New York, 1947.
———. "Newer Approaches to Jewish Emancipation," *Diogenes*, Spring 1960, pp. 56–81.
———. "The Revolution of 1848 and Jewish Emancipation," *JSS*, 11 (1949): 195–248.
———. *A Social and Religious History of the Jews*, vols. 3 and 4. 2d ed. New York, 1952.
Barral, Pierre. "La Franc-maçonnerie en Lorraine aux xixe et xxe siècles," *Annales de l'Est*, 22 (1970): 3–38.

Barry, D. H. "L'Immigration des alsaciens-lorrains à Nancy après la guerre de 1870," *Annales de l'Est*, 31.2 (1979): 133-66.
Bauer, Jules. *L'Ecole rabbinique de France (1830-1930)*. Paris, n.d.
Bayer, René. "La Communauté juive de Niederrödern," *Outre Forêt*, no. 10 (1975), pp. 6-12.
Béchaux, A. "La Question juive en France," *Le Correspondant*, 136 (July-Sept. 1893): 401-28.
Ben-Sasson, H. H., ed. *A History of the Jewish People*. Cambridge, Mass., 1976.
Bensimon-Donath, Doris. *Socio-démographie des juifs de France et d'Algérie, 1867-1907*. Paris, 1976.
Berg, Roger. "Le Judaïsme en Lorraine à l'occasion du bicentenaire du rattachement à la France de la Lorraine et du Barrois," BNC, July 1, 1966, p. 10.
Bernheim, Samuel. *Du rétablissement en France de la Faculté de Médécine de Strasbourg*. Strasbourg, 1871.
Betting de Lancastel. *Considérations sur l'état des juifs dans la société chrétienne, et particulièrement en Alsace*. Strasbourg, 1824.
Bloch, Jean Richard. "*—& Co.*" Tr. C. K. Scott Moncrieff. New York, 1929.
Bloch, Joseph. "Grand-Rabbin Ernest Weill," BNC, 12.16 (1956): 11-12.
———. "Histoire de nos communautés—Haguenau (Bas-Rhin)," BNC (7 parts), 12.19 (1956): 13-14; 12.20 (1956): 13; 12.21 (1956): 1-13; 12.25 (1956): 12; 13.3 (1957): 11; 13.4 (1957): 10; 13.5 (1957): 13.
———. *Historique de la communauté juive de Haguenau, des origines à nos jours*. Paris, 1969.
———. "Il y a cent ans: Les écoles israélites en Alsace," UI, 80.2 (1924-25), suppl., "La Famille israélite," pp. 2-5, 42-44, 53-54, 77-79, 92-94, 108-9.
Bloch, Joseph, and Salomon Picard. *Grussenheim: Communauté juive disparue*. N.p., 1960.
Bloch, Maurice. *Alexandre Weill: Sa vie, ses oeuvres*. Vincennes, 1905.
———. *L'Alsace juive depuis la révolution de 1789: Conférence faite à Colmar le 27 mars 1907*. Guebwiller, 1907.
———. *L'Oeuvre scolaire des juifs français depuis 1789: Conférence faite à la Société des études juives le 6 mai 1893*. Paris, 1901.
———. *Les Vertus militaires de juifs: Conférence faite à la Société des études juives le 30 janvier 1897*. Paris, 1897.
Blum, Jules. *Un Héros alsacien, David Bloch*. Colmar, 1923.
Blumenkranz, Bernhard, ed. *Histoire des juifs en France*. Toulouse, 1972.
Blumenthal, Daniel. *Alsace-Lorraine*. New York, 1917.
———. "Opinion sur les sentiments de l'Alsace-Lorraine," *Revue de Paris*, Jan. 15, 1914, pp. 265-75.

———. "La Revanche du droit." In Abbé Wetterlé and Carlos Fischer, eds., *Notre Alsace, notre Lorraine*. Paris, n.d., pp. 197–206.
Bogue, Donald J. "Internal Migration." In Philip M. Hauser and Otis Dudley Duncan, eds., *The Study of Population: An Inventory and Appraisal*. Chicago, 1959, pp. 486–509.
Bopp, Marie-Joseph. "Indifférence de la bourgeoisie alsacienne à l'égard de la propriété rurale aux xviiie et xixe siècles." In *La Bourgeoisie alsacienne*, listed below, pp. 377–99.
La Bourgeoisie Alsacienne, études d'histoire social. Strasbourg, 1954.
Bourguignon, Eugène. *Bischwiller depuis cent ans*. Bischwiller, 1875.
Braun, Jean. *La Littérature alsacienne d'expression allemande et dialecte de 1870 à 1918*. Strasbourg, 1962.
Bredin, Jean-Denis. *The Affair: The Case of Alfred Dreyfus*. Tr. Jeffrey Mehlman. New York, 1986.
Bresslau, Harry. *Bismarcks Stellung zu Preussentum und Deutschtum (Rede 31. März 1915 zu Strassburg bei der akademischen Gedenkfeier des 100. Geburtstages des Fürsten Bismarck)*. Strassburg, 1915.
Brogan, D. W. *The Development of Modern France, 1870–1939*, vol. 1: *From the Fall of the Empire to the Dreyfus Affair*. New York, 1966.
Brown, James S., Harry K. Schwarzweller, and J. J. Mangalam. "Kentucky Mountain Migration and the Stem-Family: An American Variation on a Theme by Le Play." In Jansen, ed., *Readings*, listed below, pp. 93–120.
Cahen, Emile. *Les Héros de Wissembourg: Discours prononcé en 1872, lors de l'anniversaire de la journée du 4 août 1870*. . . . Paris, 1898.
Cahen, Gilbert. "Les Juifs dans la région lorraine des origines à nos jours," *Le Pays Lorrain*, 53. 2 (1972): 55–83.
———. "Les juifs et la vie économique des campagnes (1648–1870)," *Revue d'Alsace*, no. 97 (1958): 146–47.
Cahnman, Werner J. "Village and Small-Town Jews in Germany: A Typological Study," LBIYB, 19 (1974): 107–35.
Cahun, Léon. *La Vie juive*. Paris, 1886.
Camus, Jules. *Le Développement économique et social de Bischwiller*. Strasbourg, 1939.
Caron, Vicki. "Patriotism or Profit? The Emigration of Alsace-Lorraine Jews to France, 1871–1872," LBIYB, 28 (1983): 139–68.
———. "The Social and Religious Transformation of Alsace-Lorraine Jewry, 1871–1914," LBIYB, 30 (1985): 319–56.
Caron, Vicki, and Paula Hyman. "The Failed Alliance: Jewish-Catholic Relations in Alsace-Lorraine, 1871–1914," LBIYB, 26 (1981): 3–21.
Cerfbeer de Médelsheim, A. *Ce que sont les juifs de France*. Paris, 1844.
Cetty, H. "Les Elections complémentaires de Mulhouse," *Revue Catholique d'Alsace*, 1899, pp. 856–63.

———. "Le Paysan alsacien," *Revue Catholique d'Alsace* (3 parts), 1884-85, pp. 224-36, 286-94, 345-54.

Chatelain, Abel. "Les Migrations françaises vers le nouveau monde aux xixe et xxe siècles," *Annales: Economies; Sociétés; Civilisations*, 2 (1947): 53-70.

Chevalier, Louis. "Emigration française au xixe siècle," *Etudes d'Histoire Moderne*, 1 (1947): 124-71.

Chouraqui, André. *Cent ans d'histoire: L'Alliance Israélite Universelle et la renaissance juive contemporaine, 1860-1960.* Paris, 1965.

Clement, Roger. "Le Professeur Léon Zéliqzon," *Annuaire de la Société d'Histoire et d'Archéologie de la Lorraine*, 48 (1947): 26-32.

Cobban, Alfred. *A History of Modern France*, vol. 3: *France of the Republics, 1871-1962.* Middlesex, Eng., 1965.

Cohen, David. "L'Image du juif dans la société française en 1843, d'après les rapports des préfets," *Revue d'Histoire Economique et Sociale*, 55.1-2 (1977): 70-91.

———. *La Promotion des juifs en France à l'époque du second empire (1852-1870).* 2 vols. Aix-en-Provence, 1980.

Cohen, Gary. "Jews in German Society: Prague, 1860-1914," *Central European History*, 10 (1977): 28-72.

———. *The Politics of Ethnic Survival: Germans in Prague, 1861-1940.* Princeton, N.J., 1981.

Collin, Henri. *Inauguration du monument de Noisseville élevé aux soldats français tombés en 1870 sur les champs de bataille à l'Est de Metz.* Metz, 1908.

Comité Alsacien d'Etudes et d'Informations, ed., *L'Alsace depuis son retour à la France*, vol. 1. Strasbourg, 1932. Suppl., 1937.

"La Communauté israélite de Schirrhofen," *BNC*, 16.20 (1960): 14.

"La Communauté israélite (Weiterswiller)," *Société d'Histoire et d'Archéologie de Saverne et Environs*, 47-48.3-4 (1964): 26-27.

Consistoire israélite de Colmar. *Réfutation par un israélite du Haut-Rhin, de plusieurs articles calomnieux, publiés contre le Consistoire israélite de Colmar.* Strasbourg, 1841.

Contamine, Henry. *Metz et la Moselle de 1814 à 1870.* 2 vols. Nancy, 1932.

Coypel, Edouard. *Le Judaïsme: Esquisse des moeurs juives.* Mulhouse, 1876.

Craig, John. "A Mission for German Learning: The University of Strasbourg and Alsatian Society, 1870-1918." Ph.D. dissertation, Stanford University, 1972.

———. *Scholarship and Nation Building: The Universities of Strasbourg and Alsatian Society, 1870-1939.* Chicago, 1984.

Curtis, Michael. *Three Against the Third Republic: Sorel, Barrès, and Maurras.* Princeton, N.J., 1959.

D'Andlau, Christian. "La Fédération agricole d'Alsace et de Lorraine et les caisses mutuelles de dépots et de prêts (système Raiffeisen). In *Trois*

Provinces de l'Est: Lorraine, Alsace, Franche-Comté. Strasbourg, 1957, pp. 141–51.

Daudet, Léon. *L'Avant-Guerre: Etudes et documents sur l'espionnage juif-allemand en France depuis l'Affaire Dreyfus.* Paris, 1915.

Debré, Moses. *The Image of the Jew in French Literature from 1800 to 1908.* Tr. Gertrude Hirschler. New York, 1970.

Delabrousse, Lucien. *Edmond Goudchaux, 1843–1907.* Meulan-Hardricourt, 1909.

Delahache, Georges [Lucien Aron]. *Alsace-Lorraine: La carte au liséré vert.* Paris, 1918.

———. "De Bischwiller à Elbeuf," *Revue de Paris*, Dec. 1, 1911, pp. 563–74.

———. *L'Exode.* Paris, 1914.

———. "Figures d'Alsace et de Lorraine: Blumenthal," *Le Figaro*, Oct. 17, 1911.

———. *Juifs.* Paris, 1901.

———. "Les Juifs d'Alsace: Leur amour pour la France (Fev., 1918)," *Souvenir et Science*, 1.1 (1930): 5–9.

———. *Plaidoyer pour les "annexés."* 2d ed. Paris, 1898.

Delpech, François. "De 1815 à 1894." In Bernhard Blumenkranz, ed., *Histoire des juifs en France.* Toulouse, 1972, pp. 305–27.

Delsor, Abbé N. "Revue du mois," *Revue Catholique d'Alsace*, April 1899, p. 297.

D'Elstein, G. *L'Alsace-Lorraine sous la domination allemande.* Paris, 1877.

Dennery, Justin. "La Communauté israélite de Metz avant 1870," UI, 80.2 (1924–25), suppl., "La Famille israélite," pp. 289–92, 295–98, 305–8.

Dollinger, Philippe. "Bourgeoisies d'Alsace." In *La Bourgeoisie alsacienne*, listed above, pp. 485–92.

———, ed. *L'Alsace de 1900 à nos jours.* Toulouse, 1979.

Dohm, Christian Wilhelm. *Concerning the Amelioration of the Civil Status of the Jews.* Tr. Helen Lederer. Cincinnati, 1957.

Dreyfus, Alfred. *Souvenirs et correspondances.* Paris, 1936.

Dreyfus, François G. *La Vie politique en Alsace, 1919–1936.* Paris, 1969.

Dreyfus, Lucien. "La Vie juive depuis 1918." In Comité Alsacien d'Etudes, ed., listed above, suppl. 1937, pp. 201–8.

Dreyfuss, J.-H. *Sermons de Guerre.* Paris, 1921.

Duhem, Jules. *La Question d'Alsace-Lorraine de 1871 à 1914.* Paris, 1917.

Eccard, Frédéric. *L'Alsace sous la domination allemande.* Paris, 1919.

"Einiges zur Geschichte der früheren Juden Gemeinde von Lembach," *Eichbaum*, 6–7 (1975): 7–9, 21–22.

Elias, Alfred. *Assimilations-Bestrebungen im Elsass.* Mulhouse, 1900.

———. *Die jüdische Handwerksschule in Mülhausen i. E.* Brunn, n.d.

Elkin, Judith Laikin. *Jews of the Latin American Republics.* Chapel Hill, N.C., 1980.

Erckmann-Chatrian. *Le Blocus: Episode de la fin de l'empire.* 3d ed. Paris, n.d.
Festschrift zum Geburtstage Sr. Majestät des Kaisers und Königs Wilhelm II [Jan. 24, 1891]. Niedersept, 1891.
Festschrift zum 25. jährigen Jubiläum der Firma Wolf Netter und Jacobi in Strassburg i/E., 6 Feb. 1873–1898. Strassburg, 1898.
Feuerwerker, David. *L'Emancipation des juifs en France de l'ancien régime à la fin du second empire.* Paris, 1976.
Fleurent, Joseph. "L'Idée de patrie en Alsace," *Revue Politique et Parlementaire*, 51 (1907): 324–45.
Florent-Matter, Eugène. *Les Alsaciens-Lorrains contre l'Allemagne.* Paris, 1918.
Friedmann, Joë-Yehoshua. "Un Témoin de la vie juive en Alsace aux xixe siècle: Alexandre Weill," *Saisons d'Alsace*, n.s. nos. 55–56 (1975): 103–18.
Fritsch, Antoine. *Bischwiller: Histoire d'une petite ville industrielle du Bas-Rhin des origines à nos jours.* Bischwiller, 1972. Privately published.
Fuerst, A. "Die Juden im Elsass." In Franz Delitzsch, ed., *Saat auf Hoffnung: Zeitschrift für die Mission der Kirche in Israel.* N.p., 1878, pp. 192–202.
Gain, André. "La Lorraine allemande, foyer d'émigration au début du xixe siècle," *Le Pays Lorrain* (2 parts), 18 (1926): 193–205, 259–66.
———. "La Population juive en 1808: Liste des juifs à Nancy," *Revue Juive de Lorraine* (2 parts), 9 (Oct. 1933): 257–70, 290–95, 321–34; 10 (June 1934): 14–21, 39–48, 64–77, 101–7, 125–34, 144–50.
Gartner, Lloyd P. *The Jewish Immigrant in England, 1870–1914.* London, 1960.
Gauthier, Robert. "Les Alsaciens et l'Affaire Dreyfus," *Saisons d'Alsace*, Winter 1965, pp. 56–80.
Gay, Peter. *Freud, Jews and Other Germans: Masters and Victims in Modernist Culture.* Oxford, 1978.
Gehler, Léon. "Les Juifs de Marmoutier," *Société d'Histoire et d'Archéologie de Saverne*, 1954, nos. 3–4, pp. 25–28.
Geigel, F. "Kirchen- und Schulpolitik im Reichslande, 1871–1906." In *Annalen des deutschen Reichs für Gesetzgebung, Verwaltung und Volkswirtschaft*, 1907, pp. 27–32.
George, Pierre. "Types of Migration of the Population According to the Professional and Social Composition of Migrants." In Jansen, ed., *Readings*, listed below, pp. 39–47.
Gerber, Philippe. *La Condition de l'Alsace-Lorraine dans l'empire allemand.* Lille, 1906.
Gerdolle, H. "La Future Banque d'améliorations agricoles et l'endettement rural," *Revue Catholique d'Alsace* (2 parts), 1884–85, pp. 636–44, 657–68.

Ginsburger, Moïse. "Elsässische Juden als Soldaten." In *Jahrbuch der Gesellschaft für die Geschichte der Israeliten in Elsass-Lothringen*, 1917, pp. 28–31.

———. "La Société pour l'histoire des israélites d'Alsace et de Lorraine," *Souvenir et Science*, 2.3 (1931): 1–7.

———. "Les Troubles contre les juifs d'Alsace en 1848," *Revue des Etudes Juives*, 64 (1912): 109–17.

———. "Der Wucher im Elsass," *Strassburger Post*, Sept. 20, 1908, p. 2.

Girard, Alain, H. Bastide, and Guy Pourcher. "Geographical Mobility and Urban Concentration in France: A Study in the Provinces." In Jansen, ed., *Readings*, listed below, pp. 203–53.

Girard, Patrick. *Les Juifs de France de 1789 à 1860: De l'émancipation à l'égalité*. Paris, 1976.

Girardet, Raoul, ed. *Le Nationalisme français, 1871–1914*. Paris, 1966.

Glaser, Alfred. *Geschichte der Juden in Strassburg: Von der Zeit Karls d. Gr. bis auf die Gegenwart*. Strassburg, 1894.

Goldscheider, Calvin, and Alan Zuckerman. *The Transformation of the Jews*. Chicago, 1984.

Goldstein, Alice. "Aspects of Change in a Nineteenth-Century German Village," *Journal of Family History*, Summer 1984, pp. 145–57.

———. *Determinants of Change and Response Among Jews and Catholics in a Nineteenth-Century German Village*. New York, 1984.

———. "Some Demographic Characteristics of Village Jews in Germany: Nonnenweier, 1800–1931." In Paul Ritterband, ed., *Modern Jewish Fertility*. Leiden, 1981, pp. 112–43.

———. "Urbanization in Baden, Germany: Focus on the Jews," *Social Science History*, 8.1 (Winter 1984): 43–66.

Gordon, Milton. *Assimilation in American Life: The Role of Race, Religion and National Origins*. New York, 1964.

Grégoire, Abbé. *La Révolution française et l'émancipation des juifs*, vol. 3: *Essai sur la régénération physique, morale et politique des juifs, 1789*. Paris, 1968.

Guerber, Victor. *Sozialismus der Erzfeind steht vor der Thüre*. Strassburg, 1891.

La Guerre et les israélites. Vol. 1 of *l'Univers israélite*, pub., *Le Judaïsme français et la guerre*. Paris, 1918.

Gugenheim, Max. "Les Israélites de Bouxwiller," *Société d'Histoire et d'Archéologie de Saverne*, 1955, nos. 3–4, pp. 25–26.

Hagen, William W. *Germans, Poles and Jews: The Nationality Conflict in the Prussian East, 1772–1914*. Chicago, 1980.

Halff, Sylvain. *La Fidélité française des israélites d'Alsace et de Lorraine (1871–1918)*. Paris, 1921.

---. "The Jews of Alsace-Lorraine, 1870-1920." In *American Jewish Yearbook, 1920*, pp. 53-79.

Hammel, Raymond. "La Population juive en Alsace de la fin du xixe et du début de xxe," *Tribune Juive*, suppl. to no. 200 (April 28, 1972): 4-5.

Hayes, Carlton J. H. *Essays on Nationalism*. New York, 1966.

Heilmann, Auguste. *Les Paysans d'Alsace, l'impôt et l'usure*. Strasbourg, 1853.

Helfand, Jonathon I. "French Jewry During the Second Republic and Second Empire (1848-1870)." Ph.D. dissertation, Yeshiva University, New York, 1979.

---. "The Symbiotic Relationship Between French and German Jewry in the Age of Emancipation," LBIYB, 29 (1984): 331-50.

Hemerdinger, M. *La Position des israélites de l'Alsace appréciée par le "Courrier du Haut-Rhin": Réponse par M. Hemerdinger*. Colmar, 1845.

Hermann, E. *Le Monument français de Wissembourg*. Paris, 1909.

Hersch, L. "Jewish Migrations During the Last Hundred Years." In Vol. 1 of Central Yiddish Culture Organization, *The Jewish People: Past and Present*. New York, 1946, pp. 407-30.

Hertz, Georges. "Portrait du juif alsacien," *L'Arche*, Nov. 1959, pp. 30-32.

Hertzberg, Arthur. *The French Enlightenment and the Jews: The Origins of Modern Antisemitism*. New York, 1970.

---, ed. *The Zionist Idea*. New York, 1970.

Hertzog, Aug. "Der Wucher in Elsass," *Strassburger Post*, Sept. 13, 1908.

Hiegel, Henri. "L'Option et l'émigration dans l'arrondissement de Sarreguemines de 1870 à 1914," *Annuaire de la Société d'Histoire et d'Archéologie de la Lorraine* (2 parts), 74 (1974): 89-122; 75 (1975): 85-107.

---. "Les Protestations des lorrains en 1871 contre l'annexion de la Lorraine mosellane à l'empire allemand," *Information Historique*, 19 (1957): 199-200.

---. *Sarreguemines, principale ville de l'Est Mosellan*. Sarreguemines, 1972.

Hirsch, Samson Raphael. *The Nineteen Letters of Ben Uziel; Being a Spiritual Presentation of the Principles of Judaism*. Tr. B. Drachman. New York, 1960.

"Histoire des communautés: Bischwiller," BNC, 11.20 (1955): 12-13.

"Histoire de nos communautés—Sarre-Union—Bouquenom," BNC, 14.6 (1958): 28.

Huisman, Michel. "Chronique strasbourgeoise," *Revue de l'Université de Bruxelles* (3 parts), 4 (1898-99): 68-72, 149-53, 230-38.

Hülfsbüchlein gegen viele Wucherjuden und etwelche Wucherchristen. N.p., 1852. Anon.: "Ein freund des elsässer Bauernstandes."

Hvidt, Khristian. *Flight to America: The Social Background of 300,000 Danish Emigrants*. New York, 1975.

Hyman, Paula E. *From Dreyfus to Vichy: The Remaking of French Jewry, 1906–1939.* New York, 1979.
———. "Jewish Fertility in Nineteenth-Century France." In Paul Ritterband, ed., *Modern Jewish Fertility.* Leiden, 1981.
———. "Joseph Salvador: Proto-Zionist or Apologist for Assimilation," JSS, 34.1 (Jan. 1972): 1–22.
———. "Migration and Social Mobility of Alsatian Jewry, 1820–1866." Paper presented to the Social Science History Association meeting, Columbus, Ohio, Nov. 3, 1978.
Igersheim, François. "La Politique scolaire allemande en Alsace-Lorraine (1870–1871): De la confessionalisation à la loi Falloux," *Recherches Germaniques*, no. 5, (1975): 243–87.
———. *Recherches sur l'insertion de la social-démocratie dans la vie politique strasbourgeoise, 1871–1890.* Mémoire diplôme d'études supérieures d'histoire. Strasbourg, 1966.
Illsey, Raymond I., Angela Finlayson, and Barbara Thompson. "The Motivation and Characteristics of Internal Migrants: A Socio-Medical Study of Young Migrants in Scotland." In Jansen, ed., *Readings*, listed below, Oxford, pp. 123–56.
Imbert, François. "Le Saviez-vous? L'ancienne communauté israélite," *Trait d'Union*, Rixheim, no. 6 (1977): 38–39.
Imbs, Paul. "Notes sur la langue française dans la bourgeoisie alsacienne." In *La Bourgeoisie alsacienne*, listed above, pp. 307–27.
"Les Industries alsaciennes: L'Industrie de la laine," *Revue Alsacienne*, July 1897, pp. 389–90.
Israelitische Gewerbeschule des Ober-Elsass in Mülhausen. Reports, 1888–1908.
Israelitische Wohltätigkeits-Verwaltung Strassburg im Elsass, *Rechenschaftsbericht für 1915 und 1916.*
Jaeger, Jules-Albert. "Les Alsaciens à l'étranger." In Comité alsacien d'études, listed above, vol. 1, pp. 607–46.
———. "Un Patriote scrupuleux, modeste, ardent, . . ." *L'Alsace Française*, 18. 436 (May 19, 1929): 442–44.
Jahrbuch der Gesellschaft für die Geschichte der Israeliten in Elsass-Lothringen. Guebwiller, 1918.
Jansen, Clifford J. "Migration: A Sociological Problem." In Jansen, ed., *Readings*, listed below, pp. 3–35.
———. *Social Aspects of Internal Migration.* Bath, 1968.
———, ed. *Readings in the Sociology of Migration.* Oxford, 1970.
The Jews of Czechoslovakia, vol. 1. New York, 1968.
"Die Juden im Elsass und in Deutschlothringen," *Magazin für die Literatur des Auslandes*, Nov. 12, 1870, pp. 648–49. Originally published in *Israelitische Wochenschrift*, Oct. 26, 1870.

"Die Juden in Strassburg," *Deutsch Soziale Blätter*, Dec. 20 and 27, 1894, pp. 403-4.

"Les Juifs en Alsace," *L'Ami du Peuple* (6 parts), 1969, nos. 12-17.

Juillard, Etienne. "Indifférence de la bourgeoisie alsacienne à l'égard de la propriété rurale aux xviiie et xixe siècles." In *La Bourgeoisie alsacienne*, listed above, pp. 377-85.

———. *La Vie rurale dans la plaine de Basse-Alsace*. Strasbourg, 1953.

Kahlenberg, Pinhas. "Villages juifs d'Alsace," *Tribune Juive*, no. 430 (1976): 68-78.

Kahn, Zadoc. *Isidore Loeb, 1839-1892*. Versailles, 1892.

———. *Souvenirs et regrets: Recueil d'oraisons funèbres prononcés dans la communauté israélite de Paris, 1868-1898*. Paris, 1898.

Kann, Robert. "Assimilation and Antisemitism in the German-French Orbit in the Nineteenth and Early Twentieth Century," LBIYB, 14 (1969): 92-115.

———. "German Speaking Jewry During Austria-Hungary's Constitutional Era, 1867-1918," JSS, 10.3 (July 1948): 239-46.

———. "Hungarian Jewry During Austria-Hungary's Constitutional Period (1867-1918)," JSS, 7.4 (Oct. 1945): 357-86.

Katz, Jacob. *Exclusiveness and Tolerance: Studies in Jewish-Gentile Relations in Medieval and Modern Times*. London, 1961.

———. *Out of the Ghetto*. Cambridge, Mass., 1973.

———. *Tradition and Crisis: Jewish Society at the End of the Middle Ages*. New York, 1961.

Keller, Emile. "Une Voix d'Alsace-Lorraine," *La Vérité*, May 27, 1898.

Kessner, Thomas. *The Golden Door: Italian and Jewish Immigrant Mobility in New York City, 1880-1915*. New York, 1977.

Kiechel, Lucien. "Le Cimetière israélite de Hegenheim et l'histoire des juifs d'Alsace," *Société d'Histoire et du Musée d'Huningue et du Canton*, 4 (1955): 20-27.

———. "Documents sur les israélites de Hegenheim vers le milieu du 19e siècle," *Société d'Histoire et du Musée d'Huningue et du Canton*, 9 (1960): 40-44.

Klein, Paul. *L'Evolution contemporaine des banques alsaciennes (Histoire d'un essai de régionalisme bancaire)*. Paris, 1931.

Kloss, Heinrich. "Die Auswanderung aus dem Elsass und aus dem deutsch-sprachigen Lothringen nach Frankreich." In Paul Wentzcke, ed., *Schicksalswege am Oberrhein*. Heidelberg, 1952, pp. 250-97.

———. "Die Elsass-Lothringer in Innerfrankreich," *Elsass Lothringer Heimatstimmen* (2 parts), 1932, no. 1:34-39; 1932, no. 2:81-86.

Kober, Adolf. "Emancipation's Impact on Education and Vocational Training of German Jewry," JSS (2 parts), 16 (1954): 3-32, 151-68.

Koch, Jules. "Les Alsaciens à Paris et dans les départements." In Comité Alsacien d'Etudes, listed above, vol. 1, pp. 585-606.
Koch, Marcel. "Les Mouvements de la population." In Comité Alsacien d'Etudes, listed above, vol. 1, pp. 335-52.
Kohler, Max J. "Jewish Rights and the Congresses of Vienna and Aix-la-Chapelle," *Publications of the American Jewish Historical Society*, 26 (1918): 33-125.
Kohn, J. "Abraham Sée: L'Histoire d'une banque et d'une famille," *Tribune Juive*, suppl. to no. 168 (Sept. 17, 1971): 2-3.
Köllman, Wolfgang. "The Process of Urbanization in Germany at the Height of the Industrialization Period," *Journal of Contemporary History*, 4.3 (July 1969): 59-76.
Kuznets, Simon. "The Economic Structure of the Life of the Jews." In Louis Finklestein, ed., *The Jews: Their History, Culture and Religion*, vol. 2. 3d ed. New York, 1949, pp. 1597-1634.
———. "Immigration of Russian Jews to the United States: Background and Structure, 1881-1914," *Perspectives in American History*, 9 (1975): 35-124.
Lamberti, Marjorie. *Jewish Activism in Imperial Germany: The Struggle for Civil Equality*. New Haven, Conn., 1978.
Landes, David. *The Unbound Prometheus: Technological Change and Industrial Development in Western Europe from 1750 to the Present*. Cambridge, Eng., 1969.
Lang, Paul. "Les Juifs de Lunéville et la petite histoire," *Revue Juive de Lorraine* (2 parts), 10 (Oct. 1, 1935): 271-80; 11 (Dec. 1, 1935): 331-36.
Lantz [Family], ed. *Lazare Lantz, 1823-1909*. Mulhouse, 1909.
Laufenberger, Henry. *Cours d'économie alsacienne*, vol. 1. Paris, 1930.
Laufenburger, Henry, and Pierre Pflimlin. *Cours d'économie alsacienne*, vol. 2. Paris, 1932.
Lémann, L'Abbé Joseph. *L'Entrée des israélites dans la société française et les états chrétiens*. Paris, 1886.
Lerch, Dominique, and Freddy Raphael. "Le Colportage juif en Alsace au xixe siècle," *Revue des Sciences Sociales de la France de l'Est*, special issue, 1977, pp. 102-19.
Lestschinsky, Jacob. "Jewish Migrations, 1840-1946." In Louis Finklestein, ed., *The Jews: Their History, Culture and Religion*, vol. 4. 1st ed. Philadelphia, 1949, pp. 1198-1238.
Leuilliot, Paul. *L'Alsace au début du xixe siècle: Essais d'histoire politique, économique et religieuse*. 3 vols. Paris, 1959-60.
———. "L'Emigration alsacienne sous l'empire et au début de la restauration," *Revue Historique*, 165 (1930): 254-79.
———. "Politique et religion: Les élections alsaciennes de 1869," *Revue d'Alsace*, 100 (1961): 67-101.

Lévy, Daniel. *Les Français en Californie.* San Francisco, 1884.
Lévy, Elisabeth Esther. *Journal d'une colmarienne pendant la guerre mondiale, 1914–1918.* Translated from the German by "un Colmarien." Colmar, n.d.
Lévy, Isaac. *Adieu à l'Alsace: Sermon prononcé au Temple israélite de Colmar* [July 6, 1872]. Paris, 1872.
———. *Alsatiana: Echos patriotiques de la chaire israélite.* Paris, 1873.
———. *Eloge funèbre de Samuel Dreyfus, Rabbin de Mulhouse* [May 27, 1870]. Mulhouse, 1870.
———. *Isaïe ou le travail.* 2d ed. Paris, 1865.
———. *Nathan le sage; Conférence faite à la société républicaine d'instruction de Vesoul* [Dec. 5, 1880]. Paris, 1881.
———. "Le Passé et le présent: Sermon prononcé à l'inauguration du Temple de Vesoul." In Lévy, *Sermons.* Paris, 1875, pp. 173–86.
———. "Sermon prononcé au Temple de Belfort lors de l'inauguration du monument élevé aux victimes du siège." In Lévy, *Sermons.* Paris, 1875, pp. 187–99.
Lévy, Lazare. *La Grande Guerre 1914–1918 en Alsace.* Mulhouse, n.d.
Lévy, Michel. *Coup d'oeil historique sur l'état des israélites en France, et particulièrement en Alsace.* Strasbourg, 1836.
Lévy, Paul. "La Démographie juive en Alsace et en Lorraine," UI, 87 (July 8, 1932): 362–63.
———. "Les Ecoles juives d'Alsace et de Lorraine d'il y a un siècle," *Tribune Juive* (3 parts), 1933: no. 32, pp. 519–20; no. 33, pp. 540–41; no. 34, pp. 569–70.
———. *Histoire linguistique d'Alsace et de Lorraine,* vol. 2. Publications de la Faculté des lettres de l'université de Strasbourg no. 48. Paris, 1929.
———. *La Langue allemande en France: Pénétration et diffusion des origines à nos jours.* 2 vols. Paris, 1952.
———. "Le Parler des juifs en Alsace-Lorraine," UI, 80.2 (1924–25), suppl. "La Famille israélite," pp. 256–58, 263–66, 271–75, 280–81.
Levy, Richard S. *The Downfall of the Anti-Semitic Political Parties in Imperial Germany,* New Haven, Conn., 1975.
Lévy, Robert. *Histoire économique de l'industrie cottonnière en Alsace: Etude de sociologie descriptive.* Paris, 1912.
Lévy, Sylvain, ed., *A la mémoire du Capitaine Raoul Bloch.* N.p., 1920.
L'Huillier, Fernand. "En guise de conclusion: Protestation, résignation." In L'Huillier, ed., *L'Alsace en 1870–1871.* Paris, 1971, pp. 369–81.
———. *Histoire de l'Alsace.* Paris, 1947.
———. *Recherches sur l'Alsace napoléonienne.* Strasbourg, 1947.
Liberles, Robert. *Religious Conflict in Social Context: The Resurgence of Orthodox Judaism in Frankfurt am Main, 1838–1877.* Westport, Conn., 1985.

Lichtenberger, F. *Le Protestantisme et la guerre de 1870*. 2d ed. Strasbourg, 1871.
Lipman, Armand, ed. *Un Grand Rabbin français, Benjamin Lipman (1819 – 1886)*. Paris, 1923.
Livet, Georges, and Raymond Oberlé. *Histoire de Mulhouse des origines à nos jours*. Strasbourg, [1978].
Lowenstein, Steven M. "The Pace of Modernisation of German Jewry in the Nineteenth Century," LBIYB, 21 (1976): 41–56.
———. "The Rural Community and the Urbanization of German Jewry," *Central European History*, 13.3 (Sept. 1980): 218–35.
———. "Voluntary and Involuntary Limitation of Fertility in Nineteenth-Century Bavarian Jewry." In Paul Ritterband, ed., *Modern Jewish Fertility*. Leiden, 1981, pp. 94–111.
Lutz, Robert. "La Communauté juive de Westhoffen: Les familles Blum et Debré," *Société d'Histoire et d'Archéologie de Saverne et Environs*, 79–80.304 (1972): 67–71.
Lyon-Caen, Charles. "Avant la guerre à Paris," *L'Alsace Française*, May 19, 1929, pp. 433–35.
Mangold, Ern. "Die ehemalige Judengemeinde von Froeningen." In *Annuaire de la Société d'Histoire Sundgovienne, 1970*, pp. 33–47.
Manuel, Eugène. *Anniversaire: Poésie . . . à la fête de l'arbre de Noël de l'Association générale d'Alsace-Lorraine* [Dec. 25, 1878]. Paris, 1878.
———. *Le Dernier Délai: Poésie dite par M. Coquelin . . . à l'arbre de Noël de l'Association générale d'Alsace-Lorraine* [Dec. 25, 1873]. Paris, 1874.
Marrus, Michael R. *The Politics of Assimilation*. Oxford, 1971.
Marrus, Michael R., and Robert O. Paxton. *Vichy France and the Jews*. New York, 1981.
Marx, Dr. "Die jüdische Bevölkerung Elsass-Lothringens," *Strassburger Israelitische Wochenschrift* (2 parts), Jan. 23, 1908, pp. 2–3; Jan. 30, 1908, pp. 6–7.
Marx, Roland. "Les Juifs et l'usure en Alsace: Réflexions sur un mythe," *Saisons d'Alsace*, n.s. nos. 55–56 (1975): 62–67.
———. "L'Opinion publique et les juifs en Alsace sous la révolution," *Saisons d'Alsace*, 9 (1964): 84–92.
———. "La Régénération des juifs d'Alsace," *Annales Historique de la Révolution Française*, Jan.–March 1976, pp. 105–20.
Maslin, Simeon J. *An Analysis and Translation of Selected Documents of Napoleonic Jewry*. Cincinnati, n.d.
Matzen, Raymond. "Le Judéo-alsacien et les hebraïsmes alsaciens," *Saisons d'Alsace*, n.s. nos. 55–56 (1975): 189–206.
Maurois, André. *Memoirs, 1885–1967*. Tr. Denver Lindley. New York, 1970.

Mayer et Cie. *Rapports présentés à l'Assemblée générale des actionnaires*. Metz. Various years, 1873-1902.
Mayeur, Jean-Marie. *Autonomie et politique en Alsace: La constitution de 1911*. Paris, 1970.
McCagg, Jr., William O. "Hungary's Feudalized Bourgeoisie," *Journal of Modern History*, 44 (March-Dec. 1972): 65-78.
Meiss, Honel. *Choses d'Alsace: Contes d'avant guerre*. Nice, 1913.
———. *Traditions populaires alsaciennes*. Nice, 1928.
Mendel, Pierre. "Les Noms des juifs français modernes," *Revue des Etudes Juives*, n.s. 10 (Dec. 1950): 15-63.
Mendelssohn, Moses. *Jerusalem and Other Jewish Writings*. Tr. and ed. Alfred Jospe. New York, 1969.
Meyer, Michael A. *The Origins of the Modern Jew: Jewish Identity and European Culture in Germany, 1749-1824*. Detroit, 1967.
Michel, Albert. *Appel au Poilu!* N.p., 1918.
Migneret, M. *Description du département du Bas-Rhin*. 3 vols. Strasbourg, 1864.
Ministerium für Elsass-Lothringen. *Untersuchung der Lage und Bedürfnisse der Landwirtschaft in Elsass-Lothringen, 1884*. N.p., 1885.
Mitchell, Allan. *Bismarck and the French Nation: 1848-1890*. New York, 1971.
———. *Victors and Vanquished: The German Influence on Army and Church in France After 1870*. Chapel Hill, N.C., 1984.
———. "The Xenophobic Style: French Counterespionage and the Emergence of the Dreyfus Affair," *Journal of Modern History*, 52 (Sept. 1980): 414-25.
Moch, Gaston. *Alsace-Lorraine: Réponse à un pamphlet allemand*. Paris, 1895.
Moch, Leslie Page. *Paths to the City: Regional Migration in Nineteenth-Century France*. Beverly Hills, Calif., 1983.
Morrison, Jack Gaylord. "The Intransigents: Alsace-Lorrainers Against the Annexation, 1900-1914." Ph.D. dissertation, University of Iowa, 1970.
Mosse, George L. *The Crisis of German Ideology: Intellectual Origins of the Third Reich*. New York, 1964.
Mosse, Werner E., Arnold Paucker, and Reinhard Rürup, eds. *Revolution and Evolution: 1848 in German-Jewish History*. Tübingen, 1981.
Mossman, Xavier. *Etude sur l'histoire des juifs à Colmar*. N.p., 1866.
Mull, Charles. "Histoire économique et sociale de Haguenau: Depuis la révolution jusqu'à la guerre de 1870." 3 vols. Thèse de doctorat, 3ᵉ cycle, University of Strasbourg, 1974.
Muller, Sharon. "The Origins of Eichmann in Jerusalem: Hannah Arendt's Interpretation of Jewish History," *JSS*, 43 (1981): 237-54.

Neher, Albert A. *La Double Demeure: Scènes de la vie juive en Alsace.* Paris, 1965.
Neher, André. "La Bourgeoisie juive d'Alsace." In *La Bourgeoisie alsacienne,* listed above, pp. 435-42.
———. "Une Carte antisémite de la Suisse au xixe," *Evidences,* June-July 1952, pp. 40-44.
———. *La Littérature juive en Alsace.* Strasbourg, n.d.
———. "Présentation du Judaïsme d'Alsace," *Saisons d'Alsace,* n.s. nos. 55-56 (1975): 5-8.
Netter, Nathan. *La Patrie absente et la Patrie retrouvée: Sermons et allocutions patriotiques.* Metz, 1929.
———. *Vingt siècles d'histoire d'une communauté juive: Metz et son grand passé.* Paris: Lipschutz, 1938.
Neu, Heinrich. "Elsässer und Lothringer als Ansiedler in Nordamerika." In *Jahrbuch der Elsass-Lothringischen Wissentschaftlichen Gesellschaft. 1930,* pp. 98-128.
Niewyk, Donald L. *The Jews in Weimar Germany.* Baton Rouge, La., 1980.
Nordmann, A. "Uber Wanderungs- und Siedlungs-Beziehungen zwischen elsässischen und schweizerischen Judentum." In *Jahrbuch der Gesellschaft für die Geschichte der Israeliten in Elsass-Lothringen, 1917,* pp. 1-10.
Oualid, William. "La Démographie juive en Alsace et en Lorraine," UI, 87 (May 27, 1932): 165-66.
Ozouf, Jacques, and Mona Ozouf, "Le Thème du patriotisme dans les manuels primaires," *Le Mouvement Social,* 49 (1964): 5-31.
Peterson, William. "A General Typology of Migration." In Jansen, ed., *Readings,* listed above, pp. 49-68.
Pfister, Christian. "L'Historien de l'Alsace." In "A la mémoire de George Delahache," *L'Alsace Française,* n.s. 9.20 (May 19, 1929): 427-28.
———. *Pages alsaciennes.* Strasbourg, 1927.
Philipson, David. *The Reform Movement in Judaism.* New York, 1907.
Pietri, François. *Napoléon et les israélites.* Paris, 1965.
Plaut, Gunther W. *The Rise of Reform Judaism.* New York, 1963.
Poidevin, Raymond. "Les Elections de 1893 en Alsace-Lorraine," *Bulletin de la Faculté des Lettres de Strasbourg,* 44 (1965-66): 465-79.
Ponteil, Félix. "En manière de conclusion: L'Alsace en 1848." In *Deux siècles d'Alsace française: 1648, 1789, 1848.* Strasbourg, 1948.
———. *L'Opposition politique à Strasbourg sous la monarchie de juillet, 1830-1848.* Paris, 1932.
Poppel, Stephen M. *Zionism in Germany, 1897-1933: The Shaping of a Jewish Identity.* Philadelphia, 1977.
Posener, S. "The Immediate Economic and Social Effects of the Emancipation of the Jews in France," JSS, 1 (1939): 271-326.

———. "Immigration des juifs allemands en France sous le premier empire" (3 parts) UI, 1934, pp. 785–87, 821–23, 856–59.

———. "Les Juifs sous le premier empire," *Revue des Etudes Juives*, 93 (1932): 192–214.

Pourcher, Guy. "The Growing Population of Paris." In Jansen, ed., *Readings*, listed above, pp. 179–202.

Ralston, David B. *The Army of the Republic: The Place of the Military in the Political Evolution of France, 1871–1914.* Cambridge, Mass., 1967.

Raphael, Freddy. "Les Juifs d'Alsace et la conscription au dix-neuvième siècle." In *Les Juifs et la révolution française: Problèmes et aspirations.* Toulouse, 1976, pp. 121–42. [Also in Raphael and Weyl, *Regards*, listed below, under the title "Grandeur et servitude: Les juifs d'Alsace et la conscription," pp. 235–52.]

———. "Présence du juif dans l'oeuvre d'Erckmann Chatrian," *Revue des Sciences Sociales de la France de l'Est*, 5 (1976), pp. 81–142. [Also in Raphael and Weyl, *Regards*, listed below, pp. 150–207.]

———. "Une Rencontre manquée: Les relations entre les juifs d'Alsace et leurs coreligionnaires d'Europe orientale," *Saisons d'Alsace*, n.s. nos. 55–56 (1975): 207–28.

———. "Stéréotype du juif dans un village d'Alsace en 1976," *Revue des sciences sociales de la France de l'Est*, special issue, 1977, pp. 142–53. [Also in Raphael and Weyl, *Regards*, listed below, pp. 287–97.]

Raphael, Freddy, and Robert Weyl. "Les Juifs d'Alsace entre la France et l'Allemagne (1870–1914)," *Revue d'Allemagne*, 13.3 (July–Sept. 1981): 480–94.

———. *Juifs en Alsace: Culture, société, histoire.* Toulouse, 1977.

———. *Regards nouveaux sur les juifs d'Alsace.* Strasbourg, 1980.

Ratisbonne, Louis. *L'Alsacienne: Poésies dites à l'arbre de Noël de l'Association générale d'Alsace-Lorraine* [Dec. 25, 1874]. Paris, 1875.

Redslob, Robert. "La Bourgeoisie alsacienne sous le régime allemand." In *La Bourgeoisie alsacienne*, listed above, pp. 443–51.

Reinharz, Jehuda. *Fatherland or Promised Land: The Dilemma of the German Jew.* Ann Arbor, Mich., 1975.

Rémond, René. *The Right-Wing in France: From 1815 to De Gaulle.* 2d American ed. Tr. James M. Laux. Philadelphia, 1969.

Reuss, Rod. *Histoire d'Alsace.* Paris, 1920.

Richarz, Monika. "Jewish Social Mobility in Germany During the Time of Emancipation (1790–1871)," LBIYB, 20 (1975), pp. 69–77.

———. *Jüdisches Leben in Deutschland: Selbstzeugnisse zur Sozialgeschichte, 1780–1871*, vol. 1. Stuttgart, 1976.

Rinckenberger, Walter. *La Culture de houblon en Alsace.* Bischwiller, 1931.

Ritterband, Paul, ed. *Modern Jewish Fertility.* Leiden, 1981.

Roblin, Michel. *Les Juifs de Paris.* Paris, 1952.

Rossé, J., et al. *Das Elsass von 1870-1932.* 3 vols. Colmar, [1936]-38.
Roth, François. "Antoine, député protestaire de Metz," *Annales de l'Est*, 18 (1966): 361-97.
―――. *La Lorraine annexée: Etude sur la présidence de Lorraine dans l'empire allemand (1870-1918).* Annales de l'Est, II Mémoire, no. 50. Nancy, 1976.
Rothenberger, Karl Heinz. *Die elsass-lothringische Heimat- und Autonomiebewegung zwischen den beiden Weltkriegen.* Bern, 1975.
Rouby, H. "Historique de la communauté israélite de Soultz," *Annuaire de la Société d'Histoire des Régions de Thann-Guebwiller*, 2 (1951-52): 51-52.
Rozenblit, Marsha L. *The Jews of Vienna, 1867-1914: Assimilation and Identity*, Albany, N.Y., 1983.
Ruland, H. *Deutschtum und Franzosentum in Elsass-Lothringen, eine Kulturfrage.* Strassburg, 1908.
Ruppin, Arthur, ed. *Zeitschrift für Demographie und Statistik der Juden*, vol. 1.6.
Rürup, Reinhard. "The European Revolutions of 1848 and Jewish Emancipation." In Werner E. Mosse et al., eds., *Revolution and Evolution: 1848 in German-Jewish History.* Tübingen, 1981, pp. 1-53.
―――. "Jewish Emancipation and Bourgeois Society," LBIYB, 14 (1969): 67-91.
Saloman, Henry. *Edouard Bamberger (1825-1910): Un alsacien et une famille lorraine aux xixe siècle.* Paris, 1922.
Sayous, André E. "L'Evolution de Strasbourg entre les deux guerres (1871-1914)," *Annales d'Histoire Economique et Sociale* (2 parts), 6.25 (Jan. 1934): 1-19; 6.26 (March 1934), 122-32.
Scheid, Elie. "Mémoires d'un juif alsacien." Manuscript, 1906.
Schmidt, H. D. "The Terms of Emancipation, 1781-1812," LBIYB, 1 (1956): 28-47.
Schnapper, Dominique. *Juifs et israélites.* Paris, 1980.
Schnurmann, Erwin. *La Population juive en Alsace.* Paris, 1936.
Schoell, Franck L. "Colonies alsaciennes dans la prairie américaine," *Revue de Paris*, 29 (1922): 168-90.
Schoenbaum, David. *Zabern 1913: Consensus Politics in Imperial Germany.* London, 1982.
Schorsch, Ismar. *Jewish Reactions to German Anti-Semitism, 1870-1914.* New York, 1972.
―――. *On the History of the Political Judgment of the Jew.* Leo Baeck Memorial Lecture 20. New York, 1976.
Schwarzfuchs, Simon. *Les Juifs de France.* Paris, 1975.
Seager, Frederic H. "The Alsace-Lorraine Question in France, 1871-

1914." In Charles K. Warner, ed., *From Ancien Régime to the Popular Front*. New York, 1969, pp. 111-26.

Sée, Julien. *Guerre de 1870: Journal d'un habitant de Colmar, juillet-novembre 1870*. Paris, 1884.

———. *Nos élections au Reichstag: Lettre à M. A. Maudit*. Clermont-Ferrand, 1874.

Silverman, Dan P. "Political Catholicism and Social Democracy in Alsace-Lorraine," *Catholic Historical Review*, 52 (1966-67): 39-65.

———. *Reluctant Union: Alsace-Lorraine and Imperial Germany, 1871-1918*. University Park, Pa., 1972.

Snyder, Louis. *The Dreyfus Case: A Documentary History*. New Brunswick, N.J., 1973.

Soboul, Albert. "Les Troubles agraires de 1848." In Soboul, *Problèmes paysans de la révolution, 1789-1848: Etudes d'histoire révolutionnaire*. Paris, 1976.

Société de protection des Alsaciens et Lorrains demeurés français, Rapports. Paris. Various years, 1873-86.

Sommer, Robert. "Réflexions sur le judaïsme alsacien," BNC, 12.20 (1956): 1.

Soucy, Robert. *Fascism in France: The Case of Maurice Barrès*. Berkeley, Calif., 1972.

Spach, Louis. "Die Israeliten im Elsass," *Strassburger Zeitung*, Sept. 30, 1871, p. 2. [Also in *Opuscles diverses* (Alsace), no. 17, n.d.]

Spire, André. *Les Juifs et la guerre*. Paris, 1917.

"La Statistique de la population juive de Strasbourg," *Tribune Juive*, 2 (Jan. 13, 1933): 17.

Statistischen Bureau des (Kaiserlichen) Ministeriums für Elsass-Lothringen. *Das Reichsland Elsass-Lothringen*. 3 vols. Strassburg, 1898-1901.

———. *Statistische Mitteilungen über Elsass-Lothringen*. 23 vols. Strassburg, 1873-1910.

———. *Statistisches Handbuch für Elsass-Lothringen*. 2 vols. Strassburg, 1885, 1902.

———. *Statistisches Jahrbuch für Elsass-Lothringen*. 7 vols. Strassburg, 1907-14.

Stauben, Daniel. *Scènes de la vie juive en Alsace*. Paris, 1860.

Stenne, Georges [Schornstein]. *Perle*. [Paris], 1877.

Stern, Fritz. *Gold and Iron: Bismarck, Bleichröder, and the Building of the German Empire*. New York, 1977.

Sternhell, Zeev. *La Droite révolutionnaire, 1885-1914: Les origines françaises du fascisme*. Paris, 1978.

Strauss, Herbert. "Pre-emancipation Prussian Policies Towards the Jews, 1815-1847," LBIYB, 11 (1966): 107-36.

Strauss, Léon. "Les Militants Alsaciens et lorrains et les rapports entre les

mouvements ouvriers français et allemands entre 1900 et 1923," *Revue d'Allemagne*, 4.3 (July-Sept. 1972): 465-79.
———. "Le Plébiscite du 8 mai dans le Haut-Rhin." In F. L'Huillier, ed., *L'Alsace en 1870-1871*. Paris, 1971, pp. 105-83.
Strebler, Joseph. *Alsaciens au Texas*. Strasbourg, 1975.
Szajkowski, Zosa. "Anti-Jewish Riots During the Revolutions of 1789, 1830, and 1848" (in Hebrew), *Zion*, 20 (1955): 82-102.
———. "The Anti-Jewish Riots in Alsace in 1848" (in Yiddish), *Kihum*, 6 (1948): 394-97.
———. "The Growth of the Jewish Population of France: The Political Aspects of a Demographic Problem," JSS (2 parts) 7 (1946): 179-96, 297-315.
———. *Jews and the French Revolutions of 1789, 1830 and 1848*. New York, 1970.
———. "Notes on the Occupational Status of French Jews, 1800-1880." In *Proceedings of the American Academy of Jewish Religion Jubilee Volume*, Jerusalem, 1980, pp. 531-54.
———. *Poverty and Social Welfare Among French Jews, 1800-1880*. New York, 1854.
———. "Some Facts About Alsatian Jews in America" (in Yiddish), *Yivo Bleter*, 19 (1942): 312-18.
———. "Yidn in di Pariser Commune." In *Yidn in Frankraych*, E. Tcherickover, ed., vol. 2. New York, 1942, pp. 93-154.
———. "Yidn in Elsass-Lothringen." In *Di Yidische Ekonomik*, vol. 3. N.p., 1939, pp. 87-89.
Tama, Diogene. *Transactions of the Parisian Sanhedrin*. Tr. F. D. Kirwan. Cincinnati, 1956.
Thabault, Roger. *Education and Change in a Village Economy: Mazières-en-Gâtine, 1848-1914*. Tr. Peter Tregear. New York, 1971.
Thomas, Dorothy Swaine. *Social and Economic Aspects of Swedish Population Movements, 1750-1933*. New York, 1941.
Thomson, David. *Democracy in France Since 1870*. 5th ed. New York, 1969.
Tilly, Louise A., and Joan W. Scott. *Women, Work, and Family*. New York, 1978.
Toury, Jacob. "'Deutsche Juden' im Vormärz," *Bulletin des Leo Baeck Instituts*, 8.29 (1965): 65-82.
———. "Jewish Manual Labour and Emigration Records from Some Bavarian Districts (1830-1857)," LBIYB, 16 (1971): 45-62.
Treschan, Victor. "The Struggle for Integration: The Jewish Community in Strasbourg, 1818-1850." Ph.D. dissertation, University of Wisconsin, Madison, 1978.
Uhry, Edmond. "Galleries of Memory." 2 vols. Manuscript, Leo Baeck Institute Memoirs Collection, New York, 1946.

Vigée, Claude. "Souvenirs" (tr. from the English by Simone Raphael), *Saisons d'Alsace*, n.s. nos. 55–56 (1975): 234–44.
Voilliard, Odette. "Immigration des alsaciens-lorrains à Nancy à la suite du traité de Francfort." In *Trois Provinces de l'Est: Lorraine, Alsace, Franche-Comté*. Strasbourg, 1957.
Wahl, Alfred. *Confession et comportement dans les campagnes d'Alsace et de Bade (1871–1939)*. 2 vols. Strasbourg, 1980.
———. "Immigration allemande en Alsace-Lorraine entre 1871 et 1918: Un aperçu statistique," *Recherches germaniques*, 1973, no. 3, pp. 202–17.
———. "Metz en 1870 et les problèmes des territoires annexés, 1871–1873." In *Actes du colloque de Metz (6–8 novembre 1970)*. Metz, 1972.
———. *L'Option et l'émigration des alsaciens-lorrains (1871–1872)*. Paris, 1974.
Wahl, Jean-Jacques. "Le Judaïsme rural alsacien au xixe siècle à travers la littérature d'expression française," *Saisons d'Alsace*, n.s. nos. 55–56 (1975): 91–98.
Wallerstein, Ernst. "Die jüdische Bevölkerung in Elsass-Lothringen (1871 bis 1900)," *Allgemeine Zeitung des Judentums*, Dec. 3, 1909, pp. 580–83.
Weber, Eugen J. *Action Française: Royalism and Reaction in Twentieth-Century France*. Stanford, Calif., 1962.
———. *Peasants into Frenchmen, 1870–1914*. Stanford, Calif., 1976.
Weber, Jean Julien. *Au soir d'une vie*. Paris, 1970.
Wehler, Hans-Ulrich. "'Das Reichsland' Elsass-Lothringen 1870–1879." In Helmut Böhme, ed., *Probleme der Reichsgründungszeit 1848–1879*. Cologne, 1968.
Weil, Arthur. "L'Ecole primaire israélite en Alsace et en Lorraine (1870–1923)," UI, 78 (April 20, 1923): 109–10.
Weill, Alexandre. "Actualités," *Revue Israélite*, 3.29 (June 28, 1872): 420–22.
———. *Briefe hervorragender verstorbener Männer Deutschlands*. Zurich, 1889.
———. *Elsässer Briefe*. N.p., 1842.
———. *Epopée alsacienne*. Paris, 1895.
———. *Frony*. Paris, 1877.
———. *Knittelverse eines Elsässer Propheten*. Paris, n.d. Privately printed.
———. *Lettres d'amour—entre deux époux avant et après le mariage, 1847–1878*. Paris, 1900.
———. *Lettres de vengeance d'un alsacien*. Paris, 1871.
———. *Ma jeunesse*. 2 vols. Paris, 1870.
———. *Rimes alsaciennes—Contre l'Allemagne Bismarckienne en général et contre les antisémites en particulier*. Translated from the German by the author. Paris, 1889.

———. *Sittengemälde aus dem elsässischen Volksleben: Novellen*. 2 vols. Stuttgart, 1847.
Weill, Georges. *L'Alsace française de 1879 à 1870*. Paris, 1916.
Weill, Jules. *L'Alsace et les alsaciens pendant la guerre*, vol. 1. Strasbourg, 1921.
Weill, Julien. *Zadoc Kahn, 1839–1905*. Paris, 1912.
Weiller, Lazare. *Discours prononcé par M. Lazare Weiller, député de la Charente à la séance de la Chambre des députés du 13 juillet 1917 sur l'Alsace-Lorraine*. Paris, 1917.
———. "L'Alsace d'aujourd'hui," *Revue de Paris*, 34 (June 15, 1927): 830–48.
Weinberg, David H. *A Community on Trial: The Jews of Paris in the 1930s*. Chicago, 1977.
Weiss, J. J. *Au pays du Rhin*. Paris, 1886.
Wertheimer, Jack L. "German Policy and Jewish Politics: The Absorption of East European Jews in Germany, 1868–1914." Ph.D. dissertation, Columbia University, 1978.
———. "'The Unwanted Element': East European Jews in Imperial Germany." *LBIYB*, 26 (1981): 23–46.
Weyl, Robert. "Les Juifs à Rosheim: Naissance, épanouissement et fin d'une communauté juive," *Saisons d'Alsace*, n.s. no. 66 (1978): 101–19.
Weyl, Robert, and Martine Weyl. "Mappoth d'Alsace," *Saisons d'Alsace*, n.s. nos. 55–56 (1975): 119–33.
Wiener, Max. *Abraham Geiger and Liberal Judaism*. Tr. Ernst J. Schochauer. Philadelphia, 1962.
Wilson, Stephen. *Ideology and Experience: Antisemitism in France at the Time of the Dreyfus Affair*. Rutherford, N.J., 1982.
Woog, Mayer. *Bas Jechido oder das kranke Töchterlein*. N.p. 1884. Privately published.
Wurmser, Isaak. *Der Lehrer als Staatsdiener*. Mulhouse, 1881.
Zeldin, Theodore. *France, 1848–1945*. 2 vols. Oxford, 1977.

Index

In this index an "f" after a number indicates a separate reference on the next page, and an "ff" indicates separate references on the next two pages. *"Passim"* is used for a cluster of references in close but not consecutive sequence.

Abraham, Ephraim, 213
Acculturation, 22n
Adler, Isaak, 109
Adler and Oppenheimer (tannery), 106, 109, 223
Africa, antisemitism in, 11
Agricultural cooperatives, 166
Alcan, Félix, 62, 69
Alcan family, 98
Algeria, emigration to, 72, 98
Allgemeine Zeitung des Judentums, 11n, 33, 39, 42f, 45, 109, 142, 188n
Alliance Israélite Universelle, 11
Alsace-Lorraine: Monument to Grant (Aron), 99
Alsace-Lorrainer Society of Providence and Mutual Aid, 98
Alsacien-Lorraine, 99
Alsatians, vs. Old Germans, vii
"—& Co." (Bloch), 66f
Anticatholicism, 118–23 *passim*. *See also* Kulturkampf
Antisemitism, 5, 32; in France, 10f, 13f, 118–20, 128–33; in Alsace-Lorraine, 13, 24, 30–34, 118–21, 124–35, 140–41, 146–47, 150, 167–69; and moneylending, 124–26; as official German policy, 188. *See also* Dreyfus Affair; "Infamous decree"

Antoine, Jules, 100–101, 123
Archives israélites, 11n, 18, 32n, 40, 42f, 52, 62, 72, 141f
Arendt, Hannah, 188–89, 191
Argentina, 85
Aron (Grand Rabbi of Strasbourg), 110n, 111, 234
Aron, Henri, 98
Aron, Joseph, 99–100
Aronssohn, Paul, 60
Aschkeness, *see* Jews, German
Ashkenazim, 6, 14, 24
Assimilation, 5–25 *passim*, 192
Association Culturelle Zadoc Kahn, 113
Association Générale d'Alsace et de Lorraine, 97–98
Association of Jewish Academicians, 108
Augsburger Allgemeine Zeitung, 124f
Auscher, Léon, 215
Auscher, Léon Weill, 215
Autonomism, 145, 190

Baden, 92
Bailly, Father (French Catholic leader), 135n
Bamberger, Dr. Edouard, 33–34, 69, 100

Index

Bamberger family, 98
Banking and commerce, 4, 17, 24, 166, 169–71, 173
Barkai, Avraham, 218
Baron, Salo, 2
Barrès, Maurice, 149
Bas-Rhin, 18–23 *passim*; Jewish emigration from, 76, 78–79, 199–200
Bavaria, 16, 92
Bayonne, 13–14
Bebel, August, 107, 127n
Beer and Hirzberg (Berlin firm), 106
Belgium, 89
Bensimon-Donath, Doris, 69, 80
Bergheim, 119
Bernheim, Armand, 180, 184
Bernheim, Dr. Samuel, 60
Bernstein Affair of 1911, 134
Berr, Sylvain, 100
Bigart, Isaac, 139
Bing, Isaiah Berr, 18
Bischwiller, 64–67, 80, 199
Bismarck, Otto von, 28, 32, 35, 54, 96, 102, 118, 121f, 188
Blin, Jules, 99
Blin, Maurice, 65, 215
Blin, Théodore, 65, 67, 99, 215
Blin family, 98
Bloch, Baroukh, 105
Bloch, David, 65, 116n, 181, 215
Bloch, Edgar, 65, 215
Bloch, Isidore, 215
Bloch, Jean-Richard, 66f, 182
Bloch, Joseph, 107
Bloch, Maurice, 15
Bloch, Michel, 213
Bloch, Rabbi (head of Colmar rabbinical school), 111
Bloch, Raoul, 182–83
Bloch, Richard, 182
Bloch, Robert, 182
Bloch, Simon, 14, 31, 41
Bloch family, 98
Le Blocus (Erckmann-Chatrian), 21
Bloque, M. (Parisian rentier), 225
Blum, Alphons, 93
Blum, Léon, 89
Blum, Simon, 144–45

Blum-Auscher, Léon, 101
Blumenthal, Daniel, 133
Bonaparte, Napoléon, 6–7, 20f, 119
Bordeaux, 13–14
Boulanger, Georges, 79
Bourguignon, Eugène, 68
Brazil, 85
Bréal, Michel, 131–32, 146
"Brennende Fragen" (Fritsch), 140
Breslauer (Justice councilor), 142, 144
Brussels Peace Conference, 32
Bülow, Bernhard von, 129

Cahen, Isidore, 42
Cahen, Samuel, 215
Cahen, Simon, 114
Cahen, Solomon, 153–54, 156
Cahnman, Werner, 24
Cahun, Léon, 32, 36, 227
Calvinists, 64
Catholicism, vs. socialism, 126–27
Catholics (Alsace-Lorraine), 12, 18, 23, 28, 89, 97, 100; and Protestants, 49–50, 186; antisemitism of, 118–20, 126–35, 140; relations with Jews, 118–35, 186; and Germans, 121–23. *See also* Anticatholicism; Jesuits; Kulturkampf
Cattle dealing, 125, 166–67, 169
Centralverein, 149f
Cerf, Alfred, 100, 116
Cerf family, 98
Cerfberr, Max, 72–73
Chile, 85n
Christians, *see* Catholics; Protestants
Cigar/cigarette manufacture, 169
Civil posts, Jews in, 43, 141
Clemenceau, Georges, 183–84
Clemmer, Karl, 85
Clermont-Tonnerre, 2, 9
Colmar, 18; optants from, 71n; rabbinical seminary of, 111; population of, 162
Commerce, *see* Banking and commerce
Communism, 193
Concerning the Amelioration of the Civil Status of the Jews (Dohm), 3
Conscription, *see* Military service

Conservative movement, 112
Consistory(-ies), 7, 9ff, 32–33, 72, 102, 137–40, 183–84; of Bas-Rhin, 18, 101f, 107 (Strasbourg, 20, 101, 109, 146); of Haut-Rhin, 103, 120, 184 (Colmar, 20); of Lorraine, 106, 109, 153f (Metz, 101f, 147); Central (Paris), 113
Contamine, Henry, 23
Conversion, from Judaism, 5, 175–76
Conversos, 13n
Cooperatives, agricultural, 166–67
Courrier de Colmar, 120
Courrier du Bas-Rhin, 50, 55, 91, 109, 137, 151f
Credit, *see* Moneylending
Crémieux, Adolphe, 100
Crimean War, 56

Dalsace family, 98
Damascus, 10
Darmsteter, James, 9
David, August, 109
Delahache, Georges, 45, 75n, 99, 113, 131, 146, 231
Democratic pluralism, 193
Derenbourg, Joseph, 10, 41n
Déroulède, Paul, 98, 99n
Desertion, 93–94
Deutsch-Israelitischer Gemeindebund, 108
Deutschtum und Franzosentum in Elsass-Lothringen (Ruland), 148
Diedenhofen (Thionville), 109, 164
Dietary laws, 3
Discrimination Against Jews in the Judicial Service (Breslauer), 142
Divorce, 122
Dohm, Wilhelm, 3
Draft evasion, 90–92, 97, 182
Dreyfus, Alfred, 64, 127–32 *passim.* See *also* Dreyfus Affair
Dreyfus, Jacques, 64
Dreyfus, Mathieu, 128
Dreyfus, Raphael, 64
Dreyfus, René, 63, 69
Dreyfus Affair, 10, 45, 118, 127–31, 135n, 136, 146, 155, 179n, 188, 230f

Drumont, Edouard, 128, 149
Dupont, Pierre Mayer, 63, 69
Dupont des Loges, Bishop of Metz, 100, 228
Durkheim, Emile, 29n, 179n
Durlach, Emmanuel, 63f

East European immigrants, 140, 173, 186, 192
Ecole Israélite des Arts et Métiers (Strasbourg), 33
Ecoles de travail, 11n, 15, 171
Ecoles rabbiniques, 72, 104, 110f, 149
Edouard Siegel (textiles), 106
Education, 18, 31–32, 104, 122, 141–46, 173–75
Eisenmann, Alphons, 213
Eisenmann, Jacques, 213
Eisenmann, Léon, 213
Elbeuf, 66–67
Elias, Dr. Alfred, 133, 181
Elkin, Judith, 85n
Der Elsässer, 172, 231
Emancipation, of European Jews, 2–26 *passim*
Embourgeoisement, 161, 172–73
Emigration, 49–95, 98, 175–95, 197–200, 214, 245–47. See *also* Hagenau; Optants
Emigration permits, 77, 79, 88, 93, 199f
Emigré organizations, 97–100
England, 10
Enlightenment, 4, 9
Entlassungsurkunde, see Emigration permits
Erckmann-Chatrian (pseud. Emile Erckmann and Alexandre Chatrian), 21, 116n
Europe, antisemitism in, 11
Ez Chaim, 112–13

Famine, 18
Fertility decline, 158–61, 162
Les Fils d'Emmanuel Lang (textiles), 64
Foch, Ferdinand, 183
Foreign Legion, French, 55, 97
Fraenkel, Henri, 65ff, 215

Index

Fraenkel, Louis, 65f, 215
France: Jewish emancipation in, 5–25 *passim*; antisemitism in, 10, 118–20, 128–33 (*see also* Dreyfus Affair); and purchase of military replacements, 55–56; tariffs of, 57; loyalty of annexed citizens to, 96–117; anti-Alsatian sentiment in, 128–33; nationalism of, 206. *See also* Franco-Prussian War; French Revolution; Jews, French; Napoleon I; Napoleon III; World War I
Franco-Judaism, 8–9, 25, 27, 37
Francophile organizations, Jews in, 100–102
Franco-Prussian War, vii, 35, 100, 115, 118, 121; Treaty of Frankfurt, 34, 48, 149; French Jews in, 37, 56
Frankfurt, Treaty of, 34, 48, 149
Frankfurt Rabbinical Conference, 8
Freemasonry, 100
French Revolution, 6, 9, 13–15, 36, 119, 169
Fritsch, Theodor, 140
Fürst brothers, 169

Galut (exile), 2, 9
Geiger, Abraham, 8, 10, 41
Geldmonopol, 140
Gentiles, *see* Catholics; Protestants
German as official language, 60, 102–4
German Empire, *see* Germany
German-Jewish Community League, 108
German Jewish immigrants, 105–13; 150–51, 192
German Reform Party, 140
Germans, Old, vii
Germany: Jewish emancipation in, 6; Jewish religious movements in, 8; antisemitism in, 10; tariffs of, 57; Jews at universities in, 146; and Alsace-Lorraine in World War I, 178–80, 181–82. *See also* Bismarck; Franco-Prussian War; Jews, German; World War I
Glassworks, 106

Gneisse, Professor (director, Colmar Gymnasium), 181
Goldstein, Alice, 161n
Goldstein, Rabbi (editor of *Jüdischer Sprechsaal*), 110
Goudchaux, Edmond, 100–101, 114
Goudchaux family, 98
Gougenheim, Jules, 98
Grace, William, 99
Grain dealing, 166, 173
Grant, Ulysses S., 99
Gravelotte, 147
Grégoire, Abbé, 3ff
Griser (Lixheim priest), 227
Grumbach, Solomon, 127n
Guebwiller, 90
Guerber, Joseph, 121
Guerber, Victor, 126–27
Gugenheim, Isidore, 213
Gugenheim, Julius, 213
Guizot law, 18

Haarscher, Marx, 71n
Hagenau, Jewish emigrants from, 52, 76–95, 199–200; urban vs. rural, 79–81, 83f, 86; vs. non-Jewish emigrants, 76–92 *passim*; occupational patterns of, 81–89 *passim*; factors in move, 83, 90, 92–93; destinations of, 85–89; age of, 92
Halff, Sylvain, 45, 178, 180, 183
Halphen (emigré banker), 101
Hamburg, 202
Hammel, Leon, 107
Hannaux, Emmanuel, 115, 116n, 181
Hannaux, Marx, 104, 115, 154–55, 156
Hansi (Alsatian artist), 105
Hardenberg, Karl August von, 6
Hartmann, Frederick, 119f
Haut-Rhin: optants from, 52; 1869 elections in, 119–20; population of, 162–64
Heimann, Jacques, 213
Helfand, Jonathon, 32n
Henry, Hubert, 131
Henry II (Fr.), 13n
Herzl, Theodor, 191n
Herzog, Ernst, 65, 67, 215

Herzog, Solomon, 52, 215
Hiegel, Henri, 75n
Hirsch, Isaac, 213
Hirsch, Leon, 107
Hirsch, Samson Raphael, 8
Hirsch, Samuel, 215
Hirtz, Georges, 99
Hirtz, Mathieu, 60
Hohenlohe-Langenburg, Prince von, 110n–111n, 234
Holocaust, 192f
Holy Roman Empire, 13
Hops industry, 62–63, 213
Horse dealing, 114–15, 167, 169
Humboldt, Alexander von, 6
Hvidt, Khristian, 47, 54

L' Indépendent de la Marne et de la Moselle, 69
Industrial Revolution, 157
"Infamous decree" of 1808, 7, 105, 119
Ingwiller, 166
Integration, 22n
Intermarriage, 6, 175ff
Isaïe ou le travail (Lévy), 15, 19, 21–22
Israelit, 141
Israelitische Wochenschrift, 38–39
Itterswiller, 119

Jerusalem (Mendelssohn), 4
Jesuits, 122, 226
Jewish Youth's Benevolent Society, 108
Jews: historically, 1–7 passim; and the state, 188–94 passim
—East European, 167–69, 192
—French, 6–26, 29n; and Alsatian Jews, 40–42, 97–99, 113–15; demographic impact of annexation on, 71–72. See also Franco-Judaism
—German, 6–11 passim, 27–30 passim, 40n, 186; as Alsace-Lorraine immigrants, 24, 105–6, 150–51, 167, 173, 192; and Alsatian Jews, 38–42, 105–13
Journal d'Alsace, 123n, 124–25, 148
Journal des debats, 29
Judaeo-Alsatian (lang.), 102

Judaism, 1–9 passim, 111–13; officially recognized in Alsace-Lorraine, 147. See also individual movements by name
Jüdischer Sprechsaal, 110
Juifs (Delahache), 131
July Monarchy, 7
July Revolution, 119

Kahn, Alexandre, 180
Kahn, Nathan, 89
Kahn, Simon, 89
Kahn, Zadoc, 17, 19, 112
Kaiser: and Jewish community, 139, 147
Kaiser Wilhelm University, 142–44, 173–75
Katz, Jacob, 16f
Kaufmann, Karl, 106
Keller, Emile, 130
Klein, Salomon, 19–20
Koch (rabbi of Wissembourg), 116, 226
Kol Nidre, 103
Kollenscher, Max, 151n–52n
Kolnische Zeitung, 30f, 91, 141
Kühlwetter (German Civil Commissioner), 31f, 60, 121f
Kulturkampf, 28, 32, 49, 121–22, 123
Kuznets, Simon, 16–17, 47

Lambert, Eliezer, 69
"Lamentation d'un alsacien" (Weill), 35
Landflucht, 164
Landtag, Jewish representation in, 147–48
Lang brothers, 64
Language patterns, 18–19; Yiddish, 5, 11, 15, 18, 102
Lantzenberg, Alfred, 213
Latin America, Jews as immigrants to, 85n
Lauterbourg, 19
Lazard Frères, 100
Lazare, Bernard, 191n
Lazare, Isidore, 50, 55
Lefevre fils (Haut-Rhin politician), 119

Lemaître, Jules, 149
Lettres de vengeance d'un alsacien (Weill), 35
Levi, G., 142
Lévy, Abraham, 71n
Levy, Adolph, 154
Lévy, Elisabeth Esther, 178, 179-80
Levy, Emile, 184-86
Lévy, Emmanuel, 93
Levy, Ernest, 143
Lévy, Gustav, 146
Lévy, Isaac, 15, 19, 21-22, 36-37, 50, 72, 120, 140, 148, 229
Lévy, Israel, 185
Levy, Léopold, 215
Lévy, Molling, 93
Lévy, Paul, 18, 164
Lévy, Simon, 71n
Lévy, Solomon, 114-15
Lévy, Sylvain, 114-15, 225
Levy Brothers (textiles), 106
Liberal Judaism, see Reform movement
Lieber, Arthur, 237
Liebschutz, Benjamin, 213
Ligue d'Alsace, 52
Ligue de Revanche (Nancy), 98
Ligue des Patriotes, 98-99, 101
Lipman, Armand, 146
Lipman, Benjamin, 32, 37, 50, 72, 146, 168
La Lorraine annexée (Roth), 75n
Lowenstein, Steven, 161n, 218
Loyalty oaths, 37
Lunéville, 14n
Lutherans, 18
Luxembourg, 89

Maase, David, 61, 71n
Maccabees, 22
Malesherbes, Chrétien de, 5
Mannheimer, Lucien, 184, 232
Manteuffel, Edwin von, 122n
Manuel, Eugène, 98
Mappot (Torah cloths), 105
Marbach, Abbé (editor of Volksfreund), 121

Marriage rates, 160-61
Marrus, Michael, 189, 191
Masons, see Freemasonry
Le Matin, 107
Maurois, André, 52, 65f
Mayer, Isaac, 101, 169
Mayer, Joseph, 69
Mayer Frères et Cie (Metz bank), 101, 154, 169
Meiss, Honel, 32, 108
Mendelssohn, Moses, 3-4, 8
Messianism, 2ff, 8f, 11, 203
Le Messin, 153-54
Metallurgy, 106
Metz, 13, 18; Ecole Rabbinique of, 20; "Frenchness" of Jews of, 23; optants from, 69, 71; community support of Bishop Dupont des Loges, 100; population of, 162; expulsion of Polish Jews from, 168
Metzer Zeitung, 131, 140
Meurthe, 23
Mexico, 85n
Meyer, Arthur, 149
Meyer, Eugène, 180
Michaelis, Johann David, 3f
Michaelis, Otto, 143
Middle Ages, Jews during, 36
Military service, 7, 20-22, 54-56, 90-94, 97, 182, 219
Mirabeau, Honoré de, 5
Missions Rabbiniques des Communautés de France, 72
Mitchell, Allan, 128n
Moch, Arthur Wolfgang, 213
Moch, Gaston, 75n
Molsheim, 50
Moneylending, 47, 83, 105, 119, 124-26, 166, 170-71. See also "Infamous decree" of 1808; Usury
Moock (rabbi of Mulhouse), 112
Moore, Deborah Dash, 192
Morhange, Louis, 71n, 101
Moselle, 20, 23, 34
Mossmann, Xavier, 23
Muhler, von (Prussian Minister of Religion), 38

Mulhouse, 50, 64, 90, 162–64
Müller, August Ernest, 153–54, 156, 223

Nancy, 14n, 63f
Napoleon I, 6–7, 20f, 119
Napoleon III, 33, 35, 119f, 122
Nationalism, vs. patriotism, 151–52, 191
Near East, antisemitism in, 11
Neher, Albert, 24
Neher, André, 172
Neo-Orthodox Judaism, 8–9
Netter, Nathan, 116, 151–52, 155, 184
Neue Mülhauser Zeitung, 51
New Christians, Jews as, 13n. See also Conversion
Noisseville, 115
North Africa, antisemitism in, 11

Oath *more judaico*, 7
Obernai, 110
Occupational patterns, Jewish, 16–17, 58–62, 70–71, 81–89 *passim*, 158–73 *passim*
Old Germans, vii
Oppenheimer, Ferdinand, 223
Optants, 48–74, 157, 191, 197–98, 245–46; factors in choice, 49, 54–56, 62–71, 218f; Christian, 49–50; Jewish, 50–77, 83, 94, 215; characteristics of, 57–62, 70–71
"L' Option et l'emigration dans l'arrondissement de Sarreguemines de 1870 à 1914" (Hiegel), 75n

Palestine, as "promised land," 2, 4, 8
Paris: Sephardim of, 14; optants to, 72; as revanche headquarters, 98
"Passport regime," 91, 96n
"Patrie/Religion" ideology, 9, 12, 14, 25, 192
Patriotism, 6–7, 26, 27–74, 115–16, 151, 189–94; vs. nationalism, 151–52, 191
Peasants into Frenchmen, 1870–1914 (Weber), 73n

Peddling, 167
Peirotes (SPD candidate), 127n
Penal code, German: introduced into Alsace-Lorraine, 124
Perle (Stenne), 19, 22n
Peru, 85n
Philippson, Dr. Ludwig, 39–41, 188n
Picard, Frédéric, 215
Picquart, Georges, 132n
Piyuttim (liturgical poems), 11, 112
Plaidoyer pour les "annexés" (Delahache), 131
Pluralism, democratic, 193
Poppel, Stephen, 22n
Population decline, Jewish, 75–76
La Population juive en Alsace (Schnurmann), 158
Poverty, Jewish, 17–18
Preiss (Colmar politician), 134n
Presse israélite, 40–41, 42
Protest movement, 100–101, 122ff, 138, 145, 155
Protestants, 12, 18, 28, 49–50, 64, 119–21, 186, 190; Jewish converts, 176–77. See also Lutherans
Prussia, 35, 120; reform movement, 6. See also Germany
Puttkamer, von (State Secretary), 111n, 112, 235

Rabbis, 1, 11. See also Ecoles rabbiniques
Raiffeisen banks, 125, 166, 170
Raphael, Freddy, 21, 45, 172
Ratisbonne, Achille, 71n
Ratisbonne, Louis, 98
Ratisbonne family, 69n
Reform movement, 110, 111–12; in Germany, 6, 8–9; and messianism, 203
Reform Party, German, 140
La Régénération, 14
Reich, *see* Germany
Reichstag, 33
Reinach, Théodore, 9
Reisenberg and Massbaum (textiles), 106
Rerum Novarum, 126

Index

Reubell, Jean François, 13f, 119
Reuss, Rod, 75n, 106n
Revanche, 34, 36f, 97ff, 131, 134, 182, 187, 220. *See also* Protest movement
Revolution of 1848, 119
Revue israélite, 30, 61, 137
Rohling, August, 140
Roman Catholics, *see* Catholics
Roos, J. (cantor), 93
Roth, François, 75n, 136, 172, 200
Rothschild, Edmond de, 205
Rouff, Capt. (emigré leader), 98
Rueff, Adolph, 101
Rueff, Leopold, 71n
Ruland, H., 148

Salvador, Joseph, 9
Sanhedrin, 6–7
Sarreguemines, 14n, 71
Saverne Affair, 154
Scènes de la vie juive en Alsace (Stauben), 18
Scheid, Elie, 205, 213
Scheurer-Kestner, Auguste, 128–29, 132
Schirrhofen, 80, 227
Schmoll, Georges, 183
Schnurmann, Erwin, 94, 158–77 *passim*
Schorsch, Ismar, 189n
Schull (Jewish industrialist), 180
Schwab (rabbi of Mutzig), 114
Schwartz, Jacques, 101
Schwarzfuchs, Simon, 173
Science of Judaism movement, 203
Second Empire, 35, 47, 85, 124; purchase of military replacements during, 55
Sée, Julien, 120, 123
Sée family, 98
Sephardim, 6, 13–14
Le Siècle, 29, 129–30, 131
Silverman, Dan P., 96, 117, 121f, 187
Simmel, Georg, 143
Singer, Paul, 107, 127n
Social Democratic Party (SPD), 126f
Socialism, 30, 126–27, 193
Socialist International, 30

Société de Bienfaisance de la Jeunesse Israélite, 71, 108
Société d'Encouragement au Travail Parmi les Jeunes Israélites Indigents du Bas Rhin, 11n
Société de Prévoyance et de Secours Mutuels des Alsaciens-Lorrains, 98
Société de Protection des Alsaciens Demeurés Français, 98
Société de Réintégration des Alsaciens-Lorrains, 98
Société des Etudes Juives, 11n
Société Israélite des Amis du Travail, 11n
Société pour l'Encouragement des Arts et Metiers Parmi les Israélites de Metz, 11n
Sonnenburg, Liebermann von, 140
Soultz-sous-Forêts, 21
Souvenir Français, 100
Sozialismus der Erzfeind steht vor der Thüre (Guerber), 126
Spiess (Landesausschuss deputy), 235
Spire, André, 113
Staripolsky (Old German rabbi), 110, 112f, 224
State, Jews and the, 188–94 *passim*
Stauben, Daniel, 18
Stenne, Georges, 19, 22n
Strasbourg: optants from, 52, 56, 71n; Jewish factions in, 109, 112–13, 146; vital statistics of, 160–64; Eastern European Jewish population of, 167; post–World War I problems of, 184–86; University of (*see* Kaiser Wilhelm University)
Strassburger Bürger Zeitung, 109
Strassburger Israelitische Wochenschrift, 134, 144, 148–49, 150, 169
Strassburger Neue Zeitung, 117
Strassburger Zeitung, 42–43
Sufflenheim, 227
Switzerland, 64, 89, 180, 214
Sylvain Michel Lévy et Cie (horse-dealing firm), 114
Syria, 10
Szajkowski, Zosa, 45, 52

Talmud, 19
Terquem, Olry, 69
Textile industry, 63–67, 106, 215
Thiers, Adolphe, 34
Thionville, 109, 164
Third Republic, 193
Torah, 105
Trois Fontaines (glassworks), 106
Tuteur, Felix, 155, 223

Uhry, Adolph, 112, 114, 148, 185
Uhry, Edmond, 56, 85–93 *passim*, 104, 166, 183
Uhry, Léon Auguste, 181
Union Alsacienne, 97
Union of German Jews, 150
United States: emigration of Alsace-Lorraine Jews to, 46f, 50, 76f, 85–88, 97–100 *passim*
Univers israélite, 11n, 14, 99, 108, 148f, 168, 184
Universities, Jews in, 173–75
Urbanization, Jewish, 16, 158, 161–67, 173
Uruguay, 85n
Usury, 5, 13, 124–25, 126f, 229. *See also* Moneylending

Verband der deutschen Juden, 150
Verein für Cultur und Wissenschaft der Juden, 11n
Verein Jüdischer Akademiker, 108
Verein Jüdischer Studenten, 144
Veterans' associations, 100
Vichy France, 193
La Vie juive (Cahun), 32, 36
Vienna, 202
Voilliard, Odette, 64
Volksbote, 120
Volksfreund, 121, 130, 231

Wahl, Alfred, 58, 123
Wahl, Henri, 221
Wahl, Solomon, 213
Wallach, Naphtalie, 181
Wandervogel, 150

Weber, Eugen, 73n, 157, 161n
Wedel, Statthalter von, 153
Weil, Alfred, 180
Weil, Bruno, 147, 150
Weil, Isidore, 111n, 180
Weill, Alexandre, 17, 29n, 34–35, 208, 226–27
Weill, Georges, 127n, 181
Weill, Jacob, 213
Weill, Julius, 215
Weill, Simon, 213
Weiller, Lazare, 113, 221
Werth, Léon, 15
Westphalia, treaty of, 13
Wetterlé, Abbé (autonomist deputy), 148f
Weyl, Abraham, 213
Weyl, Raphael, 21
Weyl, Robert, 21, 105
Wilhelm I, 121
Wilhelm II, 110n, 116
Wimphen, Ferdinand, 101, 114
Wissembourg, 52, 115–16, 226
Wissenschaft des Judentums movement (Science of Judaism movement), 203
Wolf Netter and Jacobi (metallurgy firm), 106
Wolff, Isidore, 33f
Wolff, Dr. Zacharias, 111
Woog, Maier, 107
World War I, 151, 177; effect on Alsace-Lorraine Jews, 178–94
Worms, Justin, 69, 101
Worms, Mme. (emigré leader), 98
Wucherspille, 140

Yiddish (lang.), 5, 11, 15, 18, 102
Yom Kippur, 103

Zabern Affair, 154
Zeppelin, Ferdinand von, 115, 147
Zionism, 108, 149, 151n–52n, 191, 193, 237; in Alsace-Lorraine, 133, 181; and Arab question, 191n
Zollverein, 28, 57
Zunz, Leopold, 11n

Library of Congress Cataloging-in-Publication Data

Caron, Vicki, 1951–
  Between France and Germany.
  Bibliography: p.
  Includes index.
  1. Jews—France—Alsace—History. 2. Jews—France
—Lorraine—History. 3. Alsace (France)—Ethnic relations.
4. Lorraine (France)—Ethnic relations. I. Title.
DS135.F85A4715   1988   944'.38004924   88-2131
ISBN 0-8047-1443-6 (Alk. paper)